Let Linda Gol-
oger, show y ... in
your life!

Is your *husband* your kind of man? How do you get him and keep him!

Is your *wife* passionate, capable, suspicious, extravagant, submissive? What are your wife's secrets? What does she *really* want and need?

What makes your *lover* want you? How do you make him want you more?

Where is your *child* going, and how can you help him get there?

Why did your *boss* hire you, and how can you keep your job?

How do you make your *employee* come in early, stay late, and love it?

With insight, humor, and *remarkable accuracy*, Linda Goodman will show you the way to a greater understanding of your loved ones, friends, and enemies through their SUN SIGNS.

LINDA GOODMAN'S
SUN SIGNS

BANTAM BOOKS
TORONTO • NEW YORK • LONDON • SYDNEY • AUCKLAND

*This edition contains the complete text
of the original hardcover edition.
NOT ONE WORD HAS BEEN OMITTED.*

LINDA GOODMAN'S SUN SIGNS

*A Bantam Book /published by arrangement with
Taplinger Publishing Co., Inc.*

PRINTING HISTORY

*Taplinger edition published September 1968
Universe Book Club edition published Spring 1969
Book-of-the-Month Club edition published Spring 1970
Condensed in* PAGEANT *and serialized by the*
DES MOINES REGISTER TRIBUNE SYNDICATE
*Bantam edition / October 1971
45 printings through August 1988*

ISBN 0-553-27882-7

Published simultaneously in the United States and Canada

*Bantam Books are published by Bantam Books, a division of
Bantam Doubleday Dell Publishing Group, Inc. Its trademark,
consisting of the words "Bantam Books" and the portrayal of
a rooster, is Registered in U.S. Patent and Trademark Office
and in other countries. Marca Registrada. Bantam Books,
666 Fifth Avenue, New York, New York 10103.*

PRINTED IN THE UNITED STATES OF AMERICA

KR   54 53 52 51 50 49 48 47 46 45

For Mike Todd
the Gemini
who really knew the people he knew

    and for Melissa Anne
    the Pisces
    to keep a promise . . .

Thus grew the tale of Wonderland:
    Thus slowly, one by one,
Its quaint events were hammered out—
    And now the tale is done . . .

Acknowledgment

I would like to express my grateful thanks for the help and advice given me by my friend and teacher, astrologer Lloyd Cope, a Virgo. Without his encouragement and faith, this book might have remained just another Aries dream.

The verses used throughout the text have been taken from the works of Lewis Carroll.

The term "Sun sign" means that, if you are, for example, a Gemini, the Sun was in the zone of the zodiac called Gemini when you were born, approximately between May 21st and June 21st, inclusive. You'll find that the dates covering the Sun sign periods are slightly different, depending on which astrology book you read. Most astrologers don't wish to confuse the layman with the information that the Sun changes signs in the morning, afternoon or evening of a particular day. It's all very nice and neat and easy to pretend each new sign begins precisely at midnight. But it doesn't. For example, except for leap year variations, the Sun, for the last several decades as well as at the present, both leaves Aries and enters Taurus sometime on April 20th. It's important to know that April 20th contains both signs. Otherwise, you might go around all your life thinking you're a Taurus when you're really an Aries. Remember that if you were born on the *first* or the *last* day of any of the Sun sign periods listed in this book, you'll have to know the exact time and the longitude and latitude of your birth to judge whether or not the Sun had changed signs by that hour.

CONTENTS

GEMINI

May 22nd through June 21st

CANCER

June 22nd through July 23rd

LEO

July 24th through August 23rd

VIRGO

August 24th through September 23rd

LIBRA

September 24th through October 23rd

SCORPIO

October 24th through November 22nd

SAGITTARIUS

November 23rd through December 21st

CAPRICORN

December 22nd through January 20th

AQUARIUS
January 21st through February 19th

PISCES
February 20th through March 20th

Foreword

HOW TO UNDERSTAND SUN SIGNS

A tale begun in other days,
When summer suns were glowing—
A simple chime, that served to time
The rhythm of our rowing—

Someday, you will doubtless want the complete details of your personal natal chart. Meanwhile, you can be sure that studying your Sun sign is an important first step. However, studying your Sun sign shouldn't be confused with studying the predictions based on your Sun sign alone in magazines and newspapers. They may hit you with impressive accuracy more often than they miss, but they're far from being infallible. Only a natal chart calculated for the exact hour and minute of your birth can be completely dependable in such a specialized area.

On the other hand, don't believe the common accusation that these predictions are "just a bunch of general phrases that can be scrambled around to fit anybody." That's equally untrue. The predictions (indications would be a better word) apply as they are printed, to the Taurus or Pisces or Virgo person individually. They don't apply helter-skelter to any of the twelve Sun signs. They are written by competent professionals and based on mathematical calculations of the aspects formed between your natal Sun and the planets moving overhead, and they give you a fair degree of accuracy, as far as they go. The fact that they're not based on the *exact degree* of your natal Sun, nor on the additional aspects from the other eight planets in your natal chart, plus your natal Moon, is what creates the flaw. Still, they can be interesting and helpful, if allowances are made for the discrepancies.

The Sun is the most powerful of all the stellar bodies. It colors the personality so strongly that an amazingly accurate picture can be given of the individual who was born when it was exercising its power through the known and predictable influences of a certain astrological sign. These electro-magnetic vibrations (for want of a better term in the present stage of research) will continue to stamp that person with the characteristics of his Sun sign as he goes through life. The Sun isn't the only factor in analyzing human behavior and traits, but it's easily the most important single consideration.

Some astrologers feel that a book about Sun signs is a generalization comparable to lumping together all the Polish, Irish, Chinese, Negro, Italian and Jewish people— or like lumping all butchers, bakers, candlestick makers, merchants or Indian chiefs. Though I respect their feelings, I can't agree with them. True, Sun signs can be misleading if they're used with the wrong attitude. But in the absence of a natal chart, they're far ahead of any other known quick, reliable method of analyzing people and learning to understand human nature.

An individual's Sun sign will be approximately eighty percent accurate, sometimes up to ninety percent. Isn't that far better than zero knowledge? That extra ten or twenty percent, is, of course, most important and must be considered. But if you know a person's Sun sign, you're substantially better informed than those who know nothing about him at all. There are no pitfalls in applying Sun sign knowledge when it's done with discretion. Just plant an imaginary policeman in your mind to keep warning you that you might be off by that ten or twenty percent, and you can use them with confidence.

What is a Sun sign? A particular zone of the zodiac— Aries, Taurus, Gemini, etc.—in which the Sun was located at the moment you drew your first breath, an exact position taken from a set of tables called an ephemeris, calculated by astronomers. As pointed out in the note to the reader that precedes the Table of Contents, if you were born on the *first* or the *last* day of any Sun sign period, you'll have to know your exact birth time and the longitude and latitude of your birth place to judge whether or not the Sun had changed signs by that hour. In other words, the dates which begin and end the Sun sign periods in this or any astrology book are approximate, and this is most important to remember. These two days are called the cusps, and don't let them confuse you. Some astrologers even give them a longer period. But either way there's been entirely too much stress laid on them for the layman. No matter what you've heard, if the Sun was in Gemini when you were born, it was in Gemini, however near it may be to the cusp, and that's that. The influences which may be impressed on your personality from the sign preceding or following Gemini will never blot out your Gemini characteristics enough to turn you into a Taurus or a Cancerian. Nothing can dim the brilliance of the Sun, while it's actually in a sign, and the variations you get from being born on a cusp are never strong enough to substantially alter your basic Sun sign personality. The important thing is to establish through your birth hour that you were definitely born within the cusps. Make a small allowance for them, and then forget it.

What is a natal chart? You can think of it as a photograph of the exact position of all the plants in the sky at the moment of your birth, formed by precise mathematical calculation. In addition to the Sun and Moon (the two luminaries), there are eight planets, all of which influence your life, according to the signs they were in when you were born, their distance from each other by degrees (aspects) and their exact location.

If you were born on October 9th, you're a Libran, of course, because the Sun was in Libra, and about eight out of every ten Libra traits will show in your character. However, the Moon, ruling your emotions, might have been in Aries, coloring your emotional attitudes with Arien qualities. Mercury, ruling the mind, could have been in Scorpio, so your mental processes would often be Scorpion in nature. Mars, ruling your speech and movements, among other things, could have been in Taurus, so you would speak rather slowly, like a Taurean. Venus might have been in Capricorn, giving you an essentially Capricorn attitude in love, artistic and creative matters—and so on with the other planets. Yet, none of these placements will totally erase the basic qualities of your Gemini Sun. They simply refine the details of your complex personality.

There are other factors to consider if you're to be one hundred percent correctly analyzed. For one thing, the aspects formed between the planets and the luminaries at your birth can modify their positions in the signs. But the most important consideration is your ascendant—the sign rising on the eastern horizon when you took your first breath—and its exact degree. Your ascendant greatly modifies the personal appearance (though your Sun sign has a lot to say about that, too) and it forms your true inner nature, upon which the motivations of your Sun sign are based. If your ascendant is Aquarius, for example, you may have strong Aquarian leanings, and wonder why the descriptions of your Gemini Sun sign don't include all of your idiosyncrasies and secret longings. The two most important positions in any natal chart, after the Sun sign, are the ascendant and the Moon sign.

You'll find it interesting to obtain your ascendant from an astrologer (which can be done quickly over the telephone), and then read the description for that sign, along with your regular Sun sign. You'll find that the two of them blended make up your total personality to a remarkable degree. A third blending of your Moon sign with the other two will give you an even more complete picture.

Next, the houses of the horoscope must be considered. These are mathematically computed locations in the natal chart which have influence over different areas of your life. There are twelve of them, one for each sign. The first house is always ruled by the sign on your ascendant, and so on, in counter-clockwise order around the circle which forms the horoscope. The astrologer who has carefully calculated your natal chart, based on the exact time of your birth and its geographical location, must interpret the meaning of each sign's influence on these houses—or locations—also taking into consideration the planets which fall into their specified areas. Blending all the foregoing factors in analyzing your character, your potential, and the indications of your past and future mistakes and possibilities (which are based on the aspects of the progressed and transiting planets to your natal planet positions) is called the art of synthesis in astrology. That's what takes the time, talent, effort and knowledge of the astrologer. Calculating the chart itself is a relatively simple task, once certain mathematical formulas are followed.

But back to your Sun sign, because, after all, that's what this book is about. In a way, saying that you're a Gemini is rather like saying you're from New York, which isn't the generalization it seems to be. Wouldn't it be fairly easy to spot a Texan in a New York bar—or a New Yorker in a Texas restaurant? Isn't there a considerable difference between a Georgian politician and a Chicago industrialist? Of course. A rather marked difference.

Imagine that you're a Texan, discussing a man who is about to arrive for a business meeting. Someone says, "He's a New Yorker," and immediately an image is formed. He'll probably have faster, more clipped speech than a Texan, be less warm in his personal relationships, and will want to plunge into business without too many preliminary pleasantries. He'll probably be in a hurry to get the contracts signed and catch a plane back to the east coast. He'll be sophisticated to some degree, and probably more liberal than the Texan in his politics. Why is this instant impression likely to be pretty accurate? Because the New Yorker lives a fast life in a fast city, where slow reactions may lose him the seat on the subway or the taxi in the rain. He's constantly rubbing shoulders or elbows with the famous, so he's not easily awed. He has access to the latest plays and the best museums, so it's hard for him to remain unsophisticated. Due to higher crime rates and crowded living conditions, he won't be as hospitable or as interested in his neighbors as the Texan—his personality will be somewhat cooler.

Of course, a New Yorker can be a slow-talking Taurean or a slow-moving Capricorn, but he wouldn't be quite as slow as the Texan Taurean or Capricorn, would he? Nor would a fast-thinking and acting Gemini be quite as fast if he lived in Texas as he would if he lived in New York. It's all relative.

All right, he's a New Yorker. Now assume you discover he's Italian. Another image. He's a writer for television. A third image. He's married, with six children—and yet another dimension of the man is revealed. Therefore (although this is an analogy, and all analogies are imperfect), saying he's a New Yorker is like saying he's a Gemini, for instance, and adding the further information is comparable to knowing that his Moon was in Virgo and he had a Scorpio ascendant when he was born, etc. But even without the extra knowledge, just knowing that he's a New Yorker puts you considerably ahead of those who don't know if he's from Tibet or the South Sea Islands. In the same way, even without a natal chart, just knowing a man is a Gemini or a Leo can give you more understanding of him than could ever be possessed by those who don't know if they're coping with a fiery Sagittarius or an earthy Taurus.

It's true that a detailed nativity can infallibly reveal the finer nuances of character. It can indicate marked inclinations toward or against dope addiction, promiscuity, frigidity, homosexuality, multiple marriages, a disturbed childhood, alienation from or neurotic attachments to relatives, hidden talents, career and financial potential. It can show clearly tendencies to honesty or dishonesty, cruelty, violence, fears, phobias and psychic ability; plus many other strengths and weaknesses of inner character which may be latent for years, then burst forth under provocation during planetary progressions and transits which affect the natal planet positions for a temporary period of time. Susceptibility and immunity to accident and disease are revealed, secret attitudes toward drink, sex, work, religion, children, romance—and the list could go on and on. There are no secrets hidden from the accurately calculated natal chart. None except your own decision concerning how much of your individual free will you may decide to exercise.

However, in the absence of such a complete analysis, everyone can profit from a study of Sun signs, and the knowledge can make us more tolerant of one another. Once you understand how deeply ingrained certain attitudes are in people's natures, you'll become more sympathetic toward their behavior. Learning Sun signs can help cool, poised Scorpio parents to be more patient with the quick brightness they would otherwise think was restless fidgeting in a Gemini child. It helps extroverted students understand introverted teachers, and vice versa. You'll forgive the Virgo his pickiness when you realize he was born to keep every hair straight and to untangle issues by examining each detail. It's easier to bear the carelessness of the Sagittarian when you understand he's too busy finding causes to cherish and defend to look where he's going every minute or notice whose toes he's stepping on. His frankness will cut less when you're aware of his compulsion to speak the truth, whatever the cost.

You won't be as hurt when a Capricorn doesn't "ooh" and "ah" over the gift you gave him, after you've remembered that he's deeply grateful, but incapable of showing his pleasure openly. His insistence on duty will chafe less when you know that he disciplines himself as severely as he does others. Putting up with the endless Libran arguments and hesitations is somehow more bearable with the Sun sign knowledge that he's only trying to be fair and reach an impartial decision. The Aquarian won't seem as rude when he roots into your private life if you stop to think he was created with an uncontrollable urge to investigate people's motives.

Once in a great while you may come across a Leo, for example, with, say, five or six planets in Pisces. The Piscean influences will obviously project themselves strongly, making his Sun sign harder to guess, since they'll greatly subdue his Leo qualities. But that will happen only rarely, and if you're completely familiar with all twelve Sun signs in detail, he can't disguise his true nature forever. No matter how hard the fish tries to hide the lion, that Leo Sun sign will never be totally eclipsed—and you'll catch him unawares.

Never make the mistake of skimming the surface when you're trying to recognize Sun signs. Not all Capricorns are meek, not all Leos are outwardly domineering and not all Virgos are virgins. You'll find an occasional Aries with a savings account, a quiet Gemini or even a practical Pisces. But look beyond the one or two traits that threw you off. You'll catch that flashy Capricorn peeking at the social register—the shy Leo pouting over a slight to his vanity—and the rare flirtatious Virgo buying insecticide by the case, because it's cheaper. The quiet Gemini may not talk fast, but her mind can operate at jet speed. The exceptional thrifty Aries will wear a bright red Mars coat to the bank or talk back to a rude teller—and the practical Pisces secretly writes poetry or invites six orphans for dinner every Thanksgiving. No one can successfully hide his or her Sun sign from you, if you keep your eyes and ears open. Even your pet will show unmistakable Sun sign traits. Don't move the food dish of a Virgo cat to a strange spot—and never try to ignore a Leo dog.

It's fun to practice with famous people, politicians, fictional heroes and heroines. Try to guess their sign, or what sign they most represent. It sharpens your astrological wits. You can even try comic strip characters. Good old Charlie Brown is obviously a Libran, and Lucy could only be a Sagittarius with an Aries ascendant and her Moon in Virgo. As for Snoopy, well, anyone can easily see he's an Aquarian dog, the way he wears that crazy scarf and the World War I aviator's cap, while he chases an imaginary

Red Baron from the roof of his dog house. (Snoopy may also have an afflicted Neptune.) Try it yourself, and you'll have gobs of fun. But what's more important, as you play the Sun sign game, you'll be learning something very serious and useful: how to recognize people's hidden dreams, secret hopes and true characters—how to understand their deepest needs—how to like them better and make them like you—how to really know the people you know. It's a happier world, and people are pretty great, when you look for the rainbows hidden inside them.

Isn't that really life's major problem? Understanding? Abraham Lincoln said it simply and clearly: "To correct the evils, great and small, which spring from positive enmity among strangers, as nations or as individuals, is one of the highest functions of civilization."

Start right now to study your Sun signs, use reasonable caution when you apply them, and people will wonder where you got all your new perception when you begin to unmask their real natures. In fact, understanding the twelve Sun signs will literally change your life. You're on your way to understanding people you've never even met. You'll soon feel closer to strangers, as well as to friends, and isn't that really rather wonderful?

It's nice to know you . . .

Linda Goodman

Linda Goodman's SUN SIGNS

"I daresay you haven't had much practice,"
said the Queen . . .
"Why, sometimes I've believed as many as six impossible things before breakfast."

ARIES the Ram

March 21st through April 20th

How to Recognize ARIES

They would *not remember the simple rules
their friends had taught them: such as
that a red hot poker will burn you
if you hold it too long;
and that, if you cut your finger*
very *deeply with a knife,
it usually bleeds.*

Have you recently met an unusually friendly person with a forceful manner, a firm handclasp and an instant smile? Get ready for a dizzy dash around the mulberry bush. You've probably just been adopted by an Aries. Especially if you found it a little tough to take the lead in the conversation.

Is he committed to some idealistic cause and angrily defending the underdog? That figures. Male or female, these people will fight what they feel is an injustice on the spot, and they're not bashful about voicing their opinions. The ram will talk back to a traffic cop or an armed gangster with equal vigor, if either one happens to annoy him. He may regret it later, but caution won't concern him in the heat of the moment. Mars people come straight to the point, with no shilly-shallying.

Aries is the first sign of the zodiac. It represents birth, as Pisces represents death and consciousness of the soul. The ram is conscious only of himself. He's the infant of the zodiac—the newborn baby—completely absorbed with his own toes and fingers. His needs come first. An infant doesn't care whether or not his parents or the neighbors are sleeping. When he's hungry or wet, he yowls in discomfort. He wants his bottle, and he wants his diaper changed *now,* and don't be pokey about it. When the Aries person has an idea or something he wants to get off his mind, he'll call you at four in the morning without a qualm. Why shouldn't you be awake to listen to him? He's awake. That's all that counts. He wants something. He gets it.

4

Like the infant, Aries is concerned with the world only as it relates to himself. But who could call the small baby truly selfish? He's perfectly willing to lavish his smiles and favors on those who satisfy his demands. It's hard to resist a baby, because he's so totally unaware that he's causing anyone the slightest inconvenience. So it is with the ram. His innocence hangs over him and mellows his aggressiveness, like the innocence of the newborn softens his egocentricity.

This disarming naivete is also why Aries people are so fearless. The baby fears nothing and no one, until he gets burned. Even then, he'll trustingly try again, when he's forgotten the hurt. There's not a trace of cunning wile in the ram, and he'll remain this way throughout his lifetime; forever believing with all his heart, always falling down and getting up again to try once more. Any doubts he collects along the way are immediately displaced by the next person who's kind to him, just as the baby forgets the pain of the safety pin that accidentally stuck in his leg the next time someone sprinkles the powder.

The ram can make believe from here to tomorrow, and spin fabulous dreams, but he can't lie worth a tinker. What you see before you is what he is. There's nothing hidden or complicated about him. He's just as vulnerable as the baby, and just as helpless. When stronger, more mature people force him or take things away from him, he reacts in the only manner he knows—yelling and causing so much disturbance, that people give in just to get peace. He doesn't need delicate strategy. Lung power and self-absorbed determination suffice beautifully to allow him to get his way. Perhaps helpless is not the right word. Vulnerable, yes—but helpless, no.

It's a cinch to recognize the physical appearance of the ram. Aries people have decided features, usually sharp, seldom soft or blurred. The well-marked brows often join with the narrow bridge of the nose in forming the sign of the ram (Υ), perhaps as a warning to anyone with the silly idea of trying to stop or conquer him that those symbolic horns mean business. You may notice a mole or a scar on the head or face, a reddish cast to the hair in the sunlight, and more color than average in the complexion. You may also sense invisible sparks shooting out in all directions. The movements will usually be quick and capable, with a mental process to match. Both the male and female rams normally have broad shoulders, and they may walk with the body slightly bent forward, leading with the head, so to speak, and almost always in a great hurry. (Often, they're in a hurry to get to a brick building to knock down, though their horns may get bent in the butting.) There's little that's graceful about the ram, unless it's his smooth way of handling a crisis (which never fails to surprise people who underestimate him). The bone structure is fine and strong, and few Aries people slump. Their posture reflects their supreme ego and self-confidence. If you see an Aries with drooping shoulders, he's probably a sheep type, who was badly hurt in the ego when he was young. It may take him some time to recover, if the wounds went deep, but he'll straighten up someday. You can count on it. Nothing keeps these people down forever, failure least of all.

The Mars-ruled person will look you straight in the eye, with unabashed honesty and rather touching faith. You're his friend, aren't you? You like him, don't you? No? Then the tears will start, but inside. He'll never show it on the surface, if he can help it. If you see him openly weeping, you can be certain that he's been cut to the very soul in some way. Aries would rather be caught dead than be caught weak—and some of them literally risk the former to avoid the latter.

The ram will seldom glance nervously around the room. When he does, he's no longer interested in talking with you. Something else has caught his attention, and for the moment, you are forgotten. So is what you're saying. Don't be offended. Remember the baby and his toes and fingers.

He will undoubtedly be at the head of his chosen career or involved in a profession on his own. If he's not, then you can easily recognize him by the discontent he clearly shows at being forced to submit to others. You can look for a liberal attitude, lavish generosity with both time and material things, and a marked desire to lead all the marches —with loud cymbals. But don't look for subtlety, tact or humility. The average Arien was behind the barn door when those qualities were passed out. He's a little short on patience, too. In a coffee shop, he'll quickly criticize the waitress and the sandwich, if the first is fresh and the second is stale. But he'll probably leave an unnecessarily big tip when the service is good.

Aries is very direct, to put it mildly. Deceptiveness and deviousness are entirely foreign to the Mars nature. Frankness and refreshing honesty are Arien trademarks, yet rams don't make the best credit risks. Some of them lack stability and evidence a child-like lack of responsibility. Even those who have matured can forget debts in the excitement of the ever-present new challenge of the moment, which will always consume their entire attention. They'll eventually pay their bills cheerfully and willingly, but you may be out of breath when you catch up with them.

Although Aries is the firebrand, who forges his way through life with daring, initiative and enterprise, there's a strange quirk to his bravery. He'll face the abominable snowman or the Frankenstein monster without the slightest trace of fear, yet he can't stand physical pain. He's never a moral coward, but he can be a huge sissy about anything that hurts. The dentist is not one of his favorite people.

Every Arien, at some time in his life, will indulge in rash behavior that brings an injury to the head or face. Cuts and burns are also likely, and severe or even migraine headaches, which could stem from kidney infections. The ram would be wise to steel himself and see that dentist regularly, guard his eyesight, watch his diet, treat head colds seriously, and stay away from alcohol (not only bad for the kidneys, but quite combustible when combined with the Mars temper). Skin rashes, painful knee caps and stomach disorders also plague those born in late March or April. The ram's constitution is strong and tough, if he doesn't abuse it, which he usually does, by ignoring it. When you see him confined to bed with little to say, you know he's really sick. Even so, it may require handcuffs to keep him down. He can survive fevers high enough to kill the average person, and many of them are brought on by his headstrong Mars tendency to carry through under adverse circumstances, at the wrong times with the wrong people. The angry impatience and frustration this always triggers is the real cause of his health problems. His reaction to delay makes him ill, and the conscious cultivation of patience and cautious deliberation would keep the doctor away. Not that he'll take such advice. He keeps the doctor away for years at a time anyhow, until he either drops in exhaustion or reaches an age when he gets more sensible. There's not much danger of an Aries becoming addicted to drugs. Normally, the ram won't even take a sleeping pill. He'd much rather stay wide awake. (He's afraid he might miss something.)

Because of his forceful optimism, Aries (along with the other fire signs, Leo and Sagittarius) seldom falls victim to the chronic, lingering diseases—which astrology has always taught and medical science now realizes are triggered or intensified by melancholy and pessimism. The fire signs are more susceptible to raging fevers, fulminating infections, strokes, high blood pressure and violently acute illness. Say what you will about his impulsiveness, the ram is seldom guilty of gloom. The seeds of depression, even if planted, will die a quick death in Arien soil. But that precious idea Aries holds, that no one else can do anything as efficiently as he can, may run away with him and lead to a thousand disasters. He'll carry through his schemes with dash and confidence, seldom realizing that he's overreaching himself and headed for ulcers or a nervous breakdown. No one ever accuses him of laziness.

Because of their guileless nature, subtle tricks of strategy are impossible for these people. One Aries I know well, with his fiery, contagious enthusiasm, got a financial angel to back one of his original ideas. Just as the deal was about to be closed, and this ram was about to realize his fondest dreams, the angel logically suggested that a well-known expert oversee the operation. The Aries was positive that no one could run it as well as himself, and he was fearful of getting involved with someone from whom he might have to take orders, so he responded quickly, with the usual Aries humility. He waved his cigar in the air in a superior gesture, and asked bluntly, "How do you want your no, fast or slow?" The financial angel just as quickly withdrew his backing, and the poor Aries promoter soon developed a severe case of business leprosy. For many frustrating months, those who had formerly been behind him one hundred percent were mysteriously out to lunch or in Europe every time he called.

A little tactful diplomacy could have kept his dream from exploding, but it takes the average ram many years to reach the diplomacy of an Arien like Dean Rusk. People who have arrived at the top through hard and patient work justifiably resent an aggressive Aries, who thinks he knows far more with far less experience. He learns modesty and humility only after many dismal failures. But once he's learned, he can make a project pay off like a gusher, adding stacks of creative ideas, and intuitively making the right moves. He reaches leadership only by first respecting those above him in credit and stature, yet success, when it comes, is normally gigantic and impressive. Strangely, most Aries people often create wealth for others rather than for themselves. Lots of rams pay rent most of their lives, and seldom own their own home. It doesn't seem to break the Mars spirit that cash doesn't always cling to him, perhaps because what he seeks is not necessarily in the bank.

Though Aries pushes ahead with confidence, caring little for the feelings of others, and his attitude, especially in youth, is "me first," he can be the warmest and most generous of all the Sun signs. He's not cruel. He just honestly believes that he can do anything better than anyone else, and he's psychologically unable to stand by while others fumble and flop. Give him a choice of money or glory, and he'll take glory any time. He's as fond of a dollar as the next person, but he's just a few shades fonder of praise and fame. The ram has a way of making instant decisions without the authority of his superiors. His speech can be satirical and cutting in invective. Arien anger flashes forth with the speed of sound, but it's usually gone before the victim knows what it's all about, and the happy, child-like smile quickly returns. One can't help being reminded of a certain impulsive ram, Nikita Krushchev, who once banged his shoe in a fit of childish temper, on a table at the United Nations, in full view of a television audience, and the devil-take-the-hindermost. He was being ignored, and what Arien cares about tact when he's being ignored? Yet this same Aries was truly heartbroken when he missed enjoying the magic wonder of Disneyland.

Mars people are often accused of having a terrible temper. They have. But they also have a complete inability to remain angry, and once over with, the grievance is generally buried and forgotten. He's hurt and surprised that you still remember the rash things he said but didn't mean. Given the chance, Aries will apologize to his worst enemy, regardless of any dire threats he made in the throes of emotion. He seeks acceptance, even while he heedlessly and deliberately courts rejection. Aries people seldom become angry with individuals. You may get the shower of sparks, but the fire is actually directed toward an idea or a situation he finds intolerable.

The ram is capable of trying to tell a small white lie, if it will put him foremost or save one of his cherished ideals, but most of the time, he has little use for lies, which is fortunate, because he gets caught every time. Blunt candor is quicker, and since the main interest is in getting to the point in a hurry, he prefers to tell the truth. He has no time at all for gossip. That involves discussing others, and Aries is far too interested in himself to waste any excess energy speculating on the inner secrets, behavior or motives of anyone else. Besides, people are normally either black or white to him. He doesn't bother with the gray tones. Don't mistake this for prejudice, however. If he has heavy planetary afflictions of his natal chart, the Aries impulsive disregard for the facts may come forth in the form of cruelty or prejudice; but this is extremely rare. The typical ram will dine with beggars and kings with equal ease and genuine affection. Any reputation he gets for prejudice comes from his tendency to lump people into two distinct camps—his friends and his enemies—and he'll expect you to line them up the same way, if you're close to him.

Despite his shocking forwardness, the ram can also be the epitome of social grace. He can converse for hours in an exciting, interesting manner on subjects he knows absolutely nothing about. There's a lot of surface polish to cover that aggressive Mars drive. Patience with detail isn't his strong point. He'd rather leave the minor, petty statistics to someone else. That's sensible enough. Someone else would handle them far more efficiently. Time spent pinning down the facts is resented, because the ram cares nothing for yesterday's lessons, and tomorrow is too far away to worry about. Today is his natural residence. This hour and this minute. He's totally consumed in the action of the present.

A realist, yet a decided idealist, Aries often defies emotional description. No one can show such tough, forceful behavior. Yet, few others are capable of such sentimentality, wistful innocence and belief in miracles. Mars people are literally incapable of accepting defeat. They won't recognize it—even when it stares them in the face. They're incurable optimists about the end result of anything from love to a baseball game. Being very clever in-fighters, the rams battle best with their heads, meaning their minds. They enjoy opposition because of the challenge it presents, and they'll go out of their way to meet an obstacle and conquer it long before it comes to them—and often when it might have been headed in the opposite direction. They don't wait around for success to drop in their laps, either. They'll chase it at a furious pace, which is why you'll find very few Ariens on welfare lists.

Just thinking about the energy of the ram wears out most people. But Ariens are also capable of being calm, wise and serious when they choose. Unfortunately, they usually don't choose until youth has passed and maturity has mellowed their rash idealism and sense of driving haste. They can arouse popular sympathy easily, yet they don't necessarily make good politicians. Thomas Jefferson and Eugene McCarthy are rare exceptions to the rule. Of all the Ariens who have tossed their hats in the ring, most have had comparatively brief or troubled political careers. We haven't had an Aries president in the United States since John Tyler in 1840. The field of politics is difficult for the average ram. For one thing, he's not the very best economist in the world. For another, he's impulsive in his speech and he hates to hedge, both deadly traits for a politician. Most politicians wait to see what people want before airing their positions. The average Aries has his own ideas of what the people need, never mind what they want, and he'll see that they get it, sooner than might be politically expedient. Still, he's so idealistic that once the Arien has come before the public he fires their imagination and makes them believe in themselves again. The freshness of Mars candor can blow through the smoke of political back rooms like a breeze.

But most Aries people are usually happier in business or the creative arts, where they're so desperately needed. Others may excel in planning strategy. Calmer heads and more practical minds may be better at efficient organization. But without the direct action, energy and originality of the rams, the most desirable projects would fall to the ground or make little headway.

You may find an occasional Arien who is shy, but you'll never find one who's uncertain where he stands. It's difficult to express your own individuality around these people. Aries is far happier when he's talking about himself and his plans than about anybody or anything else (with the exception of the loved one, when he's caught in the clutches of a romance). Once you get his interest—and lots of

luck—he'll be an attentive listener, especially if your ideas
are exciting and progressive. He'll promote you to the
skies, and offer you his time, money, sympathy and loyalty.
When you're in the hospital, he may forget to send a card,
but he may choose the hospital for you, drive you there
himself and refer you to his own doctor (who will be
superior to Pasteur and both of the Mayo brothers, of
course). Once involved in helping you through a rough
time, Aries will walk the extra mile without hesitation. But
show your gratitude, please. He'll be deeply hurt, if not
downright angry, when you don't appreciate his strenuous
actions, which went far beyond the call of duty, and also
probably far beyond what you needed or wanted. He enjoys
doing favors; the larger the charitable gesture the better;
but the ram wants his credit when it's coming to him. If
thanks are withheld, however, it probably won't keep him
from helping again. His amazing faith in himself is matched
only by his naive trust in others, which is why he's almost
constantly disillusioned, and complaining that someone has
let him down. Of course, he won't stay down long. He'll
pick himself up, dust himself off, and soon be ready, willing
and able to blast away again, after a typical binge of violent
but brief depression.

The ram gives such an impression of sincerity that it's
startling to face his sheer audacity when he claims for a
fact something he knows—or should know—to be untrue.
Accuse him of dishonesty, and he'll look at you in amaze-
ment, with candid eyes open wide in utter horror that you
could doubt him. He can wear blinders and ear plugs to
shut out anything he doesn't want to believe. Even when
his position is completely untenable, he'll bravely stick to
his guns and work for the lost cause with earnest conviction. Still, he can change his mind about an opinion you
thought he was born with in a moment of fast decision,
and when he does, it's impossible for him to regain his
former point of view, let alone remember it. His urge to
toss the past in the trash can and go forward at full speed
(one of the chief reasons he adapts to new locations and
people so painlessly) makes him think those who try to
reason with him are interfering with his progress. Then
he's liable to throw what little tact he has to the four winds.
The ultra conservative, who weighs every word and decision, is maddening to the Mars souls, who can communicate their annoyance and frustration with clear and abun-

dant meaning. So it's easy to see why they sometimes make such bitter enemies of older, wiser heads.

Aries has an innocent wistful facet to his nature, and a kind of eternal, joyous, naive faith, blended with the blind zeal of the born crusader. Like the diamond, his Mars horns are hard, and tough to crack.

He sees bright red frequently, but when the sparks have disappeared, he becomes as cheerful and openly friendly as the happy Arien daisy. His metal is iron, and its unbendable strength gives him nine times as many lives to live as others; nine times as many chances of winning the battle. The fire that consumes his spirit can be a flaming torch that lights the way to courage for anyone who recognizes his great idealism.

He is the pioneer, always leading others onward to an impossible goal. His beautiful iron faith is pure—unmixed with the alloys of hypocrisy and greed. He seldom amasses a fortune, and if he did, he would be too busy to stop and count it. Help yourself to his money, clothes or time. He always has some to spare, however pressed or poor he may be temporarily. The ram knows that bread cast on the waters not only feeds his ego and returns again increased, but it makes people happy, one of the things he enjoys most in life. To Aries, miracles are a dime a dozen. If you run out, he'll make you some more, wrapped in brave, scarlet dreams.

Famous Aries Personalities

Dean Acheson	Henry Luce
Bismarck	Eugene McCarthy
Marlon Brando	Andrew Mellon
Charles Chaplin	J. P. Morgan
Ilka Chase	Wayne Newton
Julie Christie	Lily Pons
Joan Crawford	Joseph Pulitzer
Bette Davis	Simone Signoret
Thomas Dewey	Harold Stassen
Bernard Gimbel	Leopold Stokowski
Harry Houdini	Gloria Swanson
Henry James	Lowell Thomas
Thomas Jefferson	Arturo Toscanini
George Jessel	Peter Ustinov
Nikita Krushchev	Vincent Van Gogh
Clare Boothe Luce	Wernher von Braun

Tennessee Williams

The ARIES Man

He said, "I go my ways
And when I find a mountain-rill
I set it in a blaze . . ."

"So either way
I'll get into the garden,
and I don't care what happens."

That creature over there making a phone call—is it an
electrically charged dynamo? Is it a flaming torch? is it a
bird, an explosion—or is it Superman? Well, practically.
It's an Aries male, which is pretty close. Let's hope you
know what you're looking for. Should it be excitement,
an Aries man will provide it by the bushel, with seldom a
dull moment to blur the sparkle. But if you're looking for
the security and contentment of a soothing love, you're in
the wrong telephone booth.

Aries can overwhelm you with passionate ardor one
mintue, and be as icy as a polar bear the next. Insult him
or lose his interest—either or both—and that warm, impulsive Mars nature will freeze instantly. To ignite it again
may mean starting all over from Act One, Scene One.

Aries men are fairly bursting with ideas and creative
energy. Keeping up with him may be tiring, but keep up
you'd better. At least mentally. Aries has a way of leaving
the snails behind and not glancing back. He'll probably
look and act younger than springtime, which is all very
delightful, but his youthful aura may carry over into his
mental and emotional attitudes until he's matured, which
won't be early in life. The Aries man is impatient with
slow pokes, bold and confident, always ahead of others,
and sometimes ahead of himself as well. He can be the
soul of generosity, giving his time, money, sympathy and
possessions by the carload cheerfully to strangers. But he
can also be exasperatingly intolerant, thoughtless, selfish

and demanding, when his desires are delayed, or he's forced to be around negative people.

When it comes to love, his heedless attitude is absolutely amazing. He'll plunge into an affair, positive that this is the only true love ever known by any two people ever born, with the possible exception of Romeo and Juliet. When it breaks in half, he'll pick up the pieces, and try every angle he can think of to salvage the dead romance. If it's beyond repair, he'll start all over again with a new Juliet, and it will be like the very first time. No matter how many romantic mistakes he makes, the ram is sure his true love or soul mate is just around the next dream. Unless you're a Scorpio female, the Aries man is as passionate as any woman could ask. There's little left to desire. He's so idealistic and susceptible to sentiment, he'll squeeze all the tingles, sighs, ectasies and poetry it's possible to squeeze out of a relationship. Aries isn't capable of going halfway. He gives all of himself to the burning interest of the moment.

You may be involved with one of the quieter sheep. Don't let him fool you. He's still ruled by Mars. He doesn't talk much right away? He's not openly exuberant and pushy? Yes, I know one, too. But take my word for it, if you could see inside that hard head, you would discover that his brain is spinning at approximately two hundred revolutions per second. Any time you meet this kind, one who docsn't at first appear to have the typical Mars drive, check the present record of the business he's conducting. You'll soon be convinced you're dealing with an Aries. Then ask his ex-girl friends. They'll probably answer with a giggle. "Him? Bashful? Timid? You must mean someone else." After a while, you should begin to get the picture. That quiet demeanor is a mask for a fiery heart and a tough business drive. Naturally, it's easier when you're in love with a plain, simple ram, who makes it obvious just how enthusiastic he is about everything from potato chips to moonlight and motor trips.

No other Sun sign can be so scrupulously faithful as Aries when he's really in love for keeps. His honesty will usually keep him from fooling you, and his idealism will keep him from wanting to. Promiscuity or even light flirtations are not an Arien habit, no matter what the books tell you. Not when he's deeply involved with all his heart. He's looking for a storybook romance, and storybook romances never include a casual attitude toward love and sex. Those other girls were B.Y.C.A. (before you came along). In fact, I know one Aries who frequently precedes discussions of yesterday with his current flame with, "That was B.U." (before us).

Of course, you must keep alert to future possibilities, because as sincere as he is in his present devotion and promises of complete loyalty (which are undoubtedly absolutely true), his need for romance is so strong that he's capable of looking elsewhere if you don't keep his illusions alive constantly. The minute you let your mutual love lose its storybook flavor, he may wander off the steady path. In case you're not sure, storybook love, to him, does not include going to dreamland at night with a female who has Vicks salve on her chest to clear up her cough. It also does not include watching your intimate personal toilette, such as polishing your nails, whitening your teeth, brightening your hair with "blondes have more fun" bleach, peeling your sunburn, filing your nails or fighting with your mother for hours on the phone. Somehow, in his mind, this is not the way storybook princesses behave. And goodness knows, Juliet would never have sat with her feet up, chewing taffy and watching TV. Wear your perfume when he's around, and giggle with your girl friends when he's not. He finds it difficult to visualize himself as Prince Charming when he kisses you awake and you either snore, or shout unpleasantly, "For gosh sakes, let me sleep, will you?" Now, really, is that the way Sleeping Beauty would have acted when she woke up? Be prepared to greet him dewy-eyed and breathless each morning, fresh from your dreams, thrilled to find his handsome face so near. And let him know it.

Aries males whose sweethearts neglect romance are heartbroken at first. Then they become angry. Then they go looking for a princess who doesn't snore and things like that. This isn't dishonest as far as he's concerned. He didn't break a promise. You did. You made him think you were a lovely nightingale, singing in the moonlight, like it says in his favorite song. Now he finds out you're a chattering squirrel or a nagging blue jay and the jolt rouses him from his heavenly world of angelic choirs and bells ringing every time he touches your hand. How can bells ring when your hands are always full of dirty ashtrays, and how can he hear choirs when you're screaming at him that he stayed out until after midnight for two nights in a row? (Which he did, of course, but who are you to think you can dictate his every move? Marriage is not a prison, and you are not his warden—that's his attitude.)

If you learn how to open your eyes and look at him mistily and all the rest of it, he'll stay with you happily, and ignore every female on earth for you. The ram is highly unlikely to commit himself physically to more than one woman at a time (unless there's a Gemini ascendant or some Venus affliction in his natal chart). It just wouldn't fit his image of one true and lasting love. The decision to break off the old will always be made before becoming too deeply involved with the new. You'll have plenty of warning. An Aries man can rarely pretend a passion he doesn't feel. This alone prevents any undue amount of deception. Besides, now you know how to keep him inside the pages of that storybook.

Just don't be dull, negative or overly timid. To hold him, you'll have to be a combination of Grace Kelly, Ursula Andress, Marie Dressler, Madame Curie and Queen Victoria, with a little bit of Clare Boothe Luce thrown in. No one princess will ever satisfy his image of the ideal. It's quite a trick to convince him you're superior to all other females, but it will keep him spotlessly faithful, if you can swing it. It's really worth a try, because, if the Aries plunge into romance is headlong, his race out of it is equally reckless. He's both an idealist and an egotist, which means he hates to admit he's wrong, or that the love he chose could die. Still, always remember that he's capable of finding situations unbearable that others would consider par for the course. After a separation, if you catch him in the right mood, you can fire his romance all over again, if you act as if there had never been any previous intimacy. You'll have to play hard to get, because he loves a challenge. To make it easier to forgive him, if trouble ever arises, remember that any straying was due to a sudden impulse after his nightingale stopped singing in the moonlight, not to a deliberate seeking of casual variety. Adultery is actually distasteful to his honest nature. Don't fret about the future. You have the magic key to his heart. Lock it.

If you have any ideas about playing games with him by flirting—drop them. Your first indiscretion will probably be your last. You can lose him with just a whisper or an intimate look at another man, let alone any actual infidelity.

He insists on being first in everything, and you can bet your old pressed gardenia this includes being first in your heart. Aries is possessive and jealous in the extreme. Only a Leo male can get wilder at the thought of a transgression on the part of his beloved. To make it worse, the ram will never give you the blind faith he expects you to give him in such matters. You'll simply have to understand that his animated conversations with other women are innocent, because he'll demand all the freedom of social contact he denies to you, and then some. Your Mars lover will glue you to a pedestal, and expect you to stay there. Don't move a single toe. Don't even look as if you want to.

The Aries male is a natural rebel. He loves to defy authority and he thinks he was born smarter than anyone else. Perhaps he was, but most people don't relish being told so. Thanks to his rash way of pushing his superiority, he's liable to fall flat on his face more than once. Because of his need to lead and refusal to follow, those in more powerful positions will teach him frequent lessons in humility. At these times, you're way ahead, because he'll run to you for comfort and assurance when his ego is bruised. Then you'll learn that, beneath his self-confident, aggressive front, lies an inferiority complex he'd rather die than admit having. The woman who handles his shattered confidence with gentle and total devotion has the best chance of keeping his heart permanently. Never make the mistake of agreeing with his momentary enemy, or trying to be fair and seeing the other side of the controversy. You must love what he loves and hate what he hates. He demands the same fierce and unquestioning loyalty that he gives, in both love and friendship. It's his code. Unless you honor it, find another man.

There are no subtle tricks in the Aries nature. It's not at all hard to recognize when a Mars man is finished with a relationship. The ice and boredom in his voice and manner will be unmistakable, and will usually be accompanied by a frank statement that makes it crystal clear. On the other hand, an explosive flame of scorching anger is less serious, signifying that his displeasure is probably just a passing mood, and the romance can be saved. You have more reason to fear his ice than his fire.

Aries males don't like games. He'll be direct in all his approaches. And that means in romance, as well as in business. He won't waste a second, once the love has been recognized, but be sure to let him be the one to recognize it. Don't chase him, phone him frequently, get starry-eyed or declare your feelings until you're absolutely sure the passion is mutual. The quickest way to lose him is to make the first advance. He must be the leader here, as elsewhere. If you don't allow him to be, he can lose interest so fast it can astonish you and crush you at the same time. Once you're each firmly committed, however, don't be too cool and casual, or he'll seek attention somewhere else. Love with an Aries man is like walking a tightrope between warm interest and aloof detachment. You practically have to be a trapeze artist. Don't run after him. Don't run away from him, either. Stick a penny in your shoe, carry a four-leaf clover and wish on a star. That will get you as far as any normal, methodical strategy. Maybe farther. You have to keep him guessing, even after you're his. At the same time, he needs the assurance that your love is always there. Learn to live with it—or learn to live without an Aries.

On the plus side, although your Aries lover will insist on being first in the relationship, he'll also be the first to say he's sorry after a quarrel, and the first to be there when you need him. He'll be right by your side when you're ill or unhappy. He'll spend money on you freely and willingly (if he's a typical son of Mars). He'll compliment your appearance, appreciate your talents and be a stimulating mental companion. Although he can be bossy and lose his temper over a trifle, he'll seldom let the sun go down on his anger before making up. You may be the most important thing in his life, but he'll expect you to know that, and wait for affection and attention when he's all excited by some new idea which is consuming his interest. He wants to be your whole world, but unlike other men, he'll let you share his world, if you're his equal.

The Aries male will expect his lady fair to be ultra-feminine and a tomboy at the same time. He wants you to be completely independent, yet willing to stay a few paces behind him. He'll expect you to praise him and be devoted to him, but never play the role of humble slavey. Are you still with me? Good. Brave girl. There's more to come. He's capable of saying bitterly cruel and sarcastic things to you when his ego has been wounded, things he won't mean at all, but which may break your heart if you don't understand him. Then he'll expect you to forgive and forget as readily as he does. You'll have to like all his friends, while he reserves the right to be bored by yours. Well, you wanted a man, didn't you? You've sure got one in your Aries mate. If you're a real woman, your love affair can be the envy of everyone in town, just like Romeo and Juliet (without the tragedy, of course).

Once you've married him, the Aries male will dominate the home or leave it. He won't stand for being nagged in public or private, especially about how he spends his lettuce. He earned it, didn't he? It's *his* money, isn't it? (Sometimes that possessive pronoun can stretch to include the money you earn, too.) He may not balance the budget too well—and I'm being kind to put it so tactfully—but don't take it over yourself, even if you made straight A's in math. Never question his financial affairs. It's essential that he control the purse-strings all the way. He'll be generous with his cash, if he's a typical Arien, and give you whatever you need. You can have that cobra skin handbag after he's bought that alligator brief case, if there's anything left over. (He may be a little selfish, but he's never stingy.)

Though the ram may change jobs frequently until he becomes his own boss, he won't let you starve. He'll find a way to keep the dollars flowing in, even though they may flow out again just as fast. Better save a few quarters in the blue china pig and surprise him with it when he needs it most, because he's not likely to salt away much of his earnings himself (unless he has a hidden asset, like the Moon in Capricorn or Cancer, or an ascendant which dictates economy).

Each new baby will find him behaving like the devoted, proud papa of your dreams. Later, he may be a little bossy with the children, and try to dictate their careers. He'll be a warm and wonderful fun daddy, but he might have to be reminded that the youngsters need independence as much as he does. Fatherhood is definitely a role he'll enjoy. Baseball, talks about the birds and bees, football, father-daughter dinners, the whole works. Just don't let him think little Herman or Henrietta is more important to you than he is, however, or his enjoyment of the role may cool considerably.

Go ahead and continue your career after marriage if you like. He probably won't resent it, as long as you don't outshine him. It's easier for him to forgive instant suppers or quick-frozen kumquats than to forgive your lack of faith in his ideas. That's important to remember.

Encourage his independence, but try to curb his impulsiveness—tactfully. He must lead or life is worth little to him. His great and bubbly enthusiasm can die a sad death if you douse it with wet blankets or short circuit his positive energy with negative thinking. The minute he loses authority on the job or in the home, his refreshing optimism will turn to moody discontent and finally, complete disinterest. It's not his nature to submit. He's a man's man. Never destroy his masculinity, but never lose your own individuality. Don't try to push him around, and don't let him push you around. An Aries husband won't put up with a wife who runs around to club meetings every night. Neither will he tolerate a wife who sits home and crochets bedspreads and tablecloths all day. You'll have to aim somewhere in the middle. If you're successful, just think— you'll be the only white-haired Juliet in your crowd someday, with a husband who's still sentimental on your golden wedding anniversary. That's quite a challenge if you're a romantic, and of course you are, or you wouldn't be involved with an Aries man in the first place.

The ARIES Woman

"But aren't you going to run and help her?"
  Alice asked . . .
"No use, no use!" said the King.
"She runs so fearfully quick
  you might as well try to catch a Bandersnatch!"

So you're in love with an Aries girl. I don't know whether to congratulate you or sympathize with you.

When Byron wrote that "Man's love is of man's life a thing apart; 'tis woman's whole existence," he forgot about the Aries woman. She may think love is her whole existence, but she's too vitally absorbed in the world around her, not to mention in herself, for it to be the beginning and end of her life. She can get along without a man easier than any female you'll ever meet.

Of course, getting along without a man is not the same thing as getting along without romance. She'll always need that hero of her dreams to yearn for in her heart. He may be long ago and faraway—or hiding just out of sight and touch, somewhere in tomorrow's mists—but she'll think about him in an April rain. He'll haunt her when the first snow falls, when she hears a certain song or sees lightning flash. However, while she's yearning, if there's no male around in actual physical presence, she won't miss him terribly. Anything he could do, she can do better—she thinks.

The Aries girl will open her own doors. She'll also put on her own coat, fight her own battles, pull out her own chair, hail her taxi and light her cigarette without any masculine help. Doing it herself is, to her, the fastest way to get it done. Naturally, this doesn't set too well on the vulnerable male ego. The Mars girl is determined to take the lead, to be the first to move to action, and that includes the action of making the first advance in romance. Aries females are the most likely of all the Sun signs to do the proposing, especially if the man is slow about naming the date. And that's about as early as you can safely show your feelings—when she proposes. Before that you're taking a chance. Be very careful about moving in on an Aries girl. She wants to be the leader in the love affair. Better be sure you have her heart safely in your pocket before you try to grab her around the waist and kiss her goodnight. Otherwise, she may give you a sharp right hook to the jaw and run like a frightened deer.

Don't be misled. The reason for her running isn't maidenly modesty. She's not afraid of your passionate intentions. Those she can handle. Her flight is based on the fear of getting tangled up with a worshiping slave or a lovestruck puppy dog, either one of whom would bore her to tears. Be casual, keep her guessing, and the chances are she'll chase you into a corner instead. A man who resists her impact always intrigues an Aries female. She can't understand why she isn't overwhelming him with her obvious charms. Then her Mars ego will leave no stone unturned to prove she's desirable, even when she has no lasting interest in him.

Scarlett O'Hara is the very epitome of the Mars-ruled

Aries female. Like Scarlett, the Aries girl will gather every available male for a hundred miles around to her feet, while her willful heart yearns for the one man she can't have for one reason or another. Like Scarlett, the Mars woman can quickly adapt for survival if necessary, without whimpering. Both the O'Hara and the Aries characters are tough enough to defy convention, face an advancing army, or even shoot a man through the head with icy calmness, if he threatens her loved ones.

Never was Scarlett more Mars-like than when she was starving, alone and friendless, and without waiting for a man to come to the rescue, she clenched her fist toward heaven and shouted, "I'll survive this . . . and when I do, I'll never be hungry again . . . If I have to lie, cheat, steal or kill—as God is my witness, I'll never be hungry again!" Much later, her emotions shattered, her beloved child dead and the one man she loved about to walk out of her life, this typical Aries woman was still able to say, "I'll think of some way to get him back. There's never been a man I couldn't get, once I set my mind on him. . . . After all, tomorrow is another day."

Yes, Scarlett O'Hara creates a vivid image of the first Sun sign of the zodiac, with all the Mars strength and ability to bounce back after tragedy; able to play the female role to the hilt, with fluttering lashes and a well-timed tear, but just as able to take over a man's job when the men aren't around. A careful study of Scarlett's character can give you an excellent understanding of what you're in for with an Aries woman—and naturally, also the rewards you can look forward to after you've been brave enough to claim her. Her aggressive drive may be hard to take, but her shining optimism and faith in tomorrow can be mighty uplifting.

The Aries girl is rather a pushover for flattery, if it has an honest base. Let her know you admire her, but don't be too flowery or sugary about it. Her loyalty in love is gigantic, as long as you keep the sentiment alive, for she is deeply sentimental. There's the typical Arien contradiction in her: she doesn't want to be obviously chased, yet she quickly loses interest if you're too detached. She doesn't want a completely domineering male, but neither will she warm up to a man who sits adoringly at her feet. Before love can bring her happiness, the Aries woman must meet the eternal Mars challenge—her strong desire to control the lover, conflicting with her secret wish to be controlled *by him*. Unbelievably idealistic, sometimes she searches in vain for that brave knight in shining armor, who will sweep her off her feet, conquer the world, hand it to her gently and yet never sacrifice his manhood. Since he exists only in fairy tales and the myths of King Arthur's court, the Aries woman often walks alone, without a star to guide her. Her days are bright and full of excitement, her nights are sometimes dark and full of longing. Yet, when her defeated dreams become smoldering ashes—just as you think the flame is dying, Aries leaps up to build another fire.

She must be proud of you to love you. But don't be so important that you neglect to notice *her* talents and abilities. Though she'll demand a lot from you, she'll give double measure in return. The Aries girl can be generous to a fault with her time and sympathy, cheerfully sharing her possessions and money, but when it comes to love, she's downright stingy. "What's hers is hers" in the romance department, and it will take very little to set off a jealous explosion. Don't admire your favorite movie actress in her hearing, or pay too many compliments to her girl friends. The man with an Aries wife is safer with a male secretary. If she's not first with you in every way, you'll soon wonder where all the intense passion and thrilling emotion went so fast. When the Aries woman has been really hurt, she turns from fire to ice. Her fire burns hot and dies quickly. Her ice can be eternal. Memorize that, if you care deeply about her—and it's doubtful that she'll stand for you caring about her any other way. Aries plays for keeps.

She puts the loved one on a pedestal, expecting him to live up to an impossible image of perfection, stubbornly refusing to look at his clay feet, until they become too muddy for even her to miss. Never criticize the lover, husband or children of an Aries woman unless you're wearing an asbestos suit. She's capable of being demanding, selfish, and making cutting remarks when you dampen her hopeful plans. Yet, she can also be gentle, devoted and cooperative when she's met halfway.

Since she prefers the company of men to women, and solicits admiration from every male she meets, be he nine or ninety, you'll have plenty of chances to feel the stabs of those little green monsters of jealousy. Forget it. As fiercely possessive as she is of you, she won't put up with your possessiveness of her for an instant. The Aries girl insists on complete freedom, before and after marriage. You'll have to trust her wherever she goes and whatever she does, though she won't have that kind of faith in you (unless she's learned the hard way to keep her emotions under control if it kills her, which it almost will). It's not as bad as it sounds, because she'll be faithful, once she's really yours. An Aries girl is seldom able to love two men at the same time. She's simply too honest for such deception. Barring unusual circumstances, she'll let you know clearly that love is dead before going ahead in total commitment to someone else.

This woman is capable of deep passion and mystical idealism, woven together in strange patterns. In any relationship she feels is real and forever after, there will be no holding back, no feminine wiles, coquettish tricks or silly games. Her love, like her speech and actions, is direct. There's something clean and fresh about the utter simplicity of her emotions, but even so, they often get her into waters way over her head. You may have to tame her a little, but she'll accept it with surprising docility if she really loves you.

Mars females are often career girls. They can handle almost any profession a man can handle, from stockbroking to real estate. They can also turn a nice ankle or profile in strictly feminine occupations like modeling and acting. It may be difficult to get her to give up her job for you, if it's a real career or profession. She may toss it overboard for a period, while she's suffused with the glow of romance and picturing a storybook cottage for two beside the sea (typical of the Arien imagination that leads straight to the happy part and ignores the dull part). But when the cottage begins to need a paint job, the roof starts to leak and the first fine rapture dims slightly, she may be anxious to dig out her social security card again. Let her. She'll be far happier and more loving—even more gentle—if she's allowed to fill her idle hours with something that interests her. Mars emotions, unfulfilled, can look for molehills of frustrations to build into huge mountains of trouble.

There's practically nothing this woman won't tackle. If it's a challenge or just something she thinks she wants to brighten her life, she'll make some kind of a stab at it whether it's practical or not. I know an Aries woman who was forced for financial reasons to live for several years in two rooms with a husband, five active children and a dog.

That kind of an arrangement can get a little cramped, and
just contemplating it might give a woman with any common sense a few doubts. Not a Mars female. This one
coped somehow, though she may have let it goad her into
a few tantrums. In the middle of the situation, when an
astrologer read her natal chart and pointed out that her
planetary aspects showed a long period of great hardship
in her life, she was puzzled and intrigued. "When does it
look like it might happen?" she wanted to know.

This same impulsive Aries woman got a sudden urge
one day to add another dog to the group camping out in
two rooms. She felt the family's male pet needed a female
companion. He looked lonesome. Besides, the children
thought it was a rollicking good idea. The discovery that
the second dog wasn't housebroken threw her only temporarily. Like a determined drill sergeant, she assigned every
member of the family their turn at scrubbing the carpet.
After she saw that it would never be the same again, she
surveyed the situation and made a decision. To get rid of
the second dog? Of course not. She was secretly hoping
there would be puppies someday soon. The money would
just have to come from somewhere to get a new rug. Funny
thing—it did. As for the puppies, she was sure some miracle
would happen to move the entire crowd into a new apartment before the happy event. Funny thing—it did. Miracles
have a way of happening to those who believe in them.
Aries women certainly believe. Sometimes to the point of
foolishness. Her rash ways can get her into some complicated pickles, and she may have a few gray hairs before
she learns how to avoid the same pickle twice. Aries is not
noted for learning from experience. The spirit is willing,
but the disposition is headstrong. There's no use to try to
caution a typical Aries female with the biblical warning,
"Pride goeth before a fall." Her interpretation of the
phrase, since she first heard it in Sunday School, is "When
your pride goes, you fall."

Never worry that your Aries girl will succumb to the
charms of a wolf. She's immune to wolves and playboys,
and in far more danger of being seduced by an idealist
with a cause, preferably a lost cause. But even with him,
she'll assert her individuality frequently. It will never be
completely conquered in the Mars woman, though it can
be subdued by the right man. She'll buy you gifts, loan you

money, nurse you through illness, and help you get a job. And she'll expect the same from you.

She'll deny it vehemently (she does almost everything vehemently), but when she's miserable, you should be miserable. When she's happy, you should be happy. To Aries, love is equal sharing. She'll expect to share your razor, your bank account, your friendships and your dreams. In return, you can share hers. Of course, her razor may be broken, her bank account a little overdrawn, her friendships slightly scattered and her dreams too large for you to swallow. But she's not selfish with them. Keeping a secret from her can drive her wild, and it's not a good idea to drive an Aries wild. Don't ever embarrass her by your grammar, clothing or behavior in public. She won't embarrass you, at least not in these matters.

To injure her pride or dampen her enthusiasm will almost break her heart. Others will constantly be doing just that to her. The world resents a female who talks back to it, and who thinks she's smarter than everyone else. When she discovers she really doesn't run the universe after all, she'll come running into your arms in tears, her world all dark and dismal. Then you'll have a chance to see her as she really is, defenseless and vulnerable in the extreme, for all her outer confidence. She's not really Tugboat Annie. She'd just like to be. She admires strength and tries to imitate it. The Aries idealism and optimistic faith in human nature is often dashed to bits by reality. Comfort her with tenderness at these times, and you'll probably never lose her. Always defend her against her enemies. She can never forgive you if you fail to fight for her or take her side. (But be prepared to make up with them when she does, which may be quickly.) At least she's fair about it. She'll also defend you. An Aries woman will throw away fame or fortune defiantly right in the face of anyone who hurts a friend of hers. If she loves you, her indignation will have no bounds. These women are nothing if not loyal.

As a wife, she may be quite a handful. There will probably be outside interests, because home will seldom be enough for her creative energies. Don't expect her to be a happy little cricket, chirping away contentedly by the hearth. She'll be a competent enough cook, and she'll keep the house spanking clean—at least the part that shows. She'll sew on buttons and iron shirts, too, but she won't like it. Still, she'll do it when it's necessary. (An Aries woman can do almost anything when it's necessary.) Her fire is more like that of a glittering diamond than like the warm, comforting glow of the fireplace. There's undeniably a brittle side to her nature, and she may agitate you more often that she soothes you. But she's exciting and certainly never boring. Then there are always those moments of softness that belie her strong drive—for a man who has the patience to bring them out. Mars women are always softer inside than any but those who have been really close to them ever know. Her conversation will be very intelligent and very frequent. Don't hide behind the newspaper at breakfast. She'll expect companionship from you, or you can just scramble your own eggs.

You'll rarely find her complaining of illness or fatigue. But when she's in pain, she'll expect tons of sympathy. Although you may have to sit on her to get her to go to bed when she has a raging fever, be prepared to wait on her hand and foot when she has a toothache.

This is not the woman to call and tell you'll be working late at the office, unless you enjoy creating Fourth of July fireworks in the middle of February. She won't mind keeping the gravy hot, but she won't like not knowing where you really are, and what you're really doing, and she may call back to find out. The Aries wife will probably make an excellent impression on your boss, if you can keep her from telling him how to run his business. She won't mind going out to bring home the bacon when you're temporarily out of a job, but she can never respect a man who makes less money than she does (though an Aries woman would never leave a man for this reason—she'd be more inclined to make excuses for him). If she has a rare spell of letting herself go, the first word of disapproval from you will send her flying back to the mirror and perfume bottle. (In this way, she's as feminine as Eve herself.) A flattering comment about your secretary's new hair style will do the same thing, but it's more dangerous. Besides, you were warned to hire a male secretary. There's a vain streak in a Mars woman which makes her sensitive about everything from her age to an innocent remark about how tired she looks, which she may take as a hint that you think she looks like an old hag.

Keep the passion and romance alive in your marriage, or she'll be miserably unhappy. Aries will waste little time changing any situation which causes unhappiness, and that can lead to a hasty separation or an impulsive divorce. In most cases, letting her handle the family checkbook would be unwise, but you can try it, if the bank is game.

As a mother, she'll see that the baby is clean, happy, healthy and loved. She probably won't pick him up every time he cries, fuss over him or over-protect him. But her children will get lots of warm, impulsive kisses and bear hugs. An April mother will teach her youngsters to believe in leprechauns. She'll take them for walks in the park, and point out the sparkling necklaces left on the lawn by the fairies when they danced under the moon where others might see only the early morning dew on the grass. Aries women create a magic world of fantasy for their children. It's where they live themseves. She won't be a permissive parent, she'll insist on strict discipline, and will probably be very fortunate in raising her offspring to be independent adults. Her favorite weapons of child psychology are: a wooden paddle, bedtime stories and goodnight kisses.

This woman can be unreasonably temperamental, and create some violent scenes. But her quickly aroused temper will splatter like summer hailstones and soon melt away. She'll never hold a grudge, seek revenge, indulge in self-pity or bitterness. After an emotional storm, her optimistic, April nature will return like the rainbow suddenly appearing after a shower. Lots of people will tell you an Aries woman is completely masculine, but don't you believe them. She's all woman underneath her flashing, forceful exterior, perhaps too much woman for the average man. But, of course, a knight in shining armor isn't an average man. Are there any lonely, courageous knights out there? This is the fair lady of your dreams, worth all the dragons you'll have to slay to win her.

Don't forget that she bruises easily, in spite of her bright, brave smile. (That's just her shield against hurt.) If you can turn the ram into a lamb, you'll have a woman who is honest and passionate, loyal and exciting—though she may be a little impulsive, bossy and independent. Well, you can't have everything, you know. The Aries girl will help you find your lost illusions and she'll have a fierce faith in all your dreams. You don't have any? Borrow some of hers. She has plenty to spare. If you believe in her just half as much as she believes in you, you could make some miracles together.

The ARIES Child

"All I know is something comes at me
Like a Jack-in-the-box
And I go up like a Sky Rocket!"

While Papa is passing out the cigars, the crimson-faced little Aries baby will yell for attention in the bassinet. How dare you ignore him and talk to the nurse? Who's the boss around here anyway?

You won't any more than get him in the taxi on the way home before that question will be emphatically answered. Your Mars infant is the boss. Do you have any doubts? They'll fade away when he's old enough to sit in the high chair and bang his spoon on the tray if you leave him alone too long. He'll never tease you or be subtle about his preferred diet. There's not a subtle bone in his strong, active, broad-shouldered little body. The Aries tot will spit out his vegetables as if they were shot from a cannon, and rub the cereal bowl on his tiny, bald head to make it quite clear that this is definitely not the food baby likes. The girls will be as direct in their actions as the boys. Maybe more so, though you hardly expect such fierce determination from a soft, little miss. Did I say soft? April's metal is iron, and April's stone is the diamond, the hardest substance known to man.

He'll probably walk earlier than other babies, and certainly will talk earlier. He won't be easy to control. Say, "No, no," to an Aries toddler, and he'll shake his chubby little finger right back at you in defiance. Discipline should be started quite young. Be on guard against falls and injuries to the head or face. He's accident-prone, to put it mildly. Keep sharp knives out of reach, watch out for burns and scalds. If there's anything hot or forbidden around, you can just bet the Aries child will stick his curious fist in it impulsively. You think that will teach him a lesson? Not this youngster. He'll try to break his own record.

Teething time may be feverish and severe. Baby will come through the ordeal with little difficulty, but will you?

When he gets a little older, you may get the breath squeezed out of you with one of his loving bear hugs. Aries children are usually affectionately demonstrative, except for the few Mars youngsters whose early emotional experiences freeze their normally warm hearts. These are the sad, quieter little sheep. But their horns are just as dangerous.

Better not ask relatives to babysit without warning them. If poor Aunt Maude bravely takes him while you have a brief vacation, things could become a little strained. She'll catch your Aries tot with his busy hand in the sugar bowl, and probably make the mistake of stamping her foot in displeasure. That will both surprise and outrage the little ram into stamping his own small foot, and bursting out with his first complete sentence, "Aunt 'Mod'—don't you *tell* me sumpin'." So quaint. Bet she won't "tell him something" again soon. (You might have to come home a little early. He broke his big toe when he stamped his foot.)

As he grows older and stronger, after having fought measles, mumps, chicken pox and scarlatina, and won hands down (a battle with germs is no contest with the quickly recuperating Mars nature), your Aries child will begin to show a pattern of temper. You'll notice that he or she can be most unreasonable when thwarted, but the anger won't last long. After a periodic explosion, the Aries boy or girl will beam a large, bright and winning smile your way.

He'll share his toys with amazing generosity with you, his playmates, the mailman, the neighbor's bulldog and the alley cat. However, his generosity will end if one of them hurts his feelings or gets in the way of something he wants to do or somewhere he wants to go. Then look out for fireworks.

Aries boys and girls may fall into the early habit of neglecting homework, and using your more obedient little Capricorn, Cancer, Virgo or Pisces child as an example will hardly impress him. (I'm assuming you don't have more than one Aries offspring. The planets don't do that to parents very often.) Instead of shaming the Mars youngster into studying, challenge him. He'll lap up a challenge like that favorite stray alley cat of his laps up cream. Just tell him (or her) that he's probably just slow, or not as bright as the other students, inferior in some way, but you don't mind. You love him anyway. My! How the dust will fly off those schoolbooks, as he sets out to prove what a ridiculous theory *that* is. Someone who can top him? That will be the day—or night.

After you've watched the magic of such strategy at home, tip off his teacher. She'll get down on her knees and thank you. If she has more than one Aries student in her class, she may send you a five-pound box of candy. Actually, Mars youngsters can learn anything in nothing flat, never forget it, and breeze through their studies, if they apply themselves. Not all parents know how to accomplish this. They may spend years wondering why Mike and Maggie test with such a high I.Q., and still manage to stay in the third grade for four years. They needn't worry too much, however, because little Mike and Maggie will make up for lost time with the speed of a bullet, once they get out in the world and find out people are smarter than they are. A couple of humiliations to the Mars ego, and they'll cram so fiercely, they'll skip a few grades.

Your April youngster will have a vivid imagination; he'll be as dreamy and sentimental as a storybook, but he'll know very well how to get his bread toasted at the same time. If there is such a contradictory thing as a hard, practical idealistic dreamer, it's your Aries child. He's as naive as he is tough; as gentle as he is pushy. All these conflicting traits are woven into his fiery little nature. You'll marvel at it and wonder about it. So will your friends later on, not to mention his boss, his future enemies and the unsuspecting soul he marries.

Aries children will take the lead with playmates, start new games and invent new ideas for the gang. They'll insist on having their own way or butt their heads against authority, so you'd better decide to set down some firm rules in the beginning. The Aries child who isn't trained to obey in his youth will be taught some crushing lessons in maturity. Remember that his heart is as soft as butter, and it hides deep-seated fears of being disliked and unloved, despite his brave front. Rejection of his bright dreams or dampening of his exciting enthusiasm will send him running home to you in tragic tears. Hold him very close when this happens. His heart will be broken. For all his rash domineering ways, the Aries idealism is sensitive and it bruises with the slightest bump. He'll be getting plenty of those bumps on his naive, hope-filled optimism during his lifetime, and he needs more protection against them than you might think.

He believes in fairy godmothers with magic wands, and giants who can topple over whole cities with one sweep of a powerful hand. Unfortunately, Aries children naively identify with these two omnipotent types. When they discover that there are giant killers out there in the brutal world—and blunt realists, who can make those magic wands pathetically impotent, they'll take some hard tumbles. But they'll get back up, brush themselves off, and push forward again indefinitely. *They'll* teach that dull, unimaginative old world a thing or two! There may be a few scars before it's over, but don't count your Mars child out of the fight, no matter how many times he's knocked down. Wait for him to holler "Uncle." You may have a long wait.

Hide birthday presents in a safe place. He'll be impatient, and unwilling to wait for surprises. Don't destroy his faith in Santa Claus and the Easter Bunny too soon. To first believe fiercely, and then learn not to believe, toughens his emotions. It's a necessary lesson. His allowance will burn a hole right through his pocket, but he'll cheerfully give you his last dime for the milkman. Your Aries daughter may pay the neighborhood bullies a nickel a day to stop stepping on ants. An Aries child handled harshly in the impressionable years can show a defensive cruel streak, but guided gently and wisely, he'll insist on his rights with less force, and show a gigantic generosity and sympathy for his fellow man. Don't give him orders, always ask him to do things with a cheerful smile, and he'll knock himself out to please you. Never destroy his confidence. It's as important to him as the air he breathes. He may run away from home; the Mars independence shows early, but he'll come back wiser. Teach him that it's unkind to dominate meeker youngsters. He truly does not want to be unkind.

Being around cold, negative people can wound him deeply, but nothing will ever break his spirit. (Remember the diamond.) He'll probably be wild about books and be an excellent reader, yet he may not be anxious to settle down to four years of college. Aries is too interested in getting into the action of chopping down all those challenging beanstalks. But don't give up too quickly. He can use the additional discipline of higher education to help his mind catch up with his flaming emotions and sudden, puzzling bursts of sharp intuition. The more he balks at the idea of a rigid scholastic schedule and prefers the freedom of trying out a few jobs, the more you can be sure he needs the schedule.

He'll have to learn responsibility, but you'll teach him this and other things faster through direct logic and honest affection. Both appeal to him. Parents and teachers should never forget that Aries children glow under praise and doggedly proceed to top their own efforts, but they sputter like firecrackers under attack and lose all incentive to try. Tell him what you like about him, and he'll do less that you don't like. Aries youngsters live up to exactly what's expected of them, including those who hide their burning drive under a calmer personality. This child must always be kept busy, or he'll wander into trouble. Idleness spells danger. He needs stacks of sleep to renew all that scattered, misplaced energy.

He'll love stories about brave, shining heroes who conquered new worlds. But he also believes in leprechauns and wishing wells, and he'll continue to believe in them long after you've bronzed those little Aries baby shoes and welcomed the first grandchild. If you lead your Mars child gently, with constant love, he'll grow up with the wonderful power to dream the impossible dream—and make it come true.

The ARIES Boss

"Well now that we have seen each other," said the Unicorn, "if you'll believe in me,
  I'll believe in you.
  Is that a bargain?"

The Aries boss won't be popular with lazy employees. If you're looking for a temporary soft spot to fill in the time while you seek a permanent career, or a place to pick up a little spending money during a lull in your life, you'd be well advised not to work for an Aries. This man simply can't abide half-hearted work or a lack of enthusiasm in those around him. He'll expect you to be as devoted to the company as he is, and just as intently concerned with its future potential. He'll probably hire you fast, promote you fast—and point out your mistakes just as quickly.

If he suspects you are coasting, you're liable to get a blunt and direct-to-the-point tongue-lashing, with no feelings spared, but you'll also get a second chance, perhaps even a third or fourth one, if you admit you're wrong and promise to do better. You might as well be prepared to work overtime for the Aries boss frequently. He'll expect it. On the other hand, if he's a typical Aries, he probably won't frown at the clock or glance at his wristwatch when you arrive late in the morning or take an extra half hour or hour for lunch. He's not a clock watcher himself. Because of his highly individual personality, he'll understand that you can't turn on creativity like a light switch at nine in the morning and turn it off again at five in the afternoon. He's a boss who will often ask you to work an extra Saturday, but he's also likely to accept the excuse of your grandmother's funeral when you want to attend that baseball game, though you'd get the time off just as easily by telling the truth. He can see why, on sudden impulse, you'd like to root for your team on a spring day.

Though he'll usually be generous with vacations, salaries, raises and all such matters, he'll fully expect you to drop everything—personal plans, emotional ties, travel commitments or what-have-you—if something of great importance pops up at the office. I hate to say it, but I do know of one Aries boss who had a business crisis requiring the round-the-clock services of a valued employee. The fact that the business emergency occurred on a day this employee was scheduled for an appearance as a bride was incidental. What if she had made plans for six bridesmaids, a flower girl, a ring-bearer, and a reception for three hundred afterwards?

The Aries boss couldn't understand why all that couldn't be postponed, including the honeymoon, for an urgent meeting concerning a million dollar deal which could put the company on the big board. He would be willing to delay his own marriage for such a crisis, so why wouldn't you? What's the matter, aren't you loyal? This is admittedly an extreme case, but you've been warned.

It's a rare Aries boss who isn't more lavish than the ordinary employer at Christmas-time. Depending on how strong an Aries he is, you can count on getting a larger bonus check than your friends in other offices—or even a hand-picked, expensive gift, which could be something you've been wanting for a long time. A Mars boss is not likely to be stingy (unless there's a conflicting Moon sign or ascendant).

He's not as susceptible to flattery as other astrological signs, but it won't hurt you to pay him a sincere compliment now and then. If you let him know in a straightforward way that you appreciate him as an employer, you admire his efficiency and you think he's just about the smartest boss in town, your job security is guaranteed. However, do or say this only if you really believe it and mean it. He will have contempt for an employee who gurgles his praises just to make points, while he's secretly doubtful of the ram's ability to head the company. The Aries is not ordinarily a good judge of character, but he's so sensitive to other people's opinions of him that he can pretty well tell if he's disliked by those around him day after day. To be liked is his secret need. You might never guess it from his self-confident air and his brave front, but underneath all that swagger he's desperately in need of the approval of his fellow man. That includes you, his wife and his dog—even the stranger on the elevator. Despite that surface independence, nothing makes him happier than to be looked up to and recognized as the capable person he knows he is. On the other hand, nothing can make him as depressed, cranky and sometimes downright petty as suspecting that those who work for him don't approve of his methods or don't realize his value and potential.

If you hear a rumor that the company is about to go bankrupt, don't look around for another job too quickly. You may not need a new job, after all. If anybody can pull the company out of trouble, save it at the last minute from financial disaster under the most dire circumstances, and make the entire operation seem rather like Moses parting the Red Sea, it's your Aries boss. He's independent, daring and venturesome. His drive (unlike the more emotional drive of the Scorpio) is vital, from the spirit, and almost always idealistic. (He may lose out to the equally determined Scorpio pitted against him, however, and be unable to match the steady ruthlessness of Pluto—though he'll recover from the loss and win somewhere else.)

Aries initiates. If there's a suggestion box around the office and you drop in enough workable, creative ideas, you're almost sure to advance to a high position quickly with this man. He appreciates employees who care enough about the company to make suggestions and who are original in their thinking—as long as they make it perfectly clear they have no intentions of trying to outshine him.

Will power is one of the strong features of the Aries man. He fights off all minor ailments and he won't give in to serious illness either. Sometimes he can delay or entirely prevent disease by sheer positive thinking. If he does have a cold or virus infection (probably accompanied by a high fever), he'll get dressed to come in to the office for some urgent business and by the time he arrives, the fever may be gone, to the mystification of his doctor and the suspicion of his employees that he was really at home goofing off.

The Mars will is so fantastically strong that your Aries boss (who will probably be fairly lucky at gambling) can go to the racetrack and practically root his horse into the lead. You're bound to feel the effect of such a forceful personality, so expect plenty of fireworks, excitement, chaos and intense activity around the office. Your business day will seldom be uneventful. Something will always be happening.

There will be nothing lethargic about him, and there had better not be anything lethargic about you. Your Aries employer will probably have little interest in any previous bad job record you held before or in the reasons why your former boss may have fired you. He's the best bet to approach under these circumstances. Because of his conviction that he's going to make the future what he wants it to be, Aries is seldom bothered or concerned by the past. Yours or his.

The Mars executive is too proud to let others know they've hurt him. In spite of quick outbursts of temper (which won't last long or be vindictive, and will be forgotten as soon as they're over), he will hide quite well those things which truly affect him deeply. The ram won't admit his dependence on anyone but himself. He does need others—far more than he will ever admit, but his strength comes from inside, and he can always find a way of going it alone when he must.

If you can admire his energy and courage, though you find it impossible to imitate; if you can make up for his impulsive, slapdash ways by patiently filling in the details he's overlooked in his haste (and do this unobtrusively), he'll probably pay you more money than you can make anywhere else and you'll be with him for life. Tactfully attempt to keep him from doing or saying rash things he'll regret later. Remind him gently that those to whom he directs his temporary righteous anger may be Very Important People and they could react in a way whch will hurt his business if he alienates them.

That's the important thing to remember about your Aries boss. In spite of his great independent spirit, when his idealistic, optimistic enthusiasm gets him in over his head, he really needs your help, faith and loyalty. Give these to him in abundance and you'll never find a pink slip in your pay envelope. You won't have to worry when missing a taxi in rainy weather makes you late for work, if you need an extra week's vacation time for an operation—or about someone younger and more efficient replacing you. More than any other kind of boss, he'll repay loyalty with loyalty. Keep a full supply of aspirin in the desk drawer for frequent emergencies, polish up your smile, don't take his outbursts seriously—and you can throw away the classified ads. You'll want to stay where the action is.

The ARIES Employee

"I said it very loud and clear
I went and shouted in his ear
And when I found the door was locked
I pulled and pushed and kicked and knocked. . . ."

"But it's no use going back to yesterday
Because I was a different person then."

A job interview with a prospective Aries employee, if he's a typical ram, might run something like this:

EMPLOYER: I see from your resume and references that you've been with six different firms in the past two years, Mr. Bootsikaris.

ARIES: Call me Charlie, Mr. Flaxman. Yes, I believe in trying to advance myself. When you outgrow a job, what's the point of staying in a position where there's nothing more you can learn and nothing more you can contribute to the company?

EMPLOYER: That's just what bothers me, Char—uh, Mr. Bootsikaris. I'm afraid you may outgrow us in a short time, also, after we've spent the money to train you.

ARIES: I thought that might concern you. But you don't have to worry. I've investigated your company, and I'm sure I wouldn't feel restless, because I can see there's plenty of opportunity with you for anyone who really tries. I've always wanted to work with a really great, creative and progressive management. They're so rare that I'd rather wait 'til there's an opening here than go anywhere else.

Needless to say, the boss who can overcome his initial shock at such an unusual interview is likely to hire the Aries on the spot. That kind of sincere enthusiasm for the company is hard to come by in these days of security-minded and union-conscious employees—never mind the abruptness and the superego.

Hiring an Aries can be the smartest move you ever made or the largest headache you've ever known, depending on how you aim this combustible, misguided missile. Aiming him toward a routine, nine-to-five job is the wrong direction. In the beginning, he may shine like a silver dollar to impress you, but it won't be long before he's restless and unhappy. And he'll let you know it in unmistakable ways, like coming in a little later each day, taking extra time for lunch, or writing personal letters at his desk. These are all danger signals that your Aries employee is not satisfied. He's still extremely valuable to your firm, but he's bored, and when the ram gets bored, his virtues are quickly buried under his shortcomings.

Put your Aries worker in a position where he has complete freedom to make decisions, answerable if possible, only to you. If you can do it without hurting office morale, allow him to come to work at odd hours. After a short period you'll notice that, although he may appear as late as ten or eleven in the morning, or take two hours for lunch, he'll also be the very last one to leave at night, especially if there's extra work to get out. He's more likely than any of your other employees to accept additional assignments as a challenge, without complaining.

Many an Aries will labor until the wee small hours, if it's necessary, or if there's an exciting project under way, and probably be more familiar to the nightly cleaning woman than to the early morning switchboard receptionist. You won't find him getting edgy or peeking at the clock around five o'clock, so why should you be fussy if it's twenty minutes past ten when he arrives in the morning? That's his reasoning, and there's a certain logic in it.

The Arien is constitutionally unable to keep to a tight and uniform schedule, regardless of standard office procedure. His great, creative energy comes on him at all hours, and it can't be adjusted to fit someone's idea of the proper working day. He may ask to leave early some afternoon for pressing personal reasons, but he'll come back later the same night to burn the midnight oil, or pop in before the birdies chirp the following morning to make up the work he's missed. One thing Aries can't stand is to turn in work which is less perfect than he knows he can do. Despite his carelessness with detail and his disdain of normal office routine, that quality is too good to miss. It's worth putting up with the Mars independence to take advantage of his wonderful determination to succeed, which will obviously benefit your company, if you're astute enough and patient enough to utilize it properly.

Money is never his prime reason for working. He will insist on being paid what he's worth (what *he* thinks he's worth) for the sake of ego and status, but money is never his main objective. He's motivated by success, and cash is always secondary. He may frequently ask to borrow money, because the ram usually lives beyond his income. Still, an extra pat on the back will often get more out of him than an extra five dollars a week in his pay envelope. Of course, you may have to tame his natural desire to take over everyone else's department, since he's bursting with ideas of how everyone in the firm could get where they're going faster, including you. But if you can learn not to take offense at his frequent and impertinent suggestions, you'll find a bonus of original and profitable thoughts.

Always put Aries in the action job, in a position where he can get out and promote the firm and mix with people. Never put him behind a desk where he has to do the same thing day after day under the scrutiny of another employee. Aries will take orders willingly from very few people, since he believes very few people are superior to him. He undoubtedly thinks you are, or he wouldn't have gotten mixed up with you in the first place. Once he's sure you understand and appreciate his efforts, he'll probably be the most loyal, hard-working and competent employee on your payroll. But put him in an inferior position and he'll be reluctant to make any but the most perfunctory effort.

Naturally, he can't always start at the top, though he'd like to. If he must begin at the bottom and learn a new trade or profession, try to add some kind of important-sounding responsibility to his daily duties, so he'll at least think he's at the top. It allows him to save face with himself. To bring out his best, he needs to feel that the place couldn't run without him. The ram is a natural promoter. He'll promote your business to his wife and friends enthusiastically, to cab drivers, waiters and anyone else who will listen—at the movies, in the swimming pool—and not just during the hours he's being paid to do so. He'll turn everyone from his broker to his insurance man into a booster for your firm. Few people (except Leos) can equal him in bringing in new accounts, saving customers you thought were hopelessly lost and putting over the largest, most ambitious schemes you can devise—especially when he thinks you're depending on him to come through.

If there's ever any kind of financial trouble, your Aries employee is not one to desert a sinking ship. He'll stick with you through the crisis, and possibly add a few ideas of his own about how to solve it. The Arien is literally unable to conceive that anything or anyone he believes in, including himself, can fail. Obviously, such a trait can be mighty welcome some black day.

Ask this employee to work on weekends or holidays, take a temporary cut in salary during an emergency or perform someone else's job in addition to his own in case of illness or vacation, and he'll seldom complain. Just be sure you thank him warmly and let him know you honestly appreciate it. There's little he won't do to get enthusiastic approval from you. Never give someone else credit for work he's done, never make him feel guilty about being late, don't compliment others too often when he's around, don't harp on his mistakes—especially in front of other people—and never give him the impression you wish he'd

stay in his place. Otherwise, he'll be irritable, frustrated
and lazy. You won't have to fire him. He'll most likely
quit before you get around to it. It's usually not necessary
to scold the ram, anyway. He'll be the first to apologize
for errors he's committed through his natural haste and
impulsiveness, if he's met halfway, and he'll sincerely try
not to repeat them. Even if he's not always successful in
that attempt, his intentions are admirable. You may want
to train him tactfully and privately not to be so rash and
over-confident, but never break his spirit. If you try, you'll
fail, and the attempt will just lose you all that refreshing
and valuable optimism.

When you recognize his talents, Aries will literally knock
himself out to top himself. Criticism will never accomplish
its intended purpose with him. Besides, he's more often
right than wrong with his hunches, no matter what some
of the experts who have been around for years might
think. Aries has an uncanny ability to understand today
with a clarity not possessed either by those who cling to
yesterday or those who pin all their hopes on tomorrow.
So it pays to listen to him, even though his eagerness and
his sureness that he's right makes him drop his manners
now and then, with a loud and unpleasant thud.

As soon as you can, give him a raise or a title to let him
know he's doing well and that you're pleased, and by all
means, as quickly as you can, let him either work alone or
lead others. Let him feel he's your personal associate. It's
imperative that those dealing with an Aries in any working
or professional capacity realize that he will pour out an
amazing number of valuable contributions to the project
at hand only if he feels that, in some way, he's important.
When his excitement and his idealism are dampened, he
quickly loses interest, becomes disheartened and stands
back to let others take over—glum and miserable—an
unnecessary waste of rare and useful talent. Unless the
ram is allowed to promote, create and originate, he's no
use to himself or anyone else. Logic and kindness will
reach him every time.

Because he's a natural innovator and leader, Aries is at
home in almost any career or profession. There are no
special places where he thrives best. Whether it's a green-
house or a police station—whether he wears a fireman's
hat or a surgeon's mask—he must be in charge. The fields
of advertising and public relations attract him, since they

give him a chance to promote, and he takes to selling like a duck takes to water. But you can place him in any job, from teaching to trucking—from broadcasting to building —and he'll fit right into the slot, if the slot is wide enough to take up his excess energy and ego.

You may run across a ram who hides his drive under a calmer, more controlled manner, but don't kid yourself into thinking you can push him into the corner. That's for little Jack Horner, not him. His place is in front—avant-garde. Channel his abilities and he'll make a heap of money for you, as well as give you unswerving, unquestioned loyalty—especially when the chips are down. If you do a little comparative shopping around, you'll find those virtues are cheap at half the price.

"I shall sit here," he said,
"on and off, for days and days."

TAURUS the Bull

April 21st through May 21st

How to Recognize TAURUS

*"Take care of the sense,
and the sounds will take care of themselves."*

A travel bug friend of mine, who has been everywhere at
least twice, told me he will never forget his first trip to
southern Spain on a tramp steamer. One day, while he was
on deck admiring the view, a huge mass of solid rock
loomed ahead in the distance, rising grandly out of the
bright, blue Mediterranean. Someone on the ship shouted,
"Look! The Rock of Gibraltar!" Awed and impressed, my
friend snapped a picture of it for the folks back home,
then turned to a bored teenager in the next deck chair,
and waxed poetic. "Isn't it beautiful?" he asked. "Tons of
water have beaten against it through the centuries, storms
have lashed at it, armies have assaulted it, civilizations
have come and gone, but it just sits there. Nothing ever
changes it, and nothing can make it move." The teenager
yawned. "Yeah. Reminds me of my old man."

His father was born in May. And that's how you
recognize Taurus, the bull. The most fertile places to look
for him would be a farm, a bank or a real estate office,
but you'll also find him grazing in other pastures. There
are Taurean engineers, movie stars, clerks, gardeners, kings
and queens, chimney sweeps, butchers, bakers and candlestick makers. You can always tell the bull by his strong,
silent attitude. Until you get to know him better, his
lengthiest monologues will probably be "Yep," "Nope,"
"Thanks," "So long," and frequently "Uh-uh," a substitute
for "Nope." If he had a strong Gemini, Aries or Sagittarius influence at birth, he may be a little gabbier and
walk with more bounce. But the typical Taurean prefers
to move deliberately and speak sparingly.

Like Gibraltar, he is solid and steady and nothing disturbs his tranquility. You can throw water on him or light
a fire between his toes. You can beat on his chest with
clenched fists, glare at him hypnotically or shout at the top

of your lungs. Taurus won't budge an inch. Once his mind is set, he folds his arms calmly and digs in his heels. He sticks out his rather prominent chin, flares his nostrils, pins back his ears and you've had it.

The bull seldom rushes forward to stomp on your toes. He simply wants to be left alone. Don't disturb him and he'll remain contented. Press him and he becomes obstinate. Shove too hard, tease too much, and be prepared for violent rage. He can go for months and years on end, exhibiting perfect poise and control, inhaling the fragrance of the posies and ignoring the nervous clacking and clucking all around him. Then some unexpected day, a pushy person will pile one straw too many on his broad back. He'll snort, begin to paw the earth, narrow his eyes—and charge. Get out of the way as fast as you can and run for your life! The Taurean temper is seldom displayed impulsively, but when the bull gets mad, he can destroy everything in his path, up to and including Scorpios. Destroy is not the right word. Demolish is better. It may be some time before the dust settles and peace reigns again. Some Taureans have such control that they only charge once or twice in a whole lifetime. Even the quick-tempered ones won't erupt more than once or twice a year, if that often. Still, it's best to remember that Taurus usually doesn't get just a little mad or annoyed. If the incident is large enough to rock his normally placid emotions, you can count on blind fury, no ordinary anger.

I know one Taurus male whose wife had never seen him angry during all the years of her marriage, until one night in a crowded supper club. An obnoxious drunk stumbled over to their table and made an off-color remark. She expected her husband to handle the man firmly, with his usual self-control, and she was as shocked as the rest of the customers when the Taurean suddenly stood up, shoved over two tables, lifted the man in the air, and sent him flying to the other side of the room, nearly demolishing the bandstand. Not a word was exchanged. I trust this will make you properly cautious. Before even winking at a strange woman, it would be wise to know her escort's birthday.

You can expect many May people to actually resemble a bull, the men that is, and the women born under the Sun sign will have an intangible, elusive bovine quality about them. The look in the female Taurean's eyes will be

serene and limpid, yet steady. She will move gracefully,
indolently, but with a suggestion of hidden strength. As
for the males, the neck will often be thick or muscular,
the shoulders, chest or back, or all three, broad and
strong. The entire body will be well proportioned, whether
short or tall. The ears are usually small and close to the
head. When they eat, they chew slowly, and ordinarily
have excellent digestions. You may notice a lock of hair
(resembling the bull's forelock), or a curl that hangs in
the center of the forehead. Not all, but many Taureans
have curly or wavy hair. It's usually dark, like the eyes
and skin. Even the occasional blonde, light-eyed and fair-
skinned Taurus people will never suggest fragility of mind
or character.

Naturally, you can't expect every Taurean to look like
Ferdinand the bull or Elsie the cow. It's true that they
frequently have large, generous bodies, ranging from
muscular to plump to fat. But if you get that image too
set in your mind, you won't recognize the skinny ones,
and it's important to learn to spot them, too. What are you
going to do when you turn on television and *The Late, Late
Show* features Taureans Bing Crosby, Fred Astaire or
Gary Cooper? Don't let it throw you. For all his Piscean
lightness of foot, and his airy Gemini charm, Fred Astaire
is an earthy Taurus. The other planetary influences in his
chart can't change that. Just ask his friend, choreographer
Hermes Pan, or anyone else close to the dancing legend.
Ask them how tough it is to get this Twinkletoes to go
somewhere he doesn't want to go or do something he
doesn't want to do. Bing Crosby is also famous for his
unruffled personality and his calm, easygoing manner.
(That was probably one of Bing's sons on the tramp
steamer.) As for Gary Cooper, take another look at the
tall, lanky frame of that hero of the vintage cowboy
shows. His solid feet seem to be growing right out of the
ground as if they were rooted there. He moves across your
television screen with slow deliberation, and the total
number of complete sentences the actor speaks in those
old westerns is roughly under a dozen. Actor? Following
the venerable Hollywood system of type casting, Gary
Cooper always superbly played Gary Cooper. And like
many another Taurean you'll meet away from stage and
camera, the Cooper love scenes feature a romantic girl,
who cries, "I love you madly, passionately. I can't live

without you. You're my whole life, darling. Tell me you
care. Say you feel the same way. Do you love me? Do
you?" What answer does the poor girl get for her torrent of
sentiment? "Yep." (But it can be strangely comforting.)

Taurus is strongly attracted to the opposite sex, but aggressive pursuit of any kind of pleasure isn't in his bag of
tricks. He prefers to attract people to him. Why should
he waste his energy chasing them over the countryside?
A short trip to a farm and some astute observation of the
laws of nature will make it clear how the Taurean emotions
are activated in both love and friendship. Passivity is the
typical behavior. Taureans would rather entertain hospitably at home than go to the trouble of visiting. The effort
required for scintillating popularity doesn't appeal to the
bull's nature. If you want him, you can call him. He'll
be there. Throw out the line of comradeship or romance,
and he'll pick it up, if it interests him. He'll know what
to do with it, too, which isn't always true of the more
gregarious signs.

Taurus seldom worries, frets or chews his nails. He can
pout and brood when things don't suit his fancy, but he's
not the nervous, twitchy type. It's his nature to be stoic,
and take things in his stride, and nothing really alters this
basic tendency.

I know a Taurean, who is both an attorney and a certified
public accountant, a double career that would give anyone
plenty to take in stride, especially at tax time. Now, this
Taurus may bite his nails a little. All right, he bites them a
lot. He talks faster than I do (which is pretty fast), and
he does have a couple of worry creases in his forehead.
But there's a heavy Gemini influence in his natal chart
that causes the deceptive speed, and if you look behind
the whirling action of his dynamic outer image, you'll still
discover a Taurus. His brain may calculate like lightning,
but his decisions are made slowly and carefully. His actions
are predictable, his character is strong, and you can ask his
wife just how much of a pushover he is when she tries to
get him to dress up and go somewhere on the nights he'd
rather stay home. You can also ask his clients who try
to rush him into closing deals quickly. He'll listen patiently
and pleasantly, but the papers don't get signed until the
bull makes up his mind it's the right move. Oh, yes, he's a
Taurus, never mind the Gemini wit and agility. Flighty

action is not among his vices. He rushes slowly, and that's *not* a non sequitur.

Taurus people are home folks. There's scarcely a bull who doesn't love to luxuriate under his own roof and stretch out amid comfortable, familiar surroundings. Change upsets him (unless there's a Gemini, Sagittarius or Aquarius Moon or ascendant). If the Taurus you know doesn't own his own home, he's dreaming about it, and he will someday. He's close to the earth, and the love of the land will come to him eventually, one way or another. If he's forced to live in a crowded apartment building, he'll probably have a window box full of geraniums or petunias. When the noisy clatter of the city threatens to press in too close, he'll determinedly grab his fishing pole and head for a quiet, pastoral spot. Let the world spin at too dizzy a pace for him, and Taurus simply gets off for a spell until it slows down. If he has no fishing pole or window box outlet, he may dabble in real estate, and make arrangements for other people's mortgages, which gets him out to the suburbs occasionally. There's always a connection with the land, however remote, like hanging around the race track, or taking his Sunday stroll through the park and drinking in the sights and fragrances of nature.

The average bull is superbly healthy, with a strong constitution. It takes a lot to put him on his back, but once he's down, he may recuperate slowly, partially due to his stubborn refusal to obey the doctor. His natural inclination to distrust optimism doesn't promote speedy recovery, either. The sensitive areas for accident and infection are the throat, neck, legs, ankles, reproductive organs, the back and the spinal area. Colds often turn into sore throats, and overweight brought on by the legendary Taurean love of food and drink, mostly food, can put a strain on the heart, and plague the bull with poor circulation, weak ankles, varicose veins and other chronic complaints. Gout is another possibility. Most May people, however, can easily stay healthier than the rest of us if they avoid obesity, lethargy and kidney infections. Let's be blunt. If the bull drinks to excess or gets fat and lazy, he'll lose his splendid physique and his robust good health. One of the main causes for his illnesses is a lack of country air and exercise. His system always needs it, even though his obstinate will may deny it.

Speaking of obstinacy, there's no use telling a Taurean

he (or she) is obstinate. In the bull's mind, he's not stubborn at all. He's patient. It's a matter of semantics. He's not hardheaded—he's just sensible and firm. For the life of him, he can't see why people judge him so unfairly.

The truth is that Taurus is as stubborn as a human can be and not actually turn into solid stone. Taurean men and women seem to be glued to both their seats and their opinions. A Taurus husband will refuse to accompany his wife to a friend's house if there are no comfortable chairs there for him to sit in. She can plead in vain. He just won't go. A Taurus woman who doesn't approve of her husband's cronies simply will not talk to them. Still, the bulls can also claim the virtue of patience with justification. Many a Taurean bears emotional and physical burdens in silence for years without complaint. The higher the troubles pile up, the more strength Taurus finds to bear them. His loyalty and devotion to family and friends often surpass all understanding. Lots of Taurus men and women deserve gold medals for courage under blows of fate that would have long ago broken the back of those born under other Sun signs. Fine. I'll go along with awarding a blue ribbon in recognition of the Taurus fortitude. *But he's still stubborn.*

There's very little that turns his appetite faint. The bull can usually eat anything from fried peppers to chocolate whipped cream cake, sour pickles and turnips—all at the same meal—without a trace of indigestion. Steak and beef are usually his favorites, and he loves to clean up the leftovers. If alcohol is added, the Taurean can closely resemble King Henry VIII, happily gorging at a royal banquet. (Of course, a Virgo ascendant can keep him on raw carrots and lettuce, washed down with prune juice.)

The Taureans' funny bones are tickled by broad and slapstick comedy. Many of them fail to catch subtle satire, but they'll howl when someone slips on a banana peel or gets a custard pie in the face. Taurus humor is warm and earthy, playful and reminiscent of Falstaff. These people are seldom, if ever, really cruel or vindictive. It's a strange fact that cruel Taureans often have many planets in Aries at birth. The two signs don't seem to mix well in the same horoscopes. Hitler is a good example.

Now, about the subject of money—the bull and his money are seldom parted. Not every Taurean is a millionaire, but you won't find many of them standing in line for free soup. Taurus likes to build empires slowly and surely. He starts with a solid foundation, then gradually adds a story at a time, until he's built a stable business and a bank account with muscles. Oddly, Taurus likes to accumulate power, along with cash, but simply for the sensual enjoyment of possessing it. They often turn over the action to subordinates. Just knowing the power is there along with the dollars seems to satisfy the Taurean need for security. Why should he be bothered with the effort of manipulating all the strings? There are Capricorns and Cancerians around to do that, while he snoozes, smells a daisy or eyes the pretty girls. It's enough that everybody knows who owns the pasture. Sooner or later, money will come to Taurus, and it usually sticks like glue when it does. The bull prizes his cash and his possessions as he does his family, but he's not stingy. The Taurean generous heart and pockets are wide open to real friends in real trouble.

He's impressed by bigness. The larger a building, the grander it is to him, and he'll walk right past the monkeys at the zoo to stare in fascination at the powerful elephants. Taurus will face huge animals with magnificent courage, but he fears a mouse. A tiger on the loose won't cause the bull to flicker an eyelash, while a tiny wasp can send him climbing up the nearest tree in nervous panic.

Fine paintings and great symphonies stir him deeply. Every Taurean owns some evidence of the Venus love for art and music, if it's only an old Caruso record, or a museum postcard of an early Van Gogh tucked under the sweat shirts he wears when he's out jogging on weekends. Many Taurus men and women have beautiful voices. Some of them sing professionally; others warble in the bath, soak in rich oils and dream of gilt-edged security. Music will always touch their lives in some way, and drawing or painting are often either hobbies or careers.

The sensuous bull is tranquilized by the color of the sky. Shades of blue bathe his emotions with peace; also rose and pink, in a lesser way, but never red, as any matador could tell you. The greens and browns of nature calm and soothe him too. Green paper money and a brownstone house will keep him perfectly contented.

Although Taurean ideas are always sensible, they can also sparkle with the clarity and depth of fifteen precious sapphires that add up to six kinds of good fortune, as he doubles his money under the benign smile of the gods. There's nothing small about Taurus, including his capacity for lasting love and his potential for wealth. Copper, the Taurean metal, is an excellent conductor of electricity and heat, and it glows with burnished beauty through years of use and wear. Let the excitable ones scurry and squabble for first place. The bull's fixed nature needs no flaming torches to light the way to the security he seeks. Eventually success will come to him, and he will be ready. Because the far-off Venus showers him with the love of luxury, he pays dearly for his possessions and treasures them for a lifetime; yet he's the sworn enemy of waste and extravagance. His home is his castle—and let no man disturb the peace of the bull. Taurus is as patient as time itself, as deep as the forest, with a dependable strength that can move mountains. *But he's stubborn.*

Famous Taurus Personalities

Fred Astaire	William R. Hearst
Balzac	Audrey Hepburn
Lionel Barrymore	Hitler
Irving Berlin	Henry J. Kaiser
Johannes Brahms	Willie Mays
Catherine, the Great	Yehudi Menuhin
Perry Como	Vladimir Nabokov
Gary Cooper	Robespierre
Oliver Cromwell	Sugar Ray Robinson
Bing Crosby	Bertrand Russell
Salvador Dali	William Shakespeare
Stephen A. Douglas	Bishop Fulton Sheen
Queen Elizabeth II	Toots Shor
Duke Ellington	Kate Smith
Ella Fitzgerald	Barbra Streisand
Henry Fonda	Norma Talmadge
Margot Fonteyn	Shirley Temple
Sigmund Freud	Harry S. Truman
Ulysses S. Grant	Orson Welles

Your Friendly Banker

The TAURUS Man

"Why, I wouldn't say anything about it,
even if I fell off the top of the house!"

". . . Only you'd better not come very close . . .
I generally hit everything I can see—
when I get really excited."

Perhaps you picture the typical Taurus man as a quiet, practical soul, as sensible and down-to-earth as an old pair of shoes. It's true—he is. You may also observe that he's slow to move to action, deliberate and careful. True again. Therefore, you deduce, it's only logical to assume he's not very romantic. Positively false.

Where did you get the idea you can analyze the Taurean nature by using pure logic alone? Probably from some Libra fellow who's trying to make an impression on you. Well, he's wrong. Logic isn't very helpful when you're trying to solve the riddle of a strong, masculine symbol like the bull, who's ruled by a loving, peaceful planet like Venus. Send that Libra man with his clever mind back to the library.

The bull may take a long time deciding if he wants you for his woman. He's not going to execute a flashy swan dive into the pool of romance and discover on the way down that someone forgot to fill it with water. But once he's made up his mind that you're the one, and once he sets his mind on winning you, he'll make the Libra lover look like a fumbler. He'll even put the smitten lion and the passionate Scorpio to shame. That sensible, practical, slow, determined Taurus male is capable of sending you one pink rose each day until you surrender to his proposal—of marriage—or whatever. He can even write a poetic song or verse, and bashfully mail it to you without signing it, knowing you'll guess the sender. Taurus can be a tender, gentle and protective lover. His sensual nature will make him vulnerable to your exotic perfume, the smoothness of

your skin and softness of your hair. He may not say so in
flowery language to your face, but he will find a way to con-
vey the message. The Taurus sense of touch is a tangible
thing.

This negative, fixed earth sign is full of contradictions in
love. A Taurean will like to see you dress in luxurious furs
and rich colors. He may buy you a fragrant bunch of
fresh, spring violets for your furs from the little old
lady on the corner, and leave a large tip in her basket because she reminds him of his mother. (You, however, will
definitely not remind him of either his mother or his sister
—except when it comes to protecting you from the rude
glances of other bulls who try to move in.) Music will
stir his emotions and put him in the mood for love. He's
almost sure to have a favorite song that reminds him of
you each time he hears it. It's the one he keeps playing
on the juke box.

If you need more proof of the romance in his soul, the
typical Taurus man will help you build your hope chest
with birthday gifts of china and silver, and at Christmas
he'll remind you of Santa himself when he comes calling,
loaded down with mysterious packages and sentimental
trinkets. He'll suggest moonlight swims, picnics in cool,
secluded woods, and walks down country lanes under the
stars. His will be the largest, fanciest, most eloquent Valentine the postman ever delivered on February 14th. When
a Taurus man courts you, he courts you. He doesn't fool
around. You'll probably be taken to dine in glamorous
restaurants, with soft lights and violins, and he'll never
forget the date you first met or any other intimate anniversary between you. For the love of buttercups, how
much romance do you need?

It's perfectly true that the bull isn't a wild dreamer like
the Aquarian male. Taurus will never sweep you off your
feet like a Leo, or promise to take you floating away to
live with him in a fairy castle, drifting on pink clouds
forever and a day, like an Aries. He's more likely to drop
by on foot some Saturday night, with the architect's blue-
prints for the house he plans to build for you, out of real
lumber and with real cash. He'll probably make the down
payment on the property, or at the very least, on the apartment lease, before you become engaged. This man means
business. When the bull lifts you across his threshold and
plants you firmly in his substantial home, which won't

bear the faintest resemblance to a fairy castle, you can be
sure the mortgage is secure at the bank. That's hardly
something to complain about. You'll wonder why you ever
wanted to be wrapped in those pink clouds, once you've
been warmly and snugly enfolded in the soft Taurean
blanket of security. You'll be too busy enjoying your new
furniture and checking account (or the certainty that
they're just around the corner) to weep for misty dreams
that probably wouldn't have come true anyway. That is,
if you're a female who appreciates solid value. Not every
woman does, more's the pity. But sensible girls, from
eighteen to eighty, value the peaceful, easygoing ways
of the bull and his calm, stable nature. His sentimental
gestures and pleasantly earthy wooing can be just as
satisfying as the soulful, poetic sighs of more colorful
lovers, or the dashing excitement of the flashier Don
Juans, quite often even more so. Ask any woman who's
been sensible enough to get herself good and loved by a
strong Taurean. There are lots of contented cows and
happy heifers around.

A Taurus man plans for tomorrow carefully. As the
squirrel stores his nuts when they're plentiful in the summer, to provide security for the cold, barren winter—the
temporary pleasures of a bright afternoon will never
distract Taurus from preparing for the days when the
slush piles up at the curb. It's a funny thing, but the husbands who are financially able to take or send their wives
to Florida in January are often born in May.

Naturally, there are drawbacks to a romantic escapade
with a Taurus male—all is not peaches and perfection.
For one thing, you'll have to brush up on your ladylike
behavior. No Taurus man is going to put up with a loud,
masculine female who cracks a whip like an animal
trainer. If you have any forceful opinions, don't shove
them down his throat or brag about your brainpower in
public. Privately, he respects a female with intelligence
(though he places a higher premium on plain common
sense), but you'd just better let him be the bright one of
the team when you're out together dancing cheek to
cheek—even if you're just sitting in a restaurant, knee to
knee. Make like the emancipated woman in front of his
friends and he'll have one of two reactions. If he's a primi-
tive Taurean (and you'd be surprised how many of those
there are), he's likely to give you a shove and a shaking,

maybe even a good smack in the right place when you get home—or worse, before you get home. If he's a more sophisticated type, he'll simply clam up on you in front of everyone and sit there like a large chunk of cold stone, refusing to speak a word the rest of the night, until you're so embarrassed you wish the floor would swallow you. Your friends will be most uncomfortable, too. It can really dampen an evening, not to mention cramp your style.

Your first impulse will be to try to undo the damage, but trying to jolly him out of his stubborn mood before it's run its course is literally impossible. It's like trying to move the Rock of Gibraltar. As a matter of fact, if you attempt to tease him back into normal social behavior, you may wish you had just let him sulk. A hunk of cold stone is infinitely more acceptable than his reaction to your coaxing after you've angered him. Push him too far and he'll turn from a silent sphinx into a bellowing bull, who may very well let loose some mighty earthy language, which will cause your cheeks to flame even pinker. Either that, or he'll say calmly to the group, "Excuse me for breaking up the party, but I have to drag this woman with the tent flap mouth home and teach her a few lessons." You'll hide from everyone you know for weeks afterwards. And all because, when he's holding the group spellbound with his summary of the political scene, you interrupt him with a remark like, "Oh, honey, don't be so naive. Everyone knows Utterbach takes bribes. With his record he couldn't get elected chairman of the Boy Scout cookie sale, let alone Congressman. You don't know what you're talking about," at which point he'll dig in those heels, fold his arms across that beefy chest, and begin to pout—or clobber you—whichever. If you see him reach for his coat, you might as well put on yours, too. A Taurus man will seldom leave his woman alone with the wolves, unprotected, no matter how angry she's made him. He'll take her along, by the hair, if necessary. So don't get any ideas of staying behind to get sympathy from the others. When he leaves, you leave. And I would strongly advise you to apologize before you get home. He won't. Running to Mama's arms won't do any good. You share his bed and board, as long as he pays the rent. Mother-in-law interference is about the last thing the typical bull will stand for. The first time you try that "running home to Mother" routine will probably be the last. After they once experience his fury, your parents will prefer to keep the door locked and let you handle your own problems.

I know a Taurus man with an aggressive wife who found a unique solution. He simply refuses to go out with her in public. Her irresistible force met an immovable object— him. She can go out and rob other men of their masculinity all she wants, not Taurus, the bull. He's very fond of his positive mate, and they have rather a nice team going in many ways; they respect each other tremendously —but until she learns to submit, keep her mouth closed, and let him be the man, she's forced to go to parties, meetings and the theater without an escort. This particular Taurean has refused to accompany her ever since the time they joined several other couples for dinner at a fancy place. His wife grabbed the menu from him and ordered for the whole group. She made unflattering remarks about his haircut and his tie during the first course, and supplied the punch line to three of his jokes during the entree. Now she goes to social functions alone, while her Taurus mate refuses to budge from his castle. You can't really blame the bull. He's just being true to his Sun sign. It's still a solid marriage, but you may not be so lucky. So don't tempt your Taurean by shoving him around.

He's extremely patient, but he won't wear a ring in his nose. He doesn't necessarily want a clinging vine, either. He's too practical, and he likes his freedom too much to enjoy a female who sticks to him like rubber cement and cries at the drop of a hanky. He doesn't mind a woman with some fire and spunk. It intrigues him and balances his own steadier maturity. With a smile of detached amusement, he'll watch her cheerfully scampering around in typical feminine fashion, as one would watch a beloved, pretty kitten playing with a brightly colored ball of yarn. Just so kitty knows when the bull gives a strong tug on the yarn, it's time to stop the fun and games and listen to the voice of her master. No one can be kinder, more gentle and truly tolerant than a Taurus man, when his masculinity is secure. He'll do anything in the world for the woman he loves except allow her to wear the pants. Taurus may sometimes behave like a clumsy circus bear, and his humor is often rough and ridiculous. But he will not play the role of the fool after the party is over.

The bull enjoys shopping around and he'll seldom rush pell mell into a serious courtship. The puzzled girl he's been taking to the movies every Saturday night for a year may wonder if he's ever going to catch fire. It takes time for him to work up enough steam in the boiler to get the engine going at full speed, but once he's set his sights on a particular female, he can't be sidetracked. He may even forget to be sensible and cautious. The typical Taurus man is blind to any warnings of incompatibility when he's been pierced by Cupid's arrow. The more his friends point out possible stumbling blocks, the more obstinate he gets, and you know how obstinate that can be. Consequently, the Taurean frequently makes the mistake of getting tangled up with fire and air signs, when he's better off with earth and water, in most cases. Sometimes, it works out beneficially. Opposites can attract, and stay attracted. But when it doesn't, Taurus will take a long time to get over the scars of a divorce before he's ready to settle down again with a wife who more closely matches his own disposition and outlook.

The financial picture with a Taurus man is usually excellent. Paint it pink and rosy. Few Taureans will fail to accumulate at least security, if not wealth. Some of them play the game of Monopoly with real money. And they win. Both real estate and cash are easily conquered by the bull.

He probably loves the country, football, fishing and camping. If none of these, he likes flowers, gardening or long walks. He prefers to read books about the dashing heroes of olden days or the biographies of empire builders, rather than sophisticated fiction or deep philosophy. Most Taurus males subscribe to several men's magazines, some earthy and practical, others featuring glossy pages of feminine pulchritude.

He's the ultimate in a man's man, so don't ever serve him those dainty tea sandwiches with the crusts sliced off. He likes good, old-fashioned home cooking, with plenty of potatoes and gravy, and apple pie like Mom used to make. Get yourself a good cookbook. He'll also be willing to take you out to dine frequently. Typical Taureans don't expect their wives to be kitchen slaves. (But he may mess up your pots and pans when he plays Sunday chef and expects you to play bus boy.)

As a parent, he's a perfect delight. He'll think it's important to have a son to carry on the family name, but he'll love the little girls with special tenderness. Taurus men make loving, affectionate, warm and sympathetic fathers. He'll set high standards for the children and expect them to respect property and possessions. The Taurean dad is patient. He won't mind if the children learn their lessons slowly, so long as they get them correctly. His attitude is that young minds should be trained gradually toward maturity. You may find that he puts too much emphasis on material matters and showers them with expensive gifts that spoil them. But he'll also shower them with his time and devotion, and the firm hand of discipline will be there when it's needed. In general, life with father, if he was born in May, can be a warm experience, overflowing with love—except for those rare occasions when the bull charges in blind, furious anger, and the whole family has to hide behind the piano.

The typical Taurean husband is generous to a fault with his wife. He won't deny you nice clothes, perfume and baubles; attractive but practical furniture and a full pantry. The bull seldom skimps on furnishings, clothing or food. Still, money won't burn any noticeable holes in his pockets (unless there are impulsive financial aspects in his natal chart). He loves luxury, but he's just as enamoured with value, and he'll make sure his cash buys more than a salesman's hot air.

This man will work hard and need lots of rest. See that he gets it, because he can be quite a grumpy grouch when he's tired and out of sorts. Don't ever nag him or accuse him of being lazy. That's like waving a red flag in his face. He lives life at his own leisurely pace, and he won't be rushed or pushed. His speedometer is set at one speed—deliberate. Attempts to make him spin merrily through a continual round of whirlwind social activity are doomed to failure. He will enjoy entertaining in his own home, but he'll prefer a few people of compatible interests to large crowds. Invite old friends, or those who have serious goals and ambitions, and he'll behave pleasantly and hospitably. If you insist on cluttering his castle with emptyheaded, frivolous Go-Go types, he may just disappear from the scene—sometimes permanently.

Buy him one of those papa bear chairs that stretches out into a reclining position. No loud noises, blaring radios and TV sets, chaos and scattered toys, please. Keep your home full of music, beauty and peace. Remember that the trousers fit him better than they do you. Be his woman, and you couldn't ask for a better man. No one else will ever treat you with such gracious consideration. He really deserves to be respected for it. Taurus love is simple, plain and honest. His affectionate nature and flattering attention will make you sure you are loved, in spite of all your little faults and failings that other men would constantly criticize. Taurus gives enduring loyalty and devotion, with a faithful heart. That adds up to emotional security. Combined with financial security and romance, there's little else to ask for. So all right, he's stubborn, but remember that stubbornness turned upside down is patience, and that's a rare virtue.

Get a nice, furry, fluffy blanket (Taurus loves things that feel soft to the touch), tuck it around him when he's in his papa bear chair, and read him the stock market report. Be sure he gets his hot bath with scented oils and lots of fragrant soap. Serve him a big bowl of rich porridge. Then you're sure to have a strong, gentle man, who will protect you from all the storms. Contentment is the word. Doesn't it have a cozy sound?

The TAURUS Woman

Without, the frost—the blinding snow,
The storm-wind's moody madness—
Within, the firelight's ruddy glow,
And childhood's nest of gladness.

I remember a conversation I once had with a writer whose mother had been born in May. In discussing her parent's habits and character, the girl happened to mention that "Mother was a tall woman." "You must take after your father then," I remarked, since the girl herself was only of average height. She smiled. And I shall never forget what she said. "I didn't mean in inches. Mother was shorter than I am. That was just soul talk." The girl was a Pisces, the sign that looks deep inside you.

She was right. A Taurus female is a tall woman. Even if she measures under five feet, she can reach tall enough to meet almost any emergency life chooses to throw her way. In many ways, the Taurean female is the salt of the earth, a combination of most of the sterling qualities every male looks for and seldom finds. She may have a violent temper that would frighten a strong man into running for the woods (or at least ducking under a table-cloth), but she won't go on a raging rampage without good provocation. Ordinarily, if you don't torment her beyond human endurance, or if Fate doesn't hand her a really rough bunch of cards, she'll play the game of life fairly, with cool, admirable calm. Her candor and basic honesty are undiluted with normal feminine tricks and tears. The Taurean girl has more moral and emotional courage than many a tough male, but she has enough confidence in her own sex to let you be the boss, if you want the job. If you don't fill it, she may grab control and run things herself, but she'd much rather have it the other way around. She seeks a real man. That's because she knows she's a real woman, and she's proud of it. To her, being a woman doesn't necessarily mean being an incorrigible flirt, a mental fluff ball or a mewing kitten who pretends to be weak to get her own way. It won't be long before you see she has a mind of her own, and it's quite strong enough not to have to resort to teasing to gain an objective.

There's enough self-control in the average Taurus woman's make-up to hold back a team of horses (a fair idea of the force of her hidden will), if she chooses to exercise it. Let's hope she does. With an Aries or Leo ascendant or Moon, she may be capable of occasional cruelty or frequent emotional storms and with heavy Pisces or Gemini influences in her natal chart, she may be more restless and wavering—but the typical Taurean female practices self restraint in all areas at most times. It's a good thing, because her normally placid exterior conceals a sensual nature that could stand a little checking.

Men always appreciate her gracious tendency to take people as they are, without quibbling. She's as much at home with a scientist who studies tsetse flies in the Congo as with the sword swallower in the side show. They're doing what comes naturally; they're not phonies and that's what counts with her. Her close friends may be weird creatures straight out of the world of Toulouse-Lautrec, or they may be Norman Rockwell paintings come to life.

But they will be real people, not stuffed shirts or statues. When she runs across someone she dislikes, she doesn't start a big campaign to destroy him or challenge his ideals and motives. She simply avoids him. The Taurus woman can show frigid indifference to her enemies, but if she counts you as a friend, she'll be loyal through all your ups and downs. Her determination to stick with you would make the relationship between Damon and Pythias look like a casual acquaintance.

You can drive a Maxwell, climb a flag pole, get locked up in the pokey or wear daisies in your hair. You are her friend, and somehow she'll justify your actions. There's just a small catch here. She'll doggedly expect you to return her blind allegiance and unswerving loyalty. If you don't give her your complete devotion in return, she can sulk in the corner like a gloomy, gray cloud of repressed resentment.

This isn't the same thing as jealousy, however. The average Taurus woman will take the masculine hobby of girl watching in stride. Unlike the Aries or Leo woman, she won't turn scarlet with rage every time you openly admire a pretty girl. It takes more than a casual flirtation or kissing a good (female) friend goodnight on the cheek to arouse her Taurean anger. If you go beyond the bounds of her idea of fair play, she can be a holy terror on wheels, but the line is drawn with generous strokes. She'll have to be really pressed to the wall in some way to explode in typical Taurus fury. You can go ahead and wink at that attractive cashier, but don't test her patience too far. It does have a limit, boundless as it appears to be. If you've never seen her mad, leave well enough alone.

These women aren't dominated by strictly mental goals. That's not meant to imply that the Taurus female isn't smart and clever. She can match brains with the brightest men and women, but she's not fiercely interested in figuring out the theory of relativity or delving into abstractions. Multiple university degrees don't impress or thrill her. Just one is sufficient to gain her respect. Practical common sense and the ability to understand the fundamentals of any subject is, to her, essential. But the typical Taurean girl isn't an intellectual who reads the philosophers for kicks, and intricate ideologies are not her forte. She's a solid, practical thinker, with no frills or showy mental gymnastics. Her feet are planted on terra firma, and there are definitely no wings attached to her solid heels. Taurus women are seldom restless—they keep their heads and their balance. The Taurean perspective remains normally straight and true, with no twists and turns or distortions (though a Gemini Moon can put her in a bit of a whirl).

She's strictly a physical creature. *That* will undoubtedly interest *you*, but to interest her, an object or an idea has to appeal to her finely tuned senses. She doesn't want to hear that it's "good for her," that "everybody else is doing it," or that it will "stimulate her mentally." That sort of persuasion will make her yawn. To respond with genuine excitement, she has to derive some sensual satisfaction from everything she does.

You'll seldom see a Taurus woman stuffing a few artificial blooms in a vase. Her flowers must be real, and have an honest feel or fragrance. She'll gather huge bunches of pussywillow and bittersweet in the spring and fall, and fill the house with sturdy mums and dahlias in the summer. Her perfume will usually be exotic and lingering, though some Taurean women lean in the opposite direction, and prefer the odor of squeaking clean hair and skin. Taurus girls will be visibly moved by freshly washed sheets saturated with the sweet smell of sunshine or the delicious aroma of bread baking in the oven. She's spiritually aroused by the scent of the morning paper, the intoxicating odor of newly cut grass after a spring rain, burning wax candles or the smoke from a pile of smoldering autumn leaves. This should clue you to use a good brand of shaving lotion, rub some damp newsprint on your ears, tuck a burned leaf in your lapel and turn on the sprinklers just before you kiss her goodnight. Unpleasant odors affect her just as drastically, in a reverse way. This is not a girl who will appreciate a pet skunk, even if he has been deodorized. Don't take her on a fish fry unless you take along a can of floral spray. It's the cooking odor that causes the problem. The fragrance of fish fresh out of the stream is different; that's natural. The stables won't offend her delicate nostrils, either. Mother Nature again. You may have to make a careful list if you want to woo her with olfactory success.

Colors send her senses soaring, too, the richer the better. Every shade of blue, from powder to indigo, will weaken her strong resistance. So will rose and pink. Wear a blue tie and a shocking pink shirt when you visit her, but not at the same time. Remember, she also has a sense of harmony, and you don't want to look like a co-ed nursery.

Her food must taste just right, and she'll usually sprinkle on the seasoning generously (unless she has a Virgo or Capricorn ascendant). Be sure to take her to places with the best chefs, because flat hamburgers and bland pea soup leave her emotionally cold. If you're lucky, she'll invite you for a home-cooked meal, and you may propose before dessert is served. When this girl ties on an apron, it's not just to make cinnamon toast. It's always a good idea to drop in on her with an empty stomach. A typical Taurus woman can cook her way right into your heart, and her kitchen is a real man trap.

Harmonious sounds and beautiful visual effects draw her like a magnet. Most Taurean women have a marked talent for, or an appreciation of music and art. Her doodles on the telephone pad are often very clever drawings. Concerts and art exhibits are a good bet on dates, and Niagara Falls or the Grand Canyon are the best choices for a honeymoon. She'll be ecstatic at the sight of nature's grandeur.

If you can't afford Niagara, take her to an amusement park. She'll probably love to ride on a ferris wheel, feel the sharp wind across her cheeks, watch the colored lights and listen to the calliope music. (The roller coaster will appeal more to her Aries and Gemini sisters.) It's a rare Taurus girl who has never been on a farm nor hiked in the country—who doesn't love horseback riding and fishing. With all her sensuality, the Taurean female is a tomboy at heart. The earth beckons her with a seductive call—and she responds by throwing her arms around Mother Nature in honest rapture. If you want her to throw her arms around you in honest rapture, be sure you don't play raucous music on your record machine, eat garlic without gargling or wear clashing colors.

Finally, there's the sense of touch. Taurus women are the ones who complain that your sweater is "scratchy." It doesn't "feel nice." They can almost tell the color of a fabric by stroking it with their eyes closed. The materials she wears will be soft and luxurious to the touch, never irritating, and she'll probably dress with simplicity and taste. Her sensuous nature may not stretch to include fussy lingerie and dainty clothing (barring a Pisces or Leo ascendant or Moon). She prefers sportswear and plain, expensive outfits with no excess trimmings, and she dresses mostly for comfort; her practical nature taking over in the costume department. If she happens to have a heavy Aquarian influence in her chart, she can go a little cuckoo in stores on occasion, but even then her offbeat selections will serve a utilitarian purpose.

As you get to know her better, you'll realize that this girl can be a tower of strength. She's seldom demanding, except in the area of loyalty, and her disposition is generally even, down-to-earth and pleasant. People love her straightforward, easy-going manner—it's as relaxing as a warm bath. She's probably fond of warm baths herself, with lots of lotions and oils and bubbles. Taurean bathrooms often look like Cleopatra's private quarters. You keep expecting to see a slave appear and start waving a palm leaf fan.

You might have to find out the hard way that a Taurus woman doesn't like to be contradicted, especially in public, but why do that, when you can learn the easy way by understanding her Sun sign? Remember that she likes to do things slowly. If you hurry her or rush her, she'll become angry, and it isn't wise to make a Taurean female angry. Her tempo ranges from slow to deliberate and steady; it seldom raises to impulsive, but it can reach violent, when she's goaded too far.

Motherhood becomes her nicely. It blends smoothly with her serene disposition and matches her bovine nature beautifully. She'll cuddle little babies and adore toddlers, but as the youngsters grow older, she may be too strict and demanding. There's an unbending, stubborn streak in Taurean females that makes it hard for them to accept easily the multiple and confusing changes of adolescence. The Taurus mother becomes angry when her discipline is thwarted. She won't stand for disobedience or defiance. All the fury of the bull is aroused. She'll also find it difficult to tolerate laziness or sloppiness, and the children will probably keep their rooms neat—or else.

The Taurean love of beauty and harmony prevents calm acceptance of untidy habits. Messy youngsters and sloppy surroundings can make her see red. Outside of these few failings, she'll probably be a good parent, more of a friend to her children than a mother image as the years pass. Most offspring of a May-born woman remember her as a warm, maternal image in the early years and a pal with a sense of humor in their later years. The inbetween years—when youthful impatience clashes with the bull's firm determination—may leave a few unpleasant memories. She'll fiercely and loyally defend them from outside hurts and teach them to imitate her own honest courage.

Taurus females are never sissies. They seldom whine or complain. This is a woman who will quietly take a job to support a husband in medical school or work at home if there's a temporary financial crisis in the family. She doesn't have a lazy bone in her body, despite her often slow, deliberate movements and need for frequent rest periods. Taurus females are hard workers. She can climb a stepladder to paint or scrub the walls with the strength of a man, but she needs that afternoon nap to keep her sturdy. She'll walk proudly beside her man, and seldom try to pass him or stand in his shadow. Many a Taurean wife helps her husband with his studies, if he's taking special courses in a professional career, or types up the business correspondence he brings home from the office. She's an excellent helpmate in these areas. Taureans never expect to be supported without contributing their share, and they're miserable with a man who doesn't contribute his, though they'll try to make the best of it. Taurus women dislike weakness in any form.

Her impassivity to pain and emotional stress is almost miraculous, often even surpassing that of the Scorpio female. I remember a scene I once watched in a hospital. A Taurus woman was going upstairs for serious surgery, so serious that her chances of surviving the operation were very small, and she knew it. It was a calculated risk. As her husband watched her being placed on the cart that would wheel her to the operating area, she noticed the tears in his eyes. But she never commented. She made jokes instead, until the nurses giggled and even the doctor smiled. The last thing her family heard her say as the orderlies were pushing and pulling, trying to get the cart into the elevator, was typically Taurean. Instead of glancing back at her loved ones with a tearful look of farewell, she raised up on one elbow and spoke to the young men firmly. "Before you put me back on this thing again, get some oil and grease those damned wheels." A Taurus woman never lets sentiment interfere with practicality.

A man who marries a female born in May won't marry

a cry baby or a gold digger. She'll expect him to provide
for her and manage the family finances sensibly. She'll also
want the best quality when it comes to food and furnishings.
But she'll always keep a sharp eye out for bargains, and
be willing to wait for the luxuries she craves.

Quick fortunes without a solid foundation don't appeal
to her sense of stability. She'd rather see you build carefully
for the future. Making a good impression is important to
her, and lots of Taurean women encourage their husbands
to aim for a secure future by inviting influential people to
dinner. A Taurus wife is the soul of hospitality.

This is a girl who will stay up night after night with a
sick child and pray him back to health with a rock-bound
faith—the kind of woman who can tenderly replenish a
man's store of hope when the world has defeated him, in-
fusing him with her own brave, dauntless example. She's
as dependable and predictable as a grandfather clock, as
capable of patching a broken pipe or fixing a blown fuse
as she is of baking a cherry pie or sewing on a missing
button. There's always room enough and love enough
in her heart to welcome strangers and relatives to her
hearth, and her house will warm you when you've just
come in out of a storm. Like my friend said, a Taurus female is "a tall woman."

The TAURUS Child

> *"It'll be no use putting their heads down*
> *and saying, 'Come up again, dear!' . . .*
> *If I like being that person,*
> *I'll come up:*
> *If not, I'll stay down here. . . ."*

It may begin to be evident that your newborn baby is a
Taurean when you try to dress him to take him home from
the hospital. "Put your little arms inside your nice sweater
Grandma knit for you," you'll murmur in tender, maternal
tones. "Why are you clenching your little fists and holding

your arms so stiff? Let go, like a good little baby. Please, let go."

"Let me try," says your husband. "Okay, come on now, Kid. Let's get those arms in the sleeves. Easy does it. Hey! Did you hear me, Charlie? Let go. Move your arms. Move them!"

The nurse comes in. "Don't be upset," she says. "It's always hard to dress them when they're little. My, what a good baby. Wide awake, but he doesn't make a sound."

"Yes, he's quiet," says your husband. "But he keeps folding his arms across his chest, and I can't pull them apart. He's so strong, I can't even pry them apart."

"I don't think he wants his sweater on," you remark uneasily, a mother's intuition beginning to rise.

The nurse approaches your little bull with professional efficiency. "I'll do it. All right now, upsy daisy! In the sleeve—fist first—that's the way."

She forces the tiny arm through the opening in the sweater. Suddenly, your small bull's face turns a deep, bluish-purple-red color, and a wail is heard that brings every nurse on the floor rushing into the room. (It's more of a roar than a wail. The intern down the hall thought the boiler had exploded in the basement.) Your Taurus baby is just announcing that he doesn't appreciate being pushed. It's a warning. And it will be repeated.

Your neighbors will hear the same sound every time you try to press your May child into doing something he doesn't want to do. There will be lots of little problems like trying to stuff oatmeal into a mouth that's glued shut, pressing an iron leg into a pair of rubber panties, and trying to force a chubby, pink body, suddenly turned to unyielding cement, into the bathtub. You'll lose lots of weight and develop strong muscular control. Mothers of Taurus children always have muscles like Popeye, though they often look as haggard as Olive Oyl.

Outside of being just plain pig-headed, the Taurus baby is a delight to raise. Parents of Taurean boys and girls will find their youngsters cuddly and loving. They adore being squeezed and hugged and petted. The little bull with a cowlick or curly forelock will jump up on your lap to get a kiss and leave you out of breath with his bear hugs. He'll give your friends the same affectionate treatment, if he trusts them. The tiny Taurus girl will flirt from the high chair to get an extra helping of dessert. She's probably

Daddy's little girl. He'll find it hard to resist her limpid charm, as difficult as Mommy finds it to resist her Taurean son's quiet sweetness. The children of both sexes will be strong, healthy and athletically inclined. The boys will be all boys, sometimes little terrors, full of fun, sturdy and tough. The little girls will be all female, taking care of their dolls like small mothers, keeping things tidy and playing house. Some of them will be tomboys, and you'll catch them climbing trees or shooting marbles with the boys; but essentially, they have all the charms of femininity to call on when they choose, and they'll choose often.

Taurus youngsters seem to be generally more competent, even as toddlers, than other children. For one thing, they're emotionally stable, seldom subject to deep moods of depression, fits of impulsiveness or show-off tendencies. They can be negative and stubborn, sometimes shy and timid, but there are few of the normal hang-ups and growing pains. Taurean dispositions are normally calm and pleasant. They're not easily ruffled or disturbed. Except when they balk at being pushed too far or too hard, their personalities are smooth, cheerful and quite predictable. There's a maturity about them that children born under other Sun signs (except Capricorn and Scorpio) lack. Even the very young Taureans are usually quite well-behaved in front of company, but they'll act as if the cat got their tongues if they're forced to be the center of attention. Leave them alone to play in the corner and the chances are that visitors will be impressed at how well they've been trained.

A Taurean youngster quietly minds his own business, and the young bull will seldom embarrass you by rudeness or a smart-alecky attitude. However, if you challenge his temper by teasing him (which he can't stand), by applying steady pressure, or demanding that he do something his mind is dead set against—he can turn belligerent. The only way out of such defiance is love. Never force. A Taurean child who's been forced by older people too often may turn into a silent, moody, cruel adult. Remember that he can't remain stubborn against physical demonstrations of affection. A loving squeeze or a big, friendly kiss and a cheerful smile will coax him out of his obstinacy. Always speak gently and logically. Yelling and harsh voices raised in command will just make him shut his eyes and ears. He can resist discipline and orders until doomsday. He can't resist affection for a minute.

Even when he's very young, his mind will respond to common sense. If it sounds reasonable to him, he'll do it—but he'll want a practical explanation. Nothing complicated. Just the plain, honest, unvarnished truth. "You have to go to bed now because I say so," will get you nowhere at all. That's neither sensible nor reasonable to him. However, a softly spoken declaration like, "You have to go to bed now because we're going to turn out the lights. If you don't, we can't let you go out to play tomorrow, because you'll be too tired," will probably get him into his sleepers and ready for the sandman. It also works to say, "Hop into your warm bed now, between your nice, clean sheets, while I tuck in your soft baby bear blanket. Then I'll read you a little story." No matter how stubborn he has been, he'll almost always turn into a docile angel at those words. His is a very sensual nature, and describing the feel of things seldom fails to strike a responsive chord. Pushing him to give in to your demands is both futile and dangerous to his future personality.

Colors and sounds will affect his disposition and his emotions deeply. Bright, clashing oranges and reds in his room will make him restless and obstinate. Pastel shades, especially pink, rose and all tones of blue, will produce almost magical results. This child will react to colors visibly. If they're harmonious to his Taurean vibrations, he'll remain tranquil. If they're discordant, they can literally damage his emotional stability. Loud noises will have the same effect.

It's a good idea to give a Taurus child music or singing lessons as soon as possible. Almost every one of them will have a low, soft, melodious voice, and many of them have considerable vocal or musical talent, and you'll want to discover it while he's young enough to be trained in the right direction. Even if he's not going to make music his career, he'll enjoy listening to it on his own little record player in his room. He may prefer the classics to modern sounds or nursery rhymes. He'll probably like to draw, color or paint, and the chances are good that he may have some real artistic ability. Be sure your Taurus has lots of paper and colored pencils. It's his favorite way of expressing himself.

Teachers usually find the Taurus child a credit to the

class. Unless there are afflicting planet positions in the nativity, Taurean boys and girls will be industrious in school, learn their lessons methodically and have excellent powers of concentration. They're not whiz kids like the Gemini and Aquarian or Aries students, but they probably won't be tardy or throw spit balls in study hall, though they may break up if Teacher gets her finger caught in the pencil sharpener. The Taurus youngster is ordinarily quite obedient. His mind absorbs slowly, but he never forgets what he's learned, once a fact or date is mastered. These boys and girls usually do well on tests, because they prepare for them carefully. They're often chosen leaders of group activities, due to their love of fair play—and also due to their obvious common sense and good judgment.

The Taurus child may give his elders a few bad moments because of his stubbornness, but they'll be few and far between. One mother of a young Taurean I know took her son to school one day and was sorry she didn't stay home and keep out of it. The little bull had insulted his teacher by insisting her facts were wrong. So was the author of the textbook, naturally. The next day, his mother marched him to the teacher's desk with the firm command, "Apologize to Miss Applegarden, Sammy." That was about nine o'clock in the morning. At noon, in the principal's office, the mother was heard wearily repeating the order, "Apologize to Miss Applegarden, Sammy." Later in the day, after the students had been dismissed, the janitor was gathering up trash baskets. As he passed the office, he heard a strange, faraway, trembling voice, almost ghost-like, floating from the inner sanctum. "Apologize to Miss Applegarden, Sammy," it said. "For the last time, apologize." Through the closed door came the hollow sound of a wooden paddle being applied. Then silence. The next day, the little boy was back at his desk. He had outlasted the teacher, his mother and the principal. He never did apologize. But he made the honor roll.

Once you're resigned to the knowledge that nothing this side of a derrick will move your Taurus youngster when he digs his sturdy toes in the earth, you'll enjoy watching him grow up. He'll probably get tons of dirt on his clothes playing with his toy trucks and tractors—and the hair of little Taurean boys has the oddest way of smelling like a warm bird's nest, no matter how often you wash it—but he won't lose his report card or his marbles. He won't drive Dad's car too fast and end up wrapping it around a telephone pole when he's older. He may raid the refrigerator, and eat the fried chicken you were saving for dinner, or be tough on the new furniture. But he'll be mighty easy on your heart when he gets big. And he won't forget your birthday. Your little Taurus girl may tear her party dress climbing into her tree house, or go into a rage when someone breaks one of her precious possessions. But she'll help you bake gingerbread men, and you'll always be welcome in her lovely home after she's happily settled down with her own family. Your grandchildren will probably be well-behaved, in either case.

Raise your little bull or heifer in a cozy, snug atmosphere of love. Surround him with visible affection instead of invisible barbed wire fences. Don't pull on his horns too hard, and let him graze at his own calm tempo. Fill his ears with music and his eyes with beauty, and he'll fill your heart with peace someday. Even Miss Applegarden will forgive him.

The TAURUS Boss

*"How the creatures order one about,
and make one repeat lessons!"*

*"I sent to them again to say
It will be better to obey."*

You say you have one of those sweet Taurus bosses who never nags or fusses, and you don't need any advice or tips on how to handle that complacent, dear, docile creature? You have him just where you want him—in the palm of your hand? Well, you're certainly learning your Sun signs just in time to avoid a disaster. Before it's too late, you'd better memorize the one major rule for dealing with a Taurean executive: *Don't try his patience too far.*

It's a tougher rule than it seems. If he's a typical Taurus boss, he has such enormous patience, it's downright tempting to try it. His manner is so peaceful and his disposition so steady, you're apt to think of him as "good old Mr. Bearumple." Then you'll start treating him like a nice, shaggy bear, who's a little stubborn perhaps, but kindly and perfectly harmless. You'll remember the happy ending to the Goldilocks story, and let your guard down. That's just what you should not do. It could be the beginning of the end.

Yes, I know that Goldilocks got away with eating Papa Bear's porridge, sitting in his big chair, and napping on his bed. But bears are not bulls. Don't confuse your animals. Just because they get them mixed up in the stock market doesn't mean you should get them mixed up in the office. Bears live in the woods, and sometimes go after honey. Bulls live on the farm, and sometimes go after pushy people. Bears can squeeze strangers hard in a spirit of fun, but they mean no harm. They're playful. Bulls can destroy trespassers and china shops in blind fury, on purpose. They're dangerous. End of zoology lesson.

Today, you're safe. But who knows what tomorrow may bring? It may bring you sudden regret that you tried the patience of your Taurus boss too far. You may wish you hadn't imposed on his good nature with such casual confidence. It's not hard to see how you got on the wrong path. It happens all the time to people who work for Taurean executives. He's so meek and understanding when you turn in a letter that's sloppily typed, you may not bother to check your spelling too often afterwards. He's so considerate when you mess up the figures on your semiannual report, you may be a little careless with your math on other papers. Since he doesn't yell and glare at you when you take an extra half hour at lunch, you may try for an extra hour the next week, and gradually stretch it to two hours. It's so easy to slide into a fool's paradise. Have you allowed yourself to drift into these lazy habits under the spell of your Taurean boss's easy-going personality and quiet manner? You'd better hang one of those "Danger—Ferocious Bull" signs (the kind you see out in the country) over your desk. It might save your life very soon, or at least your job, and sometimes one is pretty synonymous with the other. You can't very well say to your landlord, "I'm sorry I'm three months behind on my rent, but I haven't found a new job yet. I got fired from my last one with no notice, because, you see, I had this boss who was born in May—and I didn't understand about the

Taurean temper because of the Venus rulership. It was that darned Venus that fooled me." If you find a landlord who won't give you an immediate eviction notice after that explanation, you must live in the land of Oz.

It's much easier to practice your Sun sign knowledge in the beginning. The reason your boss was so nice and unruffled when you typed that letter, made those mistakes in the report and lingered so long over your lunch hour, was not because he's a nice, shaggy bear pushover. Nor was it because he's too shy and timid to express his wishes or exert his authority. Frankly, he didn't see any point in embarrassing you by making a big fuss over one or two or even a few goofs. He figured you had enough common sense (remember that phrase) not to repeat yourself like a broken record. He decided to watch you patiently to see if you were practical enough to profit by past errors on your own. Aye! There's the rub! His patience was carefully calculated toward a definite purpose—to test you, and to give you a chance to prove your mettle. He admires people who learn the knack of disciplining themselves. He's a self-made man. Why shouldn't you be? He's willing to give you the opportunity.

He is determined to give everyone a fair break. He won't judge hastily. He won't expect miracles overnight, nor will he mind if you're a little slow in catching on to his methods and his very set procedures. You'll be given a chance to find your way around, and he'll look the other way more than once if you stumble in the dark. But make no innocent, naive mistakes about his ultimate goal. He wants things done his way. His way could conceivably be the way things were done when the Smith Brothers got together and decided to cure coughs, but to him, it's the tried and true, proven method. Besides those fellows still cure *his* coughs! As long as his methods keep making money, he's going to be loyal to them. He's willing to waste plenty of his huge supply of patience to find employees who fit his cement mold. However, once you've pressed his patience too far, he will first balk, then snort in anger, and finally shout, "You're fired!"—possibly at the top of his lungs. (At least it will seem loud, because it will be so emphatic.) Your only warning will probably will be that he failed to answer your cheerful, unsuspecting, "Good morning," the previous day. Know beyond any doubt that he's not going to change his mind after he's decided to sack you. Nothing changes the Taurus mind, once it's made up. He may give you a generous slice of severance pay, because he doesn't want that cold-hearted landlord to throw you and your sick grandmother and the twelve children out in the snow. But he won't give you any more chances once he's firmly convinced himself that you're dead weight to the company he cherishes only a shade less than he does his wife. It's not that he is unkind. Your memory is short if you think that. His is not. Recall, as you read the classified ads for a new job, how kind he was for all those months when you were so carefully taking advantage of his faith in you.

The Taurean boss is a thoroughly practical soul. Although he needs to feel that his business allows him to express the beauty in his nature creatively, he needs even more to succeed materially. Taurus men are never satisfied to run a small business. They want to build it into a possible empire. The Taurus boss won't be content without some expansion, however minor. There will be no dramatic, sweeping changes, and progress will proceed one step at a time. He'll build gradually, without flash or fanfare, but he'll build. He sticks to anything he starts and finishes what he begins, and he'll expect you to do the same thing.

Don't try too many short cuts. He wants his facts plain, not fancy. Taurus bosses have no more patience with the art of gilding the lily than Capricorn executives. One of his favorite phrases will be, "Get to the point," but he'll say it without rancor or sarcasm. Lengthy preliminaries in explaining ideas make him nervous, though he'll retain his outward immobility.

It will be frustrating when he refuses to budge an inch for your most exciting concepts, and when he won't let you try out that new system you read about in *Fortune* (or picked up from your brother-in-law, who's such a crackerjack promoter). Granted, sometimes he's wrong for refusing to listen to progressive ideas, and you'll feel smug when another company tries them first successfully. But over the long haul, when the final score is tallied, he'll come out ahead. What if that new gadget he stubbornly rejected as "a harebrained abortion of some schizophrenic's daydream" runs into a snag, and the company that zoomed ahead by using it suddenly goes bankrupt when the gadget backfires? Then your smugness will be replaced by a foolish feeling, and finally by respect for this some-times grumpy, often obstinate, but kindly and understand-ing boss, who has such a practical head on his sturdy shoulders.

Taurus executives usually prefer football to baseball, and peace to noisy arguments. He'll always try quiet common sense discussions to avoid emotional scenes. Remember, common sense is his key phrase. But that doesn't mean he's lacking in imagination or appreciation of the finer things in life. You'll be pretty sure to make a large hit with him if you wear good perfume and polish your nails with a rosy tint (if you're a girl, that is). He loves nice smells and soothing, pastel colors. You'll also please him if you occasionally bring him a jar of home-made vichys-soise your mother cooked—but you'd better call it potato soup. Fancy names and titles don't impress him as much as they make him uneasy. Men who work for a Taurean should wear quiet, blue ties, sensible shoes, and keep their feet on the ground, not on his desk.

You may chafe at his stubborn, bull-headed attitude at least once a week, but remember this about your Taurus boss: he's also stubborn about being loyal to people who never let him down. Be one of those people, and you'll never have to fear the dangerous bull. He's really quite gentle if the red flag of defiance isn't waved in his face too often. Grab some concrete blocks, and help him build his empire. He'll be glad to share it with you, if you deserve it. Promotion he understands. Featherbedding he does not. "Good old Mr. Bearumple" will expect you to carry your own weight, but he'll always give you a lift when the load gets heavy. He's strong and dependable. He says what he means and he means what he says. You won't need an interpreter. If he says you're a blockhead, leave quickly and quietly and don't quibble. If he says "You'll do well enough," you have real job security. That means you've passed his test of loyalty, sincerity, ability and potential. Move to the head of the class. You've made the honor roll. Congratulations! Don't let it swell your hat size, and you have a promising future ahead of you.

The TAURUS Employee

*"Well, I never heard it before . . .
but it sounds uncommon nonsense."*

First of all, I hope you don't have your Taurus employee
working for you as a salesman. If you do, have his
horoscope checked as soon as you can. He may have some
planets in Gemini, Aries, Leo or Pisces. In that case, you
can safely let him continue to peddle your wares. Otherwise, you each would be better off if you gently eased
him (for goodness sakes, don't push him) into some other
position with your company.

As a promoter or salesman, he may not make the best
possible impression on your clients. In giving a spiel to a
customer, his normal attitude would be, "If you want it,
take it. If you don't, move along." The average Taurus
employee isn't about to perform a fast buck and wing for
a prospective buyer. Nor is he noted for his golden tongue
and outpouring of imaginative, descriptive phrases. Unless
you call "Umph" and "Gumph" and "Mmm Hmm" and
"Mumph" imaginative, descriptive phrases. Not that he
doesn't have many sterling qualities. He does. But they're
usually not the kind to sway people or press them into
signing on the dotted line. He's far more likely to tell them
why they shouldn't get involved.

The most important reason Taureans seldom gravitate
to selling, however, is related to the basic Taurus need for
security. He must feel a sense of security in his work, or
his potential for success—which can be tremendous—will
be markedly diluted. No matter how large the possible
reward may be, if it fluctuates, the Taurus employee will
prefer the safety of knowing how many dollar bills he
can count each week. A Taurean on straight commission
is usually one of the unhappiest human beings in the
world. A set salary, plus a bonus incentive for sales, would
come closer to giving him the sense of achievement he

needs, but even so the position of salesman isn't the ideal spot for the bull.

Of course, there are a few exceptions to the rule, in addition to the aforementioned planetary influences. Most Taureans can handle certain low-pressure sales pitches with distinction, if the product is solid and stable, with built-in security. But the list is short. Farm equipment, tractors, manure spreaders, trucks and mowing machines or such would be right up his alley. Those he could sell. He talks the same language as the people who buy them. Money is another item he can handle on either side of the desk, and selling cash may even be a specialty. Translated, that means he's a super man to have in charge of the loan department, if your business is banking. But let's be truthful, how much persuasion is needed to convince an insolvent man he needs money?

There may be a couple of other categories where he could shine as a salesman. Real estate, for instance. A Taurean is perfectly at home showing people through houses or telling them about the value of the land. He'll point to the view and say, "Umph." Then he'll describe the landscaping possibilities with an ecstatic "Grumph." After that, he'll demonstrate the plumbing and closet space with "Mmm Hmm," and finally discuss the financing with a firm "Mumph." Hard as it may be to believe, the answer from the prospective home buyer will probably be, "Yep. I'll take it." After which the Taurus salesman will answer, "Okay. You've got it." Or something similar. The trick here is that the Taurean honesty and obvious dependability impresses people who are socking down enough money for a house. Then there's the field of education. He believes in firm foundations and facts with such fervor, and he has such faith in preparing for the future, along with a positive distaste for ignorance, that he could talk a girl into taking the engineering course at M.I.T. He wouldn't see anything silly at all about a female studying engineering. To him, practical is practical, regardless of sex.

There's also a possibility that a Taurean with a Gemini ascendant or Mars in Gemini would make a superior radio or TV announcer. The typical, musical tones of Taurean speech coupled with Gemini charm and glibness can make him a natural in such media. Then, too, if the right planets were in Aries at birth, their influence could conceivably

combine with his Taurus Sun to give him exceptional promotional or public relations abilities, though he would
never be a high-pressure type. I'm afraid that just about
covers the territory for a Taurus salesman. In most other
areas, and without the proper additional planetary influences, he's much better off doing things that come more
naturally to his imperturbable nature.

One of those things is known in politics as holding the
center together, an ability which is also extremely valuable
in the business world. Whatever desk he's assigned to, he'll
root himself behind it with determination to succeed, and
he probably will. He'll work slowly and aim for perfection,
which he usually achieves if he's left alone and not pushed
too fast. The more responsibility the position requires of
him, the smarter you'll be to put him in charge. You'll
seldom enjoy the services of a more dependable, trustworthy and honest employee. He'll seek to help your company expand, not his own ego. A successful Taurean wears
the same hat size as he did when he was still trying.

Much as he dislikes change, if he's an exceptional
Taurus, you won't keep him forever. He won't leave because he's flighty, but for a basic reason that's part of his
nature. Once he's established the growth of your company,
he's not the type to remain there and run it for you.
Taurus is more interested in building power and wealth.
He likes his freedom too much to be tied to the constant
manipulations of guiding a complicated business, or of
being the unseen cog. He's reliable and content to stick,
but he wants to be free to continue to build instead of
being tied up with intricate details. When there's no more
incentive to grow with your firm, he'll feel the legendary
Taurean itch to lay his own foundation and erect his own
empire, minor or major.

A Taurus employee, whether he's exceptional or average,
is always an outstanding worker, and one of his most
endearing qualities is his willingness to take orders without
resentment. The reason behind it is simple. He has an
inner conviction that the way to become a boss who gives
orders is to be first a cheerful subordinate who takes orders.
His respect for authority is based on his knowledge that
when he becomes an executive, he'll expect his employees
to follow his directions. As a boss himself, he'll have
definite and probably rigidly set ideas and methods. Therefore, he finds nothing strange or unpleasant about your

insistence on adhering to a fixed pattern when he works for you. As far as he's concerned, you're in charge.

Such an attitude is obviously quite a bonus, but don't let his kindly disposition nor his sensible acquiescence to superiors fool you into thinking he can be easily shoved around. He has a sort of Machiavellian detachment toward those who think they're manipulating him, and he'll handle them with smooth tact and diplomacy. Yet, if you look closely, you'll see his tongue is in his cheek while he's humoring the aggressive people who try to drive him. In the end, Taurus will have his own way. His success is even more assured by his ability to wait as long as necessary until he wins out over the pushy types. However, when his personal emotions are trampled on or his deep pride is hurt, his cool steadiness may disappear and be replaced by a childish stubbornness. Remember, that while he's pouting, he's combustible, and liable to explode finally in a fierce display of temper. It won't last long, and the bull will be ominously quiet after such a "charge," but if the cause isn't rectified immediately, he'll simply leave, and he won't glance behind him. When a Taurus goes out the door, he has left. There won't be any sheepish returns to try again. The back of his broad shoulders will be the last you see of him. Nothing you can say or do will persuade him to reconsider. The bull makes up his mind so slowly in the first place, there's never any need to take a second look at the matter. Taurean foresight precludes the need for hindsight. Since his is such a sensual, loving nature, you can probably find plenty of ex-sweethearts who will sadly tell you that when he waves goodbye he doesn't come back for encores. In both love and business, people frequently make the mistake of thinking the Taurean's patience is eternal, just because it takes him so long to lose it.

The female Taurean employee is usually a real jewel. If she's a typical Taurus, she'll have a quiet, low-pitched voice and soothing manner. These women normally make great executive secretaries. Emergencies don't throw them off balance. A crisis brings out the best in them, and that's considerable. She may be a bit slower than the others with typing and dictation. She's not exactly a fireball, and you'll never see her riding a motorcycle to work, but her job will get done. Well done. Like the males, she feels that if a job is worth doing at all it's worth doing well, to the very best of her ability. Every May person has that motto chiseled somewhere permanently. This girl won't yawn in your face when you're expounding your pet theories. If the ideas are practical, she'll probably converse with you about them like a man. Her views will be worth hearing, and her approach will be sensible and logical. But don't let that give you the impression she's not a real female.

Be careful. This is not a woman who will ordinarily become involved in casual office flirtations. She can cut up and be loads of laughs, but underneath her warm, bovine humor is a mind firmly set on marriage. If she accepts a dinner invitation twice, she's probably already sizing you up as a good provider for a lifetime, not just an exciting date for a rainy Thursday. These women are quite serious about the stakes in any romantic game. If you fit the qualifications of a Taurean female as husband material, you're not an ordinary man by anybody's slide rule. The man in the company who's the recipient of the Taurus woman's attentions is the man to watch. He's going somewhere. If it happens to be yourself, you may soon lose a peach of a secretary, but you'll get a wife in a million, which should bring you out ahead.

Female Taurus employees are pleasant to have around because they smell nice, they look nice, they're gracious and they don't smoke cigars, among other things. (Unless you happen to have one with an Aries Moon or ascendant, who would smell and look just as nice, but who might very well smoke cigars and shout a little.)

Taurus people of both sexes hate to sleep in strange beds, a phrase they're fond of repeating. Therefore, most Taurean men and women prefer to spend their vacations at home. Barring a Gemini Moon or Sagittarius ascendant, the grass will always look both greener and thicker in the bull's own backyard. When he's on vacation, sensually sipping lemonade and inhaling the scent of flowers from his hammock, you can safely call him in for an office emergency. He'll probably oblige with a good-natured grin, and even feel it's his duty to help out. But don't impose too often. There's a limit to his patient acceptance of repeated impositions, and it's foolhardy to risk making him angry to discover that limit. Stop while you're ahead.

The bull works happily as a florist, in the livestock or poultry industry, in supermarkets or in the wholesale food industry. He makes a good doctor or engineer, too. And he can be quite contented in an artistic career. The sound of music and the visual hypnotism of art pull him magnetically. He's never more at home than when he's expressing himself creatively, through his senses, as long as the financial rewards are sound and the foundation isn't shaky.

A Taurus songwriter is usually miserable, especially during the lean years, before he writes his first big hit. But when he combines his creative talent with the more stable, secure task of producing records or arranging scores, he's in his own element. You'll find that every Taurean singer or composer, without exception, eventually ends up in the production end of the music business to some degree.

After the bull has found the right meadow, where the opportunities grow plentifully, he seldom seeks change or new fields to conquer. He'll weigh, balance and soak up knowledge of his career through years of devotion to it. He can put up with a lot, if he's convinced himself there's a future, and if the occupation fits him snugly or "feels good" to him. Taurus is incredibly capable of persevering until the reward comes, but only when he's at the center of things, never when he's insecurely chewing around the edges and hoping for a break. Once he feels the necessary sense of achievement and security beneath him, and once he's planted himself in a position where he can build ever higher, he moves forward with confidence. Then he becomes irresistible to the elusive, fickle goddess of success. It won't turn his head. He'll stay faithful to her, but he'll put her in her place—and it will be a lifelong love affair.

> *"It takes all the running you can do,*
> *to keep in the same place.*
> *If you want to get somewhere else,*
> *you must run at least twice as fast as that!"*

GEMINI the Twins

May 22nd through June 21st

How to Recognize GEMINI

"I wish you woudn't keep appearing
And vanishing so suddenly.
You make one quite giddy!"
This time it vanished quite slowly,
beginning with the end of the tail,
and ending with the grin,
which remained for some time
after the rest of it had gone.

If there are times when a Gemini person makes you think you're seeing double, don't run out and change your glasses. Just remember that Gemini is the sign of the twins, and there are two distinct sides to his changeable personality. Now you see it, now you don't. Was it love you thought you caught fleetingly on those mobile features? Hate? Ecstasy? Intelligence? Idealism? Sorrow? Joy? The mercurial changes of a Gemini's expression are as fascinating to watch as the psychedelic lights in a discotheque. It's hard to tell where reality ends and illusion begins. They blend—then they separate.

Knowing where to look for this versatile creature requires a little forethought. He may be one place today and somewhere else tomorrow. Suddenly, too. A Gemini can change his clothes, his job, his love life or his residence as fast as he changes his mind, and that's pretty fast. Finding a good example to study may keep you hopping. You could try a bookstore. He's a browser, because he can get the gist of the contents in a brief scanning of the pages. (It's no accident that John F. Kennedy was a speed reader.) Mercury people also have that nasty habit of reading the last page first. If you know a Gemini who has ever read a book from beginning to end without getting bored halfway through, send him to the Smithsonian as a curio (or check his natal chart to see if he has Taurus, Capricorn or one of the more persistent signs on the ascendant). Geminis like to skip back and forth in a book, a pattern of action they also prefer when it comes to things other than reading.

You're sure to find a Gemini or two skimming through the halls and matching wits with people in a radio station, a public relations firm, a publishing house, a telephone answering service, an auto showroom or an advertising agency—if you can catch one between appointments. When you've found this quicksilver person, study him carefully, even if you do get exhausted following him around. The first thing you'll notice is a nervous energy that fairly snaps, crackles and pops in the air around him. If he has a Scorpio, Libra, Cancer or Capricorn moon, he may not vibrate with so much obvious crackle, but the snap and pop are latent, and you'll sense their presence under the influence of the other planetary positions. An occasional Gemini will speak slowly, but most of them talk fast. All of them listen fast.

Man or woman, Gemini is impatient with conservative stick-in-the-muds, or with people who can't make up their minds where they stand on particular issues. Gemini knows where he stands, at least for the moment.

Unless there's a conflicting ascendant, the Gemini build is generally slender, agile and taller than average. Many of them have small, sharp features, as if they were cut in a cameo. You'll find some with brown eyes, of course, but the majority of those ruled by Mercury will have beautiful, crystal-clear hazel, blue, green or gray eyes that twinkle and dart here and there. Geminis never rest their eyes on one object for more than a few seconds. In fact, their alert, quick-moving eyes are often the easiest way to recognize them. The complexion tends to be rather pale, yet they usually tan easily, and that's the way to spot them in the summer. (In the winter, they often have wind burns from swooping down a ski slope.)

There's an eagerness about Geminis, an immediate, sympathetic friendliness, and unusually quick, but graceful movements. The hair can be light or dark or both—like, streaked. Twins, remember? The nose is likely to be long and straight or dainty—in either case, probably well formed. There's frequently a receding hairline in the men (from all that activity in the brain, perhaps), and both sexes normally have rather high foreheads.

It's usually a mistake to try to pin Geminis down to either one place or one idea. It's always a mistake to challenge them to a battle of wits, because they can talk themselves in and out of situations with the greatest ease. They think fast on their feet (or in any other position); they can be sharply satirical, and they're more clever than almost anybody. Some Mercury people take a mischievous delight in disconcerting slower minds with their lightning fast mental processes. How would you like to get into an argument with Gemini Bob Hope?

A June person will sometimes appear to light near you, like an inquisitive bird, survey the scene with excited curiosity, then dart off in a different direction almost before you can say hello. I often join a Gemini friend in Lindy's for cheesecake and some casual conversation. He's thirty-five to forty years old, but he looks like a college student, which is typical of Gemini's ageless appearance. For a while we'll talk pleasantly, interrupting each other and easily bouncing from one topic to another. Then I'll search in my purse for a compact or a pencil, look up—and like some disappearing artist in a magic act, my Gemini friend has vanished into thin air, taking the check with him. (The more unevolved types use this agility to leave you with the check.) When he pulls one of those fast dissolves, I glance around the room anxiously, and suddenly, there he is—making a phone call or waving to me gaily as he skips out the door to who-knows-where.

This particular Gemini was recently engaged to a wonderful Aquarian girl (if anyone can cope with an elusive Gemini, it's an Aquarian), and a week before the wedding, five would get you twenty anywhere on Broadway that he would find a way to slip out of the noose—that somehow, he wouldn't make it to the church on time. But he did. Geminis can surprise you. Especially when they're in love.

One of my favorite Geminians is a Mercury woman who—typically—runs Belles Limited, a New York answering service. The play, *The Bells Are Ringing*, was based on her life. Possibly due to being glued to the telephone twenty hours a day, she's not quite as light on her feet as she was when she used to brighten Billy Rose's chorus line. You couldn't call her agile, since she seldom gets a chance to leave her switchboard, but still she gives the impression of flying around, even when she's immobile. Like most Gemini females, she has an extremely pretty, interesting face, with intelligence stamped on every feature, and her quick Mercury hands flutter in the air like lively birds.

Using more charm and wit than the law allows, she cheerfully solves everyone's problems in the twinkling of one of her clear, blue eyes. I've watched this woman find a baby sitter and a pair of gerbils for a customer, make out the grocery list, write thirty-two checks (one of her favorite occupations), phone a Broadway producer on a yacht in the Caribbean, send nine telegrams, fold the family laundry, figure the week's working schedule for her operators, find her husband's blue tie, write down the directions for the shop where he could pick up some tropical fish for their son, snap four Polaroid pictures of the dog, open and read her monthly bills (then absently file them in the wastebasket), help a casting office locate an actress who speaks six languages, and give twelve clients a wake-up call —all in the space of a little over an hour without leaving her swivel chair. Go top that.

The secret is in the Geminian duality. They can do two things at once with less effort than it takes most of us to do one. Mercury women often iron, feed the baby and talk on the phone at the same time. Some people swear that all Geminis were born with a phone in each hand.

Any kind of routine can make a typical Geminian feel like a droopy bird in a cage with his wings clipped. These people resent drudgery and monotony almost fiercely. Usually, they aren't the most punctual souls in the world (unless they happen to have a Virgo ascendant, in which case they become human alarm clocks). The typical Gemini, however, always arrives late, not because he forgets the time, but because something caught his interest on the way and sidetracked him. The restless Mercurial nature demands constant excitement and change or the spirit becomes dejected and morose.

If you have a Mercury friend, you've probably already experienced a common Gemini habit that can be so annoying it can give you ulcers. He'll suggest some activity to you, like dropping over to his apartment (it will seldom be a house—too permanent), catching an old Humphrey Bogart film with an Our Gang comedy (double feature, naturally—he doesn't play singles), driving out to a miniature golf range to practice a little putting or stopping in Jack Dempsey's for a few Bloody Marys. You're tired and you're on the way home. You thank him anyway, but ask for a rain check. The Gemini argues with you. Convincingly. He turns on those baby blues (or greens or browns) and weaves a cocoon of charm around you. He talks so fast and his smile is so persuasive that, after a while, you give in. You'll go. He has a few errands to run, so he says he'll meet you on the corner in about an hour. That you didn't expect so you start to back out, but he turns on his technique again, and you finally agree to meet him. It's a real drag, killing the hour, and besides, your feet hurt, but you manage to do it, and you show up on the corner at the appointed time. Good old Jim is a half hour late and a little out of breath when he gets there. Guess what? He's changed his mind. He's really beat. He's decided to call it a day, hit the sack—and make the scene tomorrow night. You don't mind, do you? Only a Gemini could avoid a sock in the jaw at that point. But he does. You forgive him, and what's really ridiculous is that you'll actually meet him the next night, like you had good sense or something. You've only yourself to blame for succumbing to the irresistible Gemini sales pitch. If you get stood up again the following evening, you have it coming. It serves you right for letting him sweet talk you.

There's a deep-seated need in all June people to disguise their true motives. Like the Pisces they feel a compulsion to behave in a way exactly opposite to their real desires. But this amazing Gemini versatility and facility of speech makes them terrific politicians, not to mention experts in the field of human relationships. A Gemini knows how to swerve you from your most stubbornly held convictions. He can twist you like a pretzel with his mental karate, get you to agree with him and love him for doing it to you. But if trouble develops, he knows instinctively just where the skeletons are buried in your closet, and he can use his fast mind and clever tongue to rattle those bones dangerously.

There's a strange thing about Geminis and writing. The Sun sign itself rules writing. Therefore, practically every Mercury man or woman can turn a clever phrase and string words together intelligently. You'll find whole slews of them writing speeches, commercials, documentaries, plays and books. But the books will be novels, textbooks, nonfiction or biographies. Very seldom will you find the Geminian writing his own life story. And it's extremely rare to find one who likes to write personal letters. The typical Gemini hates to answer correspondence. He'll procrastinate for weeks.

It may seem to be contradictory at first, but the reason is clear, when you realize the reluctance of Mercury people to be pinned down to an opinion. They hesitate to put their thoughts on paper because they instinctively know that what they believe today, they may not believe tomorrow—and they don't want to be committed in writing. Few Geminis need to be warned by their attorneys to "Say it, don't write it." They were born with that defense mechanism. There are an astonishing number of Gemini authors who choose to use a pseudonym—and even the average Geminian will eventually find some reason to adopt an alias —either a complete change—a different spelling, or at the very least, a nickname. The rule is so consistent, you can win a nice nest egg betting on it with all the Geminis you know.

Almost every Gemini speaks, understands or reads more than one language and French is the favorite. One way or another, the Gemini will triumph with words. He cut his teeth on Webster's Unabridged. He can sell ice cubes to an Eskimo or dreams to a pessimist. If you happen to catch him in some dodge, he can change the subject so fast, and direct the conversation away from himself so adroitly, that the whole affair ends with you on the carpet instead of him. Sometimes the Mercury tendency to fool people can lead to dishonesty or criminal activity, but not as often as you've been led to believe. Although his talents can tempt an occasional Gemini to live in a web of lies and deception, most of them are too idealistic for a life of crime. Still it must be admitted Mercury gives them superior equipment for success in that field—and they can be brilliant con artists if they choose. With their manual dexterity, if they pick a pocket, forge a check or counterfeit a sawbuck, at least they're neat about it and seldom get caught.

If you come across a smooth-talking used car salesman who was born in June, and he tells you the blue Studebaker had just one former owner—a little old lady who drove it only to church every Sunday morning—you'd be wise to ask the name of the church and check with the little old lady (unless she's a Gemini, too). But seriously, unless the afflictions and planetary positions in the natal chart are marked, the majority of Geminis are honest—and some of them are even painfully honest to a fault. They seem to go from one extreme to another. Yet, they all—petty thief— con man—and upstanding citizen alike—will be unable to resist putting a light coat of varnish on a story at times. Of course, that's not lying. That's imagination.

As promoters, all Mercury people are absolutely superb. They have no equal, not even Aries. The promotions can be strictly aboveboard, but few people are strong enough to outlast the combination of charm and sharp intellect Gemini dishes out, and that alone may be taking unfair advantage. When a Gemini tackles a worthwhile project— to sell something mankind deeply needs and wants, the angels smile on him, and we can thank those born under this Sun sign for many great and lasting improvements which have benefited all of us. At heart, every Mercury- ruled person is a salesman, even the Gemini Jesuit priests and Protestant missionaries. Take two entirely divergent examples which prove it. Gemini John F. Kennedy sold the whole world a shining ideal—and Gemini Michael Todd sold Broadway a dream or two. Each in his own way, a Mercury child. Both the world and Broadway are notori- ously jaded and hard to sell.

Geminis need to rest their busy brains with twice as much sleep as anyone else. Unfortunately, since they're so susceptible to insomnia, they rarely get enough. Neverthe- less, they should try hard to achieve rest, rest and more rest, to heal those jangled nerves and renew the over-active brain cells, because nervous exhaustion is a constant threat. Gobs of fresh, unpolluted air and barrels of bright sunshine are also necessities to keep them out of hospitals. A lack of any of these, plus suppression of activity—can make Geminis susceptible to accidents and infections involving the shoulders, arms, hands and fingers. The lungs may be weak, also the intestines. Problems involving the feet, back, elimination, arthritis, rheumatism and migraine headaches are always a possibility for the Mercury people who neglect their health. The odd thing is that the Gemini can suffer an emotional breakdown more easily from boredom and confinement than from over-activity.

Deep inside his searching, impatient nature, the Gemini seeks an ideal, and his chief problem is in recognizing what it is. It could be anything, since his imagination knows no boundaries. Money, fame, wealth, love and career are never quite enough. Mercury calls Gemini higher and higher—on and on—above and beyond, with a seductive promise of something always just a little better. The grass always looks greener just across the road. The sky is bluer over another ocean. The stars shine brighter in a different place. What is it he seeks? Perhaps some hidden, undiscovered continent within himself. Gemini is the mental explorer.

His eyes are sharp and his talents are multiple. He has a brilliant humor, tact, diplomacy and adroitness—yet he lacks persistence and patience. He throws away the precious old too quickly for the untried new, then lives to regret the instant disposal. In spite of all the people around him, he shares his deepest emotions only with his one constant companion—his other twin self. The air is his element and his real home. He's a stranger to earth.

Gemini can charm a bird right out of its tree and give it five new songs to sing. But the restless Mercurial mind can too easily overlook the bluebird of happiness waiting wistfully year after year in his own backyard. He wears clear yellows, greens and blues, silver and gray—and his moods reflect his glittering aquamarine jewel. He has the light touch, echoed in the delicate fragrance of the lily-of-the-valley, and he has breathed the fresh promise of the greenest ferns in the deepest part of the forest. But the cold metal of Mercury divides Gemini with twin desires, until he stops—and waits—and listens—to his own heartbeat.

Famous Gemini Personalities

Bennett Cerf
John Dillinger
Arthur Conan Doyle
Bob Dylan
Duke of Edinburgh
Ian Fleming
Errol Flynn
Judy Garland
Paul Gauguin
Thomas Hardy
Bob Hope
Al Jolson

John F. Kennedy
Beatrice Lillie
Marilyn Monroe
Cole Porter
Rosalind Russell
Françoise Sagan
Wallis Simpson
Michael Todd
Rudolph Valentino
Walt Whitman
Frank Lloyd Wright
Brigham Young

The GEMINI Man

"I could tell you my adventures—
beginning from this morning—"

"At least I knew who I was
when I got up this morning,
but I think I must have been changed
several times since then."

Being in love gives you a nice sense of warm security. There's that heavenly comfort of always knowing someone is going to be there when you need him—that you no longer walk alone. All the doubts you knew before just melt away. That is, unless you're having a romance with a Mercury man, which might take the edge off that "warm security." In fact, you'll adjust much better to a Gemini if you send him out for a loaf of bread on Monday and don't expect him back until Thursday. Never look for him until you see him coming—and don't hang onto his coattails when he wants to leave.

Once you've schooled yourself to accept his restless, unpredictable spirit, there's a good chance of making it work. But not if you're going to insist on "that heavenly comfort of always knowing someone is going to be there." You'll probably never know for sure when this man is going to be anywhere, and that can bring back some of those doubts romance is supposed to melt away. It's true that when you're in love with a Gemini, you won't walk alone. You most certainly won't. You'll have at least two people to walk with you—and both of them will be him. He was born under the sign of the twins, you know. In his case, they're never identical twins. The dual nature of Gemini combines two completely different personalities. You might even be involved with one of those Mercury men who are triplets or quintuplets, and if so, you have quite a crowd to keep you company, even when you're alone with him.

The typical Gemini is the favorite of every hostess. He likes people. The more the merrier. It's a rare Geminian who's not a perfectly delightful conversationalist. He has exquisite taste, he's loaded with witty remarks, and his compliments are masterpieces of warm sincerity. Usually a master of impeccable manners and social adroitness, he keeps the party moving in more ways than one.

You know those scavenger hunts, where people pair off with a list of whacky items to collect, like a hair from the head of a famous movie star and a piece of the blotter on the desk of the chief of police, and the couple which has rounded up the most items on the list gets the prize? It's the Gemini's favorite kind of party, because it combines the highest possible exposure to people of all kinds with the highest possible opportunity to move around from place to place—and he seeks both.

If you meet him first at a social affair where he's performing his fascinating multiple personality act, you haven't a chance. You'll be convinced he's the most exciting, interesting, intelligent man you've ever come across. No one could quarrel with that analysis. He probably is. It's no wonder you're excited and impressed. But before you let him change your name, be sure you're capable of tackling an uncertain future with a man whose whims may change with the wind, and whose goals in life may shift drastically before the honeymoon is even over. Geminian Walt Whitman once wrote the lines: "Do I contradict myself? . . . I contain multitudes." Whether he realized it or not, he was summing up the Mercury nature.

One day your Gemini man may call on you with a chattering monkey perched on his shoulder and suggest going to a flea circus. He'll bring you flowers, perfume, a phonograph record or a couple of books, maybe even one he wrote himself. The hours will speed by as you happily sun yourself in his cheerful disposition, laugh at his bright, clever jokes and melt under his gay, gallant charm. He'll say "I love you," a hundred different ways, like no one else in the world could do.

The next day, he'll phone you and break a date for no earthly reason whatsoever, causing you to imagine all sorts of things. Was he only joking about loving you? Is he seeing someone else? Is he in trouble? Your fears may be true. Then again, they may be false. A week later, he'll reappear, full of sarcastic remarks, moody and irritable.

He'll be impatient, critical and petulant. He may criticize
your shoes, your lipstick or your literary taste, and have
some pretty cutting doubts about the possibility of your
happiness together. Either all this, or he'll be sullen and
troubled, his mind far away, distant and aloof. No use
asking why, you won't get an answer that makes any sense.

If you survive that experience, a few more days will
find you visiting an art gallery, theater, museum, library or
opera with your Gemini man, absolutely hypnotized by
his knowledge and wide interests. He'll be unusually tender,
full of fragile, butterfly dreams and imaginative hopes for
tomorrow. Then he'll propose. Like that. Quick as lightning. You'll forget all the thunder and storm clouds, all
the rain that fell before, say "yes," before he changes his
mind—and there you are—engaged to an enigma.

Yes, I said enigma. If you expect anything else, like a
man who's stable and patient, who will gently play Darby
to your Joan while life and love glide on as smoothly as a
gondola down a romantic canal in Venice, you're headed
in the same direction as a merry-go-round. In circles. Get
off fast and never mind about grabbing the brass ring.
Don't let the gay, light-hearted music seduce you into
following a painted scene of constantly changing colors,
with shades of dreary gray as likely to show up as sunny
yellow or blissful blue. If you're an incurable romantic,
seeking perfect harmony, you're in more than a little
danger.

No matter what the rest of his natal chart says, if the
Sun was in Gemini when he was born, this man will not
remain tomorrow what he is today, nor will he have any
lasting memory of yesterday. In one way or another, he
will change. Granted, the changes may always be for the
better and he may consistently aim higher. But the element
of chance is always there. If you're a gambler, you may
very well hit the jackpot with him, and find a glorious
mental and emotional compatibility to celebrate on your
golden wedding anniversary. But all good gamblers know
the odds before they place their bet. Just be sure you do.
Two rare exceptions to Geminian instability of purpose
seem to be President Kennedy and England's Queen Victoria. However, keep in mind that John Kennedy had, at
all times a multitude of interests, which changed constantly,
and Queen Victoria (who was very close to being a Taurus
by planetary position) brought about a great many impor-

tant changes in her country's customs. Anyway, very few of us marry kings, queens or presidents, who have been forced by circumstances to mature and settle into a set pattern.

An excellent example of Geminian duality of expression is the confession of a woman who was exposed to it. The Mercury-ruled man was a producer, and the woman was a famous, dark-haired Pisces actress. After a weekend party with friends as the guest of the Gemini on his boat, during which he was openly insulting, rude and aloof to her, by turns, the actress was dismayed and puzzled. Later, she made the remark, "I don't know what's wrong with him. He must hate me. I've never done anything to him, yet he hardly spoke a word to me all weekend." Ah, but don't you see, she *had* done something to him. She had made him fall in love with her. The emotion was serious enough for him to marry her soon after the incident. But how did he react to his first knowledge of a feeling of tenderness toward her? As though she were Lucretia Borgia.

Her experience probably won't keep you from leaping into a romance with a Mercury man. Still, it might soothe the wounds of a few of you girls who have been suffering from the cold actions of a Gemini who's probably helplessly in love with you and cleverly concealing it for his own, unfathomable reasons. Geminis have an unconscious urge to disguise their true intent, to fence with others verbally and cloak their motives with dual actions. In general, they seek to confuse you. Then with true Geminian inconsistency, they'll turn right around and be so direct, they'll fairly take your breath away with their frankness and bluntness.

Loving a Gemini is easy and fun, if you don't try to get too close. There's a inner core that belongs only to him, that he'll never share with another human being, even you. Keep things cool and light, and don't be overly passionate or dramatic. Don't bore him, always excite him and your Gemini romance can be very special. Don't rebel against his changeability. Change with him. Be as alert and interested in life as he is. Otherwise, the love affair could become just one of those things. He seeks a mental companion above all else. One who can match his wits, even top him now and then, because he's not an egotist. He's a realist, and he thrives on mental challenge. The last thing he wants is a doormat or a dull mouse. Let your brain show through your feminine image. It won't scare him off, as it might some men. It will spin him around in the right direction—toward you.

Geminis tend to discard old friends for new ones, but not because they're heartless. Their own personalities fluctuate and advance so relentlessly, it's only natural for them to seek those who match their interests at the time. Anywhere Gemini hangs his hat is home. There's seldom any deep, lasting attachment to old memories, places, people and things. During a long period of loneliness, he can shed some sentimental tears, but it's the loneliness that does it, rather than nostalgia for yesterday. He's gregarious, and he hates—even fears—being alone for extended periods. If you can hit him with the message that you'll be a partner who will always be around, but who won't lean on him nor expect him to lean on you, he'll probably consider signing a long-term contract. But remember those odds. Many Geminis marry more than once, although multiple marriage is more likely to occur when they wed too young than if they wait for maturity. Not every Gemini has two wives, but he'll have two of almost everything else—perhaps two cars, two apartments, two college degrees, two jobs, two dreams, two pets, two razors, two hobbies, two ambitions. He likes to double up.

My good Gemini friend Frank Blair, NBC newsman on the "Today" show, even takes his annual vacation at two separate times during the year. His hobbies? He pilots his own private plane, sails his own boat and plays a mean game of golf. (I'm not sure, but I think Frank may be one of the triplet Geminis.) He plays two musical instruments, has multiple children, multiple awards and trophies on his office wall at NBC, multiple friends, two shifts at the network (one for the "Today" program, another for recording "Emphasis" and special shows), two electric razors in his desk and at least a dozen dreams and plans at a time, which change about every six months. He has just one wife. (He must have a Cancer or Taurus ascendant.) You'll note that he's also in a typically Gemini occupation—broadcasting. Mercury rules communication and news. He certainly has the Gemini charm and manual dexterity. Frank often pours a glass of tomato juice, dictates to his secretary, phones his wife, shaves, and packs his brief case—somehow all at once. Geminis are experts at sleight of hand.

In financial matters, the duality takes over again. A

Mercury man may be at first fabulously generous, then
abruptly turn miserly. If you average out his twin attitudes,
my guess is that the generosity would win, hands down.
Gemini has little desire to accumulate either money or
knowledge. In each case, he prefers to absorb it, sort it,
and give it back improved. He's the communicator whose
function is to create ever new, original ideas and serve
others through the versatility of his quick, brilliant mental
processes.

Will he be faithful to you? In his fashion, yes, he will.
There are a thousand answers to that question where
Mercury is concerned. He likes to converse and he likes
to mix. He's also strangely attractive to women, so there
may be occasions for whispers and suspicions. But you
can count on this: It's a rare Gemini man whose deeply
ingrained sense of fairness will let him be dishonest in his
actions if you have faith in him. I mean real faith and real
trust. Not the kind that secretly wonders. He'll always be
able to sense if you secretly wonder. Mercury minds often
intercept your private thoughts as though you were broadcasting them. However, it's not a good idea to expect a
Gemini husband to give all females a cold shoulder just
because he wears a wedding band. Females are part of the
scene, and Gemini must make the scene. If they're around,
he'll talk to them—maybe even laugh with them or have a
drink with them. It's only natural for Mercury to communicate, regardless of the sex of the listener. But that doesn't
mean he has to romance them.

It's true that there are lots of Geminians who are just
plain, outright promiscuous, yet no matter what you've
heard, there's always a cause. To be mistrusted or misunderstood in any area deeply distresses a Mercury man.
It frustrates and depresses him, and such an unhappy
Gemini can fly here and there, seeking relief from tangled
emotions. When he's free from a feeling of mental isolation, and has nothing to prove to anyone, he loses the compulsion to experiment and take flights of fancy. A woman
who has perfect *mental* harmony with a Gemini need never
fear emotional or physical unfaithfulness. That's so true of
these men, it's almost a cut and dried rule. But he won't
be chained unreasonably. To expect your Gemini not to
smile back when someone smiles at him, whether it's a
child or an adult, a man or a woman, is to expect the sun
not to shine. His cheerful, friendly nature seeks companion-

ship constantly. It could be the conductor on the commuter train or the waitress at the coffee shop around the corner from where he works. Don't try to stifle him. When anyone tries to confine the Gemini's spirit, he can become as elusive and as unpredictable as the wind itself.

With the youngsters, he'll be a buddy, but not a disciplinarian, and he'll teach them a lot before they even get to kindergarten. They'll probably love to confide in him, because he'll seldom be shocked or harsh in his judgment. He knows how to love without smothering. The relationship between the Gemini and his children is usually very close, but perhaps a bit loose, even though that may sound contradictory. As affectionate, exciting and lively as he is with young people, he may fail to insist that they follow routines, since he dislikes routines so much himself. There's also a tendency to criticize their behavior one day and approve of it the next day, which can confuse them. Although he'll manage a good lecture, you'd better expect the spankings and really serious discipline to fall in your department. Gemini fathers tend to spoil their children.

His imagination may run away with him, and cause him to make an occasional statement he can't back up. You'll have to make him see the importance of keeping his word. Regardless of all his good intentions, a few of his quick impulsive promises may be broken. If the children don't tie him down in any way, or keep him from his multiple activities, he'll enjoy them enormously. One word of warning: Although he will seldom punish the children physically, the Gemini proclivity for sudden, stinging, sarcastic speech may cause deep wounds in little hearts or create a hurt which can be remembered for a lifetime. There may also be a reluctance to show affection in the form of kisses and hugs, unless a conscious effort is made to overcome the natural Geminian coolness. Yet, I've known some Gemini parents who seem to give the warmth they can't release to adults in abundance to their children. See that the youngsters don't confine him needlessly, don't ask him to babysit unless he obviously wants to, and he'll take to fatherhood nicely, with one child or a dozen.

Jealousy is something you may never have to worry about with a Gemini husband, because possessiveness is not a typical Gemini trait. If suspicion occasionally whispers in his ear, he'll usually brush it away (unless an affliction in the natal chart indicates otherwise). Some degree of jealousy is natural in everyone, of course, but it's normally not exaggerated in a Gemini. Love is not a strictly physical relationship with this man. He hears more, sees more and feels more through his senses than others do, and Mercury helps him record the most delicate impressions vividly. His love has such an airy, elusive quality, it may seem to lack the earthy passion of other Sun signs. But if you're not seeking a wild cave man who will drag you into the woods by the hair, he should be a more than satisfactory lover. He'll speak of his emotions with romantic, imaginative phrases, and fill the hunger of your heart with the strange beauty of his idealism.

Remember that the typical emotional coldness of Mercury can be warmed considerably if you both hear the same music and dream the same dreams. He must experience a total blending of the mind and the spirit before the physical passions catch up in intensity. That may seem oblique, but it's the only real road to his heart.

You'll have to get used to the word "if." He'll say, "If I loved you, we could . . ." and "If I loved you, there might be . . ." and sometimes never finish the sentence. You may have to listen with your heart and finish it for him. Blot out the word "if." He only uses it as a smoke screen or as a safety precaution. Harsh, critical nagging and continual emotional scenes will surely dull the edge of the fine, sensitive Gemini love. Try to squeeze a puddle of mercury in your hand. What happens? It dissolves immediately into hundreds of sparkling silver balls that quickly escape through your tightly clenched fingers. One Gemini man whose wife thought she knew him very well wrote the following lines just before he left her, and she found them among his papers after the divorce:

"Into the dream you came
And across the soft carpet of my reverie you walked
With hobnail boots . . ."

You'll often read or hear it said that Geminis must always have two loves at once. This Gemini duality, hinting at deception, is so frequently mentioned, it may cause unfounded anxiety. May I modify that description? A Gemini needs two loves. Not necessarily two women. That's a riddle. If you truly understand him, you'll know the answer to it.

The GEMINI Woman

Though she managed to pick
plenty of beautiful rushes as the boat glided by,
there was always a more lovely one
that she couldn't reach.
"The prettiest are always further!"
she said at last,
with a sigh at the obstinacy of the rushes
in growing so far off.

Have you always secretly thought Brigham Young had a sensational idea when he advocated several wives for one man? Do you inwardly envy the Eastern potentates with their harems? You needn't resign yourself to romantic Walter Mitty daydreams. Just marry a Gemini girl. That way, you'll be guaranteed at least two different wives, and on occasional weekends, as many as three or four.

Naturally, there's a small catch. The difference between a girl born under the sign of the twins and a harem is her apparent lack of interest in earthy passion. It's hard to get her to settle down long enough to take passion or anything else very seriously. Her mind is always traveling, and she keeps up a pretty good running commentary simultaneously. But look a little deeper, Somewhere, hidden among the several women who make up one Gemini female, is a romantic one—one who is capable of intense passion, if you can manage to make the mental, spiritual and physical blending complete. How to develop her and still enjoy all the other women bottled up inside the Geminian personality may create a problem. I can tell you that one Gemini girl equals several women. But I'm afraid it's up to you to delve into the advanced algebra of sorting them out. Each individual case is different.

Her age will be an important clue to what you can expect, because until she matures, romance is only a game to her. She can be fickle and unpredictable to an incredible degree. First she'll be ecstatically carried away by your smile and your voice, even the way you walk. Then she'll reverse her ecstasy and criticize everything from your socks to your haircut, and she usually does it with such clever, sharp sarcasm, you may need iodine for your wounds. Now, don't let this put you out of the market for a Gemini woman. Remember you're getting at least two for one, and that's indisputably a bargain.

Mercury females aren't as heartless as they seem to be at times. Their active imaginations create many fantasies. Romance is the easiest way they can express them, and Geminis have at least twice as much to express as other women. A Gemini man can be a producer, a singer, a sailor, a lawyer, an actor, a salesman and the chairman of a few boards of directors all at once—and express himself ad infinitum. But a woman can't very well swing all that, or she would be considered a little freakish. Not that Mercury girls don't pursue careers. They do. Almost every last one of them. But under the existing conditions of society, a career still doesn't offer her as many opportunities as romance to try out her myriad theories and practice her emotional gymnastics.

The Gemini girl needs your pity, not your anger. It's painfully difficult for her to really commit herself to one person at a time. While she's being impressed with a man's mental abilities and his intelligent wit, another side of her is noticing his antipathy toward the arts or his lack of response to music and poetry. When she finds someone who's appropriately creative, who's at home at the ballet or in the literary world, the duality pops up again. Right in the middle of a stroll through the museum, her other self will begin to wonder if he's practical enough to make a living or if he has enough common sense to know where he's going. I trust you're beginning to have a more sympathetic understanding of the conflicts peculiar to those born in June.

Give her credit. She'll usually manage to keep her bewilderment at her own complex character to herself, and not burden you with it. She's a lively and gay companion. Most of the time (when the mood is on the up-swing), she'll sparkle with a vivacious personality, amuse you with her clever, witty remarks, and converse intelligently about almost any subject under the sun. She enjoys all the sentimental gestures of romance and has no trouble making conquests. No woman you've ever met will delight you

with more imaginative ways of loving you and such appeal-
ing charm. She can flutter her lashes with delicate femininity, but she's not at all helpless when it comes to earning
her own living. A Gemini woman can play the giddy party
girl to perfection, flattering a helpless, trapped male right
out of his mind and his bank book. But she can smoothly
change into a demure and adoring housewife, from which
she can quickly switch into a serious intellectual who
studies the great philosophers and talks about politics or
poetry brilliantly, then suddenly turn into a bundle of raw
emotion, full of nerves, tears and fears. She's certainly not
stuffy or monotonous.

If you think this is an exaggeration, remember the late
Marilyn Monroe. Every man she ever knew, from Carl
Sandburg to her hairdresser, saw her as a totally different
person than the other men who thought they knew her,
too. Place a photograph of her as the seductive love goddess next to a picture of her wearing horn-rimmed glasses,
a babushka and no make up, seriously intent on a lecture
about Russian authors. Then add a third and fourth shot
of her in a gingham apron, learning to bake a cheese souffle
for a husband whose athletic talents and warm, human
qualities she worshiped—and walking sedately beside another husband whose intellectual abilities and literary talent
she deeply respected and admired. Add two more photos.
One showing her with a tear-stained face, full of longing,
after losing her third baby—another shot of her in a bikini,
gaily laughing with a handsome French movie star on the
Riviera. These are not posed pictures. They were snapped
when she wasn't even looking, let alone seeking publicity.
It's a perfect example of the eye of the camera exposing
all the women contained in one Gemini female, who successfully kept her multiple nature hidden behind the image
she chose to project the most frequently.

Your Mercury-ruled girl longs to be "really, truly in
love," but it keeps eluding her. She yearns for motherhood,
but often that eludes her, too. She finds a different perfection in each man she meets, as she restlessly searches for
the one man who has all the qualities she needs for
happiness.

You'll find her a great pal. The Mercury girl will go
along with you on anything from scuba diving to speed
racing—bicycling or badminton. She'll show an interest in
all the outdoor sports, and still manage to look as soft and

feminine as a powder puff, with a mind as fast as a whip. The Geminian sharp mentality will show clearly when her curiosity is excited by any new subject. Her Mercurial mind will let her see all the intricacies of your creative ideas, and she'll probably throw in a few promotional schemes of her own. As long as you don't demand consistency from her, she'll be completely fascinating.

It's only fair to warn you that this girl can sincerely believe she's in love, and find other men attractive at the same time. Unless she's near you all the time, she can forget you quicker than a woman born under any other Sun sign. It's her nature to accept change, even seek it. Until she learns to control her devoted courtship of constant activity, neglecting to cultivate patience and stability, the Gemini female can make quite a mess of her life—and yours. Fortunately for the men in love with them, most Geminian women settle down into a deeper understanding of their own natures before it's too late.

Once you've proposed to her and she's accepted, you can pity all those men who are doomed to a life of monogamy with just one woman. You'll have several wives when you marry your Gemini.

Wife Number One will be able to adjust to anything you require of her. If you require faithfulness, she can manage that, too, providing you're interesting enough to have won her real love. I refer to that blending of mental, spiritual and physical compatibility, with the physical part added last, like the paprika, after the other three are well mixed. This wife will never sulk if you take a new job out of town. With her ingenuity, taste and sense of color, she can make a new home look lovely with a light touch of her dainty, clever hand. Besides, she'll love the adventure, and there will be no nagging reproaches that you're gambling with future security. The excitement of new horizons interests her more. She may have a surprisingly good head for business and she'll back all your original ideas. You can count on her to go to work if you need extra income, and she'll be pretty practical about how to spend it. Although she may give an outward impression of flightiness, she's not as flighty as she appears. She's a thinker, and a very clever one, underneath all the bright small talk.

Wife Number Two will be moody. You might just as well expect it. She'll have her satirical moments when she can be cynical and flippant, by turns. At the same time, she'll challenge you mentally. But a man needs to be stimulated, doesn't he? Go ahead, top her in an intellectual argument. (It's what she secretly wants anyway.) This wife won't be easily shocked by life or have any preconceived prejudices. She may decide to march in a protest parade or join a sit-in and forget to come home until midnight. What if you do have to join the fellows while she's out making a speech or going to night school to pick up a few extra credits? At least she probably won't hound you with suspicious questions about who you were with, where you were, and what you were doing. Don't question her, either. You're on the honor system. So is she. This one is a highly independent individualist.

Wife Number Three will be bored and depressed with housekeeping routines. The beds will be unmade and the dishes will stand in the sink while she daydreams, reads or writes the outline for a play. She may serve you a can of beans for dinner without even bothering to open the can. But you can have the most soul-satisfying conversations with her into the wee, small hours. She'll sympathize with your frustrations at the way life has treated you. She'll satisfy both your emotional and your intellectual cravings, be curious about your opinion of Buddhism and excited about your attempts to write a song. In short, she's pretty good company. She'll be very affectionate, too, since you haven't bugged her about dusting and baking and all that nonsense. This wife may make a mess of the checkbook now and then. But if you suggest a sudden camping trip or a few days in Las Vegas, she'll enthusiastically pack her suitcase without a bunch of silly objections, like how it's going to affect the budget or who will feed the Siamese cat and what if the bathtub leaks while you're gone.

Wife Number Four will be a gay and laughing mother. She won't let the children restrict her, because she'll probably have too many projects going constantly to smother them with over-protectiveness. They'll imitate her independence and benefit by it. If anyone asks her how much time she spends with them, she'll probably answer, "In our family, it's not a matter of how much time. It's a matter of how much love." And she'll be right. The children may not always obey her, because she's inclined to be emphatic one day, then melt and give in the next, but the youngsters will love their long talks with her. Her imagination will match theirs, and they'll amuse each other. She'll probably be a permissive mother, but she'll worry about scholastic averages, and she'll probably insist on good grades. They won't get by without doing their homework if she can help it, although they may get by without hanging up their clothes.

Wife Number Five will be a beautiful hostess, an expert at the whole candlelight, flowers and sterling silver routine. You can bring anyone, from your boss to the Governor home to dinner, and she'll be so gracious and charming, they'll never want to leave. She'll organize her life efficiently and effortlessly, dress like a fashion model and love the theater. You can take her to art galleries and concerts— she'll be right at home in any kind of society. Everyone will stare at you enviously and wonder who the glamorous woman is who hangs on your arm so sweetly. She'll be romantic and ultra-feminine, maybe even write you a poem for your birthday. You'll want to buy her velvet dressing gowns and expensive perfumes, because her gracious style will make you feel like a country squire. If you mention a trip to Europe, her eyes will sparkle. She's a sophisticate.

Well, there you are. I may have missed a few girls in your Gemini harem. Every husband in town will be green with envy when they see you with a different woman every day. If they ask you how you get away with it, play it cool. Polygamy is against the law, you know.

Your Gemini woman will never take a train when she can fly. She'll never be silent when she can speak. She'll never turn away when she can help. And she'll never walk when she can run. Her mind is full of so many thoughts and her heart is full of so many hopes, she may seem to need a computer to sort it all out. Or does she just need someone who can run beside her and toss dreams with her—from here to tomorrow? If you're that man, she doesn't dare look over her shoulder to see if you're near. Some deep, unexplained fear within her keeps her from ever looking back. When you finally match her speed, get her to slow down to your pace. You can do it, if you hold her hand tightly and never let it go. Though Mercurial north winds drive her on, secretly she may long to rest awhile more than you know. Do hurry and try to reach her. She needs you.

The GEMINI Child

"Will you walk a little faster?"
said a whiting to a snail,
"There's a porpoise close behind us,
and he's treading on my tail."

If the stork just delivered a Gemini baby to your house, sharpen your roller skates and shake the cobwebs out of your brain. You'll need to be fast and alert for the next fifteen to twenty years, and you might as well start right now, while your little bundle from Mercury is still pinned down in his crib. It won't be long before he learns to walk and talk. If you're not ready to fly beside him, he may slip in and out of your fingers like a glob of air. Did you ever try to hold on to a glob of air?

The U.S. Census Bureau figures prove that there are more multiple births during the period of Gemini, the twins, than at any other time of the year. So your June event might have been twins—or more. No? Don't be too sure. You may be able to count only ten toes and ten fingers, which adds up to one infant in most cases, but not necessarily in the case of a Gemini infant. There may have to be a change in your concept of mathematics. You'll see what I mean soon enough when he starts to crawl. It will happen a dozen times a day. You'll swear you just this second saw him with his hand inside the electric mixer in the pantry. But how could that be? There he is, all the way out on the front porch, blissfully chewing the petunias. How can he be two places at once? Remember that your offspring is ruled by Mercury. He's that Greek god you see pictured in books with wings on his feet, wearing a bright silver helmet. Stick a kitchen pan upside down on your Gemini baby's head for a helmet, and use your imagination for the wings sprouting out of his chubby little pink heels. See the resemblance?

I have never personally approved of those harness-like attachments they sell to mothers to strap around their toddlers when they take them out shopping. It always makes me think the woman is walking her dog. However, I would strongly advise the mother of a Gemini child to buy two or three of them, just to be on the safe side.

Your first thought might be that, if baby is going to be that active, a sturdy playpen is a must. I can see your logic, even sympathize with it, but I'm not so sure about playpens and Gemini children. Confinement in a small space can amount to cruelty with a little Geminian, whose entire nature urges him to seek, to explore, to learn. Even worse than the physical curtailment is the mental boredom of being stuck on one little blue and pink plastic rectangular pad, with the whole exciting world out there to see and enjoy. Periods of being cooped up in a playpen should be brief. Too much restriction and hampering of the Geminian freedom can lead to emotional depression he may not outgrow so easily. Remember, he's an air sign, and air must move. Make sure he has a variety of toys and plenty of bright books to look at when you must keep him fenced in.

Of course, he won't stay there long, once he's had it. Mercury rules the vocal chords, and when your little Gemini tot decides to exercise his talent in this direction, you'll wonder how all that noise could possibly come out of one small mouth. Bet you take him out of the playpen fast. Unless you have understanding neighbors, who are a little hard of hearing.

Gemini children often make older, more placid people nervous with their bird-like, quick movements. Grownups are always telling the little Geminian to stop fidgeting, or to be patient and do one thing at a time. But doing two things at a time is natural to these youngsters. What stodgy or poised people call fidgety is, to the Gemini, merely his normal state of activity. It's wrong to make him feel he would get more approval if he tried to imitate the slower, less lively people. He should be taught to slow down a little, perhaps, for his own good, but his basic nature can't be changed without frustrating his natural inclinations. We should try to remember that the quick Gemini child who annoys his more introverted elders—and the quiet, careful Capricorn child who irritates his more aggressive elders, are simply being themselves. Being yourself is always hard enough to do, without people trying to force a personality change.

Love your Gemini child for what he is—a friendly, alert,

inquisitive and precocious little person. You can't turn the firefly into a snail or the snail into a firefly. Nor can the leopard change his spots. I might add that, if someone tries to scrub them off, he'll be a mighty unhappy, neurotic leopard.

Of course, you aren't raising leopards. You're raising a bright, interesting, enthusiastic child. But the analogy is logical. Let those spots of duality in your Gemini youngster remain. Someday he may make you proud of a building he designed and a literary prize he won; and when he manifests such a double talent, you'll wonder why you ever tried to stamp him into a single mold. If he leaps about as though he has jumping beans inside him he's just practicing the fast reflexes he was born with. His firefly mind can confuse you, but remember that it's pursuing a thousand fancies, sorting them, deciding which to discard and which to treasure.

Teachers will usually notice right away that these boys and girls have no trouble learning to read. Gemini almost invented words. They won't mind being called on to recite, and they may smile as the rest of the students sigh, when a theme is assigned. These youngsters delight in communicating with others and sharing their knowledge verbally or on paper. Many of them are mechanically inclined and ambidextrous. It's not unusual to find a Gemini child who writes with his left hand and draws with his right. He may bite his nails, but his fingers are normally slim and flexible, which makes him adept at magic tricks and playing musical instruments. Someday it could make him a fine surgeon, dentist or watchmaker. Gemini hands are sensitive, expressive and capable.

There's usually a marked ability to mimic others. The Gemini sense of sharp wit and satire appears early. At home or in school, the Gemini child lives in a world of make-believe and reality, constantly blending, where truth is often portrayed as fantasy, and fantasy is disguised as truth. He may give the impression of exaggerating or even telling lies. But he just can't help splashing a little color around when he's relating an incident, and he often convinces himself it really happened that way. At such times, he should be handled gently, since he's actually stretching and exercising his vivid imagination. Rather than make him feel guilty for having an imagination, he should be told always to speak the truth and write the story down on paper. Once he masters this, he'll be able to see the difference between the dream and the fact, instead of being lost somewhere between the two worlds. Gemini youngsters who aren't allowed to express and communicate naturally may retreat into a half-world of illusion in self-defense. It's a good idea to start him on foreign languages early—which he'll probably learn effortlessly. Like the Sagittarius child, he'll find bi-lingual talents will come in handy because he'll talk a lot and travel a lot.

The Gemini child who argues with you that he can do his homework and listen to the radio at the same time is probably telling the truth. If his grades back him up, why not? Geminis are never satisfied with one pursuit at a time. It's as if they had two lives to live in only one lifetime, so they must absorb all they can, as fast as they can. The chief dangers are a lack of patience and an unwillingness to persist until a thing is thoroughly learned. These youngsters have to be discouraged from a tendency to let their quick intellects and glib wits skim over knowledge without completely understanding it.

Your Gemini child may find it hard to be punctual, because he's always running into some new discovery on his way to anywhere. He may also find it hard to listen without interrupting, because he's caught the thought instantly and doesn't want to hear the details. He may tend to repeat himself, but he won't allow you to do so, which quite naturally may irritate people. In the classroom, he can be distracted by a fly, a piece of colored paper or a wisp of smoke outside the window. It's never easy to get his attention, but when you do, you'll be richly rewarded by the Geminian's intent curiosity and flattering interest.

Your teenage Gemini boy will practically live on the telephone, go steady with a different person each week, change his mind a hundred times about his future career, drive the car a little too fast, putter with the engine and fix your washer. The girls will be popular and be able to turn on a shower of tears or a sunny smile like a light switch. These youngsters will keep you on your toes and keep you young.

When your Gemini child finally grows up, lots of people will tell you disapprovingly that "he has too many fingers stuck in too many pies." You'll smile then, and they may be annoyed. But you'll be remembering one spring day when he was seven. He stuck his fingers in your chocolate pies, his father's shaving cream, the fish bowl, the garbage can, a pot of hot soup and an electric socket. You were furious. Later, at twilight, you watched him run around chasing lightning bugs in the grass. After a while, you sighed, and asked yourself aloud, "Why must he rush around so? Why must he get into everything? What in the world is he searching for?" He overheard you and it troubled him. You'll never forget the look in his bright, clear eyes when he answered. "Gee, Mommy . . . I don't know. But don't you worry. I'll find it."

The GEMINI Boss

He said, "I look for butterflies
that sleep among the wheat
I make them into mutton-pies,
And sell them in the street.
I sell them unto men," he said,
"Who sail on stormy seas;
And that's the way I get my bread—
A trifle, if you please."

One day your Gemini boss will be a walking clock whose camera eye records each second you take past your coffee break. On another, he won't even notice if you come back three hours late from lunch. You can try flipping a coin to predict his changes. It's about as safe as anything else. I realize that it would be a big help to know which day he's going to take what attitude.

But the Gemini executive doesn't know himself which side of the bed he's going to get out on each morning, and since he doesn't know, you can see that I can't tell you. The safest way is not to expect him to be today what he was yesterday, and cross your fingers about tomorrow.

This man can be a brilliant, though restless, executive. He's more at home in the president's chair than the other mutable signs of Virgo, Pisces or Sagittarius would be, but he's not equipped to command or lead others for his entire lifetime. A Gemini who thinks he's constituted to run a large company with calm assurance is just kidding himself (always considering the exceptions to the rule, like a Sun sign Gemini with a Leo ascendant and a Libra Moon, for example). In the first place, it's hard for him to sit still behind a desk for more than an hour at a time. President Kennedy, one of the rare Geminis equipped to take on the burdens of leadership, solved that problem neatly. He simply released his nervous energy by making his rocking chair fly.

Your Mercury-ruled boss must move around. Gemini is an air sign, and did you ever see air stand still? It may seem to sometimes on a hot, humid day (and so will a Gemini if you catch him in a rare moment), but that's only an illusion in both cases. The typical Gemini boss will wear a hole in the carpet pacing up and down if he's caged up in an office too long. He's happier as a management consultant, an efficiency expert or a vice president in charge of trouble-shooting than when he's forced into the confining mold of a nine-to-five position, no matter how fancy the title. He deals with ideas, principles and abstractions. The humdrum and material responsibilties of the average executive eventually depress his soaring spirit. Therefore, when a Gemini parachutes himself into an executive spot, he'll be quick to exercise his acute discrimination and delegate authority to others around him. These carefully chosen specialists will really run the business, freeing his own restless mind for progressive schemes and original plans that will double the company's profit and lower its overhead. He's impatient with dull, mundane details.

If your company just hired a Gemini as your superior you can expect some changes to be made in short order. The slowest form of communication around the place will probably be cablegrams, and he may require a few more buttons on his telephone than his predecessor. Your new Gemini boss won't be on the job a week before he's inquisitively poked around into every area of the operation. As soon as he learns what's being done and how it's being done, he'll want to know why. The answer, "We've always done it this way," will cause his bright eyes to turn to ice cubes that could freeze you at thirty paces. Gemini is not even slightly interested in or impressed with tradition. When he's told something is an old custom, that's reason enough for him to change it. The typical Mercury boss will have the furniture moved around frequently, drive his secretary into a fit of the fidgets once a week with a new idea for a filing system that will work more efficiently, and change the work schedules back and forth until he finds one that clicks with him.

There's one thing you can count on, and one of the few things you can count on consistently with a Gemini. He will never be monotonous. He'll seldom be dogmatic either. His opinions are flexible. You can't mislead him or confuse the issue, because his quicksilver mind will instantly reduce the frills, penetrate the smoke screens and expose all sides of the question with crystal clarity. That means he also exposes office intrigues with little difficulty. Sometimes you'll swear he has eyes in the back of his head—and an extra pair of ears there, too. Speaking of his anatomy and such, it's even hard to credit him with just one pair of feet, since there will be plenty of occasions when he appears to be two places at once.

Never fear that your Gemini employer will hate you or be your enemy. Few people interest him long enough for that kind of intensity. You won't be in his thoughts for more than an hour or so at a time. That's not long enough to work up any violent feelings, for or against. Besides, he has a pretty fair understanding about how the other person feels.

It may puzzle you to discover that, although your Gemini employer is an individualist in every way, he may not treat you as an individualist. It seems inconsistent, but then this is a dual sign, with more than one surprise. I don't mean that he won't respect your individual opinions. He will. It's just that he doesn't always see you personally as an individual. The Geminian mind is so abstract that he often sees only basic designs in both objects and people. All kinds of people are fascinating to him, but he tends to categorize them according to their abilities, ideas and potential.

Yet this odd viewpoint doesn't make him unattractive as a human being. Quite the contrary. Even though his approach is far more rational than emotional, he likes people so much, they just can't help liking him back. Without the constant challenge of human contact, he would dry up and float away. Mercury demands that he be gregarious and live vicariously or be miserable. You'll rarely see him by himself. He may classify people by types and remain detached emotionally, but he needs them around.

Your Gemini boss will probably have considerable powers of persuasion. He can wheedle you into or talk you out of most anything, simply by dousing you with a bucket of that irresistible charm and wit of his. But it's a compensating talent he was given by the planets at birth, that hides a basic coldness of nature. Gemini lives in vague, airy palaces in the sky the average person can't reach. His true character, despite his surface warmness, is cool, aloof and lonely, in the final analysis, searching for something inside itself more than from others, no matter how frequently he seeks their company. Yet, he's not unsympathetic. His manner can be gentle and compassionate, but at the same time, he offers his sympathy and understanding the same way he offers love and friendship—from a distance.

He'll have an excellent sense of humor, and you can win him over with a joke more quickly than with tears. He's not overly sentimental, but he'll always see the ridiculous side of things. A sense of humor is a prerequisite to true intelligence, so it's not surprising to find it in the Mercury people, though sometimes it may be tinged with sharp sarcasm. There will always be a slight whirl of confusion around a Gemini-run office—and constant activity. But he won't be the one who is confused. Gemini sorts it all out and clears the muddy waters of all the gunk. His quick eye and his trigger fast brain work in perfect synchronization. The eye will probably have a twinkle in it. He'll be the company's best salesman, make speeches and entertain a lot. And he'll probably travel so much, he may keep a suitcase ready to fly at a moment's notice. If he flirts with the pretty new secretary, better tell her he's not the least bit serious, just sharpening his charm a little.

Enjoy this boss while you can, because Geminis get suddenly bored after they've made financial or business successes, and they rush off to the next challenge long before retirement time. Before he goes, learn what you can about his strategy. It's really fantastic. He's an expert at double talk. He'll run around an argument in circles, mix you up, turn you around, then win you over to his side before you realize what's happened. Yet, as clever as he is in competitive situations, he's still an incurable dreamer, and a smashingly good storyteller. Pay no attention to what nationality he says he is. Whether he was born in Israel, Australia or Afghanistan, every single Gemini in the world is Irish at heart. How else could he possess such a wonder-

ful gift of blarney? Notice all those green ties he wears.
What did I tell you—pure County Cork.

The GEMINI Employee

"The time has come," the Walrus said,
  "To talk of many things;
Of shoes—and ships—and sealing wax—
  Of cabbages—and kings—
And why the sea is boiling hot—
  And whether pigs have wings."

Yet, what can one poor voice avail
Against three tongues together?

Do you have some employees around your office who talk
fast, move fast and think fast? Do they look young and
act young, forget about their ages? Are they unpredictable,
restless, original and impatient? What a smart man you are!
You've gone and hired yourself some Geminis.

It's easy to understand why. With all that charm and
guile, not to mention flashing intellect and creative imagination, you probably couldn't help yourself. Now that you've
had a chance to watch these Mercury people in action,
you've learned that they can take an abstract idea and
reduce it to a formula better than anyone else in the office.
Your Aquarian employee can think in wildly abstract
terms, your Aries employee can toss out some red-hot ideas,
smothered in enthusiasm, and the Virgos can organize the
details meticulously. But Gemini can do all three.

Before you fire those other people, however, remember
that the Gemini doesn't have the intense drive of the Aries,
nor the willingness to work overtime. He also lacks the
fixed and steady purpose of the Aquarian and he'll never
understand the endless, devoted dedication of the Virgo.
We won't cover the other Sun signs. You get the general
idea. Your Gemini employee is not a one-man show, all
by himself, even if he is a dual personality. He'll come

closer to it than anyone else, but you'll need the other workers just the same.

Geminis share with Virgo, Aries, Leo and Scorpio a built-in ability to deal with emergencies. They can meet a crisis swiftly. The typical Gemini will make instant decisions and go into action while most of the people around him are still polishing their skis. He's easily bored with routine, happiest when he's free, so don't try to chain him down to the work bench. He'd rather do a stretch of time in Sing Sing than work for a clock-watcher. At least in prison he could turn his curious mind to studying the behavior of the inmates. I'd sincerely like to point out here that the Gemini behind bars is a lonely man who couldn't find the right niche for his multiple talents in an over-organized, conformist society. Many a Gemini forger or petty thief is basically as honest as the judge who sentenced him, and twice as idealistic. When Gemini is made to feel guilty about his vivid imagination and restless energy in childhood, then constantly criticized by the business world for being too progressive and refusing to fit into stale patterns, his high sense of moral and mental ethics becomes distorted, and he strikes out on the only original path he feels is left to him.

Most Geminis are so glibly persuasive they can talk people into buying things they couldn't possibly even use. It's never a mistake to utilize their talents in sales or promotional activities. When the Gemini's silver tongue gets through extolling the virtues of your firm, you won't even recognize it yourself, even if you're a blind egotist about your own company. Send your Gemini man out to sell the public, or to wheedle your customers and clients in restaurants and on golf courses. Or send him on the road to gather up an avalanche of good will and orders for business. If you must keep him in the office, be careful where you place him. He doesn't resent supervision as fiercely as Leo or Aries, but he will become nervous and inadequate if he's confined and unable to express himself. When this happens, your Gemini employee will break his shackles and breeze off to more freedom without an instant's regret. Now don't run in and take a hasty peek at his desk to see if he's still there. He won't fly away or disappear into thin air until he's had a chance to tell you his reasons and take his chances of winning you over to his point of view. Unless you hear differently, directly from him, he's probably as happy as a winged messenger from the gods could be here on earth, doing whatever it is you have him applying his agile mind to.

If there's an office pool of any kind, you may see your Leos, Aries and Sagittarius people doing lots of showy betting, but you can bet your old Brooklyn Dodgers button that it was probably masterminded by one of those streaks of lightning you employ who was born in June. The Gemini won't throw extravagant sums of money into a complicated bubble scheme as readily as Leo, the lion. He's more likely to risk his security in a situation where there's a challenge to his wits, where there's fast action and a quick return. His conversation will be full of phrases like "Let's give it a spin," "It's worth a flyer," and "I'll try anything once." And he will, too. Try anything once, that is. Twice is out. He's bored by then.

Your Gemini employee may be conspicuous by his absence or absent-mindedness (same thing), during baseball season or golfing play-offs. Most Mercury people enjoy these sports, and many of them have participated, thanks to the uncanny Geminian dexterity. There's little he can't do with the synchronization of his intelligence and his clever hands, and that can include calculating precisely how to swat a white ball over the fence or making a hole-in-one on the green. Sports often attract him as a way to work off all that nervous energy. In the long run, however, the Gemini prefers to exercise his wits and give his mind a workout, so he can bat plenty of home runs for your firm. Still, he should be encouraged to engage in physical activity. It will wear him out so he can sleep. All Geminis are prone to insomnia. Many Gemini employees who work in offices where they're required to be on the job early in the morning can be recognized by the circles under their eyes.

Your Geminis will keep the office humming with busy activity, lots of jokes and gay chatter. But they'll get things done. The Mercury secretary may be the fastest typist in the crowd, and quick to catch your dictation. Normally, if she's a typical Gemini, she'll be able to form an intelligent, clearly-stated letter with just a hint from you about the subject matter. In spite of her secretarial talents, you might be better off to put her out in front where she can charm the people who walk in the door and run the switchboard for you. (Doing two things at once and juggling them expertly is no problem for a Mercury girl.) You'll have fewer disgruntled people calling you. Not only will she sweet talk strangers cleverly, she's not apt to scramble the cords and cut you off in the middle of a call to Kalamazoo to connect you with Katanga.

I'd better warn you not to discuss raises, bonuses, commissions and such with a Gemini, if you can possibly help it. Use a stern Capricorn or a dogmatic Taurus or a no-nonsense Virgo as your middle man. If you don't, the Gemini may talk you into giving him a higher position with the firm than you have available without firing your wife's brother and twice as much money as you make yourself. He'll make it all seem perfectly logical. It's much safer to avoid financial huddles with a persuasive Gemini. If you're game, go ahead and try it. But you may come out of the huddle having promised him a weekly expense account that would support a couple of Virgos and Cancerians for a year.

You're likely to trip over a few broken hearts in the office hallways when you have Mercury employees. A flirtation or two a month and a rather fickle way of changing his mind is the average behavior before maturity. There's a youthful air of irresponsibility about many a Gemini (unless the natal chart indicates a more stable nature). He has a mind at least a million years old, and the emotions of a teenager. He'll look like one, too.

The truth is that the Gemini, like Peter Pan, hates to grow up. And like Peter, he needs a Wendy as smart as he is to clean house for him every spring, letting him come and go as he pleases. If you're the kind of boss to play office Cupid, don't introduce him to any other kind of girl, or you may have to loan him money to pay his alimony shortly afterwards.

Do you want to make your office really swing? Put your Aries employee and your Gemini employee together in a room to discuss a new project. Then stuff some cotton in your ears to protect them from a sound like one hundred adding machines and two hundred ticker tapes all going at once. Stand close by with a big, strong net to catch all the pink balloons that will be flying through the air. Gather them up, take them in to your office, and study them carefully before you stick a pin in them. One of them is likely to contain a million dollar idea.

He thought he saw an Albatross
That fluttered round the lamp:
He looked again, and found it was
A penny-postage-stamp.
"You'd best be getting home," he said,
"The nights are very damp."

CANCER the Crab

June 22nd through July 23rd

How to Recognize CANCER

"I can't explain myself, I'm afraid.
because I'm not myself, you see."

"Oh, my fur and whiskers!"

It is this, it is this that oppresses my soul.

The best time to hunt for human crabs is by the light of the silvery Moon. It's usually easier to recognize them at night, when they're all dressed up to go dreaming, wrapped in vivid imagination. Moonlight becomes them beautifully. It goes with their many moods, and it matches their changing emotions.

You'll gather lots of clues to the Cancerian nature by doing some Moon-gazing on a clear night in the country. It may be hard to see it through the smog in the city, but you can always study an almanac. Notice the Moon's changing shape and appearance. As it waxes and increases in light, it slowly grows into a perfect, round ball in the sky. When it wanes, it gradually disappears, so there's nothing visible but a thin sliver of light with a faint, silver shimmer.

The Cancerian's passing moods are synchronized to the Moon, answering to the same mysterious lunar influence that causes the tides of the ocean to flow in and out. Yet, the Moon doesn't really change at all. It just seems to. Likewise, the Cancerian remains the same person through all his fluctuating highs and lows. Such dependable periodicity—constant in its inconstancy—makes the crab easy to recognize, once you know the phase he's in when you see him.

You may first come across him when he's laughing the "crazy lunar laugh." It's inescapably contagious. It runs up and down the scales with a deep, throaty undertone. It giggles and gurgles, then finally erupts in a loud cackle that sounds exactly like two hundred hens laying two hundred perfect eggs. In his life-of-the-party mood, you'll have no trouble finding the Cancerian. He'll be the funniest one in the room, a laugh a minute. If he's not performing himself, then he'll be grinning at someone else's antics. No one likes a joke better than Cancer, and his funny side is all the more startling when it pops up so incongruously from his normally quiet, gentle personality. Lunar humor runs deep. It's never shallow or superficial, because it stems from the sensitive observation of human behavior. Cancer may not wear his lunar laugh every day, but he can always dig it out of his old trunk in the basement at a moment's notice.

These people don't pant after the spotlight like the extro-verted Leos or clownish Sagittarians, but Cancerians have an uncanny sense of publicity, when it pleases them to be noticed. Don't let that unassuming manner fool you. They secretly enjoy attention, and they'll soak up any headlines they get. You won't find Cancer pursuing fame with pas-sion (he pursues nothing with true passion), but he cer-tainly won't shrink from it. He's far more likely to bask in the reflected glow of applause than to run away. Cancer may hide from things, but you can be sure that apprecia-tion is not one of them.

If you're the kind of person who catches cold easily, wear your raincoat when you expose yourself to the damp-ness of a Cancerian in a melancholy mood. He can wrap you in wet blankets until you shiver and shake. Cancer can turn bluer than an inkwell, and drown you in depression deeper than the floor of the ocean. His fears are usually well covered by the nutty lunar humor, but they are always with him, haunting his days and nights with a vague sense of nameless dangers, lurking in the shadows. Pessimism is never far away, always ready to spoil those beautiful flights of fancy. A Cancerian can take the dreamiest trips to the stars on the gossamer wings of his imagination, if he learns to ignore that harping inner voice which keeps nagging him and warning him he might get lost in outer space. But until he learns to conquer his fears, they form his Achilles' heel, and they hurt every time he starts to fly too high.

His tears are never crocodile tears. They flow from the deep rivers of his fragile and vulnerable heart. You can wound his sensitive feelings with a harsh glance or a rough tone of voice. Cruelty can bring on brimming eyes or a complete withdrawal. (It's an odd thing that Cancerians seldom get fevers; they're more likely to suffer from the chills.) It won't be easy to spot the crab in this mood, because when he's hurt, he disappears into reproachful silence. Sometimes, he can retaliate with an almost scorpion revenge, but he'll usually do it secretly, seldom openly with the Scorpio's fine contempt for consequences. Most of the time, however, he'll turn away from getting even, content to hide under his protective shell. Once you've wounded him, you can poke at him with a sharp stick for days afterwards and not reach him. He won't answer his phone, his doorbell or his mail. In the midst of uncertainty, despair and sadness, Cancer people seek retreat and solitude. Just like real crabs.

That's another mood Cancerians have. Crabby. The person who gave you a cranky answer when you asked for the time, the one who nearly snapped your head off when you asked him to pass the salt—was probably a Cancer person going through one of his occasional crabby spells that makes him hate the world. He's not angry with you. He's disappointed with life. He'll get over it, and be his own sweet, gentle and understanding self when the Moon changes. Consult the daily paper for the next quarter, or wait until the tides come back in.

There are two basic Cancer types. The first kind has a handsome round face, soft skin, a wide, grinning mouth, almost circular eyes, rather a baby-faced look. Think of the man in the moon. That's a perfect image. The second type is more common. The unmistakable "look of the crab" is immediately noticeable in the face. You'll see a fairly large skull, an overhanging brow and high cheekbones. The brows themselves will seem to knit together in a sort of permanent frown which, strangely, isn't offensive, but rather interesting. There's a pronounced lower jaw, and the teeth are either prominent or irregular in some way. The eyes are small and usually far apart. Sometimes you'll see a Cancerian who combines both the lunar face and the crab face but each is so distinctive that, even when they're blended, it's easy to recognize them as Moon people, born under the sign of the crab. Some of them are indisputably plump, but the great majority have a strikingly bony structure. The arms and legs may be extra long in proportion to the rest of the body. The shoulders will be broader than average, and often the hands and feet are either unusually tiny or quite large. Most Cancerians are a little top heavy, and they waddle slightly when they walk fast. Whether the body is plump or wiry, the women will usually wear a sweater size considerably larger than the skirt size. Or they'll be absolutely flat-chested. Either way, this particular characteristic is quite marked. There is never a middle ground for this part of the anatomy with female crabs.

All lunar people have enormously expressive features. A thousand moods play fleetingly across their faces in the course of a conversation. Do you know someone who sometimes cackles wildly, then weeps despondently,—who occasionally snaps at you irritably, and then hides when you hurt him? Does he normally treat you with gentle consideration? If he's gruff, yet kindly, a fascinating conversationalist with deep wells of creative imagination, that person was probably born in late June or July.

Cancerians have such control of imagery, and their moods are so intense, they can make you feel them, too. Their imagination seizes joy and despair, horror and compassion, sorrow and ecstasy, and holds each emotion fast with a retentive memory. Like mirrors and cameras, they absorb images and reflect them faithfully. Every experience is engraved on the heart as a photograph is etched on a negative plate. They never forget any of the lessons life has taught them nor do they forget the lessons history has taught mankind. A Cancerian reveres the past and is usually patriotic to the core. Historical figures intrigue him as much as his own ancestors do. He often collects antiques, old treasures and ancient relics and has an insatiable curiosity about yesterday. Cancer is a sort of mental archaeologist, always digging for more fascinating facts.

He's also a well of secrecy. People automatically confide their secrets to the crab, but with his sensitive emotions he already knows what's on their minds. Cancerian compassion is deep and highly intuitive. There's hardly a secret he can't strip naked, if he chooses. It's a one-way street, however. He'll eventually soak up all there is to know about you, but you'll never guess his own private thoughts. He guards his inner feelings carefully from prying eyes. The typical Cancer person doesn't like to discuss his personal life, but he's delighted to hear about yours, as his lunar imagination lets him easily guess the parts you leave out. Cancer seldom judges, however. He simply gathers, absorbs, reflects.

Although the crab gives back emotions like a mirror, he won't give up tangible things without a struggle. Take a stroll along any beach and observe the habits of the real crab. When he grabs an object (and make sure it's not your big toe), he'll hang on for dear life. He'd rather lose a claw than let go. If the crab does sacrifice a claw, he grows a new one, so he can grab hold once more with the same tenacity; and let that be a lesson to you when you're trying to get a Cancerian to give up something he or she really wants. Cancer will never relinquish a treasured object, and that can range all the way from a beloved friend or relative to a title or a position—from an old tintype photo to a pair of frazzled house slippers, with the soles half worn away.

While you're still on the beach, take a few more notes on the customs of the real crab. The way he walks, for instance. If his eye is on that big toe, he'll never come forth directly and head for your foot. First, he moves backward a few paces. Then he moves sideways. Suddenly, without warning, he crawls to the other side. He always appears to be moving in the opposite direction. But he's watching every second. If that delicious toe starts to get away from him, he'll move straight forward, and you'd better run if you don't want those claws to dig in. He means business when he sees he has a chance of losing the morsel he covets. The human crab imitates these tactics precisely. Cancerians never go directly after what they want. Their strategy is to move in every direction but straight ahead. They'll play this shifting game indefinitely, until it looks as if someone else is about to grab the prize. Then the cards are played quickly and cleverly—Cancer lunges forward, takes hold firmly, and refuses to let go.

They behave much the same way when it comes to generosity and giving. Cancer's heart is too soft not to be touched by someone's need. He truly cares and he wants to help. But he'll sit back cautiously and wait to see if there's anyone else who might move in first. Why should he foolishly squander his time or money if it is not necessary? When all other sources fail, when no other help shows any sign of materializing, Cancer will rescue the struggler at the last minute. He'll let you go down twice, but he'll save you just before you submerge the third time. He's too kind to watch you drown, but he's certainly not going to get all wet if there's a life guard around, or if it looks as if you can swim to shore yourself. It's self-preservation, not self-ishness or unkindness. The crab's heart is soft at the core, under his hard, conservative outer shell. But there's just so much of his time, his money and his emotions he has to give, and he chooses to distribute each wisely. His eventual gesture will often be grand and generous. Yet, in his mind, it's only sensible to watch and wait before plunging. No one could accuse him of being impulsive.

When he does make a move, he'll want some sort of track record behind him—or behind you. The crab carefully calculates his actions on experiences, either his own or someone else's. He needs the strength of an accepted precedent or the assurance of financial security as a foundation. He fears going it alone without such an insurance policy, which is why most of his ventures are successful and each final move a coup de grace, executed with finesse. Naturally, Cancerians will seldom stumble into deep holes in the dark. With a fiery Moon sign, or a fire sign on the ascendant, he may gamble on an occasional maneuver, but if he fails, he'll be miserable about going against his own better inner judgment. Leo or Sagittarius influences may have driven him to act, but when he falls back on his own Sun sign after defeat, misery sets in. Cancer tends to brood over mistakes instead of shrugging off bad luck and trying again, and it will be some time before he takes another chance.

Male or female, the Cancerian loves his home with a respect bordering on reverence. No devout high priest of ancient times ever considered his altar more sacred than Cancer considers the place where he hangs his old hat. You're liable to notice a sampler on his wall with the words, "There's No Place Like Home, Be It Ever So Humble." (Yes, I know the verse is backwards, but his little girl made it at school, and to him it's a masterpiece, a pearl beyond price. Admire it often.) His home is where he plays, lives, loves, dreams and feels safe. Though he may travel over half the earth in connection with his career, no Cancer person is ever quite happy without a hearth to call his own. Sometime make a point of noticing the expression on the face of a crab who has just returned home from a long trip. Pure ecstasy.

No matter how much money he piles up in reserve, Cancer never feels really secure, and no matter how much love he gets, he always needs more. His emotions never

let him become sure enough to relax completely. He's
always piling up tangibles against some imaginary future
disaster. Some Cancerians actually keep big cardboard
cartons of food of all kinds under their beds. It keeps away
those nightmares. You may think that's stretching the truth,
but when was the last time you looked under a Cancer's
bed? If you don't find the canned foods there, look on the
closet shelves. You may find two dozen cans of paprika
and twenty-eight boxes of fortified bread crumbs he bought
on sale in 1943. What's he saving it for? Don't ask ridiculous questions. There might be a famine someday. He's
prepared. (Noah must have been born in July. The flood
didn't catch him with his rudders down, either.) Why
doesn't he use all that paprika and all those bread crumbs?
The answer to that one raises another question. Why
doesn't he use those fourteen pairs of new pajamas and
the seven dozen cashmere scarves he's been given over the
years as gifts? They're still in the original tissue paper. Who
knows? Maybe he's planning to wrap them around the
animals to keep them warm when the next flood comes.
Could be. He thinks that far ahead, and he remembers
yesterday's catastrophes vividly, even if he wasn't there.

You'll often find the Cancerian on the water. If he's
not swimming, he's water-skiing or at the very least, wad-
ing. Unless there's some definite planetary affliction in his
natal chart that makes him fear the waves, he'll usually be
found spending most of his leisure time on a beach. Lots
of Cancer people own their own boats. He'd much rather
have a trim little ship he can escape to than a dozen color
television sets and fifty limousines. Some crabs have fabulous yachts, but even if it's a rowboat or a canoe, he'll
blissfully row, paddle or steer it to happiness. It's as though
the Cancerian has a special, private dream that's been lost
out there somewhere in the deep waters, and he keeps
seeking it. Over half the crabs you meet will be weekend
sailors. Maybe it's the moon and the tides calling him.
Whatever it is, he's never as moody when he's happily
walking his own deck in the tennis shoes he bought when
he graduated from college. (Don't ever suggest that he buy
new ones. There's one thing you have to understand about
these people. If it's old, it has value. If it's new, it's
suspect.)

Cancerian emotions can be stronger than the physical
body. Worry and apprehension can make him ill, and

cheerfulness can make him well. Often, he fears financial collapse or the loss of someone he needs emotionally. If his security is threatened, either at the bank or in his heart, he can fall into a depression which unconsciously courts sickness or accident. His active imagination can be morbid enough to turn a minor illness into a grave or chronic one. When he gets gloomy, he responds poorly to positive statements. Then he's apt to think you're unkind for not sympathizing with him. But sympathy is the last thing Cancer needs when he's sick, never mind what he says. If he grows melancholy about fearsome possibilities, he invites real trouble, and he'll take twice as long to get well.

The most vulnerable areas are the chest or breast region, the knees, kidneys, bladder and skin. The head and face areas are also sensitive, as are the stomach and the digestive system. Cancerians practically invented ulcers. But those who keep serene, and who call on their marvelous sense of humor to see them through their moods, can easily stay well until a ripe old age. If they get a firm grip on happiness and refuse to let go, the crabs have the power to cling to life with the same tenacity that they cling to those old newspapers and pot holders. Cheerfulness, optimism and laughter, taken daily in large doses, will keep their minds and bodies healthy. As Cancer imagines himself to feel, so shall he actually feel. No other sign is so prone to let negative thoughts bring on illness, yet no other sign can create such miracles of self-healing. It's a strange contradiction, and it would immensely benefit all Cancerians to ponder it.

Lots of Cancer people have very green thumbs. They produce some beautiful gardens that are tended and watered with loving care. Most of them also have very green savings accounts, which they cultivate with the same devotion. Money clings to Cancer, and they like the feel of it, so they allow it to cling. They spend frugally, to say the very least. Even with impulsive influences in the natal chart, Cancer will keep a few dry bills aside for a rainy day. If he tells you he's broke, he means he's down to his last few thousand. To him, that's a desperate situation. No one is a more capable manager of funds than the crab (although Taurus, Capricorn or Virgo may run a close second). He's an expert at accumulating cash and making it grow like the trees and flowers he plants. It will seldom dwindle in his tenacious hands or run through his shrewd fingers, and you won't catch him tossing bundles of it out the window for the sheer joy of getting rid of it. His generosity is exceeded only by his caution. Cancerian John D. Rockefeller, Sr. probably thought he was being wickedly extravagant when he handed out all those dimes to small children; it tickled him to go on such a wild spending spree and teach economy at the same time. Still, the crab will share whatever he has willingly when someone he likes or loves is in real need. A child will never fail to move him to part with cash, but he'll come down hard on a grocer who overcharges him two cents on a can of beans.

Food somehow represents security to Cancerians. If Old Mother Hubbard had been born in July, she would never have recovered from finding the cupboard bare. Whether he actually eats it or not, the crab feels safer when the larder is full and overflowing. Just talking about food brings a rosy glow to his expressive face, and stories of starvation will actually horrify him. Cancerians care deeply about the hungry, and they feel a responsibility toward every empty stomach in the world. (The noted mathematician-astrologer Carl Payne Tobey has pointed out that Cancerian Nelson Rockefeller campaigned in supermarkets with the political slogan, "He Cares.") Wasting food is a crime to Cancer. You'll get all the second helpings you want, but be sure you clean up the plate.

There's a strong maternal instinct in both sexes. They're always trying to stuff hot food into you, or bundle you up against the damp, night air. Cancerians baby their friends and loved ones and hover over them protectively. It's hard to tell which stirs the lunar emotions more deeply—children, food or money.

The crab's sensitive nature is covered with a hard shell, and he's wise enough to avoid the stormy seas. Half the time he lives on dry land, the other half in deep waters. He wears the luminous, pale gold and shimmering colors of moonlight, and hides his powerful emotions behind the pale green, mauve and lavender tints of modesty.

There's a touch of Moon madness in every Cancerian. He knows a wild and secret place where two lilies and seven white roses grow among the iris. Sometimes the memory of this faraway garden causes him to explode with laughter. Now and then it causes him to weep with sadness. Cancer patiently gathers the emeralds, pearls and moonstones carelessly dropped in the sand by others, as he waits for the tides to wash his silver dreams ashore.

Famous Cancer Personalities

John Quincy Adams	Helen Keller
Louis Armstrong	Charles Laughton
Ingmar Bergman	Gertrude Lawrence
Milton Berle	Anne Lindbergh
Julius Caesar	Gina Lollobrigida
James Cagney	Marcel Proust
Marc Chagall	Rembrandt
Jean Cocteau	John D. Rockefeller
George M. Cohan	Nelson Rockefeller
Calvin Coolidge	Richard Rodgers
Phyllis Diller	Red Skelton
Stephen Foster	Barbara Stanwyck
John Glenn	Ringo Starr
Oscar Hammerstein	Henry D. Thoreau
Ernest Hemingway	John Wanamaker
Henry VIII	Duke of Windsor

Andrew Wyeth

The CANCER Man

"I sometimes dig for butter rolls,
Or set limed twigs for crabs:
I sometimes search the grassy knolls
For wheels of Hansom-cabs:
And that's the way," (he gave a wink)
"By which I get my wealth—
And very gladly will I drink
Your Honor's noble health."

A taciturn expert at circumlocution he is. A scatterbrain and a chatterbox he is not. Don't expect this man to bare his soul when he first meets you. Cancerians never confide in strangers, and there are certain things even their best friends don't know. It will take a long time and a fair amount of patience to really know him. If you catch him in one of his cantankerous moods, you may not be very anxious to really know him, but try again. Don't give up so easily.

He can be flirtatious and fickle, but he can also be sensitive and loyal. Without warning, that wrinkled frown can be replaced by a gentle smile. His crabby complaints and gruff manner can warm slowly into a tender tone, just before he breaks into a deep chuckle, a muffled giggle or loud, hysterical lunar laughter. When he's sad and wistful, you'll want to put your arms around him, and soothe away his melancholy. When he's showing off his sharp, intuitive mind, you'll stare at him in awe. His caution will impress you. His pessimism will depress you.

He can be so courtly, courteous, and considerate, you half expect him to ask you to dance the Virginia Reel. There's no question that he's a romantic dreamer, yet he's so sensible and practical, his enemies may call him "Old Marble Nose" behind his back. What do you do with a man like this?

You try to understand him. These aren't changes of personality. They're simply lunar moods, moving across his consciousness, here today—gone tomorrow. Both during and between each mood, the Cancer man is true to himself. His nature never deviates from its basic mold, despite the changes of expression that play on his features. Always try to remember that although a Cancerian's manner can be rough and aloof, his heart is always soft and affectionate, and so full of sentiment it often makes him feel too vulnerable. Then he crawls into his convenient shell (the one he carries with him at all times), safe for a while from his own emotions. You'll think he's a real crab and give up when he retreats into injured silence. But the next time he cautiously peeks out to see the sunshine, you'll be tempted all over again to get close to him. Unfortunately, a Cancer male can be a regular wet dishrag now and then, disparaging everything and everybody, and splashing gloom in big, blue drops all over your ego. Yet, at other times he can be as funny as an orangutan with the hiccups. No wonder you don't know whether to give him a cold shoulder or a warm hug. The temperature changes of a Cancerian could puzzle anyone. First you shiver under his freezing glances, then you get smothered with devotion. His moods are the meanest when he's the most afraid of losing something. Maybe it's you. Reassure him you're his a thousand and one times. Words of love are music to his ears.

Of course, he may wade into one of his loony spells right in the middle of a tender scene some night under a full Moon. Just when you're drifting away on lovely dreams, he may offer to tell you his favorite poem. You'll sigh, lean back on his shoulder and close your eyes. Then he'll cackle something like, "The stag at Eve had drunk his fill—where danced the Moon on Monan's rill. He blew his nose and shined his shoes—and took a swig of Mountain booze!" It may jolt you out of your magic spell, but that full Moon can do strange things to the lunar emotions. What I mean is, he can be as nutty as a cuckoo, even if he is smart enough to make a million dollars and keep it.

I'm glad we brought up money. You will be too. If you're the kind of girl who likes to pay the rent on time, you're in love with exactly the right man. He's almost as fond of security as he is of you. You may have a slight edge, but you can safely consider money your worst rival. He's going to pursue it with dedication and a sort of quiet, religious fervor for most of his days. (The nights may bring other things to pursue.) It's not the worst fate you could experience. Finances have fascinated him since childhood, and saving will be substantially more attractive to him than spending. He's not exactly stingy, but let's say it's not likely you'll ever see him lighting his pipe with a dollar bill for a parlor trick. The Cancerian sense of humor seldom takes in the topic of cold, hard cash. Money is not a laughing matter to the crab. He could probably add a column of figures in his head before he learned the alphabet, and had a paper route when he was eleven. Don't be surprised if you find he still has his first piggy bank, unopened. The tinkle of silver and the rustle of folding green paper soothe his nerves, but he won't brag about his Dun and Bradstreet rating. Cancerians seldom collect cash for status. They collect it for its own sweet sake. In fact, he will probably belittle his financial wizardry. He's "just a poor boy, trying to earn a living, and getting along the best he can." You may even feel so sorry for him, you'll offer to get him a loan at the bank. Don't. He probably owns part of it.

A fire sign on the ascendant may give him a rare extravagant urge, which he'll resist with admirable courage. Even if he gives in to an occasional spending spree to cheer himself out of a blue mood, it won't become a habit. Before you start mumbling "tightwad" under your breath, you should know that the Cancer man has an interesting idea of economy. He'd rather take you out to the best restaurant, and get what he pays for, than risk offending his sensitive tastes with over-cooked lamb chops and indifferent service in a second-rate place. He thinks it's silly to waste money on a cloth coat, when a mink or chinchilla will amortize itself over the years. A good, conservative Cadillac or Bentley is a safer investment, in his opinion, than a cheap car that depreciates as soon as you drive it around the corner. Quality and thrift are synonymous to the Cancerian. There, I thought that would bring the sparkle back to your eyes.

Even the most poetic and dreamy Cancerians, who spend their lives immersed in music, art or other cultural pursuits, have a shrewd sense of the value of cash. A lunar artist may paint in an attic, but you needn't send him any Care packages. There are probably some stocks and bonds hidden in the rafters. He won't donate his paintings, either. He'll sell them for a pretty price, if he's a professional. But they'll be worth it. When a Cancer person tackles a career, he's sure to be at the top of it. He's loaded with artistic talent. You might suggest that your Cancer man design your Christmas cards. They're sure to be lovely, even if he's only an amateur.

If he's a true Cancerian, he won't be wild about sports clothes. There's a certain formality about his toilet. Whether he's worth billions or only a few paltry thousands, he likes conservative cuts and good tailoring. He often leans to collar buttons (yes, they still sell them—to Cancerians), French cuffs and expensive shirts he gets wholesale, usually without monograms (too showy; he prefers to be inconspicuous). Even when he's short of cash for a brief period while he's working on his first million, his shoes will be polished and his socks will stay up. During any shaky financial period (and it will be temporary), a Cancer male will somehow exude an air of genteel rich, or one who has known better days. If he hasn't, he will. Fairly substantial amounts of money will someday come to this man, or he'll be given the opportunity to earn large sums of it. He won't always be wealthy, but a Cancerian in the unemployment line is as rare as a pineapple tree in Siberia. His secret motto is that "all play and no work gives Jack a skinny billfold," and he prefers his wallets pleasingly plump.

Let's hope you find his mother congenial. In fact, let's pray you do. It's fairly certain she'll pop up in his conversation frequently, in remarks like, "My mother never wears much makeup, and she's a beautiful woman. Don't you think your eye shadow is a little heavy, sweetheart?" Or "You use frozen pies and instant potatoes? My mother used to bake her own bread when I was a youngster." This paragon of virtue is quite likely to pop up just as often in person, when you least expect it. "Darling, I have to cancel our date for the theater tonight. I'm driving Mother out to the country for a few days." To put it mildly, the Cancer man may be reluctant to dethrone Mama and crown you as his new queen. He's a terribly domesticated crab, for all his occasional stirrings of wanderlust, and if his mother made his home cozy, he'll be in no hurry to leave it. Cancerians are either very, very close to their mothers or completely alienated from them. The relationship is never casual. Those who don't revere the maternal parent are either adopted, or jealousy of the father's place in the mother's affection has caused an emotional block. Then there can be an unnatural coldness and isolation.

With the typical crab, however, the problem is far more likely to be closeness. There's no use hiding the facts of life. If you're in love with this more common type of Cancerian, you'll have to cultivate his mother, and you'll have to be her rival while you're showering her with compliments. It's not easy to cultivate and compete at the same time, but that's the strategy you'll need. Don't ever let her get the edge on cooking and homemaking. Let her teach you how to bake lemon chiffon pie. He'll like that —you two girls getting along so nicely. Then turn around and do a brilliant beef Stroganoff on your own. Be sure to spoil him at least as much as she does, and that may be a lot. He's probably grown accustomed to being considered the apple of her eye. Being fussed over, fed regularly, catered to, hovered over when he's sick, and tucked in bed tenderly at night can turn him into a mighty sweet crab. Cancer men will never admit it, but they love to be petted and babied by females.

There are certain traits, however, which can even up the score in your relationship. For one, he'll be a pretty good chef himself. He may surprise you with his ability to

whip up a gourmet meal. When this man invites you to
come up to his apartment for dinner, he's usually quite
serious. Even if he asks you to look at his etchings, there
may be no ulterior motive. The typical Cancerian male is
a devotee of the finer things in life. In plain talk, he digs
culture. For all you know, he may actually own some rare
etchings or at least a fabulous record collection. You're
fairly safe in risking an unchaperoned trip to his rocky
cave, because the typical lunar man is the soul of gallantry
with women. He'll usually be a gentleman until you stop
being a lady. It's the way they did it in Grandma's day,
and to him, those were the good old days. (That's probably Grandma's photograph on the mantel.) Ask him about
his family tree. He'll love to tell you. Most Cancerians
delight in their backgrounds and their blood lines. He likes
old things, from Grandma herself to that Eighteenth Century fruitwood table he bought the first time he went to
Europe.

If he asks to take your picture, don't grab your babushka
and run. Photography is a common lunar hobby, and few
Cancer males live their lives without at least one camera.
Of course, he could have Venus in Scorpio or a Leo Moon,
so maybe it would be more discreet to check his natal chart
before you agree to anything. Whatever it is, just say, "I'd
love to, dear, but do you mind if I call my astrologer first?
I'll need your birthday." If he thinks you're jesting, you
can straighten that out right away. Just tell him that J. P.
Morgan seldom made a move in the stock market without
consulting astrologer Evangeline Adams, who was the
granddaughter and great-granddaughter of John Quincy
Adams and John Adams. The combination of both history
and money will open his eyes wide with interest.

The Cancer man may go for quite a spell without inviting
you to see either his etchings or his fruitwood table. Although he may engage in light flirtations, it may be many
years before he becomes seriously enamoured, because it
isn't easy for him to find a woman he feels is worthy of
his interest. When he finds her, he'll be beautifully sentimental, and he'll lavish her with gifts and admiration. But
his standards are high. Not every girl can meet them. Most
crabs are afraid of being burned, and not without cause.
A mismatched alliance which would cause only a few sad
weeks of readjustment for the average man can be a disaster to the crab. When something separates him from a

partner he's allowed himself to get close to, he can carry a torch for many years.

He's naturally shy of rushing in, but once he's sure, he won't be easily rebuffed. Cancerians can play the role of the romantic lover artfully. After he's declared himself, and has some hope of winning you, his timidity will switch to tenacity overnight, and you'll find yourself being courted by an earnest, determined man who won't take no as an answer for any proposal he has in mind. He's likely to stuff himself in your mailbox (figuratively, of course), camp on your doormat and monopolize your phone. It's hard to slide away from the grip of the crab. You probably won't want to, of course. Lots of girls are looking for a moonlit world like his to dream in, where someone will hold them tightly and protect them from the big, bad wolf at the door.

Now that you know he's not a sloppy dresser or a spend-thrift, that he can probably cook like a dream, has excellent taste, is looking for an old-fashioned girl like the girl who married dear old dad, and that he can be a cooing lovebird (when he's not in a snappy mood), what other information could you possibly need? How is he as a father? That's the best news of all. Cancerians are all mothers at heart. Even the men.

What I really mean to say is, he'll be a fine parent, because of the same caring, gentle, sympathetic, and understanding nature you fell in love with yourself. He'll have infinite patience with the children, be genuinely interested in every mashed toe, broken toy and toothache. He'll wear a paper hat at their birthday parties, be a pied piper for all the kids on the block, and spend countless hours entertaining the little people. Cancer dads are proud of their sons and fiercely protective of their daughters. When they're small, he'll be just the grandest daddy you could imagine. However, adolescence may churn up the water somewhat. He'd like his loved ones to lean on him forever, and when they show signs of independence, he may become a cranky crab again for a period, as he rebels against their desire to experiment with the world outside.

He'll pace the floor until he wears a hole in the carpet when young Henry has the car out after midnight or when pretty Lucy stays at the dance past her curfew. Remember how figures impress him? Use plain arithmetic to make him see the error of his ways. "It's like this, dearest. Right now

we have two children. When they get married, we might
have six or eight grandchildren, like dividends at the bank.
Six or eight adds up to more happiness than two, right?"
(You have him there.) "I'm so glad you agree, luv. Now
will you please tell us where you hid Lucy's wedding
gown, and will you please take those handcuffs off Henry
so he can pick up his marriage license?" Don't try it during a full Moon. He might misunderstand. Besides, no
Cancerian can think straight when the lunar vibrations are
strong. It's hard for him to give up control, but when he's
reminded that he still has you to cling to, his grip will
loosen.

Well, that's all in the future. Your immediate problem
is to entice your crab to move directly toward a proposal
soon, instead of cleverly dodging from side to side and
skirting the issue. You might try pretending you're leaving
him for a bolder, cave man type. Usually the crab will
stop his backward direction when the object—that's you
—shows signs of getting away. But that requires scouting
around for another man to wake him up. And that can be
a real bore, since he watches you so closely.

The easiest way to get him in the mood to take hold
tightly and stop playing scrabble every night is to work on
his emotions, which are always right below the surface of
his adding machine mind. Music, poetry, flowers, beautiful
clothes, expensive perfume sparingly used, soft words and
sweet caresses are all weapons which should mow down his
weak resistance to romance. Don't overlook that direct line
between his heart and his stomach. Cut out baby pictures
from magazines, leave your sewing machine out in full
view, take up the hems of your skirts an extra inch, and
baby him a little. Wear one of those bracelets made of
foreign coins. That will strike two sensitive chords—travel
to faraway shores—and cash. One night he'll impulsively
ask you if you'd like to meet his mother. The very next
morning feel perfectly safe to order your invitations and
your trousseau. You will have won the heart of a moody
lunar man with a thousand secret dreams—and the approval of his best girl. Then you can "sail away for a
year and a day" and "dance by the light of the moon"
while you "eat with a runcible spoon." Bon voyage!
Don't forget—never throw away his battered old hat, his
torn tennis shoes, his stamp collection or his grade school
report cards. They're his treasures. Be sure to take your

umbrella along. There will be some damp nights. May I
say that you look beautiful in your chinchilla? But of
course. A woman is beautiful only when she is loved—and
you are.

The CANCER Woman

> *. . . Echoes fade and memories die:*
> *Autumn frosts have slain July.*
>
> *Still she haunts me, phantomwise,*
> *Alice moving under skies*
> *Never seen by waking eyes.*

There's no doubt about it. In the beginning, you'll have
trouble deciding if your Cancerian girl is a gentle moon
maiden or a wild loony-bird. In the end, you still won't
know.

During the rainy season, she'll drown you in her
sorrows. When the sun peeks through the clouds again,
she'll double you up with laughter, and touch you with
tenderness. Experiencing her moods is like watching one
of those old-time silent movies where hysterical slapstick
humor comes on just before the *Perils of Pauline* thriller,
and the entire show is backed by the tinny piano in the pit.
Sometimes the tune is lively and gay; then it gets melancholy and blue. The music is variable, to suit the occasion, never stagnant or monotonous. So it is with the
Cancer girl. She's just a little mad, slightly sad and superbly imaginative. She also knows how to save the shekels.

Naturally, you can't look under her mattress until after
you've married her. Modesty is a thing with her. But you
can safely make a bet she probably has an old sock there,
stuffed with green bills and silver coins. She may have an
extravagant ascendant or Moon sign, but even so, she'll
have a quarter or two stuck under the potted azalea, or
salted away in the folds of that lace tablecloth she got for
her birthday ten years ago and still hasn't ever used. Open
one of her books of poetry, and a wrinkled dollar bill may

fall out, blinking at the light of day. A Cancer female can go on a sudden spending spree when she's been hurt and needs balm for her injured ego, but most of the time her outgo will lag considerably behind her income. Your savings account may be of unusual interest to her, and money may be one of her favorite topics of conversation. She won't look down on you if you don't have it, so long as you're the kind of man who tries to get it. She'll help you make it and save it, but you're on your own when it comes to wasting it. Don't go too far, or she'll see your mutual security slipping away. When you give this girl a terribly expensive gift, and she says, "You shouldn't have done it," let me tell you, she means it.

To take her mind off insurance, mortgages, rent, bills and her Christmas club balance at the bank, bundle her off to the seashore at midnight for a walk in the moonlight. That's when she'll be at her best. The Moon will pull out all her secret dreams, and the nearness of the water may loosen her four hundred and three inhibitions. You're liable to see her whole range of emotions in the space of an hour. Then you can choose the one you like the best and encourage her to cultivate it. A strange transformation will take place when you get the typical Cancerian girl alone on a beach under a full Moon. That cool and reserved lady you see in the daytime, or even the giggly, outrageous flirt you notice on an occasional evening in a restaurant or theater, will suddenly become a creature from another world when the magnetic rays of the Moon shine in her eyes and the compelling sound of the surf fills her ears. She'll turn into a sea nymph, who can soar with you as far as your imagination can reach. It will work nine times out of ten, and the tenth time you probably picked a new Moon. That won't accomplish the same purpose. She'll be shy and sweet when the Moon is waning but what you really want is a Moon that's full enough to arouse all her latent talents. Under its spell, at the right time in her personal ebb and flow of emotions, she can write a poem, compose a song or tear the veil off mysteries the philosophers have pondered for centuries. Naturally, she makes an interesting conversationalist at these times. To say the very least.

You should know that there are two distinctive approaches when a Cancerian female is in love with you. The first is gentle and womanly, shy, modest and pleasantly trembly. The second is rather sticky. This last type will use every trick of Eve to sit as close as possible to you in the booth. It can be very exciting, of course, if you really care for her. But if you're just being friendly, and she deliberately squeezes your hand or busses you on the cheek just as the girl you found at the end of the rainbow walks by, the game may lose some of its flavor. You can go along with the gag, but I know one man who did, and the other girl, who was for real and didn't play games, kept on walking. He was left with a clinging crab with a fit of the giggles. This kind of Cancerian woman can be a real threat to true love and happy homes. Fortunately, she is in the minority. Still, even one can cause a lot of trouble.

As you know from the other Sun signs, few women are perfect. The Aries girl is always running around hailing her own taxis and butting her head against brick walls, the Sagittarius girl is shockingly outspoken, the Scorpio girl can frighten you, Gemini can be fickle, Leo too proud— and so on. Cancer women ordinarily have none of these faults.

Nevertheless, there are some "don'ts" to remember with her. She hates to be criticized, she is deeply wounded by ridicule, and she just can't stand being rejected. One, two, three. They're basics. Seldom openly aggressive, the typical Cancerian hesitates. You'll have to make the first move. If she moves anywhere at all, it will be backwards or sideways. With her basically shy nature and fear that she won't be accepted, she echoes the male of the Sun sign. I know of a Cancer woman and a Cancer man who, for seven hours, sat close to each other one night in her apartment, under the pretense of looking at magazines. While their pulses pounded silently, they went through a stack of back issues, the morning and evening papers, and worked a few crossword puzzles. Neither crab, you see, wanted to make the first move.

Be kind to her mother, or she'll never forgive you. Mother is a lady she won't like to see abused. The Cancer girl's sense of humor doesn't react favorably to mother-in-law jokes. And never read her five-year-diary. It probably has a lock and key, anyway. Cancerians like to keep secrets. They're not much for true confessions, unless you're the one doing the confessing.

The fears of your lunar lovely can really hang you up, along with her. She's afraid she isn't pretty enough, she isn't smart enough, she isn't young enough or she isn't old enough. It makes no difference if she has a figure like Venus de Milo, a face like Helen of Troy and a mind like Aristotle: she'll still feel inadequate. Assure her that she's young, she's lovely, she's engaged, and she has you. About twenty times a day should begin to make a dent. Her moods will change on the average of four times a month, with each quarter Moon plus minor fluctuations twice a day—reflecting the tides. She's sort of predictable in an unpredictable kind of way. It may make her fascinating and mysterious, but so doggone aggravating you'll feel like whacking her. During one of her blue spells, she may even be afraid she's not a good cook, which is utterly ridiculous, because the typical Cancerian woman can make a French chef look like the mess sergeant you had at boot camp. This woman isn't an automatic can opener or a frozen food fan. She would rather shell her own peas and bake her own biscuits. Her casseroles are sensational, her potatoes are fluffy, her vegetables are crisp and crunchy, and she tops it all off with heavenly strawberry jam. Cancer women are very friendly with their ovens. The kitchen will be her favorite room by far (next to the nursery). She'll fuss over you like a mother hen, and you'll probably love it. Most men do.

In addition to the obviously unjustified fear about her culinary skill, she may be afraid you don't love her enough. That should be easy for any red-blooded male to remedy. Go ahead and prove it—as often as you like. She'll be beautifully receptive. Once you've turned on the green light, she'll happily recognize the signal, which may remove her feelings of inadequacy, but which creates a new problem. Truthfully, after you've won the Cancerian female, she may be just a little tenacious—like, she'll never let go of you as long as she lives. That's not bad. There are men who starve for such loyalty. You'll never starve for either food or affection when you've been lucky enough to win her kind of love. The loony laugh that accompanies it can be kind of kicks, too. Her rich humor is even warmer and dearer when you think of all the sarcastic sirens with their cynical wit and hypocritical laughter.

It's brutally unfair to toy with the heart of this girl, because she'll love, honor, obey and nag you a little with sincere devotion. Why encourage such rare love unless you mean to reciprocate with equal ardor? Remember her tenacity. You may only be flirting lightly, but you'll have a hard time calling the end of the inning. She won't hear the whistle. There's nothing shallow or superficial about the sentiments of a Cancer woman. When she owns a man or a teacup, it's hers forever.

She may not overwhelm your friends with her vivacity and sparkling flattery, but she won't fail to impress you with her charm. July women prefer to save their deepest emotions for people closest to them. After you've dated other girls and compared them to her, you may go running right back to your female crab, and beg her to hang on again. Tightly.

The trickiest aspect in handling her is to keep her from crawling into the always handy, tough Cancerian shell. Her feelings are so sensitive and tender, the slightest un-intentional remark can wound her harshly. It's hard to know when she'll suddenly become vulnerable to hidden meanings. You could waltz in some night and say, "Your hair looks gorgeous," and she'll get a tear in her eye. Why? Because you insinuated her hair looked frightful the last time you saw her. Cancer women can be quite touchy. They cry a lot. Always have a fresh handkerchief ready.

Females born under the sign of the crab aren't neces-sarily stingy, but they have this little habit of saving things. You could say it's a downright compulsion. She'll seldom throw away pieces of string, buttons, jars, cans, husbands, or old dress patterns. Who are you to say she won't find a purpose for those torn theater stubs, faded love letters and used tea bags? Someday in the unpredictable future, she may need the burned-out fuses she keeps in the drawer with those broken Christmas ornaments. Don't ask her how she's going to find a use for two hundred stockings and gloves, long divorced from their mates. She will, she will! This isn't the girl to take kindly to someone who burns a hole in the heirloom bedspread her great-aunt Matilda quilted. Everything has a sentimental value, in-cluding canceled checks from 1952 and her old Girl Scout badges. She treasures the things she owns and guards them jealously. That, of course, includes you. She's not so much jealous as possessive. There's a shade of difference.

Women born under the fire signs may strain and protest against life's delays and disappointments, but the Cancer girl usually feels nothing can be changed or overcome by getting all stirred up. When things don't go her way, she may shed a few quiet tears alone, but her normal reaction will be to fold her hands serenely and wait patiently for things to right themselves. Patience is one of her loveliest virtues. When she's depressed, however, you'll have to find a way to take her out of herself. Try to catch her before she has burrowed too deep. She does have a way of wanting to be babied. The desire to be a little spoiled by loved ones seems to be buried deep in the Cancerian nature. She needs desperately to know you can't live without her, and sometimes she'll go to great lengths to arouse your pity and protective instincts, just to be assured she means a lot to you. It's really very little for her to ask, when she gives so much in return. But don't be fooled by her weakness during these episodes. That helpless little baby who seeks your big, strong arms to keep out the cold, cruel world is perfectly able to manage by herself, if she must. In the middle of a quarrel, when your lunar girl looks up at you with her eyes all wet and dewy and frightened, remember that after you leave and are safely around the corner, she's likely to dry her eyes, put a stack of records on the player, and calmly clean out her closets. Of course, you can't rule out the times when her depression is real, instead of a typical Cancerian bid for sympathy. Those nights you'd better stay, listen to the music with her, and hold her hand tenderly.

There's no end to the heroic sacrifice a Cancer woman will be capable of for those she loves. The bravery she can't seem to muster for herself and her own fears is there shining when someone close needs her to be strong. She'll never let you down when things get really dismal, and then she'll remind you more of a gigantic, rugged rock than a fragile, silvery moonbeam. Her children will also find her a tower of strength and refuge. She'll help them find their way with sensitive understanding. They'll cling to her, and the warmth of her love will make their home as rich and comfortable and bright as a palace, even if it's a shack. You might suffer a slight loss of attention when the babies come along. Cancer rules motherhood, you know. There will still be room for you, but you'll have to move over a few inches. (A childless Cancerian woman will love an animal or her friends with her stored up maternal affection, and the pets and pals will be fortunate.) Like baby birds, her youngsters will probably be fed every time she finds their mouths open, and always the food will be hot and nourishing.

Nothing is too good for her family. When a child sneezes, he'll get plopped into bed with medicines, hot tea and chicken broth until he gets old enough to resist. The offspring of a Cancer mother won't get away without wearing his thick sweater on a cold night, his scarf and mittens in the snow or his galoshes in the rain. A child has to have lots of will power to fight the crab's protective solicitude. He has to be pretty tough not to get spoiled, too. It's often quite a jolt when he goes out into the world and finds out he's not the center of everyone's universe. Such complete dedication and devotion can give him a wonderful featherbed of security to fall back on when life gets too real, but it can also make him abnormally dependent on home ties, and unable to see his own faults. It's often impossible to tell whether a Cancer mother ties her children to her apron strings or they choose to tie the knot themselves. She'll save every spelling test paper, proudly hang clumsy crayon drawings on the wall and tenderly wrap baby shoes in tissue paper. Those little wrinkled bits of white kidskin are precious, because the lunar parent with her clear, photographic memory will recall a child's first steps long after he's flown away from the nest. The flight itself may be painful. Cancer women are reluctant to give up their youngsters to the ties of marriage. They tend to hang on too hard and too long, and think no one is good enough for them. Sometimes, the potential bride or groom of a man or woman with a July parent has to pass everything but the ink blot test to get approved.

I once knew a Cancer mother who used to meet her small son every day after school. He would always come bursting through the door like a jet-propelled rocket, and immediately run furiously around the schoolyard a few times before he came near her. Once, when she was accompanied by her sister, the aunt started to go after the little boy, but the Cancer mother stopped her. "No, let him be," she said quietly. "He's just working off steam. He'll be back when he's through running." Finally her son walked over to her, took her hand and said, "Let's go home, Mom. I'm hungry."

That sums up the whole attitude of the lunar female toward all forms of love, and most of all toward her marriage. It's her strange brand of possessiveness that's unshakable, but never aggressive. She knows, in her secret heart, that no matter how far away you go to follow your dream, you'll always come back again and she'll be there patiently waiting. Her eyes will still be beautiful with the Moon magic you remember, the kitchen will smell deliciously of warm spices, and she'll ask you how things went, how you feel. If things went badly and you feel miserable, she'll tell a joke to get you to laugh. Then she'll fill your stomach, and after you're relaxed, she'll gently smooth away your worries with her sensible advice and her rich humor. Later, in the firelight, you'll look at her serene face and ask yourself all over again, "Is she really a Moon maiden from some misty garden or a lovable loony bird?" But the answer won't seem very important.

The CANCER Child

Dear, dear, how queer everything is today!
And yesterday things went on just as usual.

Write it down so you'll remember it and not be surprised every day of your life: your Cancer baby will change his moods as frequently as you change his diaper. It's a strange new world for the lunar infant. He'll be fascinated by delicious things to eat and drink, and he'll love all the colorful pictures which pass before his sharp little eyes, and impress themselves on his indelible memory. What he experiences will never leave him. When he's old and gray, your Cancerian boy or girl will remember every feeling and emotion, and be able to give it back as an exact image.

One of the dearest Cancerian women I ever knew was born in Europe, and when she was ill, she would sing every word of the Russian lullabies she had heard as a child, even though she came to America almost half a century ago. Most of us would be lucky if we remembered the tune or words to "Rockabye Baby."

From breakfast until bedtime, the busy mind of the Cancerian child will be recording what he sees and hears.

It's difficult for worldly adults to follow him up his Moon mountain of dreams or go beside him as he wades in the streams of his luminous imagination. His emotions are rich, colorful and varied, but for all that, he may be lonely.

Playing with lunar babies can be loads of fun. They're funny little creatures, with droll expressions and eyes that almost talk by themselves. Their features constantly contort with tears, twist with a grimace or spread wide with smiles. It's interesting to watch those elastic expressions, but you may frequently wish you could predict when he's going to giggle, or get that faraway look in his eye as he listens to the curious music every Moon child hears.

These youngsters have more emotional needs that Pisces boys and girls. Much more than with any other children, *the strongest influence on Cancerians is always the early home environment.* From infancy through the teens, young crabs are tremendously dependent on the reactions of their parents and their brothers and sisters. Your lunar child may be too shy to express his real inner desires, but he secretly wants to be made over, cuddled and adored. If he doesn't get attention and approval from his family, relatives and friends, the rejection can simply crush him. I have a close friend who was born in July. Late one night in her kitchen (where else?), we were talking about her childhood.

She told me, "When I was a little girl in grade school, my parents gave me ten or fifteen cents a week to spend. But I never spent it. I saved it, so I could give a prize."

"For what?" I asked her.

A wistful look passed across her wonderfully mobile features. "Well, I used to offer fifty cents at the end of each month to the friend who treated me the nicest."

At first I was amused, and started to remind her of all the candy and treats she had missed by passing out her entire allowance for kind treatment, but something in her eyes changed my mind.

Although your young Cancerian may briefly turn into a rebel without a cause in adolescence, during his tender years the little crab is usually easy to manage and discipline. His inner life is very real to him, and he'll happily play by himself for many hours. He may even have an invisible playmate called something like Boris or Betty, who helps him make mud pies, plant imaginary flowers or play cowboy and Indian. The make-believe Boris or Betty are always well-behaved and courteous. They will always let the Cancer youngster win, and they'll give in to his desire to be a gentle leader without a murmur. Sometimes these imaginary playmates will disappear for weeks at a time, but they'll return as soon as a real, live neighborhood chum or schoolmate wounds those little lunar feelings or bosses the Moon child around too much. As docile and quiet as most Cancerians are, Cancer is a cardinal Sun sign of leadership. Despite their tender emotions and gentle manners, they are not followers. There's a great deal of independent thinking and individualism.

If your offspring follows the pattern of most July children, he'll get his way and be slightly spoiled around the edges. It's the squeaky hinge that gets the most oil. He won't exactly squeak, but he can get mighty weepy when he's ignored or treated harshly. Talk about tears! A Moon child can cry rivers and flood a room. It's as if someone left the kitchen spigots running. If all that dampness doesn't get him the tender sympathy he must have for healthy emotions, the little Cancerian boy or girl will grow up into a dry-eyed adult with a barren heart, unable to give or receive love easily—seeking solitude, forming very few warm friendships—and become a recluse in old age.

When such a sensitive little crab is in your care, it's really urgent to laugh and cry with him and to calm his fears. He'll have a whole passel of them. Your own lunar child may not have each one on the list, but he's sure to have quite a few. He can be afraid to go to sleep in the dark without a soft night light, afraid of fire and matches, afraid of fast cars and loud noises. He can fear strangers, large animals, bright lights, food he's never tasted before, lightning and thunder.

Lots of young loony-birds get the blues when it rains. A spring or fall shower can do strange things to the inner nature. It can make him suddenly want to write a poem, paint a picture or make music. At other times, it can cause him to hide his frightened little head under the bedspread, while his bottom half protrudes and trembles visibly.

This child requires much emotional empathy to develop his fine, loving, artistic and creative qualities. If it is given wholeheartedly in his formative years, it will help him grow into a patient, generous, quietly confident and open-hearted adult. If attentive understanding is denied him, his natural compassion and gentleness may be warped and twisted into self-pity and bitter, silent brooding. Fear, unless coped with early, can become illogical prejudice and hatred. Little crabs who have been stunted in their emotional growth sometimes turn into suspicious snappers, often revengeful and even suicidal. At best, these moody, unhappy men and women lead sad, uneventful lives, unless they make a dramatic decision to bury themselves in building a financial empire or developing a latent talent. Either one can mercifully replace the love and affection withheld from the gentle lunar heart when it was the most vulnerable —in childhood.

It can't be emphasized enough that these sensitive children can imagine hurts or slights, and dream up a rejection which never existed. Special care has to be taken to convince them that they're good, smart, pretty, handsome, loved and wanted. Many parents sense this, which is why lots of little crabs are pampered so much at home that they get quite a shock as adults when they discover the world takes a cool, disinterested view of their personal desires. No wonder so many Cancerians fondly remember Mama and practically build a shrine to her as they grow older. No one else will ever again *care* quite so much. The big question with a Moon child is always whether to be overly firm and warp him, or overly permissive and spoil him. Finding the middle road is never easy, and the problem can keep you up a few nights. The keyword is: relax. Love usually finds the way. The best formula is a good old-fashioned spanking when he needs it, with plenty of hugs and kisses and lots of physical expressions of affection at all other times.

Teachers normally find the Cancerian boys and girls whizzes in history. They seldom forget dates or events. That's because, thanks to their mirror-like sensitivity, they can read about something that happened years ago, and almost believe they were there. If Paul Revere, Thomas Jefferson, or Abraham Lincoln themselves could return and tell their stories, they probably wouldn't be recounted with much more color than the typical young Cancerian uses when he discusses the happenings of the dim and dusty past. It's as if they actually saw the Battle of Lexington, the signing of the Declaration of Independence and the shot fired on Fort Sumter. There's hardly a detail they can't imagine. It's easy to see why so many of these sensitive boys and girls go on the stage, become creative photog-

raphers or follow a distinguished career in music or art.
Instructors of the young lunar mind may now and then
complain of stubbornness or daydreaming, but it's not
often that either failing becomes pronounced enough to
be really troublesome. There may be some exaggerating.
The boy may describe the ordeal of being attacked in the
woods by a dangerous bear to explain some scratches
caused by a fall from his own front porch. The girl may
give a sad recital of how she was locked out with no supper
by cruel parents, after what was only a mild argument with
her family. But a few tall tales can be expected when you
consider the strong mental impressions created by reading
adventure stories with the lunar imagination. When there's
real heartache, instead of make-believe tragedy, the typical
Cancerian child will normally remain quiet and decline to
speak about it. There's an old Chinese proverb: "He who is
really hurt—doesn't talk."

Like the Libran child, happy Cancerian youngsters can
run up the family food bill to fantastic proportions and
soothing hurt feelings caused by the nickname Fatty is
common. If there's a lot of brooding or nervousness, the
nickname may be Skinny. It's best to bypass all nicknames
with Moon children. They should never be teased.

Most young crabs look forward to working for pay, and
they'll scour the neighborhood for odd jobs. Your Cancer
child will begin early to cut grass, sweep leaves and babysit.
He'll return bottles for refunds, help hang out the laundry,
assist the trash men, sell lemonade at the curb, or anything
else he can think of that will make his pockets jingle. The
pennies, nickels, dimes, quarters—and finally the dollars
he makes will be carefully accounted for, and a good
portion of them saved. After a while, you may be able to
save some yourself—on his allowance. He'll probably supply his own spending money sooner than other children,
and be proud of it. You'll find him easy on your pocketbook in many ways. These children often work their way
through college. The boys will have a healthy curiosity
about the business world. The girls will be efficient in cash
matters, too, but they'll also spend lots of time with their
dolls and baking brownies, practicing for their future
careers as mothers.

The Cancer child will keep you amused with his jokes
and his contagious laugh. He can make funny faces that
look like Halloween masks, and he sees the humor in every

facet of the human parade as it passes. Give him, if possible, a little plot of earth he can call his own, where he can plant things with his green thumb and watch them grow. He'll be tenderly concerned with relatives who are ill, financial emergencies in the family, and the difficulties of his friends and neighbors. Lunar youngsters love books about heroic people who braved hardships to do great deeds, and they'll be especially gentle and sympathetic with animals. But if they feel cruelly treated themselves, they may pass on the cruelty, or rather, reflect it to others smaller than themselves in a sort of "kick the cat" progression. Young crabs can live up to the name and be quite crabby, but such moods seldom last more than a few hours, before they're replaced by a lovable loony grin.

As you turn off the lamps at bed time, you may wonder, as all parents do about a day in the not too far distant future when the little head that keeps popping up "for one more drink of water" will be missing. The house will be still then, and empty of his alternating tears and laughter, after the funny, imaginative little crab crawls away to raise his own family. Will he forget? Not if he was born in late June or July. Years can go by, and he may sail on distant seas, but you can keep his bean bag—the one he gave you that Saturday afternoon you quarreled—on his dresser. And you can leave her rag doll in its place on the window seat. Your Moon child will come home again many times throughout every tomorrow—to meet old memories and return to the past. No matter how many miles separate him from yesterday, anywhere he lives is always handy to home. Keep the cookie jar full.

The CANCER Boss

"You see," he went on after a pause, "it's as well to
  be provided for everything.
  That's the reason the horse has all those anklets
   around his feet."
"But what are they for?" Alice asked, in a tone of
  great curiosity.
"To guard against the bites of sharks," the Knight
  replied.

After learning about the Cancerian sense of humor, you
may have the impression that the office of a Cancer boss
is a real fun place, with everything except confetti and a
sommelier to serve champagne. The employees will all be
straight men, and the lunar executive is the stand-up comic
with the clever one-liners. It will be like going to work in
a nightclub every day. Well, no—not exactly.

If you work for a TV or movie funnyman, all that just
might apply. Anywhere else, you'd best dust the confetti
off your shoulder, straighten your tie and forget the jokes.
The serious, hard-working Cancerian executive doesn't
go for hilarity on the job. His working humor can consist
of anything from laughing at an over-confident competitor
falling on his face to a faint chuckle when you ask him
to double your salary before you have proved yourself.
Both of these situations will strike his funny ribs and bring
a wide grin. Nothing else will arouse much mirth or many
giggles. The humor is still there, beneath his crisp business
face and his snow-white collar, but it will be used sparingly
on the job. Most of his laughs at work will be saved for
the human comedy of errors, or to ease someone's nervousness, and the tone will usually be kindly. Seven hours and
fifty-nine minutes out of every eight working hours, however, will be humorless, even grim.

I don't mean to frighten you into thinking he's Simon
Legree (though there are a few Cancerian bosses of that
type scattered around the world). It's just that your job

under a Cancer boss will be more secure if you see that
your trousers are creased, your hair is parted neatly, and
your brain is operating at a sharp level than if you tell a
few fast ones, happily trying to play second banana. The
top banana you're trying to impress is off duty in the
humor mill while he sits behind that polished mahogany
desk, with his mother's picture on one side, and the group
picture of his family on the other. Can you imagine what
would have happened to a member of Calvin Coolidge's
cabinet if he pulled the one about "who was that lady I
saw you with last night" in the middle of a meeting? I
know an employee who made a serious error in quoting a
shipping date to a valued client. When his Cancerian
superior called him in for an accounting, prepared to be
kind, he cheerfully said, "Boss, I sincerely regret my
stupidity, and if you'll give me a couple of days, I'm sure
I can come up with several excellent excuses!" He would
have been a scream in old-time vaudeville, but he got the
hook from his unamused Cancer employer.

Hopefully, you will profit from the large egg that employee laid at his last performance. The Cancer boss is in
business for one purpose only. To make money. Period.
Money. It's made of green and black printed paper, and
it has different numbers in the upper corners, signifying
how much power, prestige, and luxury it will buy. You
trade it for hard work. The harder you work, the more
pieces of this green and black printed paper you get and
the larger the numbers are in the upper corners. That's
his philosophy, in a crab shell. It would be wise to make it
yours.

So you think he's a little stuffy, do you? Maybe if he relaxed more, and stopped being so strict about goofing off,
and created a friendlier atmosphere, he would not only be
more successful, he would be happier, too. Has that occurred to you? Glance at a copy of *Who's Who in Commerce and Industry*. The summer birthdays will be the
heaviest, and July will top them all. Then take another
look at the names of the Cancerians at the end of "How
to Recognize" this Sun sign. He must be doing something
right.

Whatever business he is in, the Cancer boss is really in
his element when it comes to trading—from horses to
stocks—and anything in between. He is a past master at

figuring out what people want and supplying it at a substantial profit.

The lure of cash may even have taken him away from the education he wanted, and he became a self-made man. If not, then you can safely wager a month's paycheck that, while he was in college he was working part-time and setting a little moola aside. What am I saying, college? This man probably had his first employment at the age of six or seven, going to the corner store to get milk or bread and charging his doting mother two cents for the trip. Ask him when he began his first salaried job. You'll probably get quite a shock. But it will increase your status with him. He'll respect you and make a mental note that you're thinking right. By the way, watch those mental notes he makes. He has a memory like an elephant. Cancer bosses seldom forget a thing. That includes what time you arrive, what time you leave and how many times you visit the washroom while you're there. But he'll also remember the nights you stayed late and the time you worked all weekend to help him with an important contract, and you'll be justly, even generously, rewarded.

He may have inherited wealth and position, but the Cancer boss will seldom rest on his family's laurels. He has to prove he can stack up the gold pieces on his own. Still, he's not greedy. He's truly sympathetic and charitable, without being naive about it. To him, charity begins at home. His family comes first. Next, his business. After that, it's your turn—and everybody else's. No one can be as big-hearted and financially generous when the recipient is deserving, and when there's really nowhere else he can go for help. The crab will make his gesture then—and it won't be small. Just remember that there's a wide berth between honest charity and rash speculation. He has a soft heart, but he doesn't have a soft head.

In reality, your Cancer boss is a deeply sensitive, gentle person, and basically insecure. Success calms many of his inner fears, and that's why he pursues it so devotedly. When he's hurt, and that may be far more frequently than you realize, he crawls into his hard shell. It's also a Cancerian defense when he doesn't get what he wants, and it often works to his advantage. People always feel sorry for a crab who has retreated inside his shell, and sometimes they'll promise quite a bit to coax him back out.

There are lots of female Cancerian bosses, too. Almost

every single Cancer woman you'll ever meet has worked at sometime in her life, is working now, or is bossing you now. She may be in love with love, but it will have a rival in her job that can win in a walk. She won't be happy with emotional security alone, even if she sometimes thinks she would. To all Cancerians, happiness is a twin—money and affection in equal measure. The female crab probably detests housework, anyway. Most Cancer women do. If you've heard differently, it's because of the attachment they have to the kitchen. Actually, these women would much rather compete in a man's world, with all their sensitive feelings, than drudge through the daily routine of sweeping and dusting and dusting and sweeping, with an occasional mopping thrown in to relieve the monotony. They hate to admit it, and their homes are usually pleasant enough places, clean or messy, but they do dislike being housewives. The affection and protection that goes with it is dandy, but the furniture polish they can do without. In most ways, the women executives don't differ essentially from the men, with one exception. The girl crabs don't wear trousers and white shirts and ties. They wear gentle smiles to hide tender hearts and hard shell minds, usually topping it off with feminine and romantic clothing.

All Cancer bosses have a remarkable insight into your feelings. They'll understand everything you say with uncanny accuracy, and the unnerving part is that they're also perceptive enough to sense the meaning of the words you leave unspoken, so watch what you leave unspoken. Cancerians aren't really loners. They may act like it at times, when they're passing through a cranky or depressed mood, but they usually surround themselves with people. Solitude is fearful to most crabs, except to those who have sought it because of very deep wounds very early in life, and even they are miserable alone, though they may not consciously realize it.

It's good to work for a Cancerian executive. You'll learn more in one month from him than you will in a year from other bosses. The most important thing you'll learn is consideration. A Cancer boss drives a hard bargain, but he's fair while he's being shrewd. Playing a game of win or lose with the big guys who hold the blue chips is one thing. Taking advantage of the innocent is another. He's essentially a kind and decent man, who's moved to deep pity by both cruelty and misfortune. Courtesy and compassion aren't old-fashioned words to him. They are part of his gentleman's code. If your intentions are sincere, your motives are sound and your heart is honest, he'll back you through mistaken opinions and personal troubles.

The crab waits patiently and tenaciously, with both eyes wide open. His mind remains alert and practical, but his heart dreams, and the dreams are as magic as the moonlight that stirs him. They can take him on a glamorous, exciting trip around the world, or inspire him to build a towering industry that uses its excess profits to encourage scientific research which will help humanity. But every dream is built on a solid foundation. His poetry is beautiful, but it always makes sense.

As for that joke, make sure you tell it to him at lunch, not on company time. If it's about plain people and has a good point, he'll laugh. Then you'll find out what he's really like. Watch his eyes, and you'll see that the lunar laugh is a bright and brave answer to inner fears and hurts that only the patient crab, with his gentle heart and tough shell, could dare to give.

The CANCER Employee

"And they drew all manner of things—
everything that begins with an M—
. . . such as mouse-traps, and the moon,
and memory, and muchness. . . ."

It's always nice to have a Cancerian work for you, because he actually works for you. He doesn't work for glory or a misty chimera, and he doesn't stop by each day because he has a crush on the receptionist. He never thinks of his job as a way to express his ego or as an amusing way to pass the time between coffee breaks. He works for the simplest reason in the world. Security. Meaning, of course, his paycheck.

You should understand immediately that a Cancerian paycheck must be made of elastic. It will have to gradually stretch bigger and bigger. As time goes on, and he gathers experience, proves his loyalty and shows his talents or abilities, he'll expect more money. His income must always equal his output, and his output will steadily increase. The paycheck will have to match it or he'll be forced to do something completely against his nature—let go of his job and go elsewhere. It's never easy for the crab to let go of anything—toothbrushes, old get-well cards, shoe-strings, socks, girls, empty ball-point pens or jobs. He gets a firm grip and you can't pry him loose. Dependability and tenacity were the materials used in building his nature, and they were used with a lavish hand. They serve him well on his ambitious climb to success. He may shake and shiver and tremble a little on the way when the sharks appear and his emotions are cut to the quick, but all that will be kept safely encased inside his tough shell of deliberate purpose. Despite the crab's apparent gentleness, Cancer is a cardinal sign, which means Cancerians were born to take responsibility—to lead, not be led. They'll accept discipline from the boss with calm docility while it's necessary, but never forget what's behind their willingness to follow orders gracefully. When the crab obediently serves, he's really serving his own secret purposes. His job happens to represent an important brick in the large edifice he's building. As soon as the sturdy structure is completed, he will take over and rule. In other words, he is aiming for an executive position. It never leaves his mind for an instant. It's best you keep it in yours also, for obvious reasons.

His motivation in laying those bricks with such strong mortar is seldom a desire for power. Prestige doesn't goad him on, as it does the Capricorn, the goat, nor ego, as it does Aries, the ram. He's driven to accumulate cash and an unshakable position of authority for different reasons. Cancerians need the security of knowing that all their tomorrows are safe, so they can finally relax and live where their hearts are—in yesterday. That takes money. Antiques are expensive. So are huge, old houses and luxurious dinners, served graciously. Collecting old autographs requires a lot of cash, too, and handsome frames to hold portraits of ancestors aren't cheap. Good hi-fi sets for classical music cost plenty of dimes. Besides, the Cancer employee may need substantial sums to support relatives who have moved in during a troubled spell, or an offspring may be in need of more money for a variety of reasons. In addition, the crab has a multitude of fears, both real and imaginary. They form a complicated network of nagging self-doubts and feelings of inadequacy, which authority and leadership will ease the way novocaine dulls pain.

He needs one more thing. Affection. Naturally, that's not your responsibility. Still, it helps to be aware of it. Someday you may have to give him a squeeze of the hand and a speech of warm gratitude instead of a raise. It won't be a substitute for cash by any means, but it might make him decide to stay around a little longer. Appreciation is soothing to the Cancerian, but it will never completely replace his sentimental attachment to his bank balance.

So don't go overboard and get into the habit of saying, "Rocky, old boy, I can't pay you the money you're worth now, but I love you madly." He may misunderstand your motive after a time or two. That is, he may think you're insincere. Be equally cautious with your female Cancerian employees. You could easily be misunderstood by them. The Cancer woman is shy and timid with strangers, but she recognizes a romantic signal from miles away with frightening speed. If she's single, you'd better hope you are, because she'll get that tender, possessive look in her eyes, and you'll have quite a time getting out of the noose. If she's married, she'll freeze you cold or snap at you until you're properly respectful. Give your lunar people love, but try to remain impersonal about it. I know that's like saying, "Hang your clothes on a hickory limb, but don't go near the water," but that's the way it is. The strategy is something you'll have to figure out for yourself.

Just as surely as Cancerian Stephen Foster wrote *"My Old Kentucky Home,"* the symbol of home will enter the lives of these employees one way or another. Your lunar secretary's mother may drop by frequently to lunch with her daughter—and a female crab working responsibly as a clerk in a department store for years will walk out suddenly if her son is in trouble or ill, and needs her. That salesman who was born in July will enjoy a bit of travel, if he's a bachelor (as long as some one calls his mother every day while he's gone to see if she wants anything). But if he's married, he may not appreciate being sent out of town or being asked to sacrifice holidays at home for business emergencies.

If you have any Cancerian employees who are going through a separation or divorce, you have a problem on your hands that may disrupt your staff for weeks. They'll spread a cloud of gloom over the office. If it's a female, double your order of Kleenex for the powder room. There will be periods of moody weeping, and she may spend a lot of time in court. The judge will award her substantial alimony or else. If support money for children is involved, she may need a month off. Physical desertion is bad enough, but the threat of losing financial security will arouse every ounce of tenacity in her, and that's a lot of ounces. Crabs of both sexes take a broken home very hard. Your best bet about this Cancerian home fixation is to hang a poem on the wall of every office. "Home Is Where The Heart Is." Just beneath it, hang one of those arrangements of rare coins, on a background of lavender velvet, framed in sterling silver. Have you missed the point? They won't.

When there's something you want to discuss with the Cancer employee, and you want to put him in a receptive frame of mind, take him to lunch or dinner. Cancerians adore people who invite them for a meal. Not only does it mean he won't have to pick up the check, but food spells security in capital letters. Just watch his eyes light up. He may not be a big eater himself, but he's still more contented and peaceful when there's an abundance of food around. Be sure you take him to one of the finest restaurants in town. He'll love the luxury, since he's not paying the bill.

Cancerians are industrious workers. You can rely on them to be steady and reliable under all circumstances, except one. Cancer is a water sign, and people born under the three water signs enjoy liquids in all forms. If the aspects between the planets were afflicted at birth, one of these forms may be a hundred proof. The Cancerian with a drinking problem is rare, but if you should happen to come across a July-born employee who fills the air with the crazy lunar laugh too frequently, or who weeps melancholy tears continually, he may be enjoying something stronger than java on his coffee breaks. Don't form the opinion that every Pisces, Scorpio or Cancer person is a nipper. True, people born during these periods are more often found drowning their sorrows than others, but that's an overall statistic, covering millions of humans, and you

can never use it when judging people individually. Most
of the Cancerians you meet will be sober. In fact, they
may be so sober you wish they would relax a little over
a cocktail.

They take their work seriously, and themselves even more
so. The lunar sense of humor is warm and wonderful, full
of sensitive insight into human nature, but when someone's wit hits a tender spot, the crab may be deeply hurt.
It's best to let him make the jokes. With his kind heart and
his sharp perception, it's unlikely that he'll wound anyone
under the guise of comedy. The typical Cancerian employee
won't scatter his punch lines during working hours on
company time, but when you take him to dinner, he might
keep you chuckling from the tomato juice through the
cherries Jubilee. Crabs can be utterly fascinating con-
versationalists, unless they're in a gloomy mood, in which
case one word an hour, snapped out briefly, will be about
par. They can pout beautifully. But they can also speak
magnetically, and sway your emotions easily through their
ability to play on people.

Cancerians feel things. No one can be more tender and
sympathetic than a Cancer person when you need a friend,
and no one can be crankier when they suspect someone
is trying to take something from them, either emotionally
or tangibly. When the bank statement doesn't balance,
they may frown in sullen silence for hours afterwards, and
if a crab thinks an associate is after his or her job, there
can be some pretty childish behavior, as a prelude to a
fight-to-the-death for possession and ownership. The victim
may not even suspect war has been declared until the victory has been won. Cancerians have more secrets than J.
Edgar Hoover, James Bond and Sherlock Holmes combined. They seldom advertise their moves in advance, and
they almost never reveal their true inner thoughts, except
to those who are so close to them there's little chance the
confidence will ever boomerang.

The crab does well in any position that lets him use his
natural abilities. He's often successful in merchandising,
trading, manufacturing and buying for large chains. The
baking, canning, packing and distribution of foods attracts
many a Cancerian. Art (painting or sculpting), designing and interior decorating, music, museums, writing, accounting, real estate, children's clothing, social work, acting
and directing, photography, gardening, lecturing, teaching,

banking, oil, commerce, shipping and politics are all typical Cancer careers. Managing hotels or restaurants, controlling theaters and arranging loans are also natural occupations for lunar people.

Your female Cancer employee loves babies, children, men, flowers, warmly heated offices, courtesy, romance, cooking, movies, books and money. She's sensitive, responsive to kindness, responsible and extremely capable. She's moody.

Your male Cancer employee loves babies, children, women, respect, admiration, warmly heated offices, courtesy, romance, cooking, movies, books and money. He's sensitive, responsive to kindness, responsible and extremely capable. He's moody.

Well, can you tell the difference between the boy and girl crabs on the beach? Both sexes are gentle and dreamy, yet as sensible and practical as red flannel underwear. You'll be glad you hired them when business takes you away from the office more than you like. They love to watch the store.

*The Queen turned crimson with fury,
and, after glaring at her for a moment
like a wild beast, began screaming,
"Off with her head!"*

SHY PUSSYCATS

*'Tis the voice of the Lobster: I heard him declare,
"You have baked me too brown, I must sugar my hair."*

LEO the Lion

July 24th through August 23rd

How to Recognize LEO

It looked good-natured, she thought;
still, it had very long claws
and a great many teeth,
so she felt it ought to be
treated with respect.

Has anyone said to you lately, "Don't do me any favors," but dazzled you with an utterly gorgeous smile as he said it? You've been exposed to the big cat. Don't worry, you'll recover. What's a little scorched spot here and there? It's not at all unusual for Leo to display his arrogant pride and his sunny playfulness at the same time, which is why he gets away with murder.

Leo, the lion, rules all the other animals. Leo, the person, rules you and everybody else. (Yes, yes, I know he really doesn't. But please don't tell him. It would break his big, warm, egotistical heart.) It's best to humor him. Then he'll purr, instead of roaring and scaring you half to death. The lion alternates between being energetically gregarious and beautifully indolent, as he stifles a luxurious yawn. If you want to study the beast, hit all the bright, sparkling places around town. At least half the people you see living it up in style will be Leos. The shyer pussycats will be at home living it up. Leo hates the dark and boredom equally.

If you see one who blushes easily make sure you aren't getting a blush confused with a flush of pride or ego. There's more difference between a blush and a flush than a letter of the alphabet. His face may be pink because he's been dancing too hard. His cheeks may be suffused with a rosy glow because the love of his life just passed by. But his high color isn't caused by introversion or self-effacing timidity. There are no introverted Leos. There are only Leos who pretend to be introverts. That's important to remember. You may find a few lions who keep their ruling Sun dimmed and go about being strong, dignified

and determined quietly. Don't let that soft purr fool you.
Even the gentle Leos are inwardly sold on their royal right
to rule friends and family as they peek out from behind
the curtains and watch for their chance on stage. If you
don't believe me, just choose a quiet Leo who's pretending
to be an introvert, and attack his pride. Take something
away from him which he believes is rightfully his, give him
orders and show him no respect. You'll hear that supposedly
gentle cat roar from here to the zoo. It takes a brave
soul to challenge him when he's defending his rights and
his dignity. Some Leos mellow with age, but the lion
never really lowers his proud head. Never.

As for the physical attributes of this Sun sign, just look
around for people who resemble a lion or a lioness, with
a mane of hair that sweeps back off the face, and a deceptively lazy look. Leos walk straight and proud, with
the smooth glide of the cat. The females combine lithe
grace with a hidden, quivering intensity. This last will be
disguised by a soft, usually calm and steady nature. But
don't forget that the lioness is always ready to pounce if
she feels threatened. Her claws are sheathed, but sharp.

You'll notice a commanding air and stately bearing, as
Leo looks down on all the mere mortals beneath him.
Ordinarily, the movements and speech are deliberate.
Leos seldom talk fast, run or even walk quickly (unless
there's an Aries or Gemini ascendant or Moon, for example). You won't ignore the lion for long in a group.
He'll either get the center of the stage with dramatic statements and action—or he'll get it by pouting and sulking
behind the potted palms until someone rushes over to ask
what's wrong. The sign produces its share of blue eyes, but
many Leos, especially the females, have dark brown eyes
that are first soft and gentle, then snap and crackle with
fire, often round in shape and slightly tilted at the corner.
The hair is dark or reddish blonde and usually wavy,
worn in a wild, careless style that upsweeps, stands out
fully on the top and the sides or is sleeked down tightly,
one extreme or the other, and there's a noticeable ruddy
complexion.

Leos have a strange effect on people that's downright
funny to watch. It's hard to stand in front of the lion without drawing yourself up to full stature, stomach in—
shoulders back. I really don't know whether we peasants do
this in imitation of the royal manner of the Leo we're

facing or to gather courage for a possible lecture, for they do love to give free advice. They have a knack for telling you with a slightly superior, condescending manner exactly how you should manage your life.

This love of teaching is why so many Leos end up as educators, politicians and psychiatrists. The exasperating thing is that they're quite good at rationalizing things and smoothing out the wrinkles in your life. Too bad they can't manage their own affairs with as much ease and finesse. Still, this is what makes the lion so downright lovable; his honest superiority and excellent abilities, incongruously mixed up with a terrible, transparent vulnerability of ego. The proud, dignified cat vulnerable? Yes indeed. He's deeply wounded when you don't respect his wisdom and generosity. To subdue him, simply flatter him. Nine times out of ten, he'll turn from a roaring beast into a bashful, docile kitten, almost visibly rolling and basking in the warmth of compliments. It's this weakness which is the Waterloo for many a stern, autocratic Leo. His vanity is his Achilles' heel. Fattery acts like catnip to him, lack of respect blinds him with rage and both extremes make him incapable of balanced judgment. There are some Leos who control these tendencies successfully, but they're always latent in the Sun sign and present to some degree.

Try it sometime. In the middle of receiving one of his lectures, interrupt respectfully and tell your Leo friend he looks positively magnificent in that sweater. The result will probably be an abrupt fall from dignity, as the lion blushes and says, completely disconcerted, "Really? You really think I do?" In most cases, appreciating the intellect works as well as complimenting the appearance.

Leo just can't help feeling superior and behaving dramatically now and then. One of my children has an August-born teacher. She came home from school one day to say, "Mother, my teacher is so funny. He's awfully smart about everything, but sometimes he runs around the room and waves his arms in the air and shouts, 'I'm surrounded by idiots!' We always giggle, because we know he doesn't mean it." Poor lion, even the children know his roar is worse than his bite. It's only fair to remind you that you may stumble on one who has an afflicted Mars or Mercury with, say, Scorpio rising, and then the bite will be more serious, but we're speaking now of the typical cat.

In many ways, Leo is extremely astute. He'll seldom waste his energy trying to get water from a dry well, as Aries often does, which makes him a superb organizer and a wise distributor of duties. His commands are surprisingly effective when he tones down the dramatics, because he can be a master of the simple, straightforward speech, even if it smacks slightly of theatrics. Leo expresses approval generously and openly, and can give almost embarrassingly extravagant compliments. He's not at all bashful about his displeasure, either. Whatever he says, he usually means. It can soothe or burn, but it never fails to leave an impression.

The regal ways of this Sun sign are splendid when the Leo man or woman is host or hostess. They make you feel you are being entertained in a royal palace. You keep expecting to see a coach and footman pull up outside the door at any moment to drop off Marie Antoinette, or, at the very least, Nell Gwyn and Madame Du Barry. Leos surround their guests with heaps of superb food, fine wines, beautiful women, and soft music. I must admit I do know one lion with strong Virgo planets in his natal chart who serves diced cucumbers sprinkled with herbs, parsley and wheat germ at parties, but the other trimmings are luxuriously leonine, always including the feminine guests. Such pulchritude! Louis XIV never had it so good. But after Louis XIV the deluge—and after many a Leo's romantic dancing and dining comes a deluge of proposals, passion, tears, anger, apologies, and just plain sentimental confusion.

Now that we find ourselves on the subject of romance, which is a pretty common place to find yourself when you're involved with the lion, either in person or on paper, we should note that you won't find many bachelors or spinsters born under this Sun sign. If you come across one, don't form a definite opinion until you've discreetly checked the closet. There's usually a paramour hiding nearby any lion's lair. He may not be married when you first meet him, but he'll be in love, or just about to be, or he'll have recently broken a romantic shackle, and will be wearing a pathetic, lost look. The fiery pride of Leo causes plenty of shattered love affairs and marriages. A lion minus his mate is usually a woeful sight to behold, but when his pride has been injured by a lover or a legal mate, he can drop his sad-eyed look and become pretty fierce and wild instead. Still, there's no one who can bear more in stoic dignity, or adjust more courageously to depressing conditions with sheer faith and optimism when it's necessary.

Since forgiveness and sympathy of spirit are part of the big cat's inner nature, the reconciliations are about as frequent in Leo's emotional life as the splits, once the fireworks of outraged dignity have sputtered out and he gets lonely. He's almost continually in the throes of passion, not just with the opposite sex, but with life itself. Life without love, to both lions and shy pussycats, is like a plug without a socket. The Sun forgets to shine for them when romance dies.

These men and women never lean on others. Instead, they prefer to be leaned on. Responsibility toward the weak and helpless appeals to them. Leo may roar theatrically that everyone depends on him and he's forced to carry the whole load, but don't pay a bit of attention to his complaints. He loves it. Try to relieve him of his burdens or lend a helping hand, and you'll see how quickly Leo will disdainfully refuse your help. Accepting financial aid is something he especially prefers to avoid. Though he may be broke frequently, he's always certain he'll find some way to line his pockets again soon. Very few Leos are cautious with cash. You may find an occasional one who was frightened by a bill collector at an early age, and behaves as if he's headed for debtor's prison any moment. But the typical lion is a spectacular gambler at heart, often wildly extravagant; even the rare cat who pinches pennies will dress expensively, and always look well turned out. He wants first class and luxury all the way, and he'll spend freely on fun and pleasure. Leo will give money to almost anybody. If he's asked for a loan and he's short of cash, he'll often go out and borrow it from someone else before admitting that the King isn't in a position to help his needy subjects. That's a last resort, however, because Leos are mortified to be forced to turn to others for money, advice or encouragement. They have enough ego to supply their own encouragement, they're clever enough to accumulate their own pot of gold—and goodness knows they don't seek advice readily. One seeks advice only from those above him, and who is superior to the lion?

Leo often runs high fevers, is prone to accidents, sudden, violent illnesses and is usually immune to chronic, lingering disease. Since they seldom do anything halfway, these people either radiate incredible vitality or else complain that they're not long for this world, the latter a typical reaction to lack of appreciation and starvation for affection. Leos seem to have either superbly strong hearts or some sort of weakness in the heart area. They may suffer from pains in the back and shoulders, spinal troubles, accidents to the legs or ankles, problems relating to the reproductive organs and hoarseness or sore throats. But they recuperate with vigor from sickness, and their main danger is carelessness about health or getting up too soon when illness strikes. To stay in bed and be waited on flatters the Leo vanity at first, but when he realizes he's playing the role of weak instead of strong, his spells of incapacitation are quickly conquered.

There's no inbetween with the Sun-ruled. They are either dreadfully careless and sloppy or meticulously neat and orderly. They rather enjoy gossip, and they feel hurt or left out if something is going on around them they don't understand. Leos are fixed in nature. It's hard to sway them from a set path, though they can sway others with convincing oratory. They accumulate only so that they can distribute to others, once they've provided themselves with a glittering throne complete with a soft, feather pillow. They can show as much ferocious energy as a steam roller, and then be as sleepily lazy as the cat, stretching out and snoozing in the sun. When they work, they work. When they play, they play. When they rest, they rest. Most lions have an impressive genius for cheerfully delegating messy and unpleasant jobs to others, while they attend to important matters, like deciding who should be elected President and how the war should be won.

Surprising himself, when a real emergency falls on Leo's strong shoulders, he'll carry it lightly and never shirk his duty, helping the defenseless, protecting the frightened (though he may be twice as frightened himself inside), cheering the melancholy and tackling his true responsibilities with courage. This is the inbred Leo nature, which will shine forth after the playboy phase has been tucked away with his gaudy hand-painted ties and that guitar he used to play.

The next time you're on the receiving end of the lion's proud roar, remember the Queen of Hearts who constantly shouted, "Off with his head," while everyone's head stayed securely fastened on. Remember the cowardly lion in "The

Wizard of Oz" who tenderly nursed his beautiful tail in injured dignity, anxiously searching the world over for the gift of true courage, only to find he was really the bravest one of the group when the real crisis came.

Leo is a fiercely loyal friend, a just but powerful enemy, creative and original, strong and vital—whether he's a quiet or a flamboyant lion, for there are both kinds. He dresses in glorious raiment, appropriate to his colorful personality. We overlook his arrogance, his sometimes insufferable ego, his rather ridiculous spells of vanity and laziness, because his heart, like his metal, is pure gold.

Brimming over with fun and generosity, the gay, affectionate lion prances in a field of poppies when his Sun is high in the sky—and the dice he throws with confidence bear the numbers one and four. Leo proudly wears a topaz for luck, then pushes it too far, but he has a true inner dignity and grace that lets him carry his misfortunes with courage. The warm, yellow rays of his cheerful hope deepen to orange in the sunset's glow, and his nights are bright with a thousand stars.

Famous Leo Personalities

Gracie Allen	John Galsworthy
Lucille Ball	Alfred Hitchcock
Ethel Barrymore	Aldous Huxley
Bernard Baruch	Carl Jung
Bill "Count" Basie	Jacqueline Kennedy
David Belasco	Princess Margaret Rose
Napoleon Bonaparte	Mussolini
Walter Brennan	Ogden Nash
Robert Burns	Dorothy Parker
Fidel Castro	Walter Scott
Julia Child	George Bernard Shaw
Arlene Dahl	Percy Bysshe Shelley
Cecil B. DeMille	Robert Taylor
Eddie Fisher	Mae West
	Whitney Young

The LEO Man

*" 'Tis love—'tis love that
makes the world go round!"*

When Gray wrote the lines about a flower "born to blush
unseen and waste its sweetness on the desert air," he
certainly wasn't describing a Leo. You might see this man
basking in the bright sunlight, and you may find him making flowery speeches, but it won't be in the solitude of the
desert. Most likely it will be on a stage or in front of a
circle of adoring friends and relatives. He may waste
money, but he's not about to waste his sweetness in the
empty air. There will always be an audience.

There you are, in a nutshell. The secret of snaring the
lion is that simple. Be his audience. Totally different from
the reluctant Virgo and Aquarian males, your Leo pal
will happily succumb to the throes of delicious romance,
if you play your cards right, adore him, flatter him, and
respect him.

Is he a flamboyant August male? Wear dark glasses and
submit to his brilliant sunlight. Is he one of the gentle,
quiet Leos? Don't be taken in by his sleek softness. Stroke
him the wrong way and sparks will fly. Remember, he's
only playing the role of the meek soul. Beneath his courteous manner and patient fixity are smoldering fires of proud
dignity and arrogant vanity, ready to flame up and burn the
pushy female silly enough to think she can rule him.

The lion will be a chivalrous and gallant suitor, tenderly
protective and sentimentally affectionate. You won't need
to lay much of a trap to tempt him into romantic advances.
One might say Leos possess a kind of instant passion. Just
add opportunity—mix well with candlelight and lush
violins—and love's in bloom like the red, red rose. As a
matter of fact, you can leave out the candles and music
if they're not handy, and just use the first ingredient. Same
thing.

If love is missing from his life, the fiery lion will simply pine away—dramatically, of course. He has to be worshiped or die, and you can just about take that literally. Leo males seldom spare expenses when they're courting. You'll be taken to the best restaurants, showered with perfume and flowers, proudly escorted to the theater and you'll tie a ribbon around some pretty fantastic love letters. To tell you the truth, you'd have to have a heart made of stone to resist.

By now, you're probably thinking you've got it made. Think again. That leonine romance won't be completely trouble free. You might take a lesson from the pampered favorites of royalty. Leo will invite you into his den and warm you at the hearth of his big heart, but the lion's lair can turn into a plush, luxurious prison. Is he jealous? The answer is "Yes," and you can spell it with big electric light bulbs. You belong to him, body, soul, and mind. He'll tell you what to wear, how to part your hair, what books to read, which friends are best for you and how to organize your day better. He'll want to know why you were gone for two hours shopping when you said you'd be back in one hour, who you met on the way, what they said— and he'll even pout if you don't tell him what you're thinking as you stare out the kitchen window while you're scrambling his eggs. After all, you could be thinking of another man. Just don't ever forget the force of his impulsive temper when it's aroused. Teasing him by occasional flirtations to prove to him you are still desirable is absolute folly. He knows you're desirable. He needs no proof whatsoever. Besides, your Leo man is liable to flatten your innocent masculine friends to the floor—if not put them in the hospital—when he's pushed too far.

All is not roses and honey in a love affair with a lion, and that includes the quiet pussycats along with the flashy tom cats. There's no difference in the basic nature. Every woman in love with a Leo should get a copy of *Anna and the King of Siam* and study it well. The Siamese monarch was a typical Leo and you'll get invaluable tips from Anna's technique. First the provocative challenge to interest him, then final feminine submission after you've taught him you won't be completely devoured. Truly, her story is a must. Sleep with it under your pillow.

Be prepared to balance his great enthusiasms with calm reason and willing to soothe him as he blows up problems into huge dimensions. The gentle Leos do this quietly, but what's the difference? Whether he roars and rages because his employees refused to obey him, or pouts on the back porch because the neighbors snubbed him the end result is identical. He needs your stability to balance his irrational pride. If you don't possess it yourself, your love may turn into a constant battle royal. You'll be breaking up and making up with such speed that your astonished friends will ask, "Where's the fire?" Where? Why, right inside your cozy lion's den.

Don't try to be a career girl. He'll never stand for it. *He's* your career. The lion may permit his mate to go out hunting for a few skins when the bank account gets low, but she'd better make it clear the job comes last, after him and the home nest. He won't tolerate competition from a male or an outside interest. If you're brave enough to accept these challenges, go ahead and buy your trousseau, but be sure it's stylish. He'll want to show you off in his own Easter Parade, in December as well as in April. Embarrass him by appearing in public looking anything but queenly and you might miss a familiar face in the church while the choir is singing "Oh, Promise Me"—his.

After you're married, mated, and deeply loved, count your rewards. Your Leo husband will be as kind and good-hearted as King Arthur, provided you let the family revolve around him. If he gets the respect he demands, he'll repay it by pouring out generosity. You may be told how lovely you look repeatedly, he'll probably give you a large allowance, and—wonder of wonders, with his romantic disposition—he'll be likely to remain faithful. There's always a better chance of that after marriage than when he's single, and I'll tell you why. The lion is usually too lazy to chase pretty faces, once he's found a lioness who will capably run his kingdom, while he luxuriously snoozes in the hammock. He'll play affectionately with his cubs, protect his mate from all danger, and thrill her with his ambition to rise to a position of impressive superiority in his career.

You will lead an active social life with your Leo husband, as long as he gets his beauty sleep. But there will be a few nights out with the boys, and there may also be some juggling of finances, due to sudden gambling urges, or a chance investment he thought would pay off. A Leo man I know once bought ten shares in an oil well. Although he was only one very minor stockholder among thousands, about twice a month, he would visit the site of the drilling and look important. When anyone asked him what he wanted, he would tell them, "I'm just checking to see how things are going with my well." The drillers treated him with great respect. They thought he was a member of the Board of Directors.

Take it all in stride—there are compensations. How can he scold you for buying that expensive mink hat after he lost the price of a mink coat in a little game with the fellows or after he spent your savings at an auction on two box cars of folded cardboard cartons in assorted sizes, when he took a notion to go into the mail order business? (Then he couldn't use them because it turned out that they were stamped all over with the words "Rat Poison" and a large skull and crossbones.) Keep him away from auctions if you have to lock him up, because he has an irresistible urge to bid higher than anybody on anything at any time. He'll be quite the check grabber in public too, cheerfully saying, "The treat's on me," with the money for the new freezer. Leo would be right at home in Texas or Las Vegas, where he would instantly be recognized as a high roller (unless his Moon or ascendant dictates economy).

There's one thing about the lion you may find very handy. Almost all Leos have a marvelous knack for fixing things. It can be anything from a broken door knob or a stubborn bathroom faucet to a tape recorder or a complicated stereo hi-fi set. If he's a typical Leo, he won't be able to resist trying his hand at making something work when it's on the blink. If all else fails, he'll give the offending machine or whatever a resounding kick in splendid leonine anger, and suddenly the door knob will turn, the water will spray like Niagara Falls, the tape recorder will start talking and the hi-fi will start singing. There seems to be something mechanical about this Sun sign. Lots of Leo men can take engines apart and put them back together again, hardly soiling their hands in the process. He's not the type to let a hinge hang for months unscrewed or a carpet lie on the floor untacked. A surprising number of lions are experts at making their own furniture and building an extra room on the house with no professional help. He may have his own workshop in the basement. Don't complain about a little sawdust on the floor. It keeps him contented—and home at night.

The lion is the life of most parties, but he's no fool. He wears the jester's mask to get attention, and his audiences usually sense they'd better respect him during his temporary playful spells. Regardless of appearances, there's nothing easygoing about the inner nature of your Leo man. He's far more steadfast and tenacious than he seems. He knows what he wants, and he usually gets it. He's pretty good at keeping it, too.

If you expect him to be faithful during the courtship, be sure you keep him well nourished with romance and affection or his huge need for love and admiration will make him stalk all over the jungle in search of it. If your relationship is real and deep, he'll probably be true to you, but his eyes may wander a bit. Other than keeping him blindfolded, there's very little you can do about that. Leo appreciates beauty, so if you're the type to get jealous over an appreciative glance at another female, you'd better get tolerant fast. A Leo man whose lady love leaves him because of his flirting will be honestly hurt and astonished. He's entirely capable, then, of faking anything from a heart attack to a tear-stained farewell note to get you to sympathize and run back into his big, warm arms, and he'll be so convincing you'll feel like a cruel monster. Unless you enjoy emotional, dramatic scenes yourself, it's much less trouble to understand him in the first place. His capers will probably be innocent and harmless anyway, if you're treating him right. Never overly sensitive to the feelings of others, in spite of their basic kindness, most Leo men are so wrapped up in themselves that they can be brutally frank and untactful. But his dazzling smile soon clears the air. The warm lion doesn't have a malicious bone in his strong, graceful body. He may blow off terrifying steam, yet malice is not a part of his make-up and he can't cope with real cruelty (unless there's an affliction in his natal chart). He will enjoy sports, but as he grows older, he will prefer to watch them from the comfort of his padded throne, while you wait on him.

Not always, but very often, there's an odd twist to Leo males. Unlike the Capricorn, who seeks to rise socially through wedlock, the lion sometimes tends to marry beneath him. He has as much desire for social status, but he just can't resist acquiring a "subject" to whom he's superior. Sometimes he makes a wrong choice, and the shrinking violet who sat adoringly at his feet makes a surprise move to grab the sceptre away from him. When that happens, the dethroned Leo is a miserable husband who wears the tragic expression of an exiled monarch.

It's sad, but true, that Leos seldom raise large families. Many of them have no children, are separated from them, or raise an only child. Too bad, because they make warm, wonderful fathers, perhaps somewhat too permissive between stern talks about proper behavior. Your offspring may chafe under his demands and be bored with his long lectures, but they'll soon learn how to flatter him into submission. He'll insist on their respect and get it, but they're liable to wheedle him out of anything by the clever usage of "Yes, Sir. You're right, Sir." Therefore, the real discipline may be up to you. The children may resent his arrogant ways, but Leo fathers are almost always remembered with affection in later years. One tip. Don't give the youngsters more attention than you give him, or you may end up with quite a lot of trouble on your hands in the form of a giant bruised ego, which will be nearly impossible to heal.

How can you size up the puzzling male Leo? Is he kindhearted or dangerous, generous or cruelly selfish? Is he really a sociable fellow who loves people? Does he gain his reputation for superiority under false pretenses, or does he, like the real lion, deserve to be called King? Obviously, by his own standards at least, he does deserve to be the Lord and Master in his love life and his career. You have to admit that he's usually highly successful in both romance and business.

Whether the Leo man is truly a king, or just a pretender to the throne, we may never know. But there are several things you do know about your own lion. He has insatiable appetites, and he's as proud as a peacock. He has an enormous need to command and to be loved by those he rules. Remember that Leo secretly fears he may fail and be ridiculed. It's a constant inner torture, and the true source of his vanity and exaggerated dignity. Yet, when his nobility has been aroused by a great cause, he knows no fear. Only then does the lion learn that the magnificent strength and courage he's been pretending to have has really been there all along.

Your Leo may drive you wild by his antics during courtship, but he's not at all a bad mate for a long term possibility. If you don't mind submerging your ego, and building your life around his, once you've tamed this man, you'll be adored and you'll never be lonely again. Besides, he can fix those bathroom faucets.

The LEO Woman

> *" 'Tis an honor to see me, a favor to hear:*
> *'Tis a privilege high to have dinner and tea*
> *Along with the Red Queen, the White Queen*
> *And me!"*

There's one thing the Leo woman probably owns that you won't like. A scrapbook of pictures and mementos from all her old boyfriends. It's no use trying to get her to burn it, because the lioness is sentimental.

She's not a wallflower. She's a sunflower. Chances are she's ridiculously popular, and you'll have plenty of competition if you want her to descend to using your name for the rest of her life. You will be a few leaps ahead if your name is St. Hoyme or Mountbatten, Cabot or Lodge. Anything that sounds royal or noble or important. I honestly can't imagine a Leo woman marrying anybody with the name Carbunkle or Smith. It's possible. Anything is possible. But she'll probably change Smith to Smythe.

Most likely, she'll be the social leader of her group, lording it over lesser women like a queen, but with such disarming warmth and such a beautiful smile, no one really minds. Perhaps the other girls sense she was born to rule and dictate styles, customs and manners. Anyway, it wouldn't do much good to try to usurp her authority.

Nature seems to have shown some prejudice when she fashioned the lioness with enough vivacity, cleverness, grace, beauty, and just plain sex appeal for at least three women, with some left over. If you're the victim of an inferiority complex, you'd better set your sights on a bird with less brilliant feathers. Don't expect to tame her into a docile little maid who hangs on your every word. The man who expects a Leo girl to worship at his feet is living in a fool's paradise. Consider yourself lucky if she meets you halfway, respects you, is willing to be your partner and allows you to possess her emotionally. By the very act of permitting you to love her, she's practically knighted you, for heaven's sake. Seriously, you could do a lot worse. A lioness is a lot of woman. She's rather a luxury item, not available in the bargain basement.

It pays to remember that the Leo female can act up a storm, and pretend to be as sweet and harmless as a bowl of jelly beans. She may have a voice like a whisper, gentle, courteous manners and big, soft eyes that sparkle delightfully when she bats her lashes. A Leo female can appear to be as smooth and calm as a cool and placid lake. On guard. That's just a role she assumed because it got good reviews. Remove her as the star of your love production, cast her in the part of the understudy or second lead, and you'll soon find out just how shy and submissive she isn't. Of course, most of the Leo women to whom you pay homage will openly make it clear that they're too proud and dignified to take any nonsense. I'd just hate to see you stumble in case you get involved with the other kind of lioness, who hides her claws, but sharpens them every day just the same.

The first step when you're courting this girl is to go prepared with gifts. It doesn't make much difference what they are, so long as they're expensive, in excellent taste, and you're dressed properly when you offer them. Then you should practice different ways of complimenting her. Please be original and creative. Phrases like "You send me, Baby," and "You're really cool, sweetheart," will get you thrown right out of the palace, back with the peasants. Vulgarity and slang both leave her ice cold. Remember, you're wooing royalty. She can't exist without flattering appreciation, but keep in mind that she admires your masculinity, and she has no desire to turn you into a henpecked weakling. A Leo woman couldn't love you if you weren't strong. It's just that she won't permit you to insult her with a condescending attitude. In her mind, she is definitely not the weaker sex.

Lots of Leo girls are athletic and enjoy sports, but you'd be smarter to take your lioness to the theater than to the ball park. The stage and footlights will never fail to magnetize and transfigure her. (Better buy orchestra seats. Forget the balcony.) Choose a play in which the heroine behaves the way you want *her* to behave that night, and your chances are better than average that she'll act the part unconsciously and never miss an inflection. After the festivities are over, don't take her to a hamburger stand and expect her to sit at the counter munching french fries because she's so much in love with you. You're better off to take her out less often to more glamorous places. She's not necessarily a gold digger; in fact, she's usually generous —she won't object to frequent Dutch dates and she'll probably shower you with almost as many gifts as you give her. But she's just plain uncomfortable in shabby surroundings. The poorest Leo woman in the world will manage to accumulate enough pennies to buy draperies for the windows, rings for her fingers and bells for her toes. Now and then she may go slumming, out of curiosity, but only as a spectator, aloof from the crowd. Poverty depresses her and makes her physically ill. If you dress like a slob and offer her a shack, you haven't got a chance.

There's a story about a noble Frenchwoman who turned to her lover in the gardens of Versailles and asked, "Darling, do the common people know this exquisite emotion of love?" When she was assured that they did, she cried out in injured surprise, "It's entirely too good for them!" She was probably a Leo.

Don't blame the lioness for her occasional arrogance and vanity. It's her nature to feel herself above the common masses. People seldom resent it, because the Leo woman who's warmly loved and respected can be the kindest and most generous of females, with a womanly compassion for children and for the helpless and the forsaken. You can't really expect her to step down from a throne that's her birthright. If she's a typical Sun child, she's so gracious and dazzling that most people gladly give her credit for being out of the ordinary. Truthfully, she is. She's intelligent, witty, strong, and capable, yet deliciously feminine at the same time. No one in his right mind could call that common.

A little flattery will get you everywhere with your Leo lady. You've already found out it's her secret weakness. And here's another secret, if you plan to marry her: eventually, she'll tire of her gilded cage and want to roam the jungle to see what's doing with all the other cats out there. Confinement inside four walls and under one roof can soon rob her of her sparkle. Let her have her career. She'll wither on the vine if she's forced to be just a hausfrau, unless you have enough money to allow her to be a constant hostess and an extravagant home decorator.

The Leo girl usually makes a jewel of a wife. You'll seldom see her dressed frumpily in a tatty bathrobe, wearing curlers and wrinkle cream. Not that she skips the beauty treatments. The typical lioness will spend hours in front of the mirror and a fortune on cosmetics, but she wants you to see the results, not the strategy. There may be times when you feel you're supporting her hairdresser's entire family. Many a husband of a Leo woman finds himself pleading, "Honey, do you have to spend so much money at the beauty parlor?" But few lionesses like to do their own hair. A shampoo and set makes them feel pampered, and feeling pampered does something for every Leo.

Unless she has a Cancer, Virgo or Capricorn ascendant, you may have to watch her with charge accounts. Leos easily slip overboard when it comes to spending for fine feathers, furnishings for the home or gifts for friends. Her wardrobe can be quite extensive. She can look luscious in evening gowns, dripping with sequins and rhinestones, or low-cut, dressy outfits. But she'll probably prefer casual clothes and sportswear, if she's a typical Leo girl. She likes tailored cuts and rich materials, but not necessarily frills and ruffles. Soft cashmeres, good Italian knits and imported English tweeds are her favorites. Her taste is usually excellent, if a bit expensive. An occasional Leo woman will overdo and bury her sense of style in gaudy, shocking clothes, but she's an exception to the general rule of the traditional leonine exquisite flair for fashion.

You'll find her a superb hostess when you bring the boss home for dinner. He'll think you're a genius to have won her. She'll probably make a hit with his wife, too, because the lioness is popular with both men and women, and each sex gets treated to her friendly smile and her outgoing personality equally. Anyone who happens to be standing in her bright sunlight feels the warmth. Leos seldom cast a shadow.

As a mother, she'll pour love on her children generously and lavish affection on them. It won't be easy for her to see their faults, but when she does, she'll be strict. Since she can't stand being taken for granted, if the children don't respect her she can pout in regal silence. Many Leo mothers have a peculiar way of spoiling the child without sparing the rod, quite a contradiction when you think about it. She may romp and play with her cubs, have long, chummy talks with them, but she'll also teach them to snap to attention like soldiers, polish their manners, and be obedient to their elders. At the same time, there's a danger of providing a shade too much spending money, and giving in to requests for luxuries. In a way, you might say she treats her offspring like petted members of a royal family, deeply loved, but expected to mind their p's and q's, especially in public. She'll be fiercely proud of their accomplishments, and heaven help the outsider who attempts to hurt them or judge them unfairly. With all this, she won't smother the youngsters. She's too independent to hover over them every second. She'll lead her own life, keeping a watchful eye out for her cubs, from a distance. Many Leo women are working mothers, but their youngsters seldom starve for attention. The career-minded Leos usually manage to balance motherhood and a job with perfect aplomb.

There are times when she'll lose her dignity and poise and become a rollocking, playful lioness, with a flair for pure slapstick. She can roar with laughter like a healthy animal, but when the moment is gone, the satin voice and regal bearing return. No one can squelch a fresh remark or a rude question with as much cold contempt as a Leo female. She doesn't appreciate familiarity from strangers. Although she'll clown around and be surprisingly casual with intimates, outsiders are expected to keep their place.

In the area of faithfulness, the Leo woman may remind you of the old toast, "Here's to me and here's to you, and here's to love and laughter—I'll be true as long as you— not a single minute after." Enough said.

Don't be jealous of her knack for being the center of attention in a roomful of admiring males. Heads always turn when the lioness smoothly glides by. She feels it's only natural for men to pay court to her. She may encourage masculine compliments and indulge in light, innocent flirtations, because her deep need for applause and adulation covers a strange fear that she's not feminine enough and she must constantly reassure herself that she's desirable. It doesn't mean she's not still in love with you, just because she smiles at your best friend and tells him she adores his new sports jacket. But don't try telling *her* best friend you like her new skirt. That's a whole different ball game. What's sauce for the gander is not sauce for the goose, to reverse the old nursery rhyme. If she hears you call your secretary anything much more intimate than "Miss What's-her-name," your purring kitten may scratch.

Of course, it's not fair. But if you want to be the proud possessor of all those gorgeous brilliantly-colored feathers, you have to make a few concessions. After all, owning a peacock is hardly the same thing as owning a cuckoo bird or a cooing pigeon. Humor her vanity. She'll probably be important in her own right, because few Leo women can resist competing with men for prestige, if not income. Your lioness could be anything from an actress to a surgeon.

One of my best friends and favorite Leos is a well-known New York psychiatrist. Granted, it's a career which permits her to lecture and advise (Leo's favorite pastime), but she gives her counsel with such a warm smile, sparkling eyes and deep compassion, her patients feel better just being in the same room with her. Her husband pays her all the respect and adoration she demands as her royal right, but he has a profession of his own to match hers. He's a gifted writer and poet, talents which always impress the sentimental Leo. They share equal billing in front of the footlights, yet he's the man and the boss behind the scenes. A perfect success formula for taming the lioness.

And that's the key to a smooth relationship with your Leo girl. Don't let her smother you—but don't try to top her. Just paste a big, bright star on her dressing room door, and puff up your ego. You're quite a guy, you know—to have won the hand of the proud lioness. Tell me, how did you manage to do it?

The LEO Child

> *"Tweedledum and Tweedledee*
> *Agreed to have a battle;*
> *For Tweedledum said Tweedledee*
> *Had spoiled his nice, new rattle."*

Remember the game you used to play called Follow the Leader? Remember the little fellow who always sulked when he didn't get to be leader? If he was the same pal who loaned you money to buy licorice sticks and Eskimo pies when your allowance ran out, you must have had a Leo in your neighborhood gang.

The typical lion cub is sunny, happy, playful, and jolly when he gets his own way. When he doesn't, storm clouds gather out of nowhere, along with a thunderous roar, or a hurt, brooding withdrawal. Even if he does seem to be a bit full of himself, the young Leo shouldn't be constantly put down. Suppressing his enthusiasm and high spirits can cause deep scars that may darken his Sun for years. Little lions and lionesses have a habit of bossing the other children which often annoys the mothers of more inhibited youngsters, but they should be restrained gently and never scolded harshly in front of playmates. The great pride of the Leo reacts violently to an attack on vanity, especially in public.

It's good to encourage the natural leadership in Leo children, but they should be taught that everyone must have his turn, because that's the fair way, even if they are stronger than the others.

The leonine sense of justice will usually cause the youngster to see the light. He's not maliciously aggressive. He just has a compulsion to head for the front of the parade. These boys and girls have a strong urge to show off, and it's hard to discourage if it's allowed to get out of hand. The little lion is the one who proudly stands on his head in the schoolyard or walks on a fence to thrill the girls. Wise parents will begin early to make the Leo child realize that showing off is really very undignified. This normally works like a charm, since Sun-ruled children have an innate sense of dignity.

You'll notice it in the tiniest Leos. There's a sort of regal bearing, which creates the impression that baby is monarch of all he surveys. The term "His majesty, the baby" was coined to describe a Leo infant. Little cubs will begin early to rule the roost, wrapping mother and daddy and the entire retinue of relatives around their fingers with very little effort. It's the oddest thing, but a small lion sitting on his throne—I mean in his high chair—covered with prune juice and egg yolk, and needing a change of diapers, will somehow manage to keep his dignity intact. It comes naturally to a Leo baby to allow doting parents and admiring friends to pay homage to him, while he graciously

accepts their attention, gifts, and flattering tributes. He
finds adoration very easy to take. Notice the pleased, smug
look on his face when strangers stop to make a fuss over
him.

Your Leo child will be more reckless than the average
youngster, take more chances and be more active. Then
will come those periodic spells of leonine laziness, when
he'll lie around the house too tired to lift a finger, except
to motion for you to wait on him. Leave him alone and
make him understand no one is his servant. If he wants
something, he can get it himself when his energy returns.
Otherwise, a spoiled Leo child can become a regular tyrant.
Now and then, of course, it doesn't hurt to bring him a
book, hand him a glass of chocolate milk or otherwise perform a friendly favor. But a little such submission to the
lion's whims is plenty, unless you have a secret urge to be
a lady-in-waiting or a prince's equerry. Leo youngsters who
have been trained that they must respect the rights of others
if they are to be respected themselves can be lots of fun
to live with. They're as playful and affectionate as those
adorable little cubs you see at the zoo, and like the cubs,
they need strict and loving discipline. The warm kiss and
the tough birch rod will both have to be employed frequently by lion tamers. Either one without the other is
always ineffective and dangerous.

There are two kinds of Leo boys and girls. The first
kind are the extroverts, gay, cheerful, outgoing, warm and
generous, if a bit pushy at times. The others are quieter,
almost timid on the surface. Such outwardly bashful little
lions may have suffered a serious blow to their vanity from
domineering parents or from too much attention being
paid to brothers and sisters. Secretly, they need power and
applause as much as the others. The danger in such situations, if they're prolonged, is that the Leo child will either
get the attention he seeks later in life by forcing issues at
the wrong time with the wrong people, or retreat into painful shyness and destructive frustration. Leo ego, unnatural-
ly bottled up for long periods, is most unhealthy.

As youngsters, Leo boys may like to play with soldiers
and enjoy games of challenge with a strong element of
chance. The little female Leo will be ladylike, if strong-
willed, may enjoy nice clothes and being told she's pretty,
and will probably like being given responsibilities around
the house. An occasional Leo girl is a tomboy, but vanity

will eventually win out, and the phase passes. Don't expect these youngsters to enjoy taking out the garbage or clearing the floors. They will rebel against menial tasks, so assign them more important and dignified duties that give them a sense of authority.

Teachers can expect the Leo students to do a little instructing of their own. They love to explain things to others, and nothing delights them more than playing the role of substitute instructor when the teacher has to leave the room. It puts them in the spotlight. Normally, the Leo child left in charge at school will administer discipline happily, but now and then his playful spirit will come forth, and the teacher can return to find a three-ring circus in progress.

Young Leos can learn fast when they want to. They're intelligent, and are often richly rewarding to the patient teacher, but they have a tendency to be a little lazy about learning. They prefer to slide by on sunny personality and ingratiating charm. Teachers can be a little sun blinded by their smiles and compliments, and it's not unusual for little cubs to get better grades than they deserve. They may have to be forced to develop good study habits. On second thought, forcing is a waste of time. The easiest way to raise the grades of a Leo child is to appeal to his vanity, to make him want to be superior to the others. That will usually turn the trick. When he's good, pat him on the back so he really feels it. Light taps won't do. No matter how many compliments he gets, he's always hungry for more.

These children will probably require more spending money than their more frugal friends. Your Leo child may give away most of his spare nickels, but he won't short-change himself, either. It's a good idea to teach him the rule the Rockefeller children were taught about finances: "Give some, spend some, save some." Especially the last.

When they grow older, the young lions and lionesses will notice the opposite sex much sooner than youngsters born under other Sun signs. Expect a turbulent adolescence, because your Leo child will be up and down emotionally a hundred times a day. Both his friendship and his romances will be terribly dramatic, and full of colorful ecstasy and heartbreak. All Leo children love to go to parties. Give them plenty of freedom, or they'll simply take it. Harsh orders destroy their pride and dignity. If you build the courage and flatter the ego of your young Leo by telling him sincerely you know he can do it, he'll proudly be strong for you.

It's never an easy task to raise an August child. There will be moments when you feel your caged lion will never be tamed. But he can be, if you remember that he needs gentle and continuous discipline—and love and affection are the two magic keys that unlock his golden heart. It's not the lions who were adored as children who grow up into unhappy adults. It's the little cubs who were emotionally starved and neglected. Remember that he'll pretend to be very brave, but secretly fears he isn't. Hug him tightly every night and love him with all your heart.

The LEO Boss

"Now don't interrupt me,
I'm going to tell you all your faults . . ."

It puzzled her very much at first
But after watching it a minute or two
She made it out to be a grin.

You have a Leo boss and you've worked for him for over a year? Really? You must be a very good listener.

Your Leo boss will probably feel that corporate taxes, government regulations and union rules were all invented as a personal conspiracy against him, but he'll dispose of them easily. Most lions are excellent organizers and perfect geniuses at delegating authority. His way of implementing such annoying situations is to turn to you and dictate, with great flourish, some resounding phrases on the general subject, then wave his hand regally, and with a gorgeous smile say vaguely, "You take it from there." Then he'll probably add that he'd like the report completed and placed on his desk as soon as possible. "Take your time," he'll say. "As long as I get it before noon tomorrow." Leos are not fond of details. They prefer to paint the picture in bold strokes and let you worry about bothersome trifles like figures and statistics.

The classic example of a Leo boss is one I know who called in his secretary to dictate an answer he had prepared for an especially important client. "Have you decided what you want to say?" asked the innocent girl, shorthand book open, pencil poised. "Yes, I have," smiled her Leo employer. "Tell him maybe. Got that? Maybe. You fill in all the other stuff." With those masterful instructions, he cheerfully went to lunch where he entertained several people at an expensive bistro, played a few rounds of golf, returned to the office around five o'clock and wanted to know if the letter was ready. It was. (The secretary was a Virgo.) After reading it with solemn approval, the Leo reached for the phone and quoted the letter to an associate. His words floated through the office door to the long-suffering secretary. "How do you like it?" he asked into the receiver. "I think I did an excellent job of putting the whole situation together and making it clear where we stand, don't you? Of course, I've always had a way of expressing myself. My wife is always telling me I should be a writer," he finished modestly.

This may be a somewhat extreme case, but you will find echoes of such an attitude lingering in the air if you have a typical Leo boss. Give him all your original ideas. He'll love you for it. August-born executives tend to favor employees who add creative thinking to the firm. However, be prepared to see him grinning like a Cheshire Cat the next day as he proceeds to organize the plan you gave him the night before, tossing out the startling comment, "It's one of the best ideas I ever had." He honestly believes he thought of it first. Truly. Of course, you triggered his imagination, which is why you're so valuable to him. But it was *his* idea. Remember that.

Now and then your Leo boss may seem a tiny bit ungrateful. Like he'll toss a huge stack of letters on your desk because he can't be bothered or bored reading them himself. Then the next morning, when you're bleary-eyed from staying until midnight to finish the extra work he threw at you, he'll shake his lion's mane disapprovingly, and mumble a comment on the sloppy condition of your desk, as he walks to his own plush lair. Oh, yes, he's almost sure to have a luxurious private office. It may have soft lights, music, flowers, a down-cushioned sofa and a cherry-wood desk. Even if the budget is small, you'll seldom find him surrounded by pineapple crates and dingy window panes with no draperies. The walls may be covered with excellent prints of good paintings or photos of himself, taken with important dignitaries. Any awards or certificates he's earned will be neatly framed, and hung in a prominent spot.

Another Leo boss I know had an assistant who worked overtime every night and all day on Saturdays and Sundays for three months on a special promotion. She also managed to move filing cabinets, pack huge boxes of merchandise and change the bottles in the water cooler every other day. Meanwhile, she found time to do her boss's Christmas shopping and pick up his cleaning once a week. One bright, sunny morning she overheard him singing her praises to a vice president of the firm. "That Hester is a real jewel," he was saying. "I don't know what I'd do without her. The girl is really fantastic. Of course, she's a little bit lazy, but you can't expect to find everything in one person."

Did Hester quit on the spot? I should say not. Why should she let a little thing like that bother her? She's a smart girl, who knows that anyone's efforts seem drab when they're compared to her boss's fabulous vitality (in between his daily beauty naps on the velvet chaise lounge in his private office). Why should she leave a boss who never fails to admire her new dress? She would hardly hand in her resignation to a man who presented her with a topaz bracelet for her birthday, a set of Waterford crystal for her hope chest, and who so sweetly understood that the color of her typewriter made her nervous. He even painted it bright yellow for her, though he was a little sloppy, and some of the paint dripped on the keys. It came off on her fingers for weeks afterwards, but she didn't mind, because it was a pleasure to wash her hands every hour with the scented soap he keeps in the washroom.

Her Leo boss helped her father find a new job, paid her mother's hospital bill, and generously gave in to her requests to hire her cousin in the mail room. Besides, she's proud of his reputation in his profession. He won two awards last year; he's dictating a book to her about his life; he's listed at the top of the best dressed men in *Esquire;* he's deeply in love with his wife, adores his children, and has caused the firm's profits to go sky high, in spite of those wild chances he took a couple of times. He seldom notices if she takes extra time at lunch. Last week, he found her a larger apartment with lower rent and scolded her fiancé because he wasn't treating her right. Quit? What do you mean, quit?

If you're a man who works for a Leo executive, you have some special problems. Be original, daring, creative, and hard working. But remember that he will always be more original, daring, creative and hard working than you —in his eyes. Say "Yes" to most of his brainstorms (and he'll have quite a pack of them in the course of a week). If you must say "No," precede it with a huge compliment and close it with another one. Sandwiched in between that kind of appreciation, he might accept it. But be tactful and proceed carefully.

Even the gentler, less showy Leo executives normally like to spread sunshine, and have oodles of delightful charm. When your leonine boss gets every last ounce of credit he deserves, plus an extra helping of respect for good measure, he'll make you glow with his praise of a job well done. He'll never be stingy with compliments. He won't hold back his disapproval either. The lion is apt to point out your mistakes with very little discretion. Employees with ultra sensitive natures would be happier working elsewhere. So would those with large egos of their own. There's more than a trace of arrogance in your Leo employer, but it's probably tempered with good-natured optimism. He'll keep things humming and running smoothly. Leos were born to command, with an enviable talent for assigning the right jobs to the right people and seeing that they're finished on time.

Office intrigues will anger him. He simply can't stand people keeping secrets from him. He must know everything that's going on. Don't be annoyed if your Leo boss is a bit nosey about your private affairs or gives you lectures on how to run your personal life. It's really a stamp of royal approval. It means he likes you enough to want to protect you by giving you the advantage of his superior wisdom.

Leo bosses can be very funny. They can have fearful rages, and then pout behind closed doors for hours when they think they've been insulted. They melt under flattery despite themselves. They dress well, eat well and sleep well. They're warm and generous to a fault, and if they get the respect they demand, they can turn failure into victory overnight with an awesome strength of character. The lion gets tremendous inner satisfaction from giving orders, and delivering lectures is something he's especially fond of doing.

You may have the kind of Leo employer who hides his hunger for the spotlight under a quiet demeanor. But the typical dignity, pride and vanity of the Sun sign is just as much a part of his basic nature as it is with the dramatic types. Any doubts? Try to puncture his ego in the smallest way; then stand back out of range.

One Leo boss I had, who fell into the quiet pussycat category, used to call a special meeting of the entire staff in his office every Tuesday morning. The ostensible reason was to improve working relationships, but the real motive behind those weekly sessions was that they were the shy Leo's big chance to deliver his thoughts to a captive audience. Bless his heart, it was his moment on stage.

When he's treated right, there's no one on earth who can be as lovable as the lion. What if he does seek admiration in huge doses to feed his insatiable vanity? Most of the time, he honestly deserves to be admired. He may plagiarize your ideas and rob you of credit now and then. You may weary of listening to his condescending advice and of telling him how super he is. But no other boss would have let you keep the baby carriage right next to your desk that time you lost your sitter. Of course, you would have preferred the time off to care for the infant at home. But the boss needed you at the office. And after all, he's the baby's Godfather.

The LEO Employee

The sun was shining on the sea,
*   Shining with all his might:*
He did his very best to make
*   The billows smooth and bright—*
And this was odd, because it was
*   The middle of the night.*

If your employee is a typical Leo, it will be almost impossible to ignore him. If he's a quiet Leo, it wouldn't be wise to ignore him. The more aggressive lion will force you to appreciate his talents and recognize his value by simply telling you how wonderful he is. The shy pussycat type will pout until you give him the same treatment. It adds up to the same thing. Don't ignore your Leo employees.

Whether the lion roars from center stage or bides his time in the wings, he is proud. He is dignified. He knows his superiority and he doesn't want anyone to overlook it. Leos are not the kind to hide their light under a bushel. If tribute isn't paid to their vanity, both types of lions will find another savannah to honor with their presence. They can't bear to be underestimated.

All Leos love titles. The bigger and fancier, the better. Offer the lion a substantial raise, but give the fellow at the next desk the title of "Chief of Office Coordination," and the lion won't thank you for the extra cash in his pay envelope. He'll be too busy brooding over the increased status of his co-worker, who couldn't possibly deserve such a promotion as much as he does, of course.

It's not perversity that causes him to insist on his rights. He was born to be the master of all he surveys. Leadership is an inherent part of his nature and impossible to root out completely. Leo is fully equipped to take charge. He feels useless and helpless, as well as unwanted, when he's not assuming some kind of obligation. If there's nothing else available to build his sense of importance, he'll get it by handing out free advice to his friends and family. Strangers won't be neglected, either. Leo scatters his pearls of wisdom impartially. He'll tell you how much you should pay for having an extra room built over your garage, counsel your secretary about her alimony problems, inform the cleaning woman what kind of ointment to use on her sore toe, and explain to the mailman how he could make his deliveries more efficiently. The less important he is on the job, the more seriously he'll practice his counseling service.

I know one Leo man (the quiet type) who worked for a large company. For years, his family had the vague impression that he was the district sales manager. In reality, he was an ordinary salesman and a route supervisor, as well as one of the most indispensable men in the company. Since he couldn't be sales manager until the well-qualified man who held the title had retired, the Leo swallowed his injured pride, and satisfied his leonine vanity by allowing his family to assume he had the position.

His enormous sense of responsibility was evident in his consistent loyalty and devotion over the years. He spent a quarter of a century supplying creative advertising ideas to the firm that paid off in steadily rising profits. At the same time, he competently supervised the company's truck routes at all hours, in all kinds of weather, and waited for the recognition he deserved, but his promotion to the top position was always just around the corner. When the sales manager finally retired, a younger man was brought in from New York to take over. That was the day the Leo quit. There was a heavy Capricorn influence in his chart, so the situation was easier for him to bear than it would have been for the typical Leo, but he'll carry the scars of the deep wound to his pride all his life. There's nothing in this world as sad as the sight of the dignified lion robbed of the respect he desperately seeks and has honestly earned.

You had better make a note that the leonine sense of responsibility, which can be so impressive, usually doesn't show itself until maturity. In his youth, the lion is the classical playboy, prancing joyously through days and nights of wine, women and song, wearing the flashiest clothes in the group, making everyone laugh at his clown-like antics and roaring when someone steps on his magnificent tail.

It's usually wise to use young Leo employees in promotion and sales. They're natural showmen, and they'll keep your customers happy with their warm, sunny dispositions. Later, as they mature, the big cats can gradually be eased into the top positions, where they'll usually live up to every bit of responsibility you give them. It's a smart boss who knows at what point the lion has graduated from the role of playboy prince to the just, dignified king.

It's a strange thing about Leos of both sexes. Underneath their brave fronts, they secretly fear they have no real courage. They can behave with the most exasperating pride and outrageous vanity, display insufferable ego, exhibit periods of pure laziness. Then along comes a crisis or emergency, either on the job or in their personal lives. Suddenly, to everyone's surprise, the lion and lioness show themselves to be the steady ones. Only under great pressure, weighed down by the heaviest burdens life has to offer, does the inner strength born in this Sun sign come forth in all its glory.

Jacqueline Kennedy's childhood of ease and comfort left people totally unprepared for her incredible courage in the face of unspeakable tragedy. The Leo with the reputation of a playboy will surprise his friends when he bravely and cheerfully supports an invalid wife and two elderly aunts after a thoughtless, carefree, irresponsible youth. Those born under the sign of the Lion and ruled by the Sun never guess what awesome power they possess until the test comes. Until that time, always remember, they are only pretending to be strong. The lion's fierce roar hides an inferiority complex which is totally unnecessary.

If Leo can't be the boss, then he must have a position where he can display his talents and abilities to the world in some way. After changing jobs a dozen times because he hasn't advanced to at least a vice presidency, the typical Leo will usually head for a profession where he can be his own boss. If the role of executive or leader is denied them, they're happier as teachers, salesmen, doctors, lawyers, managers, counselors, speakers, announcers, actors, actresses, writers or even plumbers and tourist guides. The lion seeks an occupation which allows him to give his superior knowledge to others in some manner, or to stand in the bright spotlight of publicity. They shine the brightest in the fields of politics and public relations.

Keep in mind that the Leo employee will either become an executive on your own level in a reasonable length of time, or he'll leave. He can never be content to work behind the scenes. The applause he needs is out front. Still, you're lucky to have the lion for whatever period he remains with you. He'll work harder than almost anyone else to show you what a wonderful person he is, and a steady supply of compliments will inspire him to a point where he'll show an unbelievable vitality far beyond the limits of normal endurance. Withholding flattery from your Leo employee will rob you of at least fifty percent of his potential value.

See that your lioness gets her vanity plumped up regularly too. Occasionally bring her a yellow rose to tuck in her hair, and never mind the whispers of the gossips. You can't afford to lose her. The gossips don't have her virtues and abilities. Tell her frequently how lovely she looks, how smart she is, and occasionally hand her complimentary tickets to a concert or a gala affair. Always two tickets, please, because the Leo girl will invariably be married, be in love or have a special boy friend in all seasons.

As for the lion, take him to lunch often, in an expensive restaurant, where important people can see him with the big man. Let both your male and female Leo employees be the ones to train new workers when you can. They won't mind the extra work, they'll be proud of the responsibility and they'll love telling others what to do and how to do it.

A little astrological psychology, cleverly applied, can make your proud, touchy Leos a real credit to the company. They'll decorate the office with their grace and enthusiasm. Surround them with bright lights, vivid yellow or orange draperies and carpets, and the most expensive desks and typewriters you can afford. Nothing depresses a Leo's spirit more than having to work with shabby, obsolete equipment, unless it's working with pessimistic, unimaginative people.

They'll need generous expense accounts and a little extra time for lunch. Meals are social occasions for Leos, and they use such opportunities to practice their art of promoting. Just give them the barest idea to start with, and they'll explode it into a dramatic campaign which may bring in lots of new customers. You can't expect them to operate at full speed when they have to watch the clock and worry about money. Leos can be fast with figures, but somehow they seldom learn the knack of counting pennies.

As for the clock, it cramps their style. The lion is easy to tame, when you know how. Relax the rules slightly and let down the bars a little. These employees can't be fenced in, or they'll sulk away the hours and lose their bright incentive.

It's smart to hire a Leo. He'll add a dash of excitement and he can carry some gigantic loads on his back without complaining. He needs a rich diet of compliments, authority, raises, titles and freedom, but it's not too high a price to pay for his intelligence, loyalty, faith, ideas and sense of responsibility. After all, how many bosses have royalty on the payroll? Feed both your big cats and shy pussycats plenty of catnip, and they'll justify it by being your biggest boosters, as proud of your company as if they owned it themselves. The lion's heart is as big as his ego.

> *"If seven maids with seven mops*
>   *Swept it for half a year,*
> *Do you suppose," the Walrus said,*
>   *"That they could get it clear?"*
> *"I doubt it," said the Carpenter,*
>   *And shed a bitter tear.*

VIRGO the Virgin

August 24th through September 23rd

How to Recognize VIRGO

"Only mustard isn't a bird," Alice remarked.
"Right as usual," said the Duchess;
"What a clear way you have of putting things!"

Virgo is the sign of the virgin, but you can't take the symbolism too literally. I can assure you that a September birthday is no guarantee of virginity. Although lots of Virgos remain bachelors and spinsters, there are also plenty who finally settle into connubial bliss. They may not do so with any sudden burst of fire and passion, because marriage is not a natural state for the Virginian nature; yet it's surprising how many of them master its teamwork, and they're almost always devoted to their families.

Married or single, it's fairly simple to spot the Virgo in public. For one thing, he won't be making much noise. He's not exactly garrulous, and he'll stand out as a loner. See that gentle, attractive man over there in the corner, with the thesaurus under his arm? The one with the tick-tock mind, clicking away the hours neatly and methodically noticing the smallest details? If you look closely, you can almost see him measuring each minute for what it's worth. He's a Virgo. See that quiet girl with the beautiful, soft eyes, waiting for the bus? Notice her spick-and-span white gloves, her cool manner. She'll have the exact coins for the fare ready in her hand. She wouldn't dream of asking the bus driver to change a five dollar bill. She's a Virgo.

Social gatherings are not the best hunting grounds when you're searching for these perfectionists. You're more likely to find them working late at the office than being gregarious at a cocktail party. It's not easy for Virgos to relax sufficiently to enjoy the carefree social swim, because they're basically uncomfortable in crowds. They sometimes make attempts to follow the party routine, through pure frustration, but duty whistles too insistently to allow for much frivolity. Sometimes, Virgo can make Capricorn

look like a good-time Harry, and that's really going some.
You'll seldom see them blowing bubbles in the air or
building castles in the sand. Virgos are too busy to daydream, and they're usually too tired at night to wish on
stars.

The first thing you'll notice about the typical Virgo is
the definite impression he gives that there's a serious problem on his mind he's struggling to solve—or a vague
feeling that he's secretly worried about something. He
probably is. Worry comes naturally to him. One might
even say he's affectionately attached to the habit. It's an
intangible thing, and elusive, but his delightful smile will
always seem to be hiding some great trouble.

Although the ascendant and other natal positions can
modify the typical Jack Spratt spare figure, you can generally look for a rather wiry build, and unusually lovely,
quiet eyes. Virgo eyes are often so astonishingly clear
you can almost see your reflection in them. They sparkle
with intelligence and clarity of thought. There's a purity and
tranquility of expression on Virgo features that seems to
deny those secret worries. Most of them are extremely
attractive, with delicate noses, ears and lips. There's certainly no lack of grace and charm, and there may be
a bit of vanity which pops up at odd moments. Virgos are
very critical of their own photographs and fussy in the
extreme about how they look, both on film and in person.
If you're observant, you'll catch them primping in front
of a mirror when they think no one is looking. They're
always well turned out, and usually meticulous, if conservative, dressers. Virgo Maurice Chevalier would rather be
caught without a song than without his boutonniere and his
tie tack.

The Virgo is normally a small person, certainly no
giant, but he's muscular, and he has far more strength
than his fragile appearance suggests. These people can
stand more intense work over a longer period of time than
the tougher, more brawny signs—if they can avoid a
nervous breakdown in the process. Although they're ex-
ternally capable and cool, inner anxieties gnaw away at
them, upsetting their digestion and their emotional balance.
Tackling more work than they can safely manage, and
then straining themselves to the breaking point to fulfill
the obligations is behind many a Virgo's ragged nerves.
They were meant to be calm and soothing when their intri-

cate and delicate mechanisms are running smoothly and
the wheels aren't clogged with brain fatigue.

Virgos are unquestionably dependable and sincere.
Nevertheless, they're capable of pretending to be sick when
they don't want to go somewhere or do something. At
these times, the latent Virginian talent for acting comes
forth. Occasionally, they manage to convince themselves
of such imaginary ills, but the cool eye and clear head of
Mercury-ruled people insure that most instances of such
self-deception are short-lived. They are fastidious and
exacting in grooming, eating, working and romance. Your
neat Virgo friend who looks as if he just stepped out of the
shower probably just did. He takes more baths and showers
than any four people you know put together. He also has
very precise ideas about health, little patience with laziness,
and very few illusions about life and people, even when he's
in love. Male or female, romance never clouds Virgo's
eyes with a thick enough film to blind him to any existing
flaws and shortcomings in either the relationship or in the
loved one. To use the idiom of the day, Virgo always
"knows where it's at," though the slang-hating Virgos will
shrink in distaste from that phrase.

Of course, you shouldn't get the idea that everyone born
in late August or September is fussy, prissy and dogmatic.
Lots of Virginians shine with a clever Mercury wit—if you
catch their side remarks—and they project a bright, Mercurial charm that's hard to resist. Sophia Loren is a Virgo,
which should settle that point once and for all. You may
run across a Virgo who is so busy keeping the corners of
his (or her) mind neat and orderly that he's become careless about his clothing or his surroundings, which may fool
you when you catch him in an off moment. But wait.
Sooner or later you'll find him picking up a pin from the
rug, brushing his hair or pinching a piece of lint off his
shoulder.

Although they dream very few impossible dreams, Virgos often have the inconsistent trait of looking like lovely
dreamers—as if they were all wrapped up in the very rainbows their logical minds refuse to believe in or follow.

When they're annoyed by vulgarity, stupidity or carelessness, Virgos can suddenly become cranky, irritable, scolding and nervous. But most of the time they're gentle folk,
and quite nice to have around, especially around the sick
room. Some of the finest nurses are born under this sign,

full of efficient sympathy and crisp capability. When you have a headache, your Virgo friend is the one most likely to run to the drugstore for you. If you're at his place, he won't have far to go, because there will probably be a miniature drugstore right in his house. His bathroom medicine cabinet is usually loaded down with patent reliefs for stomach-ache, constipation, upset liver or acid indigestion. Peek inside sometime. He'll never take a drug unless he's familiar with each ingredient and how it works, so he'll be an expert at telling you which remedy will be best for your headache, depending on what caused it. Virgos who travel often take their portable drugstores right along with them. They may carry an extra suitcase, just for the pills and bottles. If they're used to a certain brand of soap or lotion, they'll tuck that in, too. It would be a disaster if they happened to get stuck in a town where they didn't sell what the Virgo is accustomed to using. He usually buys his soap and sundries by the case, because it's cheaper—or at least by the dozen—which is another reason he doesn't like to purchase things en route. Sometimes a Virgo will even tote his own water with him on trips. Don't laugh— do you know what can happen to a person's stomach when certain foreign bodies in strange drinking water enter the digestive system? Virgos can tell you. When these people form habits, they form habits, and taking a vacation or a business trip is no excuse to break them. If he's used to keeping his socks in the middle left-hand drawer of the bureau at home, that's where the socks go in the hotel room. If it's one of those bureaus with only three large drawers, and no choice of left or right, it can really hang him up for awhile. He may end up just leaving them in the suitcase, but his sleep will be restless. The next morning, the waitress in the hotel dining room will quickly learn that when the Virgo says three-minute eggs, he doesn't mean two minutes and forty-five seconds. Or when he says sunnyside up, he doesn't mean sunnyside down. And he'll definitely base his tip on her attention to such details.

A Virgo may criticize your statements with hairsplitting arguments which drive you wild, but if you are in a jam, he'll also quickly step in to turn things right side up again with no motive except to serve. If the job you tackled has you so bogged down in boring details you despair of meeting the deadline, Virgo will roll up his sleeves and pitch in willingly. It's not ego that makes him itch to take over when things are in a shambles. It's just that his orderly Mercurial mind can't stand procrastination, neglected details or confusion of purpose. He may even straighten things out before he's asked, with no intention of rudeness, because bringing order out of chaos is instinctive with him. He's the kind of guest who will happily help the hostess clean up after the party. But he's also the kind of guest who will notice immediately that you have carefully placed the *Saturday Review* on the coffee table to hide an ugly stain, and arranged the cushions on the couch to cover the cigarette holes.

Like the Libran, Virgo is quick to deny his habits and traits. He has an apparent blindness to his faults and he seems unable to see his own weaknesses in as clear a light as he sees everything else. But the truth is that he does see them—and he sees them in such infinite detail that he can't bear to hear them generalized. Try to tell a typical Virgo he's critical, a worrier, fussy, neat or unusually concerned with diet and health, and you'll face a flat denial. Who, him? He's not like that at all. I still have the ten-page letter from a Virgo housewife, written in a tiny, precise handwriting, in which she carefully details all the reasons why the descriptions of her Sun sign don't fit her, never realizing that the very orderly form and length of her hairsplitting complaint was giving her away.

"I'm just not neat," she wrote. "My house is terribly sloppy." But then she continued, "After all, I do have two very small children, who constantly make messes which drive me crazy. I pick up after them every second of the day." (She then proceeded to itemize her endless chores, one by one, very carefully.) "I try to keep things in a particular spot, and I never waste time reading or watching TV like my neighbors do. But things are still untidy when my husband gets home for dinner. I don't think he has any right to complain, because I do work till after midnight while he's sleeping, getting the house in shape for morning. I couldn't get breakfast in a dirty kitchen. Dirt breeds germs, and sickness spreads fast in a family. But before he leaves for work everything's a mess again. So this neatness thing about Virgos really annoys me. I'm really not neat. I'm also not a worrier nor a hypochondriac. I never criticize my husband's mistakes with the check book, at least not very often, because it's not a wife's place to do that. . . . I'd *like* to be neat, but what can I do with the children and all? Really, if you could see how they . . ." and so on. (Naturally, she carefully included a self-addressed, stamped envelope for a reply.) The last line in her letter wondered, "Can you tell me why the descriptions of my Sun sign don't fit me at all?" Someday I plan to have those pages framed and hang them on the wall under a symbol of Virgo.

You should be able to pick out a Virgo in a roomful of people with no trouble. He's incapable of sitting still for very long. After a while, he'll become visibly restless and pace the floor or change chairs like a jumping jack, and project a vague sense of urgency as if he's late for another appointment somewhere. At the same time, the facial expression will portray a certain tranquility, like a mask. The full damage caused by Virgo's nervous intensity seldom shows completely on the outside, but it surely can mess up the digestive system inside. That's why you'll often find them carrying a roll of Tums for the tummy.

It's important to mention here the still unseen planet Vulcan, the true ruler of Virgo, since its discovery is said to be imminent. The discovery of the true ruler of a sign changes the characteristics of those born under it. To give only one example, during the period when both Aquarius and Capricorn were ruled by Saturn, the February-born, such as Abraham Lincoln, clearly showed the melancholy traits of that planet. But when Uranus (the symbol of electronics and space, and the true ruler of Aquarius) was discovered—in its proper time in the universal plan—Aquarians began to reflect qualities of restless discovery, and a more electric, unpredictable, progressive personality, such as that of Uranus-ruled Aquarian Franklin D. Roosevelt. Many astrologers feel that Vulcan, the planet of thunder, will become visible through telescopes within a few years. Shortly before or after Vulcan moves close enough to the earth to be seen, Virgos now living, as well as those born in the future, will lose much of the Mercurial pressure that causes the present nervous strain, Mercury being more compatible with the airy sign of Gemini than with the earthy Virgo. The thunderous Vulcan will also give to Virgos their astrological inheritance of courage and confidence, and will release many of the typical Virgo inhibitions. After Vulcan is discovered, the last remaining planet to be identified, according to ancient predictions, is Apollo, the true ruler of Taurus. Then each Sun sign will answer to the vibrations of its rightful ruler—twelve signs and twelve heavenly bodies. It's interesting to note that Vulcan, in Greek mythology, is the lame god with the brilliant mind. Many Virgos have a slight limp, or else some peculiar and unusual quality to the walk or posture.

You won't find those people lavish in affection or in spending money. They're normally prudent in both areas, giving their love quietly and steadily with little demonstrativeness, and handling cash just as conservatively. Strangely, as willing as Virgos are to give efficient service to others, they have an almost neurotic and intense dislike of accepting favors themselves. They don't want to be obligated to anyone for any reason. And they don't want to depend on anyone but themselves for anything. The deeply imbedded fear of dependence in old age is what makes many of them live so economically as to be called stingy. But that's really too harsh a word. When there's plenty of security and no need to worry about the future, Virgo will spend money more freely, although even then it will be spent with full value received—or back to the store for a refund.

Though he has absolutely no sympathy for beggars or idle wastrels, he is unfailingly generous when a friend is in trouble. The Virgo who is almost miserly where his personal needs are involved will make charming gestures of financial aid to those who really deserve it, or to people he really likes or loves. But you'll never find him throwing money away carelessly, because waste is one of his pet peeves. Virgos labor hard for what they have, and extravagance never fails to shock them. They usually have a few sharp things to say about spendthrifts and people who are too lazy to work.

There's one thing that will remove some of the sting of Virgo's criticism, however, and that's the knowledge that he's secretly as critical of himself as he is of you. He just can't help seeing the flaws, because he was born to notice the tiniest crack in the vase. He won't take to lateness any more kindly than he does to wastefulness. Actually, to be late is waste of a kind. It's a waste of time, and to Virgo, time is the stuff of which life is made. So be punctual if you want to avoid his stinging disapproval. Frank Sinatra's friends have learned that when the singer says "dinner at eight," he means eight, and not eight-fifteen or eight-thirty. Although Sinatra is a warm, fiery Sagittarian by Sun sign, he does have a Virgo ascendant which also explains why he's so painstaking about rehearsing and such a bug for detail in music arrangements. Every note and every tone must be exactly correct when he records or the session will be repeated until he's satisfied. Add such meticulous and impeccable taste to the Sagittarius fire and warmth and you can see why he sells a song.

It's hard to understand why Virginians are sometimes called selfish, since they usually find more satisfaction in serving others than in satisfying their own personal ambition. The selfish label probably arises from the Virgo ability to say "no" and really mean it. He gives freely of his time and energy, but he won't go beyond the point of reasonableness. When demands become excessive, Virgo will balk and make his objections quiet clear, perhaps too clear. As much as he loves to point out the flaws of others, he fiercely resents open criticism of his own mistakes. When a Virgo makes an error, which will be rare, point it out tactfully if you want to keep his friendship.

Virgos are surprisingly healthy, in spite of their traveling drugstores (unless they worry themselves into illness through overwork, mental tension and pessimism). They take good care of their bodies and they're fussy about their diets. Still, they may complain about minor ailments, such as upset stomach, indigestion, chronic pains in the intestinal area, headaches and foot problems (remember Vulcan, the lame god). They should baby themselves when they have a chest cold, because they're susceptible to lung ailments if their individual planets are afflicted in the natal chart. They may be plagued with pains in the hips, arms, shoulders—gout, arthritis, rheumatic troubles and sometimes sluggish liver and back aches. But the Virgo's concern about his own health will prevent most serious illness. Many of them are vegetarians. If not, you can bet they know exactly what they should eat and how it should be cooked. Now and then you may come across a germ-conscious Virgo who wears rubber gloves to mix a meat loaf or boils his toothbrush every night, but that's an extreme. Still, even the average Virgo will be sure to wash his hands with vigor before a meal.

Virgos like cats, birds and small, helpless creatures. They also like truth, punctuality, economy, prudence and discreet selectivity. They hate gushy sentiment, dirt, vulgarity, sloppiness and idleness. Theirs is a practical nature, with excessive discrimination—the true individualists, whose keen perception keeps their desires clear of muddy, wishful thinking. A fresh breeze blows through the dream of a Virgo, sweeping it free of wisps of wild, inaccurate fancies. Once he's learned to master life's complicated details, instead of letting details master him, he can shape his own destiny with more certainty than any other Sun sign.

Cool green jade and pure platinum complement him and bring him luck. But Virginian good fortune is always followed by five kinds of loneliness, and duty's clarion call is never still within these gentle hearts. Don't forget that the shy, wistful smile of Virgo hides a secret or two. Both the quicksilver of Mercury and the distant thunder of Vulcan run through his quiet blood, as he dresses in his favorite colors of gray, beige, navy blue, all shades of green and stark white. Underneath his serious manner lies the alluring aura of the Virgin—purity of thought and purpose, symbolized by the Virgo hyacinth. Once you've known the fragrance of this Easter flower, you're never quite free of its spell. It returns each spring to haunt the memory. Virgo has its own, secret way of making the heart remember.

Famous Virgo Personalities

Prince Albert	John Gunther
Lauren Bacall	Lyndon Johnson
Robert Benchley	Elia Kazan
Ingrid Bergman	Joseph Kennedy
Leonard Bernstein	Lafayette
Sid Caesar	D. H. Lawrence
Maurice Chevalier	Sophia Loren
Theodore Dreiser	H. L. Mencken
Queen Elizabeth I	Walter Reuther
Henry Ford II	Cardinal Richelieu
Greta Garbo	Peter Sellers
Arthur Godfrey	Robert Taft
Goethe	William Howard Taft

Roy Wilkins

The VIRGO Man

"Why, if a fish came to me,
and told me he was going on a journey,
I should say, 'With what porpoise?' "
"Don't you mean 'purpose'?" said Alice.
"I mean what I say," the Mock Turtle replied
in an offended tone.

We may as well get this out into the open right away. Don't pin your hopes on a Virgo man if your heart is hungry for romantic dreams and fairy tales, or you'll find yourself on a starvation diet. A love affair with a Virgo will dump a warm sentimentalist on the cold ground with a hard thud, and it can hurt.

This man lives almost entirely on a practical, material level, and he has little use for the abstractions of storybook romance. Of course, the whole problem may be academic anyway, since it will take no little effort to bring him anywhere near the threshold of a man-woman relationship in the first place. He's not the type to serenade you beneath your boudoir window. You'll have a long, lonely wait on your moonlit balcony until he starts climbing the rose trellis (or the fire escape, if you live in a walk-up).

Actually, Virgos are deeply involved with love from earliest childhood, but not the Romeo-Juliet kind of love. His chief way of expressing the word is concerned with unselfish devotion to family, friends and those weaker or more disorganized than himself. He was born with an instinctive love of work, love of duty and discipline and devotion to the helpless. Even the unevolved Virgo, who doesn't quite reach such heights, feels slightly guilty that he isn't living up to a selfless ideal in some way.

The kind of love which displays itself in dramatic emotions, sentimental promises, tearful declarations and mushy affection, not only leaves a Virgo man cold, it can frighten him into catching the nearest bus or train out of town. (Planes are too fast and too expensive for him, unless he's really desperate.) But he can be melted if the temperature is just right, even though he seems to be made of a combination of steel and ice. There are definitely ways to the Virgo heart. Secret ways. Aggressive pursuit is not one of them. Neither is coquetry nor sexuality, as many a flirtatious vamp and slinky siren has learned, to her surprise and disappointment.

Virgos seek quality rather than quantity in romance. Since quality is at pretty much of a premium in any category, they have few real love affairs, and the few they do have are destined to be unlucky or sad in some way, more often than not. Virgo's reaction to such a disappointment is normally to bury himself in the hardest work he can find, stay away from society in general, and be twice as cautious at the next opportunity. You can see that you'll have to use considerable strategy and patience. The basic Virginian instinct is chastity, and he's turned from it only for a good cause or for a mighty good woman. Many Virgos—though admittedly not all—can live with celibacy far more easily than any other Sun sign, just as they put up with rules of discipline they don't understand, because obedience to fate without struggling comes naturally to them. If fate decrees a single life, Virgo is prepared to accept it without excess regret or emotional trauma, so there are lots of Virgo bachelors around—but still, in their quiet way, they can manage some very poetic, if fragile, love affairs.

Although he's never obvious, Virgo can be a master of the art of subtle seduction. A couple of generations of women who have trembled inside when a certain Frenchman smiles his shy, gentle smile can tell you all about it. Maurice Chevalier didn't become a legend because he has a singing voice like Caruso, you know. He may not be of my generation, but I too get butterflies in the heart region when I see or hear him.

The Virgo man is a blend of sharp intellect and solid earth. He can be detached enough to break lots of hearts with a cool kind of flirting, but his critical analytical sense and his fastidious discrimination seldom allow these frequent excursions to leave the platonic arena. It has to burn with a white heat to produce real passion in a Virgo. His modesty and selectivity alone prevent undue promiscuity. Of course, there may be an occasional fall into an earthy, physical experience, but such indiscretions are the exception, rather than the rule. The rule is aloof interest. I know one Virgo man who accepted a part in one of those really raw "for adults only" films, but he did it strictly for the cash—he was flat broke at the time—and he still blushes when anyone mentions it. Naturally, a man is a man, and not all Virgos remain technical virgins, but they do always remain pure in outlook. There's invariably something clean and chaste about Virgo love, which is never allowed to become soiled—even in the midst of passion—no matter what unfortunate events may give the outward appearance of casualness.

He'll take his own precious time about finding a love object, because he's as critical and painstaking in the selection of a woman as he is in his eating, grooming, health and work habits. Don't try to fool him or lie to him. Your Virgo lover holds no illusions. He wants a decent, honest and genuine relationship. He knows very well how small his chances are of finding it, but it's useless to expect him to accept anything less. If circumstances ever do involve him in a sordid affair, you can be certain he won't remain in its clutches for long.

He is a difficult man to stir emotionally. He can go for a long time without feeling any burning need for a permanent mate. It's enough to make you cry if you've set your cap for him. You'll wonder if he's made of marble or if he was born without a heart. No, he isn't made of marble and yes, he does have a heart. Be patient. To her who waits comes eventual success.

Now and then a curious, frustrated Virgo may try a fling at deliberate promiscuous behavior, simply to see if he's lacking in masculinity. He's not, of course, and as soon as he discovers it, he seeks no more artificial experiences to prove himself. No cool, clear and collected Virgo can be immune to the call of human nature forever, but once he does succumb, he'll be shy about admitting it. When he's on the threshold of submission, he'll cover his true feelings with elaborate casualness. There is more than a spark of subdued, but extremely refined acting talent in Virgo. He will pretend to be disinterested as cleverly as he pretends to be ill when he's not enjoying himself at a party. Don't expect him to respond with any great display of ecstatic surrender even after he's committed, and while he's still deciding if you're really the one for whom he'll forsake his single state, he'll play it mighty cool, indeed.

Once he's decided it's for real, however, he'll declare himself with touching simplicity. His love will burn with a steady flame, never fluctuating like the love of other Sun signs, and it will give warmth over the years with wonderful dependability. Is that so bad? The one quality of fairy tale romance about Virgo is that, if he's genuinely in love, he will wait for years to claim his true mate, or travel over a thousand mountains to bring her home to his hearth. He's capable of enormous sacrifice in the pursuit of that one dainty foot he's discovered will fit the glass slipper. There's no denying that the flame is strong, once it's been kindled. It's almost impossible to extinguish it. You'll be as eternally adored as Cinderella herself. The trick, I suppose, is in the original kindling. It's a rare foot that fits his glass slipper. Virgo is enormously particular.

After you've caught him, he'll seldom if ever invite your jealousy, and he'll be determined to overcome any rough spots caused by financial problems, relatives or outside interference. He'll show incredible strength through emotional and material hardships, as long as you remain by his side. You couldn't ask for a more tender, gentle companion when your heart is broken for any reason by a cruel world or when you're physically ill. He won't shower you with money, but you'll be well supplied with necessities, and he will shower you with consideration.

A Virgo man is invariably kindly and thoughtful about all those little things which matter to women. He has a crystal clear memory and probably won't forget special dates, though he may be a bit mystified as to why you think they are so important. He won't be wildly, passionately jealous, yet Virgo males are possessive in the extreme. This sounds like a fine line to draw, but it's important. Even though he doesn't throw emotional scenes of jealousy over the attentions other men pay you, his deeply rooted possessiveness should warn you that a little freedom goes a long way. The wife of a Virgo who wanders too far away from the home fires too often may find herself without a husband to return to. Virgos are utterly loyal and they dislike destroying family ties intensely, but when their sense of decency has been finally outraged they won't hesitate to make a cold, clean break in the divorce court. No messy, complicated trial separations for them. When it's over, it's over. Goodbye and good luck. Even the Virgo's sharp, unusually excellent memory won't cause him to cry

sentimental tears over the past, simply because he's able
to discipline his memory as firmly as he does his emotions.
Self-discipline is part of his very nature. The Virgo man
with his mind made up moves on—and having moved on,
all your tears and apologies are useless in getting him to
change his mind. He'll never fall victim to the illusion that
gluing together the broken pieces will recreate perfection
in what has once been seriously flawed.

If your heart is set on a Virgo man, you'd better brush
up your thinking cap and wear it when he's around. Virgos
hate ignorance, stupidity and sloppy thinking almost as
much as they hate dirt and vulgarity, and that's a lot. The
girl who snares the Virgo heart had better be smartly
dressed with a sizable brain under her neat hair style—and
you'll notice I said *neat* hair style. Virgos look for women
who are clean in body and mind, and who dress well, but
not in flashy extremes of fashion.

You won't have to be Julia Child, but for goodness
sakes, don't ever be naive enough to think a Virgo husband
will let you feed him out of cans. A pleasure-seeking,
selfish, mentally lazy woman will never make it with a
Virgo male, even if she's fairly oozing with sex appeal. This
is the very last man in the world you can expect to find
running off with a topless Go-Go girl, though he might
loan her his sweater if she's chilly. When it comes right
down to the nitty gritty, he's looking for a wife—not a
mistress in any sense of the word.

Virgo men have no strong yearning for fatherhood, as
a rule. Their particular kind of ego doesn't seem to require
children for emotional fulfillment, and Virgos tend to have
small families. Yet, once a child or children have been
born, the Virgo is an extremely conscientious parent, and
will never take his responsibilities lightly. He'll spend many
hours teaching his youngsters skills and transmitting his
own high standards of conduct. He'll be cheerfully willing
to help with homework and will probably make no end of
sacrifices for hobbies, music lessons, camp and especially
college. A Virgo father will place great emphasis on intellect and train his children rigidly in matters of ethics,
courtesy and good citizenship. Even the divorced Virgo
will eventually see to it somehow that his offspring are well
cared for, wherever they may be, and that they get an education. Children of Virgo fathers usually grow up with both
a love and respect for books and learning. You'll seldom

find a Virgo parent spoiling a child, and there will always be plenty of necessary discipline. All this is fine, but there may be a need for more physical expressions of love between a Virgo father and his youngsters, since affection is not something that comes naturally to him. Unless a serious effort is made in this area from babyhood on, there's more than a small chance that he'll one day discover an insurmountable barrier has grown between him and the offspring he loves so deeply. There's also a tendency to be too critical, to expect too much too soon and be too strict.

A Virgo will expect you to fuss a bit over his health, but he'll wait on you when you're sick, too, and allow you to be a regular Camille. He may have his cranky and moody spells now and then, perhaps even frequently. But one thing is sure. If you leave him alone, he won't go out of his way to start an argument with you. Just let him get over his grumpiness and he'll surprise you with tenderness to make up for it. Let him worry. It's good for him, sort of a Virgo mental exercise. But when you see it's affecting his physical state, snap him out of it by suggesting something interesting or different to do. It isn't hard to catch the mental attention of a Virgo, though it may be hard to keep it.

Now that you know what you're in for, if you're still in love with that Virgo man, you can look forward to a pretty contented future. You'll have a husband who's alert and well-informed, who won't expect you to wait on him hand and foot or expect you to run around looking sexy all the time with a dab of perfume behind each ear and a rose in your teeth. (Although he may expect you to go around with a cake of soap in each hand.)

He'll be reliable and pleasant, if you're tactful about his faults. He won't have many of them anyway—unless you call the way he runs his finger across the furniture every night, looking for dust, a fault. Little habits like that. No matter what he does, try not to nag him. Remember, he's not constituted to be able to take the critical analysis he applies to others. Get used to his habit of criticizing you, and laugh it off with the realization that he can't help being such a sensitive hairsplitter. Once that resentment is out of the way, you can relax, and really enjoy your bright, loyal Virgo. He's not an angel. There are no wings sprouting on his shoulders. But lots of wives will be jealous of you.

After all, how many women are married to a hardworking, handsome man who's neat and tidy around the house, who remembers anniversaries and performs miracles with the checkbook? How many wives have a smart husband who dresses well, seldom goes out with the boys or makes passes at other women, and is usually gentle and considerate? Look closely again. Is that just the reflection of the street lights around his head, or could it be . . . ? No, it couldn't possibly be a halo. Not after the way he snapped at you when you spilled the buttered popcorn in his lap at the theater tonight. Of course not. That cranky character? Still, there is a kind of an aura. And when he smiles—and you can see yourself in his clear eyes—well, he'll do until someone with real wings comes along.

The VIRGO Woman

She had never quite forgotten that
if you drink much from a bottle marked "poison,"
it is almost certain to disagree with you,
soon or later.

Sometimes she scolded herself so severely
as to bring tears into her eyes.

Do you visualize the Virgo girl as a gentle, virginal maiden, pure as the driven snow? You may be about to get some illusions shattered. She is no White Rock nymph in a gauzy tunic, kneeling by the pool. Sorry to spoil your image.

A Virgo woman can leave her husband for a man she met beside some faraway ocean, bear her lover's child before the benefit of marriage, and face a hostile world with her head held high. That's not very maidenly or virginal. There's a lot to learn about this tender, fragile little symbol of spotless womanhood. For one thing, her spine is made of stainless steel.

It's quite true that she's basically shy. No argument there. Virgo girls don't climb on soap boxes to make fiery, aggressive speeches or chop up saloons with hatchets, like Carry Nation. They don't get arrested for drunken driving, either, and I'll give you a five dollar bill for every one you find featured in a burlesque show. But a Virgo woman is a woman. She has all the necessary wiles and weapons, including a determination to pursue happiness wherever the path happens to lead her. A few prickly thorns along the way won't cause her either to faint or cry weakly for help.

When you hear of a Virgo woman who has outraged the laws of society, be sure you read between the lines. She is basically pure-minded—true. But so is love. Real love. And Virgo is not interested in any other kind. She'll climb the tallest mountains and storm the raging seas in galoshes and a pea jacket, once the spirit of Mercury has been exalted, which can considerably dim that wispy, chiffon image. Remember, too, that Virgo's true ruler, the distant Vulcan, is the god of thunder. A Virgo woman who recognizes her marriage as imperfect and finds a love without a flaw (or thinks she has, which is the same thing), won't hesitate to cut former ties. When she uses the knife, she'll be as cool and precise as a surgeon. Much as she hates to break the family circle, the Virgo hates hypocrisy more.

Once she's accepted a love as true and ideal, the purity of her own concept of the relationship reigns supreme over all the pieces of legal paper in the world. She's the one woman in the zodiac who can be deadly practical and divinely romantic at the same time. That situation of the love affair beside some faraway ocean may seem casual and immoral on the surface. Actually, it's a predictable example of a Virginian behaving true to character when caught in a difficult decision. She'll suffer agonies of embarrassment over the condemnation of society in such an affair, but that won't alter her course of action any more than it will alter the purity of her motivation. It's a perfect example of the firm practicality of Virgo's earth element, blended with the mental, airy, ideal-seeking Mercury. There's a white heat to Virgo love, once it's ignited, that can put the passions of other Sun signs to shame by its very intensity and singleness of purpose. Igniting it may take some time, however.

I will admit that the fiery, physical aspect of love may be somewhat subdued in the typical Virgo female, but there's a mysterious, quiet, waiting quality in this woman and "passion of the spirit" is a most satisfactory substitute to men who prefer the delicacy of understatement in romance.

She's a perfectionist, but that doesn't mean that she herself is perfect. She has her negative traits, and they can be very trying. To begin with, Virgo females have this dogged belief that no one can do things as orderly and as efficiently as they can. What really drives you wild is that—usually—no one can. They're also sticklers for promptness. Did you ever keep a Virgo woman waiting for a date? When she's upset or cranky, she won't rage and storm and break bottles over your head, but she can be shrewish and fussy when you've annoyed her. You might as well expect a frank scolding. An occasional Virgo woman can come pretty close to behaving like a virago, but most of them don't carry it that far. Take her flowers. Admit you're wrong and don't argue. It won't do you a bit of good, you can't win with a Virgo. The earth is her element, so she appreciates the creations of nature, and the posies will soften her irritation. As for the apologies, keep them brief and accurate. The Virginian is nobody's fool. Her clarity of vision will spot an elaborate lie by the smoothest talker, and the faintest smear of lipstick on the edge of a collar. She may be pure-minded, but she's certainly not naive.

I'm not implying that she'll go through your laundry, at least not before you're married. After that, it will be in her house, and she won't feel so guilty about it.

This girl has a mental block when it comes to admitting she's wrong—like a block of wood right in front of her brain—so you'd be smart to take the blame right away. Most of the time, she'll be right, frustrating though it may be. So why fight it? When you've put her back into her normal mood, she's such an exquisite delight, you won't care who won or lost.

If you can bear the wound to your male ego, you might profit from taking her financial advice, or letting her handle the budget. She's concise and practical, and she catches tiny errors even a CPA might overlook. (Unless there are afflictions in her natal aspects, or she has an impulsive ascendant.)

Brush up on your manners and your grammar if you're dating a Virgo female. She won't take kindly to abuse of the language, swearing or drinking from the finger bowl. Don't chew celery close to her ear and it's better if you pass up corn-on-the-cob altogether. That's enough of a challenge at any time, let alone trying to eat it daintily in front of her. Tell the waiter to cut it off and serve it to you on the plate. You'll never pass inspection with sloppy clothing, either. Once in love with a Virgo, you might as well resign yourself to shaving twice a day, and the same goes for showers. Splash on after shave lotion, brush off the lint, spruce up your hair, wear a fresh shirt, mind your manners, and polish your shoes before you go a-courting this girl. And here's a very valuable tip: the next time you're late, pretend you don't realize what time it is. Walk in her door angrily. When she asks you what's wrong, tell her that silly, ridiculous, blasted library (that's about as profane as you'll dare to get) keeps closing five minutes before they're supposed to, according to their rules. It wouldn't be so bad now and then, but they lock the doors on you *every night* when you have all those heavy scientific journals to put away. She'll forget all about the tardiness.

Don't take her to the racetrack and let her see you throw away a week's pay on Golden Chance in the fifth, on the nose. Save your off-color stories for the men at lunch, and tell her constantly you're glad she's not the flighty type. You are, aren't you? She's not a clinging vine, either. Virgo goes to no extremes. She can take care of herself, thank you. But she doesn't have to act like a man to do it.

Don't overpower her with your physical charms or bear hug her on the subway, and don't rush the goodnight kiss on the first or even the tenth date—wait for better things. In general, underplay the whole scene. Move in slowly, with grace and taste, or you'll end up in the orchestra pit with all the other banjo thumpers. Speaking of the theater, she'll probably love it. Parades, too. The pomp and pageantry, the dramatic emotion, give her an outlet for her own tightly controlled emotions. Besides, she's one great critic. Her highly developed intellect and artistic taste combine to give her a keen perception. If you could make Broadway producers understand this, you'd be showered with free passes to out-of-town openings. A Virgo woman will call the critics' reviews in advance almost every time. Discrimination is one of her keywords. She loves plays, concerts and books, but she's severely critical of the content. She's just as critical of your tie and how you wear your hair, what you do and what you say. To criticize is as natural to her as breathing is to you. Virgo is the eternal perfectionist, and without her, we would all be pretty messy and sloppy around the edges. Don't criticize her, however. That's against the rules. The golden rule definitely does not apply here. What she does to you, you'd better not do to her. Her crystal-clear thinking makes her inwardly as aware of her own imperfections as she is of yours, and she judges herself frequently and harshly, which is why she feels she doesn't need any help from you. Of her it can be truly said that she's "her own worst critic."

One nice thing about being in love with this woman is that she'll do all your worrying for you, and possibly even enjoy it. She'll keep you from goofing without robbing you of your manhood, an art that women born under other Sun signs might well imitate.

As for the matter of faithfulness, you may hear of a rare Virgo female who, for her own unfathomable reasons, has decided to toss away virtue with a vengeance, but there's usually a desire to prove something to herself at the bottom of such a spree, and it won't last long. Virgo females who take an occasional whirl down the primrose path of promiscuity are clever enough to cover up the lapse, and such behavior is most certainly an exception. Ordinarily, if she really loves you, you'd be safe to trust the typical Virginian woman with the sexiest man you know on a desert island for a month. For two months? Well, Virgos are human, you know. They're not walking, talking computers. They have hearts warmer than people suspect, and emotions that can thunder with feeling, even if they don't care to rent a billboard to advertise it. The emotional nature of Virgo is controlled, but not nonexistent. Remember that. It will give you courage.

The Virgo girl is annoyingly meticulous about small things, but she can also be the kindest, most generous and affectionate little creature in the world. Consider her perfectionism a virtue, instead of a vice. With all the impulsiveness rampant in the world, what would we do without the sharp eye and mind of Virgo? Even while she's irritating you with her critical ways, there's a lovable quality about her that's downright irresistible. But of course you've already discovered that, or you wouldn't be shaving twice a day and going to the library every night. Her modest manner and soft, clear eyes have done their job well. You've probably even found out how much fun she is when people don't pick on her, and what a clever wit lies inside that pretty head. It's a lovely and strange thing that when Virgo women laugh it often sounds like the peal of little bells.

She has no illusions, so don't try to sell her any phony ideas. To her, truth is beauty—and beauty is truth. Get used to her emptying the ash trays every three seconds, be kind to her stray kittens, and she'll perform the pipe and slippers routine with feminine grace. She'll share herself cautiously, only with one she trusts, and little things mean a lot to her. Despite her modesty and natural shyness, she's tough enough and strong enough for others to find comforting when dark clouds gather. The quiet courage and deep sense of responsibility of Virgo women often acts as a magic glue to hold large families together. She'll probably be a good cook, and she'll never poison you with her soup. Your house will be clean and cozy, and the big bowl on the coffee table will hold apples instead of chocolate candies (bad for the teeth and general health).

You'll probably never see your youngster running around the neighborhood with a runny nose, a jam-stained face or torn sneakers. You won't find tiny fingers scattering your tobacco or coloring on your private papers, either. She'll be a firm disciplinarian. Virgo women seldom have more than one or two children, and don't seem to need motherhood to satisfy their femininity. But once baby has bounced into her life, she'll never neglect his physical, moral or educational needs. She may not supply his emotional needs as easily, but if she's sure of your love and knows she's appreciated, she'll relax and give her offspring plenty of warm affection. Little ones often find Virgo mothers delightfully funny and gentle. They'll be firm, and try to instill good habits, but they have a tender touch that tells a child he's securely loved.

Remember the poem that says you shouldn't buy bread with your last sixpence, but "hyacinths for the soul"? Give this woman both. You may often catch her busy with sewing or mending, and if you have a really typical Virgo wife, your house may be full of the heavenly mixed fragrance of fresh flowers and hot home-made bread baking crisply in the oven. It's pretty nice to come home to. She'll dust off all your old dreams and make them shine again, and you'll have a woman who will never borrow your razor or use your toothbrush for her mascara. She'll nurse you like an angel when you're ill, and she won't embarrass you by flirting with your best friend. She'll dress neatly and be able to talk with you about something besides diapers and beauty parlor gossip. You'll get every ounce of loyalty and devotion you deserve. She won't throw emotional scenes of jealousy or throw your money away foolishly. She'll keep your secrets in her heart, help you organize your work, and probably won't get wrinkled in middle age. Now really, isn't all that worth minding your manners and keeping your fingernails clean? Her eyes are cool pools of pure love, and when she smiles, she can light up a whole room with her radiance. Better keep her. You may never get so lucky again.

The VIRGO Child

But four young oysters hurried up,
All eager for the treat:
Their coats were brushed, their faces washed,
Their shoes were clean and neat—

As he tries to imitate the sounds he hears in the nursery, the tiny Virgo infant carries the seed of a seldom-mentioned Virginian talent for acting. The ability to mimic manifests itself almost from birth. The Virgo baby is alert and quick, yet at the same time more peaceful and tranquil than other infants, a contradiction which foreshadows a future personality that will soothe and irritate by turn.

Don't try to feed your little Virgo applesauce when he wants peaches or you may be in for a long siege. You'll end up with applesauce all over the high chair, but baby won't end up with a speck of it in his stomach if he doesn't like it, though he'll smile charmingly as he firmly turns his head away. He may surprise you by preferring spinach to ice cream. Virgo's meticulous selectivity about food shows early.

Aside from being fussy eaters and an occasional spell of fretful indigestion, raising a Virgo youngster is a pleasant experience, with little conflict and few tantrums. Even when they're very small, these children are inclined to be neat and put away their toys cheerfully. Your Virgo youngster may be bashful and quiet in company or crowds, but around family and friends the cat certainly won't get his tongue. He'll probably talk early and fluently, except in front of strangers. A Virgo child is seldom troublesome, and he's a wonderful companion as mother does her housework. He'll happily imitate whatever she is doing and he'll usually mind the first time he's told, with little scolding necessary.

In school, Virgos are apt to be teacher's pets, simply because they're the easiest boys and girls to discipline and the ones who study their lessons carefully. It's a delight to instruct the typical, bright Virgo child with gentle manners. Criticism, however, should be used sparingly. Too much stress on mistakes will cause him to worry unduly, sometimes to the point of actual illness.

A lecture in front of the class will be painfully mortifying, and it may smother the desire to learn for a long period. Virgo youngsters need to be told only once, quietly, if an error has been made. They'll be just as concerned as the teacher with correcting it, perhaps more so.

Often the mundane chores, disliked by the rest of the class, will be accepted as important responsibilities by Virgo children. They're efficient, dependable little people, with a serious, but friendly, pleasant disposition, though they're sensitive enough to become cranky if teased by more extroverted classmates. The Virgo child is markedly adaptable, probably just as adept at painting scenery as he is at editing the school paper. It wouldn't hurt to suggest that the Virgo youngster try out for dramatics. He won't seek the spotlight, but he might show a surprising ability to interpret characters with convincing reality, if he can overcome his stage fright.

Virgo's honesty and careful attention to details make him a favorite choice to grade papers when the teacher needs help. As a class monitor, he'll be ethical and alert. But there are occasions when the teacher can get a red face when she's made an erroneous statement (teachers being only human) and the normally shy, quiet little Virgo raises his hand to point out the mistake in no uncertain terms. Virgo students want to know the whys and the facts. They'll rarely question authority, but they will question knowledge in books unless they know what's behind it. The printed word often isn't enough for the inquisitive, painstaking Virgo mind. These children need plenty of educational toys, and when they're very young they should be read to as much as possible. They'll become most unhappy misfits as adults if they haven't received a full education. To know less than others turns Virgos into irritable introverts who are painfully embarrassed by their inadequacies.

It's best to ignore the Virgo teenager when he or she begins to notice the opposite sex. Teasing a girl about her first boy friend can give her a permanent emotional scar, and probing into a boy's dates can head him toward bachelorhood. Virgos don't easily accept close relationships leading to marriage, and the path should be made as smooth as possible.

You'll have to supply your Virgo child's emotional needs with signs of physical affection. He'll never show you how deeply he desires this kind of love, but the lack of it will strongly affect his future relationships. Even very pretty and very smart little girls—and very handsome, clever little boys have to be convinced they're interesting. It's hard for them to believe that their modest unassuming ways are as attractive as the more aggressive personalities of their friends. The Virgo ego can stand lots of encouragement without becoming excessive, so don't be stingy with bear hugs, kisses, sincere compliments and pats on the back. Your Virgo child needs large, daily doses of such emotional vitamins, along with his cod liver oil.

He'll have many exact habits, and he'll complain if his belongings are moved or his privacy invaded. He does certain things at certain times, and if his personal schedule is upset, he will be, too. It may be dangerous to ask him for a frank opinion; otherwise, he'll usually be refreshingly polite to company. This child will criticize every member of the family, sometimes with amusing, but cutting imitations of their faults. He'll probably ask for his own room early and be fussy about your cooking. No lumps in the mashed potatoes, please, and not so much seasoning in the stuffing. But he'll show an excellent sense of responsibility before most other children have learned the alphabet. He'll be sympathetic with Mother's headaches and Daddy's financial problems. You can expect him to try sincerely to make good grades at school, willingly help around the house and manage his allowance carefully.

Although he's far from a model of perfection, and you'll feel like shaking him when he makes you take the beans out of the chili, or refuses to wear the shirt you just ironed because it has two small wrinkles—most of the time, a Virgo child is a joy to have around the house.

These children should have a kitten or a bird, so they can learn the lessons of love quietly and unobtrusively, by caring for the helpless. Don't buy him a St. Bernard or a police dog. If he's a typical Virginian youngster, he'll prefer a smaller pet. He'll be fascinated by one of those ant villages. Watching the tiny ants industriously going about their business at close range should really intrigue his curious, practical little mind.

Listen to him when he talks. He has a wisdom beyond his years. You can afford to keep nagging at a minimum, because he'll try very hard to please you if he knows exactly what you expect of him. Remember that his imagination needs plenty of boosting and lots of room to grow, or it can easily become stifled. You need never worry about spoiling him or giving him too many illusions. The Virgo child is made of sterner stuff than that.

Give him all the lovely dreams you can crowd into his heart. Such bright moments of fantasy will guarantee him a much-needed emotional balance when he grows up. Be very sure he has a secret star to wish on. Memories of magical daydreams will keep him from being lonely in the years to come, and there will be many occasions for future loneliness. Unlike other children, the young Virgo may not be very fond of fairy stories and make-believe. He's a true little realist. Perhaps that's why he needs them most of all.

The VIRGO Boss

"We can talk," said the Tiger-lily:
"when there's anybody worth talking to."

If you have a Virgo boss, be kind to him. He's probably secretly troubled and unhappy. Virgos are not born to be high-powered executives who lead others forcefully and they soon regret the decision to bite off more than they can chew. Of course, due to individual planetary positions and aspects in the natal chart, there are certainly some Virgos who are extremely competent in positions of power, but they're few and far between. You can probably count the ones you know on the toes of one foot.

The typical Virgo is at his best as the power behind the throne, the one who dependably carries through the original ideas of others. He's happier and more successful in the checkmate position of chairman of the board than as the president of a huge corporation who has to cope with the problems of his employees and present a jolly company image. The very last thing most Virgos want is to glorify the self and become a listening post for everyone's troubles. Goodness knows, they have enough troubles of their own to keep them busy worrying for a lifetime, even if many of them are imaginary.

Coping with the pressure of being responsible for the impulsive actions of progressive associates, firing orders at subordinates, and pushing public relations, while juggling the finances of big empires, requires a thicker skin and a fatter ego than the average Virgo possesses. One reason he's such an unhappy misfit as an executive is because he tends to see the trees clearly and completely miss the forest —yet this is the very trait which makes him such an indispensable jewel as the man who guides the president of the firm. He may not be the one who sees the big picture, but he can erase the fuzziness from the pictures the more aggressive people paint so carelessly. If anyone can manipulate complicated projects and see them through with a minimum of disastrous mistakes, it's a Virgo. He can take the wildest schemes with a thousand dangerous, dangling loose ends and make them work. A talent like that should never be wasted up front where there's not enough privacy to accomplish his meticulous miracles. In fact, if he's forced to perform his organizational magic before a public audience, the Virgo is likely to look as if he's double-talking, when he's really not. The Virgo whose hidden vanity has caused him to be put in such a position usually ends up accused of this very thing.

A Virgo will pull few punches when he's asked for a critical opinion, and let's face it, an executive often has to smile and say "yes" when he means "no," and frown and say "no" when he means "yes." It's all part of the game. But a Virgo calls a turnip a turnip, and he's bewildered when people turn on him because he didn't pretend it was a tulip.

Consequently, the Virgo in a high-powered position

sometimes resorts to deception in self-defense, and since deception is emphatically not one of his innate talents, he ends up being accused of being downright sly and hypocritical. What a pity, when Virgo hates hypocrisy so much. But that's the price he pays for sitting in a chair he wasn't meant to occupy. The endless, chatty luncheons with clients who have to be wined and dined and catered to would drive the average Virgo into a hermit's cave after a few months, and a few years of it might actually give him a serious mental breakdown.

Any Virgo who searches his own soul eventually comes up with the knowledge that he's better off doing the actual work of running the machinery inside the organization and letting someone else pose for the pictures. If he's truly dedicated to his work (is there a Virgo who isn't?), he secretly scorns the social and political extra-curricular activities the head of a firm is forced to engage in, because it causes him to neglect his duties—and be assured that neglect of duty is not something a Virgo takes lightly.

Still, if the business is a small one with, say, under a dozen employees, a Virgo may do very well as the captain of the tugboat. He certainly won't let it hit any unforeseen snags because he'll have every potential danger charted in detail, upside down and backwards. But big business and the typical Virginian simply don't blend, always allowing for the occasional exception to the rule. A Virgo with a Cancer ascendant and a Capricorn Moon, for example, would be a horse of a different gait. Such a Virgo at the head of a large company can be a real winner, just as the average Virgo at the head of a small company is usually successful. They also excel in leading scientific, experimental groups, where painstaking research is the keynote.

This boss will not overlook the sloppy mistakes of a secretary who constantly misspells words, wears ink blots on her thumbs and forgets to water his geraniums. You'll have to be alert and on your toes if you want a promotion from Virgo. Never tell him the appointment is for three o'clock when it's really for two-forty-five, or you'll face a cranky, irritable boss who won't hesitate to point out your fumble with hairsplitting frankness. As for reminding him in self-defense that he himself mislaid the papers he needed for the same meeting, forget it. Instead of causing him to be more tolerant of your errors in relation to his own exceedingly rare goofs, he's far more likely to glare at you with extreme annoyance. Try it more than once and you may end up without a job. A little criticism goes a long way with your Virgo boss. On his side, that is. As far as you're concerned, resign yourself to plenty of it. There's just one way out and one way only. Don't make mistakes. It's really quite simple.

Once you've adjusted to his perfectionist attitude, you'll find your eagle-eyed Virgo boss is kind-hearted and fair. He won't want to hear the details of your latest romance, since sentiment bores the typical Virgo, but he'll listen with sympathy to your request for a leave of absence because your left small toenail needs attention. Sick leave will be understood. Office flirtations and careless habits will not. Keep your desk tidy, don't flash around the office in mini skirts and heavy make-up, never brush your hair over his papers, and listen carefully to all his instructions. If he approves of your grooming, your work habits and your brain, he can be a surprisingly generous and kindly, considerate man to work for. He has his little idiosyncrasies, but don't we all?

Men who work for a Virgo boss face a slightly different problem. He'll expect you to come up with creative ideas and to be aggressive in the area of promotion and salesmanship. In fact, he'll depend on you to fill in these gaps in his own make-up. Just be sure you handle yourself with modesty. He knows you have more direct drive than he does, but he's also aware that he has more organizational ability, not to mention practicality and caution, and he won't be thrilled if you let it become obvious that you could run things without his close supervision. He's undoubtedly correct. He usually is, which may be a little frustrating until you get used to it and learn to respect him for it.

Your Virgo boss may have a drawer full of indigestion remedies and a mind full of facts and figures, but he also has a heart full of compassion and the ability to straighten out inter-office disagreements. He won't give out Jaguars, or mink capes as Christmas bonuses, but he will pay you what you're worth and won't cheat you. Remember that he's entirely capable of sizing up exactly what you are worth, too. It's difficult, if not impossible, to fool him.

Don't expect him to get excited about glamorous bubble promotions. He may not be overly imaginative, but he has enough imagination to visualize such bubbles bursting with a loud bang and a spray of water, which may leave you all wet. Be sure your suggestions and methods of working have a sound foundation in fact, or he'll dismiss your schemes as daydreams and he may dismiss you, too. You may get impatient frequently with his constant splitting of hairs and faultfinding criticism, but after all, you can't just say to a superior that "It's a drag to nag." So you might as well accept his critical habits gracefully. It won't hurt you to let him shape you up a bit, anyway.

Always tell him the truth. It's useless to lie to him. Frankly, your Virgo boss may strain at gnats—but he'll seldom swallow a camel.

If you give him the understanding support and respect he needs, he'll never hurt you. Inside, he's really a gentle soul and often terribly lonely, married or single. He doesn't make friends easily, and he'll be touchingly grateful for your encouragement. Like all Virgos, he lives with a secret dream and isn't nearly as isolated from emotion as he seems to be. Let him know you've discovered that his bark is worse than his bite (even though his bark is gentle and quiet), and he'll step down from his ivory tower. Never mind if the other employees call him stingy. Go to him when you're really in trouble and see how wrong they are.

The VIRGO Employee

"When you say 'hill,' " the Queen interrupted,
"I could show you hills,
  in comparison with which
  you'd call that a valley."
"A hill can't be a valley, you know.
  That would be nonsense—"
The Red Queen shook her head.
"You may call it 'nonsense' if you like," she said,
"But I've heard nonsense, compared with which
  that would be as sensible as a dictionary!"

If you have a Virgo employee who's a typical Virginian, treasure him (or her) and plan, slowly and carefully, to move him to the position of your assistant. Don't do it too quickly or he'll feel unprepared and reluctant. Fast advances don't tickle the Virgo ego, they just alarm him and make him suspect that you're too impulsive for him to trust.

You needn't shower this employee with bonuses. On the other hand, don't underpay him either. He's well aware of his comparable and current market value, and he won't hesitate to move on, regardless of his basic loyalty and stability, if he feels you're being unfair or unreasonable. It's been said that Virgos give service without thought of reward, which has created a bit of a problem in semantics. It's more accurate to say that they give service without thought of personal ego gratification (though they secretly desire this more than they let on). The Virgo employee fully expects to be paid for his efforts, because money is important to him. It's not the cash itself as a status symbol, nor the Cancerian desire to accumulate that motivates him. It's his inbred fear of going on relief someday when he's old and sick and feeble and forced to depend on others. The very thought of such a situation gives the typical Virgo goose bumps. He'll probably be far healthier in his old age than most of the other zodiac signs. Though often weak in childhood, Virgo gathers physical strength as the years advance. Still he'll secretly worry about his health and his financial future. The twin mental images of the hospital and the poorhouse are never far from his thoughts, so you can see why Virgos are quietly ambitious to advance in their work until they reach a position where they can achieve financial security for tomorrow. At this point, and at this point only, the nervous Virgo intensity begins to unwrinkle and he can relax. Of course, Virgos never completely relax, but let's say he is not quite as jumpy as he was before; he bites his nails less, and his allergies let up a little.

You'll discover that he has a perfect eye for detail, sometimes a little too perfect to be comfortable. Just because you're the boss won't keep him from catching your mistakes and pointing them out in typical, blunt Virgo fashion. Positions and titles aren't sacred to him: perfection is—though, with typical Virgo charm, he'll probably give you more outward courtesy and respect than his associates do.

Whatever his faults, you can always count on these employees, male or female, to exhibit strong analytical ability and excellent taste. His (or her) sharp sense of discrimination makes the typical Virgo worker an excellent critic, with the knack of spotting the weak log in the fence, not to mention the weakest link in the chain, with quicksilver accuracy and speed. Virgo workers are adaptable and versatile, clear-thinking, precise, intelligent and reliable. They'll never turn in sloppy work and they have no patience with a job half done or laziness. That includes your own occasional laziness. The boss who takes a day off to play golf may return to the office to find the Virgo employee eyeing him with a thinly disguised look of disapproval, though the obedient, mannerly Virginian will probably keep silent about it.

Virgos usually shine more in businesses which give service to the public in general. Publishing, the literary field, medicine, pharmacy, anything to do with food, scientific laboratories, service agencies of all kinds, bookkeeping and accounting—all these areas are competently and efficiently handled by the adept, systematic Virgo. No tiny detail is unworthy of his consideration, and he'll stay overtime without a thought if something is not quite right and needs his attention.

You can feel completely safe in letting your Virgo employee work without supervision. His sense of ethics and responsibility are total. Besides, he'd probably prefer to work either quietly alone or confidently beside you than be exposed to any possible criticism from fellow workers. Virgo works quickly, but it may not be obvious at first. That's because he feels insecure with short cuts and is never satisfied until all the facts have been checked. He may appear to be slow simply because he's doing a thorough job. Actually, his mind works as fast as Mercury, though mere speed will never be allowed to replace cautious, methodical procedures.

Although advertising isn't a natural atmosphere for his realistic, practical approach, he might be valuable in some position where he can patiently pick up the pieces of those creative brainstorms that occasionally blow sky high, and make sure that the fabulous ideas which have been so joyously tossed into the promotional hat don't have large holes in them.

It would not be advisable to send your Virgo employee out to promote your company or sell your product. He's a bit too honest and plain spoken to paint any glowing pictures for your potential customers, and his basic nature is too shy and retiring to push either himself or your firm with any great gobs of enthusiasm. Very few Virgos make good salesmen, only the rare exceptions to the rule.

He'll dress neatly, speak with gentle diction, be as clean as a bar of Ivory soap, and probably have a desk that's so tidy it looks positively naked. You may come across a Virgo with a slightly cluttered office, but never fear. His mind isn't cluttered. He knows the exact order of the apparent disorder, and just where to put his finger on whatever he wants. His desk may look like a heap of trash to you, but he knows the whereabouts of every postage stamp and paper clip.

When Virgos become really noticeably untidy, either at home or at work, it's almost always a symptom of emotional unhappiness—just as the same thing is true of a Sagittarian who suddenly becomes neat and meticulous.

Bite your tongue when you get an urge to criticize a Virgo's work. He'll probably catch his own mistakes before you do. Any necessary criticism should be given briefly and quietly, and any unnecessary criticism should be forgotten. It takes very little to warm his heart to loyalty and gratitude, but it also takes very little to cause Virgo to bristle and fret and sulk. Still, as quick as he is to pout over imagined slights, he's just as quick to help without being asked when you're in trouble. During a real crisis, you'll swear he's grown two feet taller.

Never force Virgos to work around wild, bright colors. It disturbs their quiet inner nature. Give them the most modern, most efficient equipment you can afford, and they'll make good use of it. They don't like noise and confusion when they work. They also don't like irregular schedules. Let them have a regular day off and stick to it. They'll work overtime if you need them, but they hate the insecurity and confusion of changing shifts. Their emotional requirements are hidden, but they are there just the same, and a certain amount of open appreciation may be desperately needed.

Although the typical Virgo seldom indulges in esoteric or imaginative work, you will occasionally find a few who do. But remember that they are still Virgos. The Virgo astrologer will split hairs over his occult investigation, the Virgo poet will use precise meter, the Virgo painter will concentrate on detail and the Virgo actor or actress will master the perfect dialect or accent for the role with pains-taking study. Never let it throw you when someone born under a certain Sun sign doesn't seem to be doing what comes naturally, as far as his choice of career is concerned. Keep observing and you'll see he's still being true to his basic nature.

Once you've gradually moved your Virgo employee from the bottom (where he won't mind starting, by the way) to the position of your right-hand man or your gal Friday, you can relax and really play some golf for a change, content in the knowledge that someone totally reliable is covering you back at the office. Of course, you may feel a little guilty when you return, under the re-proachful expression in those lovely, clear Virgo eyes. You mean you never noticed how attractive your Virgo em-ployee is? Look again.

Will you, won't you, will you, won't you,
will you join the dance?
The further off from England, the nearer is to France.

"Contrariwise," continued Tweedledum,
"if it was so, it might be;
and, if it were so, it would be;
but as it isn't, it ain't.
That's logic."

LIBRA the Scales

September 24th through October 23rd

How to Recognize LIBRA

*"Your face is the same as everybody has—
the two eyes, so . . . nose in the middle,
mouth under. It's always the same.
Now, if you had the two eyes
on the same side of the nose, for instance—
or the mouth at the top—
that would be some help."*

Librans hate to be rude, yet they'll straighten the crooked picture on your wall and snap off your blaring TV set. Librans love people, but they hate large crowds. Like gentle doves of peace, they go around mediating and patching up quarrels between others; still they enjoy a good argument themselves. They're goodnatured and pleasant, but they can also be sulky, and they balk at taking orders. Librans are extremely intelligent. At the same time, they're incredibly naive and gullible. They'll talk your ear off, yet they're wonderfully good listeners. Librans are restless people. But they seldom rush or hurry. Are you completely confused? You're not alone. There's a frustrating inconsistency to this Sun sign that puzzles the Librans themselves as much as it does others.

Lots of people will tell you that Libra is all love and beauty and sweetness and light. That's fine, as far as it goes, but it stops a little short of accuracy. It also stops short of Eugene O'Neill. Just because the sign is symbolized by the golden scales of justice, don't ever think that Librans are always perfectly balanced. It seems to be a logical deduction. After all, the purpose of scales is to balance. However, did you ever watch the balancing process on a pair of old-fashioned pharmaceutical scales? The ultimate goal is to get both sides even, but what happens? First one side is low, then the other. Up and down, and they dip until there's perfect balance. Drop into a friendly neighborhood pharmacy and watch them in action. (Just tell the druggist you're trying to find out what makes Aunt Martha tick.)

Never again will you have a mental picture of a Libran as a calm, perfectly balanced, sweet, gracious and charming individual. You'll have a mental picture of a person who has that kind of disposition *half* the time. The other half of the time, Libra can be annoying, quarrelsome, stubborn, restless, depressed and confused. Libra is first up, then down. He swings one way, then another. Suddenly, like the scaels—perfect balance! It's heavenly. But there is always that period of weighing and dipping before the moment of heavenly balance is achieved.

The physical appearance of these people may require almost as much concentration as the personality. There's no such thing as a typical Libra feature, unless it's the Venus dimple. Libran features are almost always even and well-balanced. They're pleasing, but not very noticeable, so it's easier to start with the dimples. There will usually be a couple in the cheeks or one in the chin. If they're not in the face, you might check to see if the knees are dimpled. Many Libran knees are. But be careful. Very few girls will believe you when you tell them you were staring at their knees "because I want to see if you were born in October." Be discreet, but check. With the men, of course, the trousers rule out that clue, unless you're on the beach or playing tennis. Don't get discouraged if you find dimples, then discover the person was *not* born in October. Those fetching dimples have a right to be there, because he or she will have a Libra ascendant, so your guess is still correct.

After you've ruled the Venus dimples in or out, notice the entire effect of the face. It will always wear a markedly pleasant expression. Even when the Libran is angry, somehow he or she will manage to look mild, or at the very least, neutral. Venus voices are typically sweet and clear as a bell, and these people seldom raise them to a shrill or bellowing pitch. A Libran is the only person on earth who can say, "I hate you and I'm going to punch you in the nose," and sound as if he's reciting Browning's "How Do I Love Thee?" The mouth is usually bow-shaped, and the lips would have been described in Gibson girl days as "lips like cherry wine." In fact, the typical Libra face reminds you of nothing so much as a box of bonbons. Or a sugar cookie. Some of them look like human lollipops, or a caramel sundae topped with rich, whipped cream. They like to eat those things, too, and if any Librans are reading this, they're probably weak with hunger by now.

The women are almost invariably pretty, and the men are usually handsome. Still, not all of the beautiful people in the world are Librans; Venus beauty is in a class by itself, and it's not always easy to separate it from the good looks of other Sun signs. My own secret way to recognize them is to begin by thinking about the sweet expressions of Dwight Eisenhower and Brigitte Bardot, and then go on from there. The trouble is that sometimes the women will look like Ike and the men like Bardot. You have to make allowances.

I'm not implying that the Libra woman is masculine. Most of them are about as female as the average man can stand (unless there's an aggressive ascendant). And I certainly do not imply that Libra men are feminine. They're usually quite virile male animals. But there's no denying that they have a purity of feature that keeps you from getting them mixed up with prize fighters or wrestlers. Even the rare Libran who might be called ugly, and it will be most unusual to find one, has such a charming expression you're persuaded to comment that there's real beauty of character in his (or her) face.

You'll never meet a Libran who doesn't have a smile like a soft, white cloud. That Venus smile could melt a chocolate bar at twenty paces. When it hits you full force, it has enough candle power to transfigure even plain or downright homely features—literally, not figuratively.

Most Librans are full of curves, rather than angles. Their hair is often curly. They're not necessarily fat (though a Taurus ascendant can produce some pretty plump pigeons). Still, they can fool you, go on a diet and cut quite a trim figure. But even so, the curves will be there in spots, rather like a slim hourglass shape. Using Bardot once more as an example, one certainly could not call her fat—but could one call her skinny? There's one more trick in mastering the Venus appearance and physical characteristics. You'll notice a bright, lilting laugh that rings with merriment. Once you've heard it, you won't soon forget it.

Now you might think that to be born attractive and dimpled, to seek fairness and loveliness, to be pleasing and easily pleased, is a blessing. You might imagine that gentleness and intelligence, grace and understanding are the gifts of a fairy godmother. You might be right. When the Libra scales are balanced, it's utterly delightful, like meeting an angel from paradise. The problem is that fairy godmother. She keeps rapping one side of the scales with her wand and then the other, making Libra dip back and forth. She can't seem to make up her fickle mind whether she made a mistake or not, and she passed her indecision on to Librans. First they'll talk up a storm and monopolize the conversation. Then they'll listen intently, with flattering interest. When others are fighting, they'll play the role of peacemaker, and smooth everyone's ruffled feathers. Then they'll turn right around, deliberately take the other side in discussion, and start an argument for the pure relish of it.

They seek harmony. Yet, lots of Librans indulge in excessive eating, drinking or love-making, completely upsetting the cookie cart, not to mention throwing harmony out of kilter. In fact, you'll come across a few Librans who will remind you of Dr. Dolittle's "push me-pull you" animal.

The Sun sign itself is known as Lazy Libra, and that's another inconsistency. For days, weeks or months on end, Librans can be too busy to play. They'll burn gallons of midnight oil, then rise and shine in time to hear the rooster crow. It wears you out just to watch them. Suddenly, they'll plop down into a chair, say, "I'm bushed," and give the best imitation of laziness you've ever seen (especially after all that frenzied activity). Once they've plopped, you won't catch them moving a muscle if they can help it. It will be an effort for them to pick up a spoon or raise a glass (though they will manage). If there's anyone around who's willing, they'll expect to be waited on, hand and foot. When the scales have dipped down toward lethargy, you couldn't move Libra with a steam shovel. He'll talk, read, yawn, snooze, watch TV or stare out the window, and seem barely able to make it into the bedroom (though he'll manage). All the nagging and shouting in the world won't impress him. It's as if he were in another world. After a period, when he's recouped his forces, he'll feel a spurt of energy, get up, and start chugging down the track again. His nose will go back to the grindstone, and his hands and feet will fly. Once more, he'll work like a mule in harness, keeping a miraculous balance and a steady, even pace, as he harmoniously plans his chores with efficient ease. Although Libra is not a dual sign, most of their friends think they know two different people. Try to tell someone who has frequently seen a Libran in the midst of an up-swing that Libra is lazy, and he'll stare at you blankly. Conversely, if you try to tell someone who has been exposed to the Libra lassitude that this creature is a bundle of powerful drive, he'll retort with, "That lazy bum? You must be kidding."

Librans know instinctively that to restore harmony to the body, they must alternate their active spells with complete rest. Their personal arrangement of genes and cells and electrical impulses demand it, and most of them are pretty adept at managaing this delicate physical balance. However, harmony of the mind and emotions isn't always as instinctive with them. They can weep with overflowing sentiment, turn sharply sarcastic, then be as bright and cheerful as the first robin in spring. It's not at all the duality of Gemini. The Libran is constantly dipping deeply into one emotion and then the other by turns, which isn't the same thing as the complete change of character of the Gemini twins. There's a deep richness to Libra's emotions, no matter which emotion is high or low at a given moment, and a philosophic approach to both sorrows and joys that seldom fails to smooth things out eventually.

An instinct for sanity keeps most Librans mentally healthy and physically fit. Usually, they avoid serious breakdowns of body and mind. The biggest threat to their health is over indulgence of some kind. Eating sweets can bring on obesity, stomach disorders and mottled skin. Excessive use of alcohol can cause severe kidney and bladder disturbances, which in turn result in violent headaches of migraine intensity. Giving in to depression can cause itchy sensations in the skin and even boils. The breast area is a sensitive part of the body, and sometimes there are foot problems and intestinal disorders though these aren't as common. Ulcers beset many a Libran, not from worry as much as from abuse of the digestive system and the topsy-turvy emotional make-up. Generally, Librans are healthier than most people, unless they push themselves too hard, and forget to take those necessary rest periods. The effect of peace and harmony on Venus health is miraculous. When they're ill, they need enormous amounts of prolonged rest, with no discordant emotional situations to plague them, pleasant books, soft music and soothing words. Such an atmosphere rarely fails to put the typical Libran back on his feet quickly.

The Libra character is made up of just about equal parts of kindness, gentleness, fairness, plain cussed argumentativeness, stubborn refusal to capitulate, philosophical logic and indecision. It's best to examine these ingredients in detail. The argumentativeness, for instance. A Libran will argue with you about what time it is if he thinks your watch is two seconds off. Don't try to get away with a generalization like: "Teenagers are ruining the country." You'll get a logical, careful dissertation about the Peace Corps and how many wonderful youngsters there are in the world, even if his own children are defiant drop-outs. Make a remark like, "The law is so corrupt today that all judges and lawyers are dishonest," and he'll go on for hours about the divine protection of justice in this country, the virtues of the jury system and the problems of law-makers, going back to Roman law and continuing through the Code Napoleon. Never say casually, "It's foolish to live in the city when you can live in the country. There's no comparison." That last phrase especially is a huge mistake. Just mention the word comparison, and the average Libran is off and running. He can compare all night long, with refreshments at intervals. He'll extol the beauties and advantages of the cities compared to rural areas: describe the bright lights, honking taxi horns, theaters, museums and parks in glowing terms—even if he himself lives in suburbia and you couldn't blast him out with dynamite. It wouldn't make a bit of difference if you took the opposite view in any of these cases. The Libran would then expound on the rising teenage crime rate, the corruption of the courts and the joys of country living. He doesn't really care which side he takes in a good argument, as long as it's the other side. Sometimes, if he gets bored, he can switch sides in the middle. Tell him you like a movie and he'll tell you what's wrong with it. Criticize it and he'll praise it. Rave about a new book and he'll list its shortcomings. If you found it dull, he'll point out its virtues. Throughout all this constant, logical deduction, the Libran will try to remain fair. Libra dreads the appearance of prejudice, unjust accusation and blind faith equally. What he seeks is the real truth, the exact balance that gives the correct answer, after weighing all possibilities.

It's an admirable trait, of course, but all that weighing can drive a positive person simply wild. It can drive the Libran himself into a state of constant indecision. Even the most controlled Venus men and women dislike making instant decisions without taking all the possibilities into consideration. Fairness can be a fetish. The Libran general, with his qualities of balanced, harmonious judgment, makes an excellent strategist, and thoughtful planning can win a battle before it's fought. His ability to see all sides, to smooth nerves and calm angry tempers can make him the finest kind of mediator, bringing people who hate and mistrust each other together, and getting them to work in harmonious cooperation. However, war makes all Librans secretly heartsick. They hate bloodshed. An October-born officer in the armed services will let someone else make instant decisions under fire, while he brilliantly charts the strategic maneuvers that will save thousands of lives in the long run, and still win for his side.

This antipathy to making a decision can turn into quite a stalemate with the ones who have adverse afflictions between their planets at birth. There are some who can't decide which shoe to put on first in the morning, let alone which side of the bed to get out of. Even the average Libran you meet at the office or at a party will always reflect to some degree this tendency to weigh things back and forth until you get the jitters, and the time for decision is long past. They'll say, "If I do this, such and such will happen. On the other hand" (which is one of their all-time very favorite phrases) "if I do that, then such and such could occur." Those scales can dip crazily up and down like a see-saw. Nothing is more painful to watch than a doubtful Libran trying to make up his mind why, wherefore, and whether to. He doesn't like to be hurried or pushed while he's deciding, either. An impatient person can turn the airy Libran into a sudden spell of earth stubbornness that would make Taurus, the bull, look like a gullible pushover. Impatience is one quality most Librans can't stand. Flighty, rash, impulsive people who don't stop to consider the consequences give *them* the jitters.

It's amusing that Librans will always immediately deny their indecisiveness. The first thing they'll say when you're describing their Sun sign will be, "I'm not indecisive at all. That's not accurate. It certainly doesn't describe me." Hide your smile. Translated, his denial means that, although he takes a devilishly long time to make up his mind (which he very conveniently forgets), once he's reached a conclusion, he's quite gung-ho about it. If he's been allowed sufficient time, his eventual, final decision will be carried out with such forceful conviction that it misleads him into thinking he's firm and decisive. Don't let it mislead you. Anyway, when he tells you he has no trouble making up his mind, he's just starting a typical Libran argument, and you can tell him so. It will do him good to realize that, even in the midst of his objections to his astrological traits, he's proving the truth of his Sun sign. When he denies your analysis of him, just say smugly, "I expected you to take that attitude. Librans always argue every point." It will drive him crackers, but it may help him realize the truth, and the truth is what he seeks. He's bound to see the logic in that. Telling him he's being unfair and refusing to consider both sides will take him down a notch or two, also.

Very few Librans are markedly eccentric or show-offs. Most of them are as wholesome and as well-balanced as a neat field of wheat, swaying back and forth gracefully in the wind. They're normally scrupulously honest in business deals, and there's very little carelessness about them. Libra would rather take his time and get it right than make a false start and have to repeat the process. They hate exaggeration, and they're repelled by embarrassing displays of anger and passion, though they themselves can be guilty of both extremes if they're pressed beyond their endurance. Most Librans have a fantastic ability to concentrate and to ponder deep subjects. They are born with an affection for books, and such a respect for the printed word that many of them scorn paperbacks. They feel it's not a book unless it's a hardcover, and smells and feels like a book. You're almost sure to find an extensive library in every Libran home.

They love the harmony of sounds, colors, poetry and the proper use of words, both written and spoken. Rarely do they escape the influence of the arts. A Libran is a gentle, tender lover of all that's good and clean and lovely underneath whatever image he may project when that fairy godmother raps one side of his scales. He's an artistic soul at heart, who enjoys spreading the soft blue and pastel shades of Venus at parties and cultural occasions. Soft light, mellow music, interesting conversation, good food and fine wines turn him on. His mind has both the brilliance of the diamond and the smoothness of the opal. He moves in the changing element of air and reflects the usefulness of copper, his harmonizing metal. There's a touch of the cool, Libran mint in his alert reasoning and his sharp sense of honor, and six dimensions of peace shine down on him from Venus.

To truly understand Libra, you must understand the riddle of the scales; one side heaped high with October's vivid, golden leaves, suggesting brisk, autumn weather— the other side holding sky blue bunches of shy violets, drenched in the fresh scent of April rain. When the scales dip, bright optimism turns into silent panic, weighed down with lonely depression. When they balance, they produce a perfect harmony between his rich, crackling intellect and his affectionate, sympathetic heart. The seasons hold Libra's secret. Winter is too cold for him. Summer is too hot. He must blend them both into a perfect fall and spring.

Famous Libra Personalities

Julie Andrews	Charlton Heston
Brigitte Bardot	Deborah Kerr
David Ben-Gurion	John Lennon
Sarah Bernhardt	Walter Lippmann
Charles Boyer	Franz Liszt
Charlie Brown	Mickey Mantle
Truman Capote	Marcello Mastroianni
Dwight Eisenhower	Nietzsche
T. S. Eliot	Eugene O'Neill
William Faulkner	Dr. J. B. Rhine
Mahatma Gandhi	Eleanor Roosevelt
George Gershwin	Ed Sullivan
Graham Greene	Michael Todd, Jr.
Helen Hayes	Oscar Wilde
Rita Hayworth	Thomas Wolfe

The LIBRA Man

"In my youth," said his Father, "I took to the law.
And argued each case with my wife;
And the muscular strength, which it gave to my jaw,
Has lasted the rest of my life."

You'll get plenty of free advice from this man. He'll have the perfect solution to all your problems and an answer for every question you ask. But there's no use expecting him to be the answer to all your girlish dreams. He'll change some of them and argue with others. A Libra male can be as cranky as a crocodile with poison ivy, and his habit of rationalizing everything, including love, will drive you to frenzy—or leave you limp with defeat.

Still, I must warn you that once you're caught and enmeshed in the Libran charm, it won't be easy to break away. Trying to escape from a bear trap is a cinch, compared to liberating yourself from a Libran man. If you try to run, he'll persuade you to stay with such logical, intelligent arguments you couldn't hope to top them unless you graduated from Harvard Law School. In addition to using his unmatched reasoning powers on you, he'll turn so sweet and gentle you'll forget the frustrating inconsistencies of his nature that upset you before. Then he'll smile at you and something will happen inside. Your heart will turn over.

From that moment on, the battle will be lost. His dreams will be your dreams, and nothing will matter so much as making him happy. You'll seek that smile and need it to survive the way a thirsty traveler needs water. Only a really hard-hearted Hannah could resist a Libran smile, and she'd have to summon all her determination to avoid being magnetized by its purity. The Libran charm is not like the hypnotic persuasion of the Scorpio. The attraction of Libra is logical and real, not supernatural in any sense. There's no black magic about it, just common sense submission to his heavenly aura.

On the other hand, to use *his* favorite catch phrase, there will be times when those Libra scales dip back and forth with crazy contradiction. You'll have to shout at him, push him into the lake, or stand on your head to get his attention and force him to make a move. Don't be so naive as to think love will be smooth and eternally tranquil, even if he is ruled by Venus. If you're up on your Roman mythology, you're aware that Venus had her off days. Still, when the scales balance, life with Libra can be as intoxicating as a goblet of golden ambrosia, with lots of laughs and a casual freedom known only to the gods who cavort on Olympus.

Making up his mind is a chore no less strenuous to the average Libran male than taming a wild buffalo, and once he's made it up, he's liable to change it with no warning if he suspects he's made a mistake. There's a woman I know who hoped to go into a business partnership with a Libran, and she learned the hard way about this legendary Libra idiosyncrasy. They had a breakfast appointment together one summer morning, and both of them were full of enthusiastic, optimistic plans for the future. After he dropped her off on the way to his office, she began to worry. His promises were almost too good to be true, so she phoned him, just to make sure she hadn't been dreaming. He was still excited, he repeated all his promises and ambitious plans, and they made a date to get together again the following week. Before they hung up, he guessed what was on her mind and reassured her. "By the way," he remarked, "I want to say something, since I won't see you again for a few days." He hesitated slightly (she missed that clue), then continued with conviction. "I wanted to tell you that, well—I guess what I wanted to say is don't worry. I won't change my mind. We'll go through with it, just the way we planned."

The next week, when he didn't call, she phoned him again. "Were you out of town?" she asked. "No," he said slowly. "I didn't call you because I wanted to think it over." A long pause. "I think I should try something with a smaller budget first. We'll get together on our project next spring. I promise. It's just that, well, I've decided it's best to wait until then, and put it on the shelf for a while, you know?"

Filled with natural resentment and disappointment after such an unexpected letdown, she made a decision of her own. She would never speak to him again. The man was obviously undependable, untrustworthy and cruel, besides. A month later she passed him on the street, and he stopped to say hello. Caught off guard, she stammered an aloof, cool sentence or two of greeting, and instantly regretted that she hadn't cut him dead. Then he smiled. That did it. She was once more his strongest booster. He could do no wrong, even to her. To this day she defends him fiercely, and if she hears that one of his dreams got shattered, she has an illogical desire to help him pick up the pieces so he'll smile again.

Now, if that could occur when a woman is involved with a Libra man only in a business way, can you imagine your state of mind and your ability to insulate yourself if you should happen to fall in love with one of these impossible charmers? You simply can't be too careful. Steel yourself to turn your head when he smiles. Stuff cotton in your ears when he starts his convincing arguments in that smooth-as-silk voice that makes the back of your neck tingle.

The word love and the word Libra are practically synonymous. Libra invented romance, and refined it to an art with even more finesse than Leo, Scorpio and Taurus, which is saying a lot. The delicate strategies of Cupid are inbred Libran talents. He'll use every trick with casual ease and seldom fail to get the girl. However, once he gets her, he isn't always sure what to do with her. Having thoroughly charmed her into willing submission, he hesitates. Should he take advantage of her helpless state or should he propose marriage? Or both? Or neither? The mental struggle begins, and life in the garden of Eden with this particular Adam becomes considerably less than ecstatic.

He won't lose interest in the opposite sex until he's at least ninety. It may be purely an academic interest if he's happily married, but the subject will never bore him, even if he only speculates what it would be like to whirl each pretty girl he sees around an imaginary ballroom.

Since the art of love-making comes so easily—and shockingly early—to the Libra male, and since he almost always wears the crown of success on his romantic excursions into love's jungle, he gets tangled up with a lot of clinging vines. Libra hates to hurt anyone's feelings, though he remains blissfully unaware of the damage done when he's in an argumentative mood. He hates to say no, and seldom realizes that postponement is more unkind than an outright break of an affair which has no chance of happiness. In the opposite situation when the mutual feeling is as close to sublime as humans ever reach on this earth, the prolonged agony can be equally tortuous. Only an Aquarian can be more shy of making a drastic move in one direction or another. If he senses he's being unfair to someone in his own life, to you—or to someone in your recent romantic past—there will be no end to his painful indecision. Being unfair is, to him, a crime roughly on a level with murder. The reluctance to be cruel can push him into a mistaken proposal of marriage, predestined for the divorce courts —or else his endless procrastination can cause him to miss the love of his life. So you can see his attitude is a two-edged sword, which can either slice away true love or cut him a piece of indigestible matrimony. Tossing out false sentiment is the cure for both.

The tendency toward fickleness in Libra men can't be denied. They do tend to trifle, especially in youth. The natural Libra impulse is to to size up every third or fourth woman they come across, and weigh her possibilities of being the true soul mate. They often get friendship and love hopelessly confused. Surprisingly, it's not often that the Libran will suffer from a broken heart, for all his dabbling and experimenting. He can forget with insulting quickness, and be less apt than anyone, except perhaps a Gemini or Sagittarius male, to allow himself to regret the memory of unrequited love or a romance that was fated never to be. He may sustain a few bruised spots, but there will be no permanent damage, except in very unusual cases. Then the hurt can be devastating beyond imagination. But it happens so rarely you won't find many examples. It's easier to find a soft-hearted, guileless Libra man in the clutches of a passionately determined female who has made him feel that deserting her would be a sin second only to breaking all the ten commandments at once. Caught in such a net, he can be a pretty miserable prisoner of love. But both extremes are the exceptions, and most Libra men manage to keep free enough to enjoy romance to the fullest, without letting sentimental ties rope them in.

He isn't too interested in rooting out your secrets. He may seem to be, at first glance, but take a second look. Often he misses what's going on two inches under his nose.

Everyone will notice what's happening but him. Though he'll argue until hell freezes over, his purpose is not to dig out personal motives, but to dwell on abstract theories so that he can reach a balanced judgment. His questions aren't aimed at uncovering anyone's hidden neurosis. He just wants to sort the facts and assemble them in the proper places. He'll discuss pros and cons with brilliant logic and astute rationalization, and his conclusion will usually be fair, accurate, sensible and practical. Not even Solomon in all his wisdom could top a typical Libran's final, balanced decision. But he doesn't have the inclination to figure the personal nuances or emotional tangles that lie just beneath the surface. The facts and the facts alone are sufficient. The Piscean, Scorpio or Aquarian's deep penetration of character would, to his mind, muddy the crystal-clear picture he seeks. He instinctively feels that such psychological examination is out of his line. It is.

If you're extravagant, he'll simply deduce that you spend money like water; therefore you aren't a good credit risk. The fact that you seek emotional security by wasting cash isn't in his field. He's not your psychiatrist. If you're stingy, he's only interested in carefully examining your thrift to form an accurate appraisal of your customs. There's no desire to uncover your secret fear of losing your independence through poverty. Promiscuity will make him argue against its pitfalls; frigidity will bring on even lengthier discussions about isolation from human companionship. But he'll avoid learning about the traumatic experiences that brought on the former, or the deep-seated feelings of inadequacy that triggered the latter. Libra is the judge. You'll see lots of judges handing down fair decisions, based on weighing the facts in the case, but you won't find many of them asking you why the color red makes you nervous, or sympathizing with your compulsion to lock your husband out because he wore those red-striped pajamas. Always remember that the Libran argues with only an abstract curiosity. He appears to be a prober, but he's not. Nor is he as nosy and gossipy as he seems to be. It's like breaking the seal of the confessional to pry a secret given in confidence from the typical Libran.

All this makes him terribly trustworthy, but a little hard on your feelings. You can confide in him with faith. But you'll suffer when he misses sensing your innermost needs. He wants to please you, but there's seldom enough understanding of your silent hopes to satisfy all your longings (unless there's a water sign on the ascendant, or the Moon is in a water sign). Just because he's an expert lover technically doesn't make him the soul of empathy in relation to your moods. He has enough trouble coping with his own. Nothing can be more irritating than when you rush to him with a story about how someone has hurt you deeply. You seek sympathy, and what do you get? His first question will be, "What did you do to him (or her)?" Then he'll point out where you were just as much in the wrong, until you could scream with unsatisfied indignation. Go ahead and scream, he still won't take sides if he thinks you've been unfair, and the emotional implications will escape him.

Trouble invariably arises from this Libran lack of awareness of the partner's need to be understood in depth. It may seem unbelievable that he can be so intuitive about the abstract, so brilliantly logical in deduction, so capable of clear, open-minded and open-eyed deliberation, and still be so aggravatingly obtuse about what makes you ache or thrill inside. But it's one of those inconsistencies you have to live with, if you live with a Libran. His gentleness and that smile, of course, make it easier to bear.

Unless there are financial afflictions in his natal chart, he won't be tight with the budget. On the contrary, the typical Libran has a rather lavish hand with cash. He believes in spending it on objects or activities that bring beauty or happiness. Be prepared to be a good hostess, because his home will be a regular hospitality center at most any hour of the day or night (except during those times when he's resting and won't take kindly to being disturbed by doorbells, telephones or people). Don't drag him to crowded places where he's forced to feel the press of flesh and where the noise offends his sense of harmony. Crowds of strangers affect his inner equilibrium. All Librans have an instinctive distaste for physical contact with masses of humanity. His social life will be generously sprinkled with intelligent, sparkling people, but when the group expands to over a couple of dozen warm bodies, he'll struggle for air. A Libra man can suddenly leave you alone in a crowded theater with no explanation. He doesn't hate you. He was just overcome with claustrophobia, a typical Libran affliction.

The fastest road to the disinterest that leads to divorce

is a disorderly home. Keep the radio and TV sets toned down, and don't let the odor of cooking penetrate his sensitive nostrils. If you must make onion soup and garlic bread, spray pine-scented deodorant around until the house smells like the great northern woods. A wife who serves a Libran husband bread right out of the wrapper, makes him use paper towels for napkins and leaves the milk bottle or cereal box out where he can see them is headed for the life of a not-so-gay divorcée sooner than she may think. Hanging stockings across the shower rod is out. Forgetting to dust or make the beds can keep him in a constant state of emotional discord. He'll retreat from the disharmony with longer and longer naps and more and more nights out alone, and eventually, there will be no communication. He may be as sloppy as six pigs himself, but he'll expect you to pick up his socks and fold the papers he scatters on the floor. If the chartreuse draperies clash with a maroon rug, he can pout for years, and you'll never know why. Better keep the decor pastel. With the typical Libran kindness, he may not complain, but his secretary and her exquisite taste may look more attractive to him every day.

The Libra male hates confusion, and he really needs harmony to remain stable. His home must be a beautiful, quiet oasis from the jangling discord of the outside world, or those scales may remain permanently out of balance. Since he seldom probes motives, you'll have to be smart enough to guess why he's never home or why he sleeps all the time when he is. Remember that he's weak on introspection, so you must be the analyst. He'll never suspect his unhappiness stems from seeing you covered with cold cream and the youngsters covered with jelly. He may not realize he hates the orange shower curtain or that the lithograph of George Washington crossing the Delaware which hangs over the mantle goes against his artistic grain. He won't quite understand why he keeps forgetting to kiss you goodnight and good morning, but his logical mind will tell him something is off balance, and he'll suffer from it more than he lets on. Pick up the papers and toys, spruce up the house, dab on your best perfume, take the curlers out of your hair, turn down the television, buy some heavenly blue shower curtains and get a good Degas print to replace George over the mantle. You'll wake up some morning and find you're married to a completely new man with a totally changed attitude.

The children will always benefit from his sense of fairness. He'll make sure the biggest youngsters don't take advantage of the baby, or the youngest doesn't break the oldest's bicycle spokes. Libran fathers will exercise discipline with quiet authority, and they'll try to give a logical reason for punishment, which will seldom be administered in anger. Like you, the children will melt under his charm; and like you, they'll also chafe under his constant debating and challenging. Strangely, a Libra man usually doesn't look forward enthusiastically to the birth of children. But after they arrive, he weighs the advantage of their love against loneliness, plunges into fatherhood with a sincere desire to enjoy it, and normally ends up as a doting parent. However, he'll never allow parental affection to replace his romantic feelings for you. With typical Librans of both sexes, the mate comes first, offspring second. You needn't fear that his love for you will decrease as the family increases—assuming, of course, you got rid of those chartreuse draperies or the maroon rug, one or the other—and that the dirty dishes don't continually pile up in the sink.

One final word of astrological advice. If you're in love with a Libra man, and you're sure it's meant to be, go right ahead and propose whatever it is you want to propose, up to and including marriage. He'll be relieved that you took the initiative. But watch out for that perverse streak which causes him to let you decide, and then when it doesn't work out, cheerfully point out that "You made the decision. I didn't." Make sure you know what you're doing, or you'll never hear the end of it. There's only one way to even the score with him. Say "Yes, I decided. If I had left it up to you, we'd still be standing under that lamppost in the rain saying 'I love you,' and we'd both have caught pneumonia." He'll argue with you, naturally, but just before or after you bounce the teapot off his head, he'll accidentally smile, and there you'll be—standing under that lamppost in the rain again, saying "I love you," once more. I believe this is where I came in.

The LIBRA Woman

*And so she went on taking first one side
and then another and making quite a conversation of
it altogether . . .*

*She generally gave herself very good advice
(though she seldom followed it) . . .*

Once a child asked me a question that wasn't easy to
answer. "Why is it," he wanted to know, "that ladies wear
trousers and men use pretty smelling cologne?" In typical
Aries style, I dashed off an impulsive reply. "Well," I
told him quickly, before he could think of any more embarrassing riddles, "that's because there's a little bit of
woman in every man, and there's a little bit of man in
every woman. Now let's play checkers."

Looking back, I'm rather proud of my instant Mars
wisdom. That statement is true to some degree of all the
Sun signs, and it's super-true of Libra. You can find a
trace of the opposite sex in the most virile, rugged Libran
male, and Venus plays the same trick on the female scale
balancer.

She may be as dainty as a fluffy, white bunny and she
may whisper with gentle persuasion. She can dress in silks
and laces, and her hair can smell of fragrant cologne. She
might even look like a little doll you could lift with one
hand (though a Taurus or Sagittarius ascendant would
make her considerably more hefty). But with all her
femininity, sweet mannerisms and lovely grace, this girl
wears a pair of trousers with surprising ease, and they'll
fit her rather neatly. Her mental processes operate with
male logic and they can match yours in any discussion
you care to start. They can even top yours on occasion,
although the female side of the Libra woman is usually
too smart to let you catch on to that until you're safely
past the honeymoon. During the mating season, she'll be
careful not to beat you at chess, but she won't hide her

sharp mind behind those soft dimples forever. Eventually, you'll be treated to a display of her brain power.

Most Libra women will air their clever wits any time a subject appears with the slightest possibility of debate. It could be anything from why you shouldn't wear button down collars to what's keeping you from getting a raise at work. (She'll feel the latter is partly your fault and partly your boss's fault. Everything with Libra ends up as six of one and half a dozen of another—just so it all comes out even.) If you refuse to rise to the bait, she'll argue with herself. A Libra girl can start a donnybrook alone, pursue it alone and finish it alone, in a grand flourish. Your only contribution may be "But why?" or "I don't think so," but sometimes that's all she needs to deliver a brilliant monologue, which may last for an hour or more. Through it all, however, you'll probably be drowning in her charm. She'll turn on that unbearably delicious smile every third sentence or so, and you'll end up changing your mind as effortlessly as she changes her sex by taking over the man's prerogative, then switching back to a cuddly love bunny. She'll convince you with pure clear logic. You won't lose much—except your pride, and you'll hardly miss that, under the spell of that gentle Libran smile. She's usually right, because her final decisions are as carefully considered as those of the Supreme Court. Libran females don't need much encouragement to start a verbal comparison going between any two points of view. A politically active season will give her lots of chances to sharpen her rhetoric and her argumentative talents. She makes a great political worker, once she's made up her mind which side and which candidate is right.

Aside from the typical Libra penchant for weighing everything twice to make sure she didn't miss a point, she can be quite a lot of woman for a man who's interested in romance or companionship or both. Her tendency to argue is really based on a sincere desire to reach an impartial decision. It could be worse. At least she doesn't make up her own rules as she goes along, or stubbornly resist all reason, like women born under some other Sun signs. Besides, most of her opinions are presented with diplomatic tact, which somewhat softens the blow.

Perhaps the best way to get you to appreciate your Libra woman is to give you a quick rundown on what you would face with other Sun signs in a simple situation. Let's say you're discussing the subject of calling cards. Should people use them today, is it old-fashioned, and what should they look like? Take a fast flight around the zodiac. Pretend you're the only man in a room with twelve women. (That should be a pleasant supposition.) The discussion would run something like this:

Aries: Don't need them. I use the telephone.

Taurus: It's rare that I go calling. People visit me.

Gemini: Calling cards! Who has time for calling cards?

Leo: Well, if they were really wild, and impressive looking—

Virgo: I'll have to check Emily Post and see exactly what she says.

Sagittarius: My gawd! You mean people still take time for that junk?

Scorpio: If they're not home, they miss me. It's their loss, not mine.

Aquarius: I wonder if it's raining outside? I thought I heard thunder.

Cancer: Cards are so impersonal. I'd rather write a note.

Pisces: I always sense when people aren't there, and I only call on them when I get a subliminal message they want to see me.

Capricorn: The custom is perfectly proper. But there's no point in discussing the design. If it's not engraved, it's not a calling card.

Libra: Well, it all depends. If you want to do the correct thing, you should have them. It's a charming gesture. On the other hand, using them might seem pretentious today, and the modern woman is too busy to bother with them. Of course, you have to consider the reason behind the custom. Then again, there are people who can't afford calling cards. If it's a strain on the budget, they aren't really necessary. Looking at the other side of it, however, I can't help feeling the beauty and grace of yesterday is missing in today's frantic pace, so it might be money well spent. I suppose they should be engraved. Yet, it's true that something different would reflect the individual personality. A creative person could design his own. But such individual cards might be misunderstood by very social people, you know? I mean, the Rockefellers would think it was gauche. On reflection, who calls on the Rockefellers? Your own friends would love your being original, but plain engraving is probably more acceptable. At least I think it should be. But still— well . . .

Now she's run out of pros and cons, and she frowns slightly, under the strain of sorting out her own arguments and trying to dredge up an actual, firm decision from the lot.

You can see the Libran female is nothing if not fair, and committed to balanced judgment all around. You may get a little bored with her digressions on mundane subjects such as calling cards, but you'll sincerely appreciate her efforts at fairness, and her ability to judge correctly by weighing all sides, when it comes to something that really matters. Other women might toss off opinions that reflect their own individual natures, and seldom care much about what you think, or about a fair answer. To a Libra woman, there's no such thing as what she thinks is right. Your opinion deserves as much respect as hers and Plato's, until the decision is made, based on the flaws in her arguments, yours and all the philosophers.

Most Venus girls work both before and after marriage. They seek cash for the lovely things it can buy. The Libra bird needs lots of fine feathers for her luxurious nest. She loves beautiful clothes, expensive perfumes, classical music and—did somebody say she was masculine? Yes, I did. One side of her. But you will barely notice her hard head when it wears such pretty hair-dos. Mostly, Libran women need plentiful sums of money to remove them from the squalor and ugliness of discordant surroundings, which can actually make them emotionally and physically ill. But there's another reason she works, another reason she wants money. Her man. If there's one thing a Libra female treasures above all else on this temporal earth, it's the man she's chosen to love, honor and manage.

She hates to play solitaire. Partnerships, in both business and romance, constitute her deepest need. She doesn't like to work alone, and she's literally incapable of living alone. Libra women who visit astrologers have only two questions they really care about. If it's not one, it's always the other. Either: "When will I meet someone I really love?" or "When will I find someone to go into business with me?" With her, marriage is a joint venture, and the rules are almost as strict as those in a corporate setup. You are the president of the association, and you're honored as such. She's the chairman of the board, who will keep you from making mistakes, in her own feminine, protective way. Her nature is built for teamwork. She'll want to participate in as many of your interests and activities as possible. She's willing to entertain in her husband's behalf, and she's female enough to follow his lead when he wants to change his career, move to another city, or cultivate new friends. That's all his department. She's only there to smooth the way and be sure he doesn't goof anything by impulsive actions and ill-considered judgment.

You really have to give her credit. The typical Libra woman has no desire to be a stone around her husband's neck. She simply wants to remove all the stones in his path. She's not nearly as domineering on the surface as she is inwardly, because the last thing she wants to do is make a lot of positive statements you can hold her responsible for later. She'll tread gently in most cases (unless she has an Aries ascendant—and if you're mixed up with a woman who had a double cardinal influence like that at birth, you have a sizable problem).

The average Libra female is highly intellectual and has amazing powers of analysis, which can be a real help in solving your business problems. She seldom lets her emotions keep her from dispassionate decision or a balanced view, and she can usually give you better advice than your banker. Naturally, her abilities along these lines can cover a multitude of vices. Not only that, but if she's a typical Venus girl, she offers her pearls of wisdom on a silver platter of charm and amiable suggestion. Her iron hand wears a soft, velvet glove, and she can nudge you off the wrong track and in the right direction so gently, you'll swear the switch was entirely your own idea. An Aries, Scorpio, Leo or Taurus man will normally put his Libran wife on a pedestal and worship her. That's only

fair, because she worships him, too. Outsiders who visit the
love nest of a properly mated Libran and her husband may
feel as though they were seeing Adam and Eve, before the
snake came along and spoiled everything. (Two Librans
wed to each other invariably become cooing lovebirds or
snarling adversaries. They'll go to one extreme or the other,
sometimes on a permanent basis, sometimes every other
day.)

There are many rewards when you're living with a Libra
female. She'll never open your mail. It simply wouldn't
occur to her to be so dishonorable. She'll never reveal your
business secrets to your friends or embarrass you in front
of your boss. She'll probably charm him into submission,
too, with the same smile she used to melt your heart when
you first met her. There are some Libra women with
afflicted Mars positions who may over-indulge in excessive
emotions at times, or eat and drink more than is good for
them, but they're few and far between. Even if a Venus
female does occasionally trip over her own scales, sooner
or later she'll gracefully achieve her normal state of
heavenly harmony. There will be moments when you'll
wonder if she's an angel or devil, but the angels fight on
her side more often than not.

You probably won't complain of lack of physical proof
of her love, because she's as sentimental as old lace, and
as affectionate as a woman has any right to be. Although
she's sincere about her billing and cooing, those sweet
glances, tender touches, warm hugs and frequent kisses are
also a pretty effective smokescreen for her hidden masculine drive. There's no law that says sincerity can't have a
practical application.

Your home may look like one of those magazine ads for
wall-to-wall carpeting. The colors will harmonize, and the
furniture will be in good taste. Pictures will hang straight,
and meals will usually be served on time. With most Venus
girls you can also count on cloth napkins, sterling silver,
flowers on the table, good china, candlelight, wine, soft
music and a balanced menu. Taking into consideration her
clever mind and her sparkling wit, there's not a whole lot
more you could ask. Being a woman is sort of a lifetime
occupation to her, and she's bound to arrive at perfection
somewhere along the line. The masculine side of her will
rarely disturb you, unless you're one of those impossible
males who want to go shouting around like King Henry

VIII and expecting the women in your life to behave like obedient consorts, fearful of losing their heads if they say anything other than "yes" or "no." Your Libran consort will definitely say more than "yes" or "no." She likes to talk. But she'll also make a flattering listener, when you have a need for a good audience. This woman is both tough and soft at the same time, and it's not every female who can manage that delicate balancing act.

Her sweet manners and smooth ability to cool your fevered brow can lead you to think she's weak and helpless, or that she'll be fluttery and feminine when a crisis erupts. If so, you're much mistaken. That dear, womanly little creature is composed of nine parts steel. Just because you missed it when she was shrewdly and bravely planning to hook you during those early chess games when she kept letting you beat her, you shouldn't remain blind forever. Open your eyes wide the next time there's a family emergency, and see who keeps the boat from rocking. Who *really* does it, I mean. The truth needn't rob you of your masculinity. No one but you will know how much you need her helping hand at the helm when things get choppy. She'll never brag about it, or take anything away from you—except a large part of the responsibility. Be grateful she's so dependable. Besides, she looks kind of cute when she wears her slacks to garden or to the supermarket, doesn't she? Women in trousers are all right, as long as they have enough sense to wear frilly organdy to parties and slinky silk in privacy. She does. One of her most valuable assets is her ability to hide her sharp, keen mind behind utter femininity.

The children will be loved and tenderly cared for by a Libra mother, but in all honesty, they will come in a poor second to you. They're junior partners, but you are the president of the company, and she'll never forget that basic fact. They'll get a large chunk of her heart, but she'll never allow them to steal the corner she gave to you before they came along. If their play interferes with your rest, she can be pretty strict, and if they disobey you, she'll be angrier than if they disobeyed her. The youngsters will be sweet and clean as infants, neat and polite as adults—unless you spoil them and she doesn't interfere because you're the lord and master. It's just another one of those decisions she may leave in your hands so she can avoid making the wrong judgment. The Libra mother is normally gentle, yet quite firm when the need arises. Her children are never neglected or ignored, but the truth of the matter is that the reason she wanted to become a mother in the first place was so she could give *you* more happiness that way. One of the first things she'll teach them when they learn their prayers is to say, "God bless Daddy." She'll never permit them to disrespect their father. Still, if you get a little over-bearing, she's a pretty soft pillow for their tears, and she may sneak them a peppermint stick behind your back when you've put your foot down too severely.

It's true that she may nibble on sweets too often and get fat. She may linger too long at the dance or over the wine bottle. There may be times when she's a little bossy, and other moments when she talks your ear off. But these things will only occur when her emotional scales are temporarily off balance. They will never fail to settle into even steadiness when the occasional dipping is over. Unless somebody stands there with his foot on one of them, Libran scales always eventually balance themselves. If one side is a little low, add some affection and it will rise. If the other side drops from the weight of too much sadness, lighten it with understanding and her beautiful harmony will return.

What other woman could look like a princess when you take her to the ball, then turn right around, lace up her boots, zip up her red plaid lumber jacket, and help you saw logs for the fireplace? She has sweetness enough for the first and strength enough for the second. If her name is Peg, you'll be whistling *"Peg-O-My-Heart."* If it's Sally or Mary, you'll happily hum *"My Gal Sal"* or sing *"Mary Is a Grand Old Name."* In case the song writers have forgotten to pay her a tribute, write your own melody in waltz time, with a good, strong beat, and dedicate it to your Libra woman. Fortissimo.

The LIBRA Child

"She's in that state of mind," said the White Queen,
"That she wants to deny something—only she doesn't
know what to deny!"

"My, what a beautiful baby!" Parents of October infants
hear that phrase so often, they can be forgiven for feeling
smug. The little Libran does seem to be a plump, pink
angel, right out of the pages of a baby book. With his
sweet expression and those pleasant, well-balanced Venus
features, he's quite a charmer. He seldom kicks off his
blankets in red-faced, screaming rage, or punches Mommy
in the nose when she tries to give him his bottle. He's too
well-mannered for such wild shenanigans. When he smiles,
it lights up the whole nursery. "My, what a dear, good
baby! So quiet and calm. So chubby and dimpled. Surely
a gracious fairy touched him with her magic kiss."

I don't like to play the role of the mean old witch at the
royal christening, but would you mind checking to see if
he has a dimple in his chin? Most Libran babies do. You
found it? Well, just for fun, you might turn to the last page
of your baby record book and write a line Grandma was
fond of quoting. "Dimple in chin—Devil within." (Grandma may have secretly studied astrology.) There will come
a time in the future when you'll glance at that line and
silently pay tribute to her wisdom.

It may be some morning when he's sitting at the table,
slowly stirring his spoon in first one dish, then another.
The dish on the right contains his poached egg, all nicely
mashed the way he likes it. The dish on the left contains
his oatmeal, all nicely covered with brown sugar, the way
he likes it. Both are getting ice cold, and he hasn't taken
a bite. Isn't he hungry? Yes, he's starved. Does he have a
fever? No, he feels fine. Is he angry about something? No,
not at all. *Then why does he sit there so stubbornly and
keep pushing his spoon around like that? Why won't he
take a bite of something?*

He can't decide which to eat first—the eggs or the cereal. You just compounded the confusion by giving him a glass of orange juice and a piece of toast to try to tempt him. That was a mistake. Now he'll never be able to make up his mind. Better just forget breakfast today. Tomorrow morning, give him one thing at a time. First, the orange juice. He drinks it. Then the cereal. He eats it. Next the eggs. He loves them. Finally, the toast. As he sits there chewing happily, you'll be amazed that he ate all his breakfast in less than ten minutes. You have just learned the most important lesson in raising a Libra child. Never give him a choice. He hates to make a decision.

If there's anything a Libran child hates worse than making up his mind, it's having to make up his mind in a hurry. Don't rush him. Let's say he's learned to dress himself and in the excitement of such an adventure, over a period of weeks, he forgot his typical indecision. Now getting dressed is kind of old hat to him. You give him a start by helping him into his training pants. You lay out his overalls, shirt, shoes and socks. He sits there. "Get dressed, Harvey." He sits there. "Hurry up and get dressed, Harvey!"

The next thing you know, you'll be telling people your Libra child is stubborn. That's not fair. A Taurus child is stubborn. Not a Libra child. You are trying to rush him into deciding quickly which sock goes on which foot first. The whole thing is difficult enough, but just when he had made up his mind to put the left sock on the right foot, you shouted at him, disturbed his equilibrium, and now he's back where he was in the beginning. Which sock first? You see, it's your fault, not his. How does anyone expect him to make such a momentous decision if people are always shouting and hollering and yelling at him? It hurts his ear drums, and besides, it makes him forget what he was about ready to decide.

It's the kind of thing that can make you a little trembly, especially if you're the nervous type, and you're not the only one. Someday there will be a wonderful girl he's in love with. They will be discussing marriage. When and if. He'll sit there. Should he? Or shouldn't he? The girl waits patiently. He'll have the same pained expression on his pleasant features he has right now. Finally, "Harvey, are we going to get married?" He sits there. Then: "Harvey, when are we going to get married?" Poor girl. That's the same mistake you made with the orange juice and toast. Now he has two things to decide. Not only should they get married, but when. You'll have to have a talk with her.

But that's quite a few years off. Today it's the shoes and socks. Walk over to him firmly and say, "Harvey, let's put this sock on this foot first." Say it in gentle tones. Don't scream or be shrill. If you can, put the words to music and sing it to him. He'll love that. Now, you have removed two obstacles. You helped him decide, and you created a pleasant atmosphere. In five minutes, he's dressed. That's what the girl will have to do someday. She'll have to sing to him softly, "We're-getting-wed-on-June 26th" (to the tune of *"Here Comes the Bride"*). If she's the shy type, you may have to wait a long time to become a grandparent. The happy ending to the story is this: If you train him to make up his mind, without pushing, shoving or trying to rush him, the girl will profit, too. By then, he will have mastered his indecision.

Libra children whose parents have confused their delicate balance by constantly insisting that they decide things too fast often grow up with quite a neurosis about choices. Suggest a solution to him gently, over and over again. Eventually, he'll pick up the knack and you'll have helped him overcome one of his greatest difficulties. Show him how it's done. That's all. He may appear to be stubborn, but he's just reacting in typical Libran fashion to discordant interruption and the emotional trauma of being rushed through his careful moment of decision. He'd like to please you, he really would, but he can be efficient only when there's harmony of sound, color and thought in his world. Tension makes it hang crooked, like a lopsided picture. When hasty grownups force a young personality into the wrong mold, it may harden into an odd shape.

It may help you feel less frustrated to know about my friend, a dental technician whose wife presented him with *two* Libra children, three years apart, both girls. You can just imagine what went on in that house every morning! Four shoes—four socks—four feet—and two confused small minds. Until the parents discovered astrology, those little Libra girls went barefoot nearly every day.

It will also help if you remember the reason behind your child's hesitancy. Libra boys and girls are born with minds that seek the truth. They're kind-hearted, and they want to be fair. Your youngster dreads making a mistake or misjudging something. He hates to hurt your feelings, but his nature forces him to seek that balanced answer before he rushes pell mell into things, including socks. Still, that Libra caution builds character and it's great for avoiding accidents and keeping out of trouble, both now and in the future. Think positive. The little Libran may take so long deciding whether or not to draw a blue turkey on your living room wall, you'll catch him before the damage is done.

If your Libra youngster is being falsely accused of stubbornness, it may be that you keep the volume too high on the radio or TV. Perhaps the colors in his bedroom lie behind his restlessness at night. Garish, clashing tones will keep his emotional scales dipping back and forth. All shades of blue and pastels will quiet him, and it really works, too. Play music—but softly—when you want him to eat, get dressed or pick up his toys. If the sounds and colors around the Libran child are discordant, his actions will match. Being forced to be a witness to any kind of violence can destroy something deep inside him forever. Even as an infant, he'll jerk or tremble if he hears a sudden noise. The Libra child needs peace, quiet and rest in large doses.

That brings us to another problem. Libra laziness. It isn't actually laziness at all. He plays hard, for long periods, then he must rest. He isn't loafing. He's just gathering himself together. The Libran pattern demands periods of activity—then inactivity. It's the only way he can manage to stay emotionally and physically healthy. If he's made to feel guilty about it, he'll really be lazy, in self-defense. When you see the Libran youngster being idle, don't fuss. He'll soon have his inner scales balanced again and be ready for action. He's just recharging his energy. His planets made him that way. He can't change it.

Venus children are experts at softening hard hearts. They have such charming manners, they wheedle so sweetly and who could resist those smiles and dimples? The little Libran's gentle, endearing ways can turn his parents into two large genies who grant his every wish and desire (not to mention various assorted magic elves in the form of doting relatives). Consequently, these youngsters often start their school days so spoiled they're well nigh impossible to handle. After all, you can't treat a tot like a prince or princess for years, and then expect him to take orders. Young Librans don't need discipline as much as they need less coddling.

The average Libra child, raised with the proper balance, is a delight to his teachers. Their minds are bright and logical, they're fond of debate and they have a great curiosity that makes them good students. However, once they start to read and learn facts, both you and the teachers may be subjected to constant arguments.

It never works to make a flat statement to a Libra boy or girl. Always give both sides of any issue, or they'll think you're being unjust. When you give the edge to one side, the Libra student will make a big issue out of defending the other side until he forces you to be fair. If you're partial to the pros, the young Librans will always make a good case for the cons, which can give them a reputation for being rebels, when nothing could be further from the truth. These children will be sticklers for obeying the rules, as long as they've convinced themselves the rules aren't loopy. The scales must always balance, or Libra feels an unpleasant tug. He'll argue away until he feels things have been faced squarely, and the scales of justice are harmoniously lined up. October-born boys and girls always sharpen the wits of their parents and instructors, because it takes some good, logical thinking to keep up with them. They'll argue with you about everything from the newspaper headlines to who's right or wrong in a family disagreement. The Libra child won't like to hear grownups gossip. To him a confidence is sacred, and he also frowns on hasty judgments of character. He'll take the side of your worst enemy if he thinks you are wrong.

Never invade his privacy. He won't invade yours. Be sure mealtimes are pleasant. The girls will coax you to use candles and flowers; the boys will want a balanced meal and will probably love sweets. There may be some problems with overweight and the bathroom scales will get a workout.

One blessing about having Libra children is that if they haven't retreated into resentment through harsh handling they'll usually be neat and clean without being forced. Most of these boys and girls hate messes and an untidy house so much they'll help to keep it neat. Since Libra is both musical and artistic, you may have a budding composer or artist in the family, so make sure he has an opportunity to develop any latent talents.

The tiny Libra girl may dust your expensive powder all over her dress, pour your best perfume over her curly head, and hate to get out of the bathtub. She's just reacting to Libra's love of beauty and pleasant things, like scents and warm water. When she's a teenager, she'll monopolize the bathroom for hours with her bubble baths and use up all your guest soap. Remember, she seeks harmony; and to her, peace, beauty and comfort equal harmony.

The Libra boy may drive you to distraction with his snoozes in the hammock, and his irritating way of always knowing more than you do about subjects that should be over his heads. (Yes, sometimes you'll swear he has two.) But those periodic naps are refreshing his energy. It didn't die, it's just replenishing itself. As for his know-it-all attitude, he may be practicing on you for a future career as a lawyer. Take an optimistic view. The jury will someday be his captive audience, but you can always go start dinner or hide behind the evening paper. Encourage both boys and girls to write if they feel an urge. Remember that Libra rules books, too.

The teenagers of both sexes will keep a constant cloud of romance hanging over the house. There may be so many cases of puppy love you'll feel as though you live in a sentimental kennel—but even this shall pass away. Those wedding bells will ring someday, and your Libra offspring will raise a nice, peaceful, balanced, harmonious, argumentative family. Some sunny October morning you may once again stand in front of a hospital nursery, and hear a nurse or visitor coo, "My, what a beautiful baby! So dear and good. So quiet and sweet." And you'll say, with all your hard earned wisdom, "Yes, but do you see that dimple in his chin?"

The LIBRA Boss

*"Unimportant, of course, I meant," the King hastily
said, and went on to himself in an undertone,
"Important—unimportant—unimportant—important—"
as if he were trying which word sounded best.*

If you're a man, you probably think your Libra boss is
one heck of a regular guy, fair and square, always on the
level. If you're a woman, you may be a little bit in love
with him, whether you realize it or not. Venus vibrations
are powerful.

The Libra executive is normally one half of a partnership since his unconscious desire is always to bring two
things or two people together. Emotionally, the urge is
consummated through an early marriage or a shockingly
early love affair. In business, he satisfies his balancing
function by combining his charm and intellect with a
partner who complements his own personality, and sup-
plies whatever talents and abilities he lacks. (He won't
lack many.)

He may not sit behind a desk as often as other bosses.
That's because he likes to sit on the fence. It's not that he
finds it more comfortable. It can be quite painful. Notice
his unhappy expression while he's seated there. It's a
struggle, as he takes two opposing ideas and weighs them,
back and forth. Once he's achieved a fair and impartial
decision, he'll be back at his desk, happily swirling in his
contour chair again. But while he's on the fence he can be
mighty hard to fathom.

The Libra boss is extremely restless and full of outgoing
activity, yet he never seems to be in a hurry, a contradiction few people can manage. It's like watching a skillful
juggler. With all that restless activity, you expect him to
drop his poise and break into a nervous run at any moment,
just as you expect the juggler to drop one of the balls he's
tossing. But neither does. Born with a natural affinity for
the element of air, the Libran accomplishes even frenzied

action with so much easy grace, he almost seems to be standing still. It's like a movie in slow motion. The activity never stops, but the projector is set at a peculiar speed.

In spite of his often shy, gentle manner, this man is not an island. There's always a need to express himself in some way, to communicate with others. Though most of his communicating is done through speech, he can also tell you whole volumes with his smile. He's sure to be intelligent, but if Mercury was afflicted by adverse aspects at his birth, he may still be trying to convince himself that he is. Many Libran bosses are persuasive talkers and great debaters who can sway a whole roomful of people effortlessly. Even the shy Libran executive who seldom tries to grab attention can argue logically and convincingly, although this type will probably plan everything in his mind before he speaks. That's why he's so quiet for such long periods. He's deciding what he wants to say. It's usually safer to take his statements straight after he's passed through one of his silent moods. He's less likely to change his mind. If he's rushed into making a decision, he'll mull it over afterwards, realize his first thoughts were hasty and do a complete turnabout.

You may find him seeking your opinion frequently. Before you decide he thinks you've a brilliant brain, remember that there are several motives for his flattering interest in your ideas. First of all, he wants to be fair. He doesn't want to make either an unjust or unpopular decision. Another reason he feels compelled to gather up all the pros and cons of an issue is because, without access to all the available facts, he feels incapable of making a wise assessment.

The typical Libra boss who's trying to make up his mind whether to say "yes" or "no" to an important deal will take a democratic poll of his wife, the elevator man, his secretary, the cleaning woman and his public relations man, and it can have some pretty weird results. It's difficult for a tired cleaning woman to give a logical opinion on how the proposed split might affect the shareholders of the non-voting stock. She may need some time to ponder it. (She can't think straight when her feet hurt.)

The elevator man may have a little trouble grasping the costs involved in a projected merger of two large corporations. For one thing, $40,000 for attorneys' fees may seem extravagant to him. He paid his lawyer forty dollars one time for legal advice, and he felt like a spendthrift.

That vice-president who continues to draw his salary while he's in the hospital with a nervous breakdown will really throw the Libran's secretary. After all, she's been on the verge of a mental crack-up for several years, and nobody ever coddled her like that.

The cleaning woman finally makes up her mind. Forget the stock split; she's never trusted that word. It was when her old man split out that she had to start mopping floors to support the seven kids.

The Libran's wife says, "Do what you think best, dear," but she makes it clear she privately thinks he should take a negative stand because she doesn't like the wife of one of the major stockholders.

The public relations man never changes his opinion: "Damn the torpedos—full speed ahead!"—is his advice on all problems.

Finally, the consensus is complete. Armed with this expert analysis, the Libra boss will still manage to arrive at a more logical, sensible final decision than nine out of ten men would make. It's amazing, but he does it somehow.

There could be still another reason he seeks so many viewpoints when he's making up his mind. He may be one of those rare Librans who maneuvers to shift the blame for a possible mistake to someone else's shoulders. When things fall through, he can always shrug and say, "Well, it wasn't my idea to back away. The cleaning woman thought it was a bad move."

However, a Libra boss who's managed to achieve harmony and unity of his mind and emotions can be a regular well of wisdom. For all I know, you may work for one. There are lots of them around, and they're nice bosses to know when you have a problem. They can come up with an answer that no one else could have thought of, taking everything into consideration and giving you an out that's both fair and smart.

The chances are that the walls of your Libra boss's office are not bare—although the picture of the girl on his calendar may be. The walls will normally be covered with pictures, trophies, and good prints, hung in balanced positions, and the filing cabinets will be dusted. You can bet that there's a radio or record player somewhere around so he can tune in to melodious sounds when things get too discordant and his nerves get dangerously jingle-jangled from the confusion of daily routine. The colors in his office will seldom be wild. No exotic lime green or brilliant tangerine that hurt his eyes. However, there may be just a touch of the oriental motif. Some Librans seem to lean slightly in that direction. Perhaps it's because of the legendary quiet, gentle manner of living in the far east or the peaceful harmony of Eastern philosophy. He may not go so far as to have flowers on his desk, but if your Libran boss is a female, she probably will.

There are more female bosses born under Libra than any other sign, though Aries, Capricorn, Leo and Cancer run a close second. Assuming that he is a she, your Libra boss will almost surely have a big potted plant in the office, plus a large mirror. Music will be around her somewhere, too. She may not procrastinate quite as much as the men of the sign; since it's more difficult for a woman to achieve a level of command, she had to control her indecision or she wouldn't have made it to the top of the totem pole. Like her masculine counterpart, the Libran female boss will try to be fair. She'll listen to office squabbles and be able to see both sides with equal clarity. You may catch her hiding behind her door, weighing her golden scales, when the decision is important, but there's one area where she won't take long to make up her mind. Love. She's either already decided marriage is not for her, or she's constantly a little dreamy-eyed from a recent romance. It's a rare Libran female, executive or not, who can live without a valentine in her life. Though she's an expert at hiding her after-five activities, I can assure you she's not playing a solitary game of Chinese checkers every night. She may curl up with a good book on a rainy Monday, but most weekends will find her doing the town in a romantic haze. The haze, however, will be temporary. Her mind is too sharply logical to let sentiment completely blind her. Few Librans of either sex let the heart rule the head. Their heads are too hard and too bright to submit to the soft rays of Venus without a fight, another of Libra's strange inconsistencies.

This lady boss will probably be undeniably pretty or beautiful. If she's neither, you'll think she is when that Venus smile flits over her plain features. Her charming social graces may fool the customers and clients, but if you've worked for her any length of time, you'll be aware that her graceful sweetness covers a mind which doesn't miss a trick or a treatment.

She'll have her cross days, and she will probably contradict herself enough to leave you up in the air now and then. In the discipline area she's somewhat harsher than the male Libran. If you make a mistake, she'll know it instinctively, and you'll get a strong message that she doesn't want to see it multiply into daily errors. Her voice will be soft, or slightly husky, well-modulated and perhaps a little drawling, and she'll seldom raise it. (With an Aries, Gemini or Sagittarius ascendant, the air might get a little blue when she sees red.)

The lady Libra boss often looks as if she should be on the list of the "Ten Best Dressed Women," and maybe she actually is. Female employees chew their nails with envy at her wardrobe, furs, jewels and perfumes. The men employees react as you might expect. Every last one of them. Except for the lions, scorpios, bulls, goats and rams, who feel that working for a woman is like serving time at Leavenworth. The rest will succumb to her dimpled charm with nary a struggle.

When you're tempted to treat her like one of the girls, don't get too chummy. Her friendly attitude may seem to encourage confidences, but she won't tolerate powder room gossip, and she'll stamp out any signs of it at the water cooler. She didn't get where she is by having a loose tongue. Librans of both sexes treat a confidence as a sacred trust. Some of them may talk a lot, and they all adore to argue, but they're not gossips. There's a difference.

Both the male and female Libra bosses lean toward long, pleasant lunch hours. If they don't take them, you should see that they do, because they won't be their usual liberal selves when they're hungry or tired. All Venus executives would be better off if they faced up to their need for periodic rest and snoozed for an hour or so each day. You might get the employees to chip in to buy an attractive sofa for his office, if you want to keep your Libra boss balanced. He's a cat napper, but he may feel guilty about it. The day he comes to work wearing a blue expression and sporting red eyes, with droopy, gray bags under them, is a day you'll want to avoid him.

Unless he has a strongly independent ascendant he'll probably believe in unions. Anything fair is okay with him. His sense of justice makes him a natural in mediating disputes. The Libran viewpoint on money is seldom neutral. He'll either be the stingiest boss in town or the most generous. Sometimes, he may take turns: be a tightwad in December and a Santa Claus in July. There will always be a definite attitude at any given moment. He tips either a nickel or a five spot.

Sooner or later, you'll be invited to his home. Almost every Libran executive eventually wants to entertain his employees under his own roof, and he'll be an impeccably gracious host.

He's probably the soul of gallantry in front of women, and at the same time a man's man. The sure way to earn his disfavor is to be loud, vulgar and opinionated. Remember that harmony is his middle name. Create it when you can—never destroy it or disrupt it—and he'll want you around without knowing exactly why.

His occasional indecisiveness may annoy you; he may procrastinate and his dreams may need a little push now and then. Still, there's that smile, the respect you have for his quiet intelligence, and his willingness to meet you halfway. He doesn't want you to top him, yet he won't expect you to be his slave. He's neither a pusher nor a nagger, and he'll never betray your trust. When you add it all up, the scales balance in his favor. His is a blending nature. Your Libra boss really needs your cooperation to be a complete person himself, and a man who needs you can get a firm grip on your loyalty, if not on your heart. Haven't you felt the tug?

The LIBRA Employee

*"I wish they'd get the trial done . . .
And hand round the refreshments!"*

There was once a Libran designer who was brought to the west coast to do the costumes for a big movie, and he sat in his suite in a posh Beverly Hills hotel for six full weeks without making a single sketch. It wasn't because he lacked ideas. He was overflowing with them. It was the carpeting

—that hideous, shrill, peacock blue carpeting. It gave him migraine nightmares. He couldn't even think straight, let alone create, and he didn't want to change his suite because he liked the view of the palm trees.

For almost two months the film was held up until the producer finally discovered the problem. As soon as he was made aware of the Libran's aesthetic difficulties, the offensive floor covering was replaced by new wall-to-wall carpeting in an acceptable, subdued rose shade. If you're wondering why the producer was so understanding, he was a Gemini. Whether or not the designer's complaint was reasonable didn't concern him. The Gemini simply wanted to get things moving as quickly as possible, and he took the speediest way out. Both Aquarian and Gemini bosses are fabulous when it comes to handling the delicate Venus temperament. There's an intangible empathy between air signs. They're all floating around on some kind of cloud, but at different altitudes.

Please don't get the impression that you should run right out and find a rug salesman if you have a Libra employee. Not all people born in late September or October are irreplaceable artists with such sensitive nerves. But even the average Libra employee will work more happily if his surroundings don't distract him.

He'll also be more efficient if he isn't offended by the people he works with every day. A rough, sordid, unharmonious atmosphere may depress him, but uncongenial coworkers will really send him into a blue fog. He's as conscious of the vibrations of personalities as he is of the vibrations of colors, especially in close quarters. If your Libra employee has seemed confused lately, or not himself; if he's been turning in sloppy work which doesn't meet his usual standard, he's not necessarily slipping. Perhaps he's allergic to the mail boy or the cleaning woman. (I hope it's not his own secretary. The constant, abrasive pain would be unbearable.) It might even be the blotter on his desk. Give him a nice, new, clean one, preferably in a baby blue, change the cleaning woman's shift and keep the mail room staff away from him. Notice how his work improves immediately? He was just off balance.

When those Libra scales get tipsy, anything can happen. Both the male and female Librans can turn disgruntled and lazy and offer no excuse for their sullen silences. Such a change from their normal sweetness and calm is bound to unsettle your own mind a little, too. How can anyone with such an attractive dimple in his (or her) chin be so disagreeable? It's easy. How would you like *your* scales to be tipped sideways? It's not a pleasant feeling—rather like being on a boat that's rolling from port to starboard on a choppy ocean. Something may have happened at home to turn him around. Whatever the cause, it's a waste of anxiety to let yourself get disturbed when the Libra scales are unbalanced. It seldom takes long for the Libran to get them swinging harmoniously again. Then peace and tranquility will reign once more in your office; your Libran's work will be as inspired as ever, and you'll return to melting as usual when you get warmed by that incomparable Venus smile.

If there's a union of any kind connected with your company, the chances are the Libran employee will be right in there defending equal rights and fair wages. In fact, lots of people born under this Sun sign make unions their life work. The most important thing to all Librans is harmony. Perfect justice is their ideal. Unions offer him just too good a chance to pass up for his natural talent in settling disputes.

If there's no union to call for his fair judgment, then he's probably the one who becomes the peacemaker when office quarrels rage. The typical Libran is beautifully adept at clearing the air of disagreements. He defends both sides with a total lack of prejudice for either, makes opposing wranglers see each other's viewpoint, and finally tops it off by getting everyone to shake hands all around. The thing which may completely confound you is that he will instigate a few heated arguments himself. But you must remember that to him, these are healthy debates. He loves nothing more than batting the pros back to the cons, then switching to pitch the cons against the pros. In his eyes, that's not fighting. A good, intelligent argument is pure entertainment. It's better than going to the movies. He's usually cheerfully unaware that he's creating any tension when he drives his points home with brilliant logic, and causes others to strangle on their weak suppositions. As soon as his game of brain busting reaches the point where tempers become obviously frayed, he's dismayed. Then, if he's a typical Venus person, he'll quickly pour healing balms over the open wounds, and flatter everyone out of their bad humor with the sunshine of his smile. Frankly, you could kill him for manipulating you so casually.

Soothing *his* hurt feelings when he's been offended is another matter altogether. It's difficult to figure just what annoys or pleases the Libran employee. What brought a twinkling laugh or a wreath of tolerant smiles one day can bring a severe frown of injured innocence the next, or vice versa. It's those scales again, of course. How can Libra tell in advance what his mood will be toward any given subject when he doesn't know himself how far he'll be dipping to one side or the other? Ask his co-workers. Does that fellow (or girl) with the dimpled grin have unpredictable reactions? You'll get answers like, "Well, the other day I asked her if she had gained a little weight, and she smiled at me so sweetly, I got the idea she thought it was becoming. This morning I called her 'Chubby' in jest, and she won't speak to me." Or you'll get a reply like, "Well, last week, he showed me a record he bought at the Colony Record Shop—one of those old Glenn Miller 78's—and I remarked that big bands are as outdated as dinosaurs. He just grinned, and said he was a student of ancient history. Today, he heard me telling the receptionist that big bands are square, and he nearly took my head off and called me a sick, psychedelic hippy. He had a great sense of humor about it last week. How was I supposed to know he collects big band albums, lights a candle every night and listens to them like he's in a cathedral?"

Libra will love you today for what he hated you for last month, and he'll despise you tomorrow for what he found delightful yesterday. It's a little delicate to deal with his changeable reactions, but underneath all the ups and downs, the Libra nature remains basically fair and sane. His frowns are only skin deep. His smiles are real. Ignore the first and hang on to the second. In fact, nothing rocks the typical Venus person more than unnecessary shouting and tension. He's far more likely to avoid nasty scenes than to court them. There's never any vinegar in the Venus anger. There may be a little ice around the edges, but ice does eventually melt, you know.

Female Libran employees often remind you of a slice of whole wheat toast. There's a sort of Campfire Girl mystique about them. Of course, a few may have maple sugar spread on the whole wheat, in the form of dove-like voices and soft manners, but it's a pleasant sweetness. You'll rarely find a Venus girl who looks tough and battered with jaded eyes and blatant sex appeal. Hers is more of a fresh and mellow appeal, like the red and gold hues of Indian summer, against clear, blue skies. The Libra cupcakes who drip with syrupy icing are in the minority. You'll probably get the instant impression that this girl can handle herself nicely in a game of touch and tackle.

She may like to go on long hikes, and spend a lot of time at the library. If not, you can safely wager that she takes long walks, and belongs to a book club. The physical activity and literary leanings are always present. It's just a matter of degree. But there will be long rest periods between the walks or hikes, as she replaces energy with lassitude and lethargy. (That's when she catches up on her reading.)

Your Libra salesman may be studying for a law degree on the side, or he could have a hobby that's practically a second career. He may be a professional in some area outside his job, and have an expert knowledge of deep subjects you never dreamed he would think about. One thing, however, you can be sure he thinks about: Girls. Women. Feminine pulchritude. At least ninety percent of all Libra males subscribe to a *Playboy* type magazine. Even if he's bashful about it, the Venus man will enjoy a few discreet glances at the pictures of curvy bunnies who are wearing little more than a dazzling, provocative smile. He likes seeing them in person even more, which is why you'll frequently find him following the nightclub circuit, though he may leave after the floor show when the noisy crowds begin to topple his harmony. The happily mated Libran will seldom carry his interest in the opposite sex any farther than obvious visual appreciation, but the single ones can be real Lotharios.

Librans are always either married, engaged, divorced or in the middle of an important love affair. They never paddle their canoes alone. Echoing across the blue lagoon, you can always hear the stealthy footsteps of a squaw or a brave in the Libran's lodge at eventide, under the pale moon. For every Libra Hiawatha, there's a maiden, and you can reverse it.

Keep your lovely, pretty Libra girls and your handsome, gentle Libra men happy with piped-in music while they work. Don't ever shout at them, and be sure you always give them logical reasons for doing things. Respect their intelligence, because they'll have more of it than the average person, and never subject them to tension.

If they're treated right, your Libra employees will never cause friction in the office; they'll be angels of tact and diplomacy, getting along with almost everyone. The Venus worker brings his own personal aura of grace and beauty to everything he touches. Let him help you with sales strategy, and encourage him to attend the top brass brainstorming meetings. Might as well let him get the hang of how the executive level operates, because Libra is a cardinal sign, and he won't be an employee without status forever. He wants to lead, and he's well-qualified. As soon as you can, put him in charge of something, then watch how effortlessly he handles red tape, petty grievances, knotty problems and bottlenecks. He'll dress like a man of distinction, and behave like one, too. He's great for company image. As for her, a Venus woman will get what she wants eventually, in her own sweet way. If it's a promotion she wants, let her have it. She probably won't let you down. There's quite a smart head on those shapely shoulders. Why not take advantage of it?

Your Libra employee may have a little trouble making up his mind at times. His train of thought never runs at breakneck speed when the destination is a decision, but it seldom goes off the track. After he's finally pulled into the station, he'll probably have the right answer, even if it was like watching a two-headed giraffe do his bending exercises to get it out of him.

Librans are extremely artistic and musically inclined, with a flair for law and a philosophical bent. They bring their calming influence most often to hospitals, show business, publishing companies, the halls of science, courtrooms, gardens, politics, department stores, interior decorating and the ministry. But regardless of where you find them spreading harmony, the Libran thermostat will usually read about seventy degrees Fahrenheit. It seldom plunges to freezing or rises to scorching. It's like having a human air conditioner in the office, with automatic repair service when it breaks down. You don't get guarantees like that from the mechanical kind. You say machines can't talk back? Well, that's true, but on the other hand—now wait a minute—stop weighing everything I say, back and forth. You sound like a Libra!

*"The horror of that moment," the King went on,
"I shall never, never forget!"
"You will though," the Queen said,
"if you don't make a memorandum of it."*

SCORPIO
the Scorpion, Eagle or Gray Lizard

October 24th through November 22nd

How to Recognize SCORPIO

*"The question is . . . which is to be master—
that's all."*

An encyclopedia describes a scorpion as a nocturnal arachnid that attacks and paralyzes its prey with a poison injected by the long, curved tail, used for both defense and destruction. Its sting is sometimes fatal.

People often draw back visibly when someone says he or she was born in November, murmuring, "Oh, you're a Scorpio!" either in frank fear, or in awe and respect. Sometimes there's also a giggle that obviously refers to the legendary Scorpio passion. Scorpios are fed up with these reactions to their Sun sign, and who can blame them? But they are ruthless and dangerous, right?

Wrong. It depends. First, you'd better learn how to recognize the sign. In self-defense perhaps—or because you seek a really superior human being.

Scorpio likes to travel incognito. Thanks to his well-controlled nature, he usually succeeds, but there are a couple of short cuts which will make it easier to penetrate his disguise at midnight or at noon.

Look at the eyes. They can be green, blue, brown or black, but they'll be piercing with hypnotic intensity. Most people feel nervous and ill at ease under Scorpio's steady gaze. You'll have to break the spell and look away first. He'll outstare you every time. It's a foolproof identification of the Pluto personality. Scorpio eyes bore deeply into you, mercilessly, as if they're penetrating your very soul. They are.

Next, listen to him speak. The tone can be velvety soft, husky or sharply cutting, the speech slow and measured or clipped and staccato, but what he says will never be self-effacing. Scorpio has total ego. He knows what he is and he knows what he is not, and nothing anyone else thinks will change this knowledge. Insults roll right off his back, and compliments don't move him a fraction of an inch. He needs no one to tell him his vices or his virtues. At best, he'll calmly agree with your appraisal; at worst, he'll suspect your motives.

The next time you're with a group of people, bring up a discussion of Sun signs. Mention that, with a little practice, it's fairly easy to recognize them. When someone fastens you with a hypnotic gaze, and states with supreme confidence, "You can't guess what I am," say firmly, "You're a Scorpio." It may be the first time he's ever blinked. But his stare will waver only for an instant, and he'll quickly regain the cool composure he exhibited before you exposed his careful disguise. If you ever come across a chattering Scorpio whose eyes wander, chalk him up as an astrological exception as rare as the dodo bird. There are some November people with heavy planetary influences of restlessness in their nativities, but you're trying to learn to recognize the typical Scorpio. You'll find very few of the nervous kind. The nature can be modified by other natal influences, but only slightly.

Most Pluto people have powerful physiques. The features are noticeably heavy or sharp, and clearly drawn, and the nose is quite prominent, sometimes beak-shaped. Ordinarily, the complexion is very pale, almost translucent, and the brows are heavy and knit together over the bridge of the nose. There's a crackling, electric vitality about the very presence of a Scorpio that gives him away. As quiet as he tries to be, such a vital force can't be hidden completely. The males will have a heavy growth of hair on the arms and legs, often with a reddish cast. Most Scorpios have darkish hair and eyes, but don't overlook the frosty blonde types, of which Grace Kelly and Billy Graham are excellent examples. Frosty on the outside, that is. The poised surface calm of the Pluto character is carefully designed to hide the boiling inner nature.

Such mastery of the personality has to be envied. No matter how his emotions are stirred, you'll rarely see them reflected on Scorpio's frozen, immobile face. These people proudly and consciously practice a blank expression. They command their features to remain firm, and their features obey. (They wouldn't dare disobey a Scorpio.) You'll seldom see Scorpio give himself away by blushing or flushing, frowning or grinning. Smiles are rare, but genuine. The body follows the same orders as the face. There will rarely be any jumping, sudden starts or nervous mannerisms.

He'll never flinch with embarrassment or swell up with pride. Reaction is always kept at a bare minimum, because Scorpio's art is to probe your nature and motives relentlessly, while remaining inscrutable himself, and he's an expert at it.

It's important to remember that there is a particular type of Scorpio who moves and speaks rather quickly, and appears to have an open, friendly manner. Look deeply into his eyes and really think about some of his past actions, his true behavior. He's really just playing a game with all his happy talk. Inside, he's as tough and determined as the more typical, poised Pluto people. Perhaps he's even a shade more dangerous because his disguise is better, and he fools you more easily. Start treating him as Charlie-nice-guy, who's completely harmless, and you may be courting some trouble. Be on guard with all Scorpios. I don't mean they're wicked. They're just not soft or naive. Some Scorpios, realizing that their eyes expose their inner intensity, wear sunglasses frequently, even at night.

Remark to a Scorpio that he has a great talent which will someday be recognized, and he smoothly, casually replies, "Yes. I know." Ask him if he'll do you a favor, and the answer will be equally simple. "Yes, of course I will," or "No, I can't do that."

If you're sensitive, don't ask his opinion or advice. You'll get the naked, brutal truth. You asked him, he'll tell you. Scorpio will not pay a false compliment to gain a point or win an ally. It's beneath him to flatter. When he says something nice to you, treasure it. You can be sure it's sincere and unvarnished. If he says you have a good voice, stop singing in the shower and grab a microphone. If he says you have a great voice, you can safely audition for the Met. He may even effortlessly move a few mountains out of your way to help you along. Don't believe everything you hear about Scorpio selfishness. Instead, listen to some of the grateful people who have been on the receiving end of his wise counsel and generosity. Scorpio naturally attracts either fiercely loyal and dedicated admirers, or envious and spiteful enemies. But even the latter give him grudging respect, and you'll notice they're careful not to challenge him openly. The examples of the few who did are vivid and painful reminders that caution is required in an attack against Scorpio and his planet, Pluto. Remember that Pluto rules nuclear power.

Yet, there's a haunting sweetness about these people, and often a gentle sympathy with the sick or despairing. Scorpio's touch can be cool and tender, as well as hot. His Sun position gives him several paths to follow. He can imitate the nocturnal scorpion, who will sting others and even sting himself to death for the pure pleasure of stinging—or he can imitate the glorious, soaring path of his symbolic eagle, who rises above earthly limitations, and uses his strength wisely and justly. Great generals like MacArthur, presidents like Theodore Roosevelt and scientists like Madame Curie and Jonas Salk are eagles. More United States presidents have been born under this sign than any other.

As for the nocturnal scorpions, you may have been stung by a few yourself. Ancient astrology refers to them as serpents. It's not hard to guess which category the ones you meet belong to. A few Pluto people fall somewhere between the eagle and the stinging scorpion, victims of their own black magic. These are the gray lizards. With them, supreme self sacrifice becomes neurotic concern about the self, and psychic abilities become fearful apprehensions of the lurking evils which may strike at any moment. Forceful courage twists itself around, and instead of seeking the ruthless revenge of the stinger scorpions—or rising above such bitterness like the eagles—they bitterly withdraw in tangled hatreds at each minor injury, hoping fate will punish their enemies, almost unconsciously willing destruction without direct action.

The gray lizards fail to draw on the power of Pluto in their natures—power that could lift them high above all the unfortunate circumstances that surround them. In the very teeth of tragedy, this awesome inner strength could give them a new life in the sunlight. But they seek the dark shadows and lie dormant, a pathetic waste of the brilliant potential of their birthright. Still, Scorpio can never slide deep enough into the slime of bitter depression to completely lose the power of Pluto. It's never too late for the gray lizard to transform himself into an eagle. That kind of deep magic belongs exclusively to every person born under the Sun sign of Scorpio. All they need do is to call on it.

Typical eagles have no fear. In battle they'll lead their men into the very face of death without a tremor. Even the average Pluto man or woman bravely faces anything

from physical pain and poverty to ridicule and failure with
a proud contempt and complete confidence in an inner
ability to overcome any blow.

Scorpio is intensely loyal to friends. "Greater love hath
no man than this, that a man lay down his life for his
friends." Some of them do this literally, for friends, relatives or loved ones—in battle or in a civilian crisis. The
Scorpio soldier leaps instantly, instinctively, to brave the
bullets and drag his buddy to safety. The Scorpio fireman
gives his life to rescue the child in the burning building.
Sometimes it seems Pluto people unconsciously seek violence deliberately, as a challenge to their strength.

Scorpio never forgets a gift or a kindness, and it's richly
rewarded. Conversely, he also remembers an injury or an
injustice, but there are different ways of reacting. The
eagle will crush the enemy so the enemy learns never to
hurt him again, win the fight, and leave the defeated to
go his own way. The deadly nocturnal scorpion will first
sting, then plan destruction, then sting again. He's not
content with merely evening the score. He must totally
destroy the enemy, or at least top him. The typical scorpion
stinger will lie awake nights figuring how to get even.
If a neighbor deliberately scrapes his fender, he'll scrape
two fenders on the neighbor's car the next day, and maybe
drive over his carefully pruned hedges for good measure.
These scorpions are seldom content with forcing the shoe
on the other foot to teach enemies how it feels. They
glue the sandal on with cement. However, with the gray
lizards, Pluto revenge takes the form of bitterness held
inside for years, which inevitably causes deep melancholy
or actual, lingering physical illness. Seething Scorpio resentment, turned inward and never expressed, poisons with
deadly certainty. Turned outward, it can create guilt, because the stinger scorpion is ashamed to harm the defenseless, when all is said and done. Therefore, it should be
turned neither way—inward nor outward. It should be
conquered by looking up and forgetting, like the eagle—
never by looking back in anger and retaliation.

The Scorpio health picture is typical of his nature. He
can destroy his body with excesses, melancholy or hard
work. But he can also build it back at will from a critical
illness. Pluto's power is that strong. Scorpios are seldom
sick, but when they are, it's usually serious. A long rest
and a change of attitude, with peaceful acceptance re-

placing burning resentment, are the best cures. They can't let well enough alone, and of course, they know more than the doctor and all the nurses. The chief areas of attack for germs and accidents are the reproductive organs, the nose, the throat, the heart, spine, back, circulatory system, legs and ankles. Varicose veins and accidents in sports are common. They should avoid fire, explosives, noxious fumes and radiation. Yet, you'll find lots of them seek occupations that flirt with danger along these very lines. Sometimes they have chronic nose bleeds, or surgery is performed on the nose for some reason.

Scorpio is deeply interested in religion, intensely curious about all phases of life and death, passionately concerned with sex and violently drawn by a desire to reform. Yet he's also heroic, dedicated to ties of family and love, and gently protective of children and weaker souls. He can be a saint or a sinner. He can experiment with the darkest mysteries this side of Hades, or he can scathingly revile sin and decadence. Whether he emotes from a pulpit, at a business meeting, or from a stage, his hypnotic appeal pierces through his audience, literally transfixing or transfiguring them. It's really rather frightening. Even if the Scorpio has temporarily allowed bitterness, drink or melancholy to drag him into the Bowery, you can bet your old copy of Dante's *Inferno* that the other bums will clear a path when they see him coming.

He's fiercely possessive of what he believes to be his, including success, but his ambition is never obvious. He quietly waits for the chance to move ahead all the while he serves, knowing he is qualified for the position above him. He takes control slowly, but very surely. Scorpio can do just about anything he wants to do. If he *really* wants it, it's most definitely no longer a dream. The dark, magical and mysterious power of Pluto turns desire into reality with cool, careful, fixed intent.

Although a morbid desire to know the worst of sick and depraved humanity can create a gray lizard who dabbles in drugs and cruelty, he can reverse the path to a life of medicine, where drastic treatments with the same symbols have a deep fascination for him. Although many of the rumored sadistic surgeons are Scorpios, it's equally true that many of the finest medical men in the entire world are inspired by Pluto to heal both the mind and the body, diagnosing and treating with strange, inscrutable knowledge.

Scorpio was born knowing the secrets of life and death, and with the ability to conquer both if he chooses. But astrology constantly advises him that "he must know that he knows." The ancient mysteries fascinate his brilliant mind. Out of his powerful empathy with human nature grows the outstanding detective, the composer of great musical works, literature of depth and permanence, or the actor who projects with unusual dramatic intensity. Sometimes he lives alone, near the sea, as strong and as silent as the tides. Sometimes he faces the public, wearing a mask of calm reserve and control, to hide his intense desire to win. He can be a politician or a television star, an undertaker or a bartender, but he'll manage to top all his competitors. And he'll do it so effortlessly it will seem like an act of fate rather than his own powerful will.

One of the strangest patterns in astrology is the death of a relative in the family within either a year before or the year after the birth of a Scorpio. And when a Scorpio dies, there will be a birth in the family within the year before or the year after. It happens at least ninety-five percent of the time. Pluto's symbol is the triumphant phoenix rising from its own smoldering ashes, and Scorpio personifies the resurrection from the grave. Both the gray lizards and the stinging scorpions can become proud eagles without ever revealing the secret of their sorcery. No use to ask—Scorpio will never tell. But he knows the eternal truth of the circle contained in the symbolic zero.

November's thistle is dangerous, yet it grows entwined with the heavy, languid beauty of the Scorpio honeysuckle. Have you ever inhaled that sweet, overwhelming fragrance on a still midsummer's night? Then you will know why there are those who brave the thistles to seek the gentleness of Scorpio—exquisite gentleness. The explosive passion of Pluto has the rich, dark red wine color of the bloodstone. But Scorpio steel is tempered in a furnace of unbearable heat until it emerges cool, satiny smooth—and strong enough to control the nine spiritual fires of Scorpio's wisdom.

Famous Scorpio Personalities

Marie Antoinette	Katharine Hepburn
Jim Bishop	Grace Kelly
Richard Burton	Robert Kennedy
Richard E. Byrd	Vivien Leigh
Johnny Carson	Martin Luther
Prince Charles	Douglas MacArthur
Chiang Kai-shek	Margaret Mead
Madame Curie	Marianne Moore
Charles de Gaulle	Jawaharlal Nehru
Marie Dressler	Mike Nichols
George Eliot	Pablo Picasso
George Gallup	Theodore Roosevelt
Indira Gandhi	Jonas Salk
Billy Graham	Eric Sevareid
Hetty Green	Billy Sunday

The SCORPIO Man

And her eyes immediately met those
of a large, blue caterpillar
that was sitting on the top with its arms folded, quietly
smoking a long hookah . . .
The caterpillar and Alice
looked at each other in silence.

If you're in love with a Scorpio male and the word passion
frightens you, put on your track shoes and run as if King
Kong were pursuing you. He is.

I'm not speaking of romantic passion alone, though
that may be at the head of the list. I also refer to passionate intensity about politics, work, friendship, religion,
food, relatives, children, clothing, life, death and any other
categories you can think up. A Scorpio man is not exactly
what your psyche needs if you're repelled by emotional
excess. Don't look back. Just run.

You'll think I've taken leave of my senses if you've
just met that particular Pluto person. He's so calm and

steady. How could anyone with such obvious self-control be passionate, let alone dangerously so? How indeed. Because he's only bluffing with the surface cool. Inside, his passions are as red hot as that stove you burned your hand on when you were three or four years old and getting into things out of your reach. This man may also be out of reach. He's sizzling underneath his deceptively controlled manner. Don't touch. You know perfectly well how long it takes for burns to heal. Remember? Your hand was stinging for weeks after that episode with the stove when you were in your Buster Browns. After this experience, your heart will burn for months, maybe years, and first aid kits will do little good. Grandma's favorite saying, "An ounce of prevention is worth a pound of cure," applies to both stove burns and Scorpio singes, so play it safe. Make sure you know where you're going and with whom.

If your Sun sign gives you an asbestos, fireproof nature, go ahead and play with explosives. You may be able to keep the flames under control and have yourself a powerful fire to warm your heart for a lifetime. Perhaps you're passionate about things yourself. Fine. Then it's simply a matter of degree of heat. If your passion has an automatic thermostat, so it can be turned down to cool when his reads hot, you're safe. Let's pretend you are. The girls who are in danger should be in the next state by now, if they ran fast enough. They'll thank me someday after they've married a nice, safe Libran or Cancerian.

As for you women who have analyzed yourselves as safe in a Pluto relationship, let's see if we can find what's hidden behind those hypnotic, piercing Scorpio eyes. It's pretty certain he hasn't made a neutral impression on you. He's either got you thinking he's boyish and sweet, or that he's wicked and passionate. (There goes that word again.) The trouble is, he's neither. Or maybe I should say he's both. Well, this isn't getting us anywhere. Let's start all over again.

In a word, this man is invincible. Just behind his frosty reserve is a huge pot of boiling steam that bubbles and seethes continually. If you're lucky, he'll keep the lid on tight for a lifetime, but a deep injury can blow it right off with a brilliant explosion. It's kind of fascinating to watch, if you're not in its direct line of destruction. Step aside, if you feel it coming. And don't do anything to cause it yourself.

He'll bewilder you with his twin Scorpio traits of passion and reason. He's master of both: intellect and emotions rule him equally. Scorpio is more than intelligent. If he's a highly evolved specimen, he's also deeply philosophical, concerned with mysteries of existence, and he'll come close to knowing the answers.

There are Scorpios who can live a spartan existence in a bare room, denying themselves every comfort for some obscure, aesthetic reason, but the true nature of the sign is sensual. Normally, Scorpio will surround himself with luxury. He'll lean toward excesses in food, drugs, drink, and yes—in love. Most assuredly in love. He's geared for it, with confidence. Romance will never frighten him, puzzle him, or catch him unaware. It's been on his mind ever since he rode his first bicycle. Maybe even his first tricycle. Of course, you could conceivably know a Scorpio who is so absolutely innocent-looking, with such disarming, youthful charm and lack of obvious seductive mannerisms, he's convinced you that passion is over-rated in Pluto males. He may even have freckles, and a whole drawer full of Boy Scout merit badges. But ask his wife. Try something like, "Say, Bertha—or Rosalie—or Sheila—or whatever—is your husband, well, is he passionate?" She might summon enough dignity to tell you it's none of your business, but your answer will most likely be hysterical laughter. Between her peals of mirth, she'll be remembering many days of his intense, passionate declarations about air pollution, housebreaking the dog, narcotics, long hair, birth control, and many nights of . . . well, and many nights. This will be true even if her husband looks like Huckleberry Finn, and doesn't even remotely resemble King Kong.

These men have an explosive temper that can strike a life-time wound. When the Scorpio lashes his deadly tail, the sting bites hard. He not only enjoys winning, he has to win. Something inside him dies when he loses, even in small ways; yet oddly enough, a Pluto man normally practices good sportsmanship. Like all his other emotions, disappointment never shows on those set features, and his reactions are rigidly controlled, including his romantic intentions. If there's a good reason to avoid the relationship, he'll burn inside while he's projecting a glacial calm outwardly. He's also capable of torturing a girl cruelly before he finally decides to grab her by the hair and drag her off to his jungle of honeysuckle vines. Naturally, there are some November fellows who will gently propose on bended knee. They'll behave very properly, with or without a chaperone, but don't be deceived. It's merely the Scorpio desire to keep dignity at all cost. Your reputation must be spotless. He won't stand for ridicule or cheapness, for all his erotic nature.

Pluto people can have either a Sunday School teacher horror of sin, an attitude which produces intensely dedicated evangelistic religious leaders, like Billy Graham, or they can be driven by curiosity to penetrate every dark corner of the human mystery. Sometimes, both attitudes are combined, resulting in the hypocrisy or self-delusion of an Elmer Gantry or a Reverend Davidson in *Rain*.

Every Scorpio is a law unto himself, and completely unconcerned with what others think of him. He would like to be respected as a good, solid citizen, but if it interferes with any of his intense ideas or goals, then he couldn't care less, and those who gossip can just go to the place Pluto rules. None of his important decisions are hampered by the opinions of his friends, relatives, neighbors or enemies. I'm sorry to say, not even by you. Don't run away yet. Such beautiful self-containment and sureness of purpose can create a mighty attractive, free spirit who's not always fussing about what people think. Are honesty and courage and integrity such bad bargains? They may have lost a little of their sparkle in today's marketplace, but rub off the dust they've collected, and you can still get them appraised as genuine.

It's quite an experience to see the Scorpio man operate under adversity's black clouds. While others are mumbling and crumbling and grumbling, he is at his forceful, courageous best. He seldom wallows in envy or self-pity, and he doesn't happen to think that life owes him a single farthing. You can just imagine how much time that saves. Instead of pouting in hurt anger when real troubles hit, he meets them head on. Conquer them? But of course. That's what he was born to do.

One thing is a little frightening, and may require courage on your part. Scorpio loves mystery and there's not a single one that crosses his path he won't solve in detail. Since the eternal feminine mystery is any girl's most potent defense and offense, being stripped naked of your mystery can leave you feeling a little exposed. You'll scarcely have a secret left when he starts probing with those burning eyes and piercing questions.

He has high standards, and he won't choose his friends loosely. They'll have to measure up. This is a marvelous, rare kind of man who can share a jug of spirits and joke with rough humor among other men like a bawdy Elizabethan; then tap that deep, inscrutable nature and turn into as gentle and tender a lover as Robert Browning. If there's anything more to ask for in a male animal, I don't know what it might be. Submissiveness and forgiveness? Detachment and caution? That's not fair. You knew he was short on those qualities back in the beginning.

He can be cruel sometimes, for his own, unfathomable reasons, and he may even exhibit a sadistic sense of wit by describing you as fat, dumpy, shrewish and square in front of friends. It's his private joke. Grin, if it kills you. You've been warned that Scorpio is compelled to conceal his motives, and this tendency isn't watered down in love. It may even be intensified. He's not about to display his true emotions in front of the world like a vulnerable, smitten schoolboy. Later, when you're alone, he'll tell you what he really thinks.

Marriage gives you a certain security, but if he pulls some of his Pluto tricks before the knot is tied, it may hurt, and you'll fail to get the humor. Still, don't even think about telling him that his harsh, self-sufficient who-needs-you? game makes you feel like jumping off a bridge. The Scorpio man will just tell you to go ahead and jump. It may take a while to adjust to his personality, but it will eventually toughen you up. If you're too soft, you'll bruise easily with a Scorpio. Never ask him what he thinks of a new dress or hair-do, unless you're prepared to be stung by the brutal truth. At least you'll know his positive statements are honest, and not pasted together with the sticky glue of bored, insincere flattery. It's better to brave a good, healthy "You look awful," now and then, and be rewarded by an occasional "You're really beautiful, you know," than to swallow a constant diet of vague remarks like: "Yes, dear, it's lovely, sugar. Mmmmm—just fine, pigeon," from other men. Don't you think so? I do. But then, you're the one who has to live with it.

When it comes to jealousy, you'd better tread very, very carefully. He could burn and erupt like Mount Vesuvius in its heyday if you should accidentally wink near a man when a cinder gets in your eye, and if you ever give him a real reason to be suspicious, you're a very brave woman. But you'd better pack away your own jealous streak in the trunk, and then lock it. It will make no impression at all to drench him in angry tears or reproachful recriminations. No matter how he behaves, just say to yourself, "He loves me, and he will never discard real love for physical promiscuity. He's loyal to his deep ties, and he's only practicing his hypnotic art with those girls." Say it once before each meal, in the morning and at bedtime. Especially at bedtime. Women will find him irresistibly attractive, but keep remembering that if anyone is strong enough to resist such continual flattery and temptation, it's a Scorpio. Doesn't that make you feel better? It should. It's true.

He'll probably be a stern father. The children won't get away with an ounce of lazy or frivolous behavior. He'll teach them to respect property, but he'll also teach them to respect themselves. Youngsters will seldom get the chance to form any false values around a Scorpio papa. Although he'll love them with as much sincere passion as he puts into everything else he cares about, he won't stand for any nonsense. He'll protect them when they need it, but they'll soon get the message that he expects them to stand alone. If they borrow money from him, he's liable to charge them interest on it, but it's for their own good. They may not realize that until he's gone someday, but the lesson will eventually come home to them. Lots of children of Scorpio fathers resent his high-handed authority and tight discipline throughout childhood, and especially during the rebellious years, but as adults, they realize how lucky they were to have his firm guidance. From no other father can children learn so much truth about the way life really is. Often his offspring will find him gentle and funny; still there won't be any question about who is boss. He'll joke and laugh with them, and give them a sense of freedom, but the chalk line will be drawn, and they'll know not to cross it. Even as they resent his attitude of command, the children will secretly admire his strength and try to imitate it, but occasionally it works the other way. A gentle child may feel bullied and cowed by Scorpio power, and retreat into neurotic introversion, fearing to risk his displeasure. Then you'll have to remind him that affection and tenderness sometimes get more results than his normal, unbending, autocratic manner. Just be sure you remind him tactfully and respectfully. A Scorpio man will never allow a woman to dictate to him. Never in a million years. He is the man and you are the woman, and if you have any doubts about it, you will be set straight so surely that you'll never need but one lesson. Yet, a Scorpio husband with a wife who truly understands him, will be tender, sympathetic, considerate, and repay her loyalty with the kind of love most women only read about and wish for.

It won't help much to try to resist this man, once the flame has been stirred and he's decided he wants you. He'll hypnotize you right out of all your good intentions. The magnetism of Scorpio men is almost tangible. You feel you can reach out and touch it. When you do, you may get a surprise. It will burn you only if you're over-sensitive and scorchable. If you're patient and strong, it will be like touching cool marble. Girls are out of their league with him. It takes a brave woman to fly with the eagle and not crash. He can soar higher than his symbolic bright star Antares in the constellation of Scorpio, then dip down suddenly to earthy expression. Hang on tightly, but keep your eyes open wide, and you'll see horizons with him the timid will never see. Look over there, just beyond the tall fir trees—did you ever in your whole life experience such a sunrise? Sunset will be just as grand.

The SCORPIO Woman

*"Consider anything
only don't cry . . ."*

The female Scorpio has a deep, mysterious beauty. She's magnetic, proud and totally confident. But she has one secret regret. She was not born a man.

I can almost feel the heat from here when Pluto women hear about that revelation. There's not a Scorpio female alive who doesn't think she's all woman, and you may wonder what I'm talking about yourself, if you're in love with one. This girl certainly has enough glamour, and she's enormously seductive. But I didn't say she looked like a boy, nor did I intend to imply she doesn't do a bang-up job of being a female. It's just that, unconsciously, she would prefer to be a man. Less restriction—more opportunity. It's the one secret she even hides from herself, and seeing it exposed won't sit well with her.

Once the Scorpio girl has figured out the difference between blue booties and pink booties, she'll resign herself to wearing the pink ones, because she's fabulous at making the best out of a situation. But pink is not her natural color. The true shade of her nature is dark maroon, or deep wine-red, not a female color at all. However, to give her proper tribute, she's able to make you think it is. I know one who's great at pretending to be a fragile, fluffy kitten. She purrs so contentedly most men guess she's an ultra-feminine Piscean. They topple into her trap and wake up later, sadder but wiser. She is no kitten.

Scorpio women have a scornful contempt for members of their sex who flop in the roles of sweetheart, wife and mother, once they're stuck with the parts. A Pluto girl will control her desire to dominate, while she gives a glorious performance of womanhood, and she'll do it with more finess than the masculine Aries, Leo or Sagittarius girl. At least she'll do it during courtship. There may be a few cases when the unsuspecting male gets a rude surprise after he shakes the rice out of his shoes and the illusions out of his eyes. Unlike the Mars female, for example, a Scorpio will subdue her drive and magnetize a man with the heavy perfume of her exotic glance as she allows him to use his lighter to ignite her cigarette. That's far sexier than aggressively striking a match herself and blowing the smoke in his face, and she knows it. She knows lots more. Another girl might rush headlong into your arms and shout her love from the rooftops. The Scorpio girl walks toward you slowly, seductively, and silently delivers her private message. It's puzzling, but these women can look seductive in jeans, jodhpurs or basketball shoes. Maybe it's her husky voice that creates the image. I know one who wore a baseball cap (honest) the entire time her future husband was courting her, and she spent a lot of time talking about batting averages. But she was as seductive as Mata Hari just the same, and she got her man. (He was hypnotized, as usual.)

You can give her a tumble, but she won't fall all over herself reacting to your overtures. Don't expect her to bat long, sweeping eyelashes at you, and adore you with blind devotion. Lots of female Scorpios are tomboys with stubby eyelashes. Besides, with those beautiful, mysterious eyes that can read your mind so clearly, she doesn't need any extra trimming. Whisper something romantic that would melt another girl out of her senses, and the Scorpio girl will simply give you an intense, penetrating look that will see right straight through to your real intentions. She's a human X-ray machine, so don't flirt. Unless you mean business, you're wasting her time and insulting her. I wouldn't advise you to insult a Scorpio. It's just not healthy. If you don't know what I mean, ask someone who has. He may have some stories to tell that will curl your hair.

I'm well aware that this dangerous femme fatale can hide her power of retaliation with a tremulous smile, gentle mannerisms, and the most breathless voice this side of an angel. But astrologers are expected to be up on these things. It's more important for you to be well aware. After all, you're the one who's seeking to tame her—or protect yourself against her—whichever. Probably both.

You can be sure that heaven certainly has no fury like that of a Scorpio woman who's lost her normal steady control over those inward, seething, Pluto emotions. She can be overbearing and domineering, sarcastic and frigid—then turn as hot as an oven at 500 degrees Fahrenheit. She can hate with bitter venom and love with fierce abandon. She can shriek like a furious banshee or whisper like an affectionate turtle dove. One thing you can be sure of—she's never wishy-washy.

The Scorpio woman has a disconcerting gift that can make icy shivers run up your spine. It's a peculiar form of black magic, and she weaves it so expertly it can seem like real witchcraft. You have very little chance to escape, once her eyes meet yours. Because of her mystical sixth sense, she can often recognize a future mate at first glance, and somehow, she'll transfer this perception instantly. You'll have one of two reactions. You'll be hopelessly caught in her spell, and down you'll go, in a dizzy spin toward surrender, or you'll be scared right out of your socks, and feel like running for help. What's your rush? Stay around awhile. You might find out what life is all about. She knows. And she'll teach you. Anyway, you should be flattered that she considers you worth that strange gaze. A Scorpio woman can't excuse weakness in a man. She looks for ambition and courage. She wants a mate who can dominate her and make her proud, without disturbing her secret individuality. He's expected to be strong, masculine and better-looking than average. A high degree of intelligence is required to match her own excellent mind, plus more than a passing acquaintance with abstract, philosophical wisdom. So put your socks back on and practice a superior smirk. Everybody you know will think you're pretty super to have her staring at you. The men and women both. It could open new vistas, when you think about it. Your personal stock should zoom several points higher than it was before she noticed you.

Having once achieved closeness with a female Scorpio, you can be positive you're a unique and unusual man. You can also be sure that her love for you is unmatched by any you'll ever experience—and you can take that in several ways. You'll be the most important interest in her life. If she's a typical Pluto girl, she'll boost you loyally, and try to please you with passionate intensity. If you're too hard to please, she'll show her frustration with passionate attempts to conquer your disinterest.

The word "passionate" probably caught your eye. Most men have heard exciting rumors about the passion of November females. It's true. She's brimming over inside with passion, though it's kept under rigid control by a poised, frosty attitude toward strangers, and a surface smoothness suggestive of black velvet. But the male sex is too inclined to relate passion strictly to romantic action; and that's selling her short, because Pluto's definition of the word is far more encompassing. It's involved with her feelings about everything she touches. She's never just slightly interested. It's impossible for her to be detached or casual. She seldom likes or dislikes a play, a book, religion, furniture or people. She either bitterly resents or she intensely worships. If one of these two passions can't be aroused, then she totally ignores, with ice around the edges. Yet, through it all, she'll remain essentially untouched by emotional storms, judging at least from her placid exterior, which always drapes itself around her after each minor or major nuclear explosion. It may be difficult to convince your mother-in-law that her daughter really broke all those dishes and tore all those draperies to shreds after the fury has subsided and her black velvet poise has returned. People may look at you as if you're a character assassinator. What do you mean? Shame on you, accusing that cool, controlled, lovely girl of such a temper. You have my sympathy, if that's any help.

She has such fabulous virtues, you might know her vices wouldn't be skimpy, either. So think about her good points. All right, then, think about her good points after that lump on your head has healed.

Because she's drawn to investigation of the shadows, she may at first seem to be tempting, forbidden fruit, and the deep, strange expression in her eyes intensifies the impression. It's true that the Scorpio girl sometimes wanders into dangerous waters in her efforts to penetrate life, and since there's not the slightest trace of fear in her (unless she has an affliction to her Moon, and is full of nameless terrors), her search may indeed take her into some weird byways. But the typical Scorpio will emerge from any discovery still strong and pure. If she allows the journey to soil her inner spirit, Pluto will punish her with anguished remorse and guilt; yet she can still call on her great strength of character to rise again, like the phoenix, from the ashes of her experiments. In Kahlil Gibran's writings, the Prophet replies, in answer to a question about Evil, "Of the Good in you I can speak, but not of the Evil. For what is Evil but Good—tortured by its own hunger and thirst? When Good is hungry, it seeks food, even in dark caves, and when it thirsts, it drinks even of dead waters." A perfect description of Scorpio.

She may have been a fascinated spectator to a million human foibles, and she may have tasted a variety of experiences to savor the knowledge. But she can mysteriously emerge from all her explorations above suspicion, and still superior to almost every other woman you know. She could be the keeper of quite a few secrets. It's surprising how many dark deeds are confessed to Scorpios, though their own inner lives are marked: "Private—Keep Out." She likes to hear secrets, but she'll seldom tell anything anyone has confided in her, not even to you (unless there's an afflicted Mercury in her natal chart). You can also expect her to have a stack of secrets that relate to her personally, and don't try to pry them out of her. There's a private part to this woman you'll never touch, a part of her mind and soul that belongs strictly to her, and there's absolutely no trespassing there. She's not untruthful, in fact she's more often too brutally honest, yet there will always be those special thoughts and feelings she won't confide to you or anyone else.

A Scorpio woman will be incredibly loyal to those she finds strong and deserving, but the weak ones will never be honored by her glance. Her dignity in human relationships can make her seem aloof and snobbish. In a way, she definitely is, because she practices a personal caste system, and it's more clearly marked than that of her Leo and Capricorn sisters. All Scorpios are highly selective in friendships. They'll keep the worthy companions through an entire lifetime, and freeze the shallow, the common or the unworthy. There's an immense store of perseverance and determination buried in the nature of a Scorpio woman, and any time she chooses, she can call on these to help her master the excesses which may tempt her, from drink and drugs to self-destructive, ruthless revenge and dangerous depression. Sooner or later, she'll probably investigate some form of the occult, and ancient mysteries and unseen worlds will eventually have her respect, though Scorpios can range all the way from religious fervor to total atheism during a lifetime.

A Scorpio woman need not be a legal wife to give wifely love and devotion. If circumstances beyond your control make marriage impossible, she'll love you from hell to breakfast, and not give a hang what the neighbors think. In most such unusual situations, the relationship is real and honest above and beyond the shallow, selfish love of many a legitimate marriage. The hypocrisies of society will never keep this courageous woman from seeking the sun. She answers to no law but her own, and in her Pluto heart, she has more total understanding of the vow "till death do us part" than half the brides who blissfully murmur the phrase.

Despite her own strong individualism, the typical Scorpio girl will let her man be the boss. Instead of overshadowing him with her force and drive, she'll apply her talents to help him attain his goals. Your future will be important to her, and she's not likely to insist on retaining her own career after marriage (unless you've disappointed her deeply or a second job is needed in a temporary domestic crisis). She may fight you wildly in private, but she'll defend you fiercely in public. She won't stand for anyone maligning you or taking advantage of you. Those who try will feel the lash of her righteous anger. Your happiness will always come first. Unless there are adverse aspects to her Sun sign or ascendant in her natal chart, she'll patiently help you persevere until you get what you want, and while you're getting it, she won't whine or complain or become restless, though she might turn a little bitter if you lose your courage on the way. She'll expect you to aim as high as your abilities will reach. Anything less may bring on some pretty sarcastic taunts and reproaches, especially if she has an afflicted Mercury.

Scorpio women love their homes, which usually shine with cleanliness, taste and comfort. Meals are served on time, and things are generally under control. If the opposite is true, something is making her mighty unhappy, because her natural inclination is to beauty and system. To the typical Scorpio woman spring cleaning is like vacation. They love to dig into corners to see what they can find. Just be careful she doesn't find any cryptic notes that smell of perfume in your old jacket pockets when she's clearing out the closets. Scorpio is unreasonably suspicious, even when there's no basis for suspicion, so you can imagine what happens when she finds a real clue to possible infidelity. Picture the shape of a mushroom cloud and you'll get a general idea of what may happen, figuratively speaking. It's no good being suspicious of her, no matter how many opportunities arise; and there will be a goodly number of them, because she never exposes her deepest feelings. Naturally, this can arouse a few questions on your part. Just swallow them, along with the lump in your throat. Like that locked chest or drawer she's had since childhood, certain things about her are off limits. It will get you nowhere to probe. I realize fully that it isn't fair. So does she. But that doesn't change things a bit. That's the way it is. Take her or leave her. You'll probably take her. It's almost impossible to leave her. If nothing else, she'll haunt you the rest of your life. Adjusting to the idiosyncrasies of her nature is easier than suffering the nightmares that will surely result if you walk away. No one walks away from a Scorpio. Not really. Didn't you know that? Those who have tried can educate you. Anyway, you have a very special woman.

As much as she needs the security of home roots, she'll

move if it's necessary to your career, and without any visible flinching at the uprooting. She makes an excellent wife for an army or navy man and a real jewel for a politician. There's no one she can't see through, no deception that escapes her. A Scorpio woman can tell you exactly who can be trusted and which ones you have to watch. The Pisces wife has the same ability, but she may be too soft to criticize, too ready to make excuses for the failings of others. Not so the Scorpio female. In fact, she may frequently have to check her sharp tongue and tone down her brutal analysis.

In the budget department, Scorpio women are completely unpredictable. She can scrimp and save and pinch a penny until it bends double, then have a sudden spell of being magnificently extravagant. One thing is sure. She'll enjoy money, whether she saves it in an old shoe or spends it on luxury. But this woman always leans heavily toward prestige, and she won't let cash compromise that. She'll be satisfied if you choose a smaller income, as long as it insures that you are your own boss, with the potential to rise to become somebody of influence. Scorpio females like power, and they will sacrifice much for it. Your power will do, because Pluto allows her to be adept at living vicariously through others when it suits her. Remember that although she'll sacrifice and put up with very little for a planned goal, she's too proud to live amid shabby surroundings forever, and she'll become mighty sour and discontented if she's forced to do so for an unreasonable length of time. She'll either try to force a change in the family fortunes after a certain period, or she'll gradually retreat into the dismal world of the gray lizard, outwardly accepting and almost seeming to enjoy poverty, but inwardly intensely bitter.

She'll be possessive but she won't want to be possessed. One of the worst traits of both male and female Scorpios is a refusal to see any viewpoint but their own when the emotions are involved. It takes weeks of introspection to bring them around to a semblance of humility. Her natural interest in the opposite sex, even if it remains platonic, may give you as much reason to be jealous of her as she is of you. She'll probably fascinate every male in sight on occasion, and you may have to sit by while they're mesmerized. It seldom leads to anything serious, but it can cause some uncomfortable moments. It can also lead to some explosive disagreements. In the heat of battle, it pays to remember that her compulsion to even the score usually makes her the winner in any kind of skirmish. She gets the last word. If you tell her a lie, she may tell two. If you stubbornly refuse to kiss her good-bye in the morning after a tiff, she may refuse to kiss you goodnight for a month. Just let your mother (or anybody's mother) criticize her cooking, and the Scorpio woman may forget to invite her to dinner for several Sundays in a row. An accidental injury, however, she'll forgive, if she knows it's unintentional. The Scorpio sense of justice is as strong as the sense of revenge. Most people forget this. She'll remember every kindness and give you back double for that, too. It works both ways.

With the children, her expression of love may lack a certain tenderness and open demonstration, but the youngsters will probably sense her deep devotion and feel emotionally secure anyway. A Scorpio mother won't let the talents of her children go unnoticed or gather dust. She'll spend many an hour encouraging them toward higher goals, and be willing to provide any support they need. Her offspring will find her strong and helpful when youthful problems arise, because her knowledge of human nature makes her a wise counselor. She'll teach them to meet difficulties with her own courage. But she can be blind to their faults, an attitude which can naturally cause a lot of trouble if it isn't recognized and checked in time. Anyone she imagines is a threat to the happiness of her children, in any way, however small, will be crushed, and I'm afraid that includes her husband. She won't appreciate it if he's stricter with them than she thinks he ought to be.

A Scorpio woman will sometimes nearly drown you in her passion for living, yet in a real storm, her cool, calm reason and steely strength will be a life raft. Though she works her magic in strange and secret ways, her haunting eyes will always gaze at you with basic honesty, even while she remains just beyond the reach of human understanding. She's a little dangerous, perhaps, but undeniably exciting. Let other husbands cope with the flighty girls. You've known the compelling mystery of a lovely witch who brews a pretty good cup of tea and never burns your toast. (Well, almost never.) When the cup is empty, let her read the tea leaves for you. She can—if she wants to.

You mean you didn't know? I told you there are things she keeps to herself. . . .

The SCORPIO Child

"What else had you to learn?"
"Well, there was Mystery . . . Mystery, ancient and modern,
with Seaography . . . Drawling, Stretching
and Fainting in Coils."

The usual reaction of proud parents at the first glimpse of their newborn Scorpio infant is pleased surprise. "He looks so much more 'finished' than the other babies in the nursery," they murmur. "He's calmer too—and just look at what a strong body he has." That's right, even the tiniest Scorpios normally have extraordinarily strong bodies. They were designed to match their extraordinarily strong wills.

Scorpio children enjoy a good fight, and they intend to win it. Compromise is not one of their virtues. Even if they pretend to give in, they're just biding their time until the contest can be resumed on another front, where they have the advantage.

As soon as you know the stork is due in November or thereabouts, go right out and buy a large, sturdy playpen. You'll need one. After baby arrives, you can climb inside it and read a book or eat your lunch, safe and secure behind the bars. The saleswoman may look at you oddly when you lie down on the blue plastic bunny pad to measure its fit, but ignore her. If you can't take the stare of a stranger, how are you going to face the burning gaze of your own child without flinching? The Scorpio infant will fix you with his intense eyes as soon as he can see people without the fuzzy haze, and you'll be hypnotized into obeying his every whim. Picture him sitting crosslegged on the floor in his diaper and turban, playing his flute, while you sway back and forth helplessly, like a snake in a basket. Good grief! So better start steeling yourself against his black magic right now. Give that saleswoman a frosty stare right back. It's your money you're spending.

If your actions seem a little peculiar, it's not her business to dictate to you. You are the customer. Therefore, you are the boss. With minor changes, this is the exact attitude you'll need to cope with your young Scorpio. It's your house. If your rules seem a little peculiar, it's not baby's business to dictate to you. You are the mother. Therefore, you are the boss. As you say it, stare him down.

You'll have your work cut out for you, but it's an interesting challenge. The Scorpio child will need constant and firm discipline. You'll have to impress the qualities of consideration for weaker people, being a good sport when he loses, respect for authority and forgiveness when others hurt him. As you train his fine character, you'll be impressed yourself with his brilliant mind and magnetic personality. His rare courage and honesty are well worth nourishing and protecting from the infection of a super ego that can pervert or destroy them.

There are two roads for the Scorpio to choose—the high and the low. For a while, you may be convinced that he's chosen the back alley before he's even learned to walk. Fluttery, nervous or soft mothers are beaten before they start. Your little Scorpio toddler will glare at you fiercely when you forbid him to touch something. Glare back at him, kindly but firmly. It may be difficult to accomplish a kindly glare, but keep practicing. Smile through your clenched teeth and say no loudly, with emphatic conviction. You'll only win a temporary struggle; it will be resumed again an hour later, but it's a step up that high road. Eventually, the Scorpio youngster will begin to admire you for your strength in resisting him. He'll learn only from someone he thinks is stronger than himself. Of course, he knows the victory is only due to his present size, and he'll top you someday, but meanwhile, he'll give you his grudging respect, as long as you're bigger. By the time he's tall enough to wrestle his older brother to the floor or win a game of Indian deadlock with his father your job will be done. You'll be a little exhausted, but proud, and he'll be well on the way to becoming a splendid eagle, instead of a stinging, revengeful scorpion. Warning: Be sure there's a generous spreading of love and affection on top of your firm discipline, or he could become a miserable gray lizard, tortured by fears and phobias, bitter and withdrawn.

Because of his blunt, often sarcastic speech and plain-spoken manner, he'll seem to be forthright and direct, but there will still be a great need for privacy. He has his little secrets and you are not to pry. Give him a large metal box with a key, where he can keep his personal possessions, or a special drawer of his own that no one else in the family can open by strict agreement. As female Scorpios grow older, they'll want a diary with a foolproof lock.

These youngsters will conceal their own thoughts, but trying to hide things from them is impossible. They'll ferret out every embarrassing family secret from Aunt Bertha's false teeth and Uncle Percy's drinking sprees to Dad's "rug" that hides his bald spot. They're also whizzes at finding lost socks, keys, billfolds and lipsticks—regular miniature sleuths who use both witchcraft and cold logic to solve any mystery.

There's a miraculous ability to withstand pain. Even the stitches required to sew up an accidental cut will usually be borne without either tears or anesthetic. Your Scorpio youngster is wise beyond his years. There will be times when his instinctive understanding is a blessing. Daddies who are discouraged by financial problems often feel the surprising pressure of a bear hug from a little tot far too young to understand economics. He only knows his father is unhappy, and he'll want to express his desire to destroy whatever is causing it. When she's ill or depressed, a mother may get an unexpected, silent and tender touch from a tiny Scorpio who has somehow sensed her sadness.

Scorpio children are filled with boundless loyalty to friends and loved ones. They can be pretty hard on anyone else. If a bad-tempered playmate deliberately breaks his rocking horse, the Scorpio youngster may break the offending child's scooter, fire truck and blackboard—and punch him in the nose besides, just to make sure he knows he's stepped on a Scorpio's tail. Naturally, this must be discouraged, and I wish you luck. You can tell your November child that revengeful anger will come home to roost, that he's only hurting himself by getting even, but it won't be easy for him to see the logic. Get him one of those boomerangs they sell in toy stores, and let him throw it with all his force. When it's shocked him by magically returning to clip him on the ear a few times, he may get the message. It won't be as popular with him, of course, as a microscope, a book of magic games or a chemistry set. These are sure-fire hits.

His teachers won't know whether to send him to the

head of the class or get out the old birch switch. They'll probably end up doing both. Scorpio boys and girls have sharp, penetrating minds and an uncanny perception of theories. They can be steadies on the honor roll or the biggest hookey players in the neighborhood. Given the good fortune of wise instructors, they'll learn to read quickly and be leaders of school activities.

The Scorpio child has a good chance of being class valedictorian if he's guided away from his fascination for the forbidden. Keep him active physically and interested mentally, and channel his passionate curiosity into science, literature, medicine or sports. Encourage his childish dreams of being a space engineer, sailor, fireman, minister, entertainer or even president. Never try to force him into your favorite idea of the proper career. That's a perfect way to send him down that low road to dangerous experimentation in the dark alleys of life. He knows exactly what he wants, and it's a serious mistake to impose your will. Be loyal to him, and never break your word or a promise.

He needs opportunities to work off his gigantic supply of bottled-up energy because he'll seem to be more calm and relaxed than he really is inside. Displays of nerves, arguments at mealtime and family squabbles at bedtime will bring nightmares, and are extremely detrimental to both his mental and physical health. He has many intense passions and boiling emotions to manage, and subduing his volatile nature is a tough task for him, but he'll control it beautifully with careful guidance. Rough, thoughtless scoldings that lack a logical explanation, and permissive humoring are equally disastrous. Scorpios are fascinated by drugs, so keep them out of reach. He'll be drawn to fire, too, so don't leave matches around.

He'll love Halloween, monster shows on TV, science-fiction and ghost stories. He'll also be fond of the opposite sex. Don't be shocked if you catch your five-year-old Scorpio son making "mysterious eyes" at the curly-headed first-grader next door. He's going to be a Lover someday. You'll never prevent that. But you can prevent some future romantic tragedies by teaching both sexes in adolescence the importance of responsibility in affairs of the heart. Scorpio deeply respects the family circle. Explain that careless romantic behavior destroys it, and he'll listen. Whatever he becomes, he'll be the best in his chosen field. The Scorpio youngster is determined enough to get what he wants, and strong enough to hang on to it. But don't let his self-sufficiency keep you from giving him your support. He needs it, even though he appears to scorn approval. You'll have to help him find a worthy goal toward which he can direct the inner passions that threaten to consume him. This is a strange, enchanted child, with possibly an important destiny, and he has miles to go before he reaches it. Walk with him as long as he needs you, then let him walk alone. He'll return safely with whatever prize he seeks. Pluto gives him great courage, strength and intelligence, but it's up to you to give him what he needs most: a daily example of how to love—and be loved in return.

The SCORPIO Boss

"Keep your temper," said the Caterpillar . . .
"You'll get used to it in time,"
and it put the hookah into its mouth;
and began smoking again.

President Theodore Roosevelt's advice, "Speak softly—but carry a big stick," is a perfect example of Scorpio philosophy, spoken by a Scorpio. Although "Teddy" Roosevelt was the first one to say it, every Pluto person is born with the phrase carved into his nature. It's the invisible motto hanging on the wall behind the desk of your Scorpio boss. Memorize it. He has. I wouldn't make a big issue out of discussing it with him. Just watch him practice it. Scorpios have a way of discouraging certain personal questions about their own techniques.

Life is a search for wisdom and power to your soft-spoken Scorpio boss with the big stick. He wants to know all the secrets of heaven and hell—and whatever lies between. Assumedly, you lie between. Therefore, he's equally intent on learning your secrets, and in seeking knowledge of what's going on in your busy little brain, or your busy big brain, as the case may be. He'll never press you openly or actively to bare your soul, but you'll probably do it anyway. It's inevitable. One good, long, steady gaze from his hypnotic Pluto eyes is enough to pull out the deepest confessions. If you have anything on your mind you'd rather keep strictly private, avoid looking into those eyes or avoid working for him.

I once knew a girl who was a singer. She ran into her Scorpio boss at the airport one summer afternoon, on his return from a trip to California, and they stopped to have coffee. (Pluto power is often as its height in the summer, for some inconsistent reason that has nothing to do with November.) She and a songwriter, who was a good friend of the Scorpio, had just that morning confessed to each other that they were deeply in love. Due to circumstances, the discovery had to be kept secret.

As they chatted over coffee, the singer was completely absorbed by the Scorpio's anecdotes about his trip. His conversation was so fascinating that she forgot all about the fateful meeting hours earlier. Finally, the Scorpio glanced at his watch; he was late for an appointment with a producer about a film he hoped to direct.

They clasped hands and she said goodbye, adding, "I wish you luck." The Scorpio continued to grip her hand, looked deep into her eyes with burning intensity, and answered slowly, "And I wish you love. But I see you have already found it. That's good. You two are right together." Breaking the gaze first (as Scorpios always do—they never permit you to do it), he released her hand, smiled his cool, mysterious, controlled smile and walked away. To this day, the girl can't understand how he knew.

Let her experience be a lesson to you. He'll discover your secret, too. It doesn't have to be love. It can simply be that your father dropped out of school in the eighth grade, or your sister is dating a married man, or you haven't made a payment in six months on your bank loan, or your Persian cat is expecting again. Maybe you used a safety pin instead of sewing the button on your coat, or your brother hit your sister-in-law on the head with a skillet this morning. Little things like that you'd just as soon keep to yourself, but he'll know. And somehow, you'll know that he knows. It's different from the Pisces penetration. The fish gets psychic flashes. The Scorpio simply *knows*. Psychic flashes have nothing to do with it. Neither does Aquarian intuition. It goes much deeper.

This Pluto power also allows the Scorpio boss to sense your moods, and he's the kind of man who will sympathetically behave according to those moods, which can be an indescribably soothing experience. Especially after constant exposure to swift, thoughtless, shallow people who not only don't know what's deep inside you, but don't care enough one way or the other to find out. Exposure to various forms of such brittle indifference can make the Scorpio empathy seem pretty wonderful by comparison, which it is.

Contrary to what you might understandably think, the office of a November boss isn't always explosive or even necessarily impressive. It may be the quietest, coolest, calmest spot in the entire building. The Pluto self-control reaches out to touch everything around it. (Unless there's a heavy Gemini, Aquarius or Leo influence in his chart. Even so, things will seldom get raucous or out of hand. The pace will be a little quicker, that's all.) This man's control over his own nature is awesome. He's indefatigable in whatever he sets out to do, and he prides himself on not letting people know how deeply he wants or needs what he seeks. His competitor will never suspect how intensely your Scorpio boss desires to conquer him until after it's a *fait accompli* and Scorpio has won. He can see into you, but no man can penetrate his deepest feelings. One of your Pluto boss's most powerful weapons is secrecy of purpose and intent. He hides his emotions and disguises his motives so totally that the enemy is forever expecting an attack from the rear—or no attack at all— and then being surprised by a sudden movement from the right flank, where it's least expected and when it's least anticipated. That's what wins ball games.

That's also what wins prestige and success for the Scorpio executive. If he likes you, there's no limit to what he'll do to help you, advance you or push your hopes and dreams to fulfillment, along with his. If he doesn't like you, there's no point in reading this. You'll never be hired in the first place, or if someone else has hired you, your employment under a Scorpio boss won't last long. Pluto executives rarely have either sympathy or mercy for those who don't belong on the team. His first concern will be the team (which is synonymous with his personal goals), and individuals come last. I'm well aware that those of you with a Scorpio boss are already bristling in defense. How could anyone accuse him of anything less than perfection and purity, right? Most people close to a Pluto person have that attitude. If you don't, you're probably filling in on someone else's vacation.

This man has a way of attracting people who are intensely loyal. He's usually surrounded by devoted friends, with his enemies removed to a safe distance (safe for *them,* that is). It's as if he drew a circle. The chosen stand inside. Others are kept away by some form of black magic that prevents their stepping too close for comfort (*his* comfort, that is). It's difficult, if not impossible for enemies to reach him. Once those magnetic eyes have sized up a person who falls short of the requirements, he or she is banished. That person simply does not exist to the Scorpio. In his mind, you're not there. He neither sees you nor hears you. His radar will tell him if you get near enough to be dangerous. It gives one an empty feeling to be looked at as if you're not there. Being a ghost can be uncomfortable, so after a while the unwanted person fades away to where people can see him and hear him—to where he can exist as a flesh and blood human being again.

Don't get the impression that, to accomplish his miracles, the Scorpio boss has to look like Dracula and breathe deadly fumes from his nostrils. He needn't wear a black cape to practice his mystery, nor does he have to speak in sepulchral tones. If you're about to embark on the adventure of working for a Scorpio executive, the first time you see him you'll think the whole power thing is exaggerated.

His physique may very well be unimposing and he may have the kind of smile you see only on a stained-glass window. When it flashes on, you'll melt, and think astrology misled you. He'll appear to be about as dangerous as an Irish washer-woman singing a lullaby. Then he'll fix you with his penetrating blue or brown-eyed stare, and I hope there's a chair nearby for you to drop into. By that time, you'll be thoroughly hypnotized by his magnetic charm. You might even catch yourself weaving back and forth, with almost imperceptible motion, awaiting instructions. He now controls your emotions. After that, no one can reach you. It's too late. You'll be blindly loyal to your new, wonderful, kind, gentle, talented, brilliant employer, and anyone who thinks he is dangerous is a jealous, vindictive crackpot. He's the sweetest boss anyone could ever hope to have.

Sweet? Use adjectives if you must, but *sweet?* Wonderful, yes. Kind, yes. Talented and brilliant—naturally. Sincere and loyal, of course. Protective and gentle, yes again. Loving? Oh, good heavens, yes. A thousand times yes. But sweet? Emphatically no. I'd like to tell the already Scorpio-employed, plus you who are about to pass through the portals, that one of my closest friends is a Scorpio composer of enormous talent, and I've passed his magic circle test. There's also a tiny Scorpio who lives in my house (you notice I still have control—I didn't say I lived in *his* house) and I'm kind of close to him, too. So I'm not among the enemies of your Scorpio boss. You can relax. But thanks to astrology, I may understand him a bit better than you do. For example, I'll bet you think that, in a crisis, he would just stand there calmly, wearing the same smooth, detached look he puts on when he gets out of his warm bed every morning. He would not. He would undergo a compete transformation.

Your Scorpio boss cannot tolerate displays of emotion. He feels that one must keep one's cool at all costs—I mean at all costs. But if the emergency demands instant and violent action (as some emergencies do), he'll blast forth so much flaming action, you'll be sure you aren't watching the same man. When it's all over, and things are well under control, his surging, passionate emotions will be back under control again also. He'll bottle them up inside his powerful personality until they're needed the next time.

Normally, however, he'll be the epitome of deliberate, gentle, calculated placidity, every hair in place, temper in total check. The same Jekyll and Hyde transformation as the foregoing can take place in the throes of romantic passion as well as in a business crisis, but of course that's not your department—at least under ordinary circumstances it's not. His calm mask of poise is seldom removed, except for really major events.

Don't make the mistake of flattering him too often. Scorpio bosses are constantly suspicious. He wakes up and goes to sleep suspicious and his feelers are always out for ulterior motives. In fact, one of his weaknesses is that he's frequently suspicious of innocent remarks from innocent people. Polishing the deep red apple on his desk with too much gusto can get you fired instead of advanced. He may suspect you're buttering him up to take over. An occasional, sincerely meant recognition of his superiority will be appreciated deeply—just don't overdo it. His loyalty to you will be lasting and all encompassing, but never give him one millimeter less in return. He's a stickler for money transactions being spelled out in detail. Never allow financial matters to get hazy in any way. And never, never, never, never, never try to top him or hurt him. If you insist on disregarding that advice, then you'd better practice walking on eggshells for a few weeks first. Preferably eggshells with a poisonous spider hidden among them. Scorpio revenge is not something to fool around with.

No problem ever invented is so tough that the Scorpio boss can't solve it, once he tackles it. All Pluto people have the ability to surmount tragedy or illness in their personal lives and business disasters with courage and superhuman will. As for the pattern of his individual personality, it will vary with the man more widely than with other signs. Although he's the personification of the scientific researcher into inscrutable mystery, the all-purpose detective, he himself remains the greatest mystery of all.

Penetrating Pluto all the way is impossible. Besides, even if you could, you'd forget everything you learned when he hypnotized you with his eyes and voice. The best I can do is warn you to stay alert and to keep an open mind. The first is for defense purposes, naturally. The second is so you can be receptive to a man whose truth and courage you'll admire forever. Despite his unfathomable, complex nature, and the deceptive image he presents to the world, your Scorpio boss never deceives himself. How many of the rest of us can say that with complete honesty? Even those of us who are not considered "ruthless"?

The SCORPIO Employee

"But when you have to turn into a chrysalis—
you will some day, you know—
and then after that into a butterfly,
I should think you'll feel it a little queer,
won't you?"
"Not a bit," said the Caterpillar.

Offhand, who would you say is the one person in your office who is the most self-contained? Which employee seems to have the most inner confidence, without being obvious about it, the steadiest eyes, the least excuses and the most poise? If there's someone on the staff with those qualities, does he give you the feeling he can take a compliment or leave it alone? Is he secretive about his personal life? Does he have a master plan for his future? Assuming all this is true, one more question: are the other employees a little afraid of him? There's no doubt about it. He's a Scorpio.

More than anyone else with your firm, the Scorpio employee is the master of his fate and the captain of his soul. He's entirely self-motivated and single-minded. No one else can be so resourceful and so sure of his own potential. The Scorpio has the power to make or break his own life, and he knows it. He never lies to himself, and rarely blames anyone but himself for his own mistakes. To whatever degree he chooses, this employee can rise, and he'll expect few favors on the way up. He's the very last person you'd accuse of having an inferiority complex. (Unless he happens to be a gray lizard who has turned power inside out into silent defeat. Even so, it was his decision alone to do so. He was not a pawn of fate.)

It won't be easy to comprehend the reasons behind his actions. You've heard about the ruthlessness of this Sun sign, his desire for revenge, the Pluto determination to even the score, and it may puzzle you that these qualities seem to be missing in his relationship with you. They're not missing. They've been put on ice for the present, because the end justifies the means in his one-track, keen mind. He knows exactly what he's doing, but you may not.

Your Scorpio employee's reaction to you will relate directly to what you can offer him—what he wants from you and from life. If the average person opposes the Scorpio, insults him, treats him rudely, breaks a promise or steps on his tail, may the gods have mercy on him. He will rue the day he challenged Pluto. However, if you represent power and the fulfillment of his private dream, his reaction to the same treatment will be detachment. If you have something Scorpio wants and needs, he'll take almost anything from you with deliberate tranquility, and with—believe it or not—no retaliation or defensive stinging. The very fact that he's able to control his deep resentment and literally erase it from his mind is proof of his awesome inner strength.

Before you test the theory, make sure you know into which category you fall—the average person—which can include ordinary bosses, friends, neighbors, co-workers, servants, even relatives and loved ones—or someone who represents power, security and that private dream. Unless you're positive you fit the latter description, it may be dangerous to experiment.

Let's say you're a TV producer, and you've commissioned a Scorpio writer to create a script, tailored to certain specifications. After the fourth re-write, you can still tear his efforts to shreds and demand that he try again. You can say, "It stinks. Put more jokes in." What will the dangerous Scorpio do? He'll write another draft and put more jokes in. You have something he wants, you see. You have the power to produce his script on film and make it live. He may not agree with you completely from an artistic point of view, but you're the boss. You're the one who calls the shots—at the present. Later, when he's a success? You won't have to nervously wonder when he'll seek revenge for the past. That's not part of the Pluto code. You have given him power and you were the instrument to fufill his private dream. He holds no bitterness, but he'll make it clear his position is now changed and you're not to question his artistic taste or dictate how he expresses his creative ideas in the future. You'll get the message, and that will be that. Anyone other than you who criticized his earlier efforts, however, without regard for his sensitive pride, may have a few scars to show.

If there's one thing a Scorpio knows, it's on which side his bread is buttered, and who owns the marmalade. He's absolutely certain he will reach his goals eventually. Therefore, he's in no rush to knock down any brick buildings. Nor is he ashamed to submit to his superiors when it's expedient to do so. That's why your Scorpio employee is fearless. Confidence always breeds courage. To him, everything is timing. With some sort of deep, mystical penetration into the secrets of the universe, he knows when his time will come. This is not the hour to command, but the hour will arrive. No wonder he's not the anxious type.

I know a young Scorpio lawyer, who recently became associated with an important law firm, loaded with prestige and lucrative clients. His superior (and I'll use an anonymous name), Mr. Fink of Fink, Brink, Link and Katz, asked him to prepare a lengthy memorandum for a corporate merger. The request meant that the Scorpio lawyer would get no sleep at all, because Mr. Fink insisted he needed the papers for a conference at ten sharp the following morning. The next day, our hero was at his desk at nine a.m., alert, calm, and waiting for Mr. Fink to buzz him. He had stayed up all night completing the necessary briefs, and his wife wasn't too happy because he had to cancel the dinner reservations he had made earlier in the week to celebrate their anniversary. At nine forty-five his boss's secretary apologetically informed him that Mr. Fink had changed his mind. He had decided to hold the conference the following week. It was such lovely spring weather, he thought he'd play a few holes of golf with some clients from out of town. She murmured that her boss had said something about "hoping it didn't cause him too much inconvenience." You may suppose that, at this point, the Scorpio reached into his desk for a .45 automatic and headed for the golf course. But that's not the way the cookie crumbled. How did the Scorpio react to such boorish behavior? He simply shrugged. He smiled a cool, mysterious controlled smile, handed the secretary the finished memorandum, and said courteously, "Will you put this on Mr. Fink's desk please? I am going home to get a few hours sleep. I'll be back in time for my two o'clock appointment." Then, with the patience of Taurus and the discipline of Capricorn, he called his wife, told

her he would be home for lunch and left. Moral: That
Scorpio lawyer is aiming for a partnership at Fink, Brink,
Link and Katz. Are you wondering if his wife had his
lunch ready on time, after her disappointment the night
before? Of course she had his lunch ready on time. The
wife of a Scorpio? If she wanted to have any more anniversaries to celebrate, she did. She's not his boss. Mr.
Fink is his boss. This year.

If you're important enough to the future of your Scorpio
employee, you too can be a Mr. Fink. It's on a par with
being immune to nuclear power, but I don't think you
should let it turn your head to the place where you get
over-confident. If I were you, I'd keep incidents like the
foregoing at the absolute minimum. But I'm glad I'm not
you. I'm not sure I would have the nerve to play Russian
roulette with Pluto.

You can expect the Scorpio man or woman to accept
the inevitable with grace, if the stakes are high enough. He
(or she) will check out the potential with an eagle eye,
figure the consequences, mark the possible reward, and
make the final decision to submit with a cool head and a
definite purpose in mind. Most bosses appreciate and admire the Scorpio philosophy. He knows the price of success, and he's willing to pay it without asking for special
concessions. When that success arrives, however, don't
forget: it's half-time—change sides.

Compared to the attitude of the average worker, you'll
discover there's another quality to admire in your Scorpio
employee. It's an old-fashioned word, spelled l-o-y-a-l-t-y,
rather a rare commodity these days. I'm not talking about
lip service to your position as "boss" or the ingratiating,
often hypocritical servility of the normal ambitious employee. Scorpios have their own sense of loyalty.

When I was with a radio station in a small town in Penn-
sylvania, I was permanently impressed with the remark
of a Scorpio program director. The owner of the radio
station was the meanest man in town. He was a cross between Scrooge and Captain Hook. About the nicest thing
you could say about him was that at times he was meaner
than he was at other times. He had one friend—his mother.
Since he owned half the town, in addition to the station, he
was smothered with respect and obedience. Although the
staff called him "Sir," smiled from ear to ear when he
entered a room, and jumped to immediate attention every

time he mumbled the slightest request, they made faces at him when his back was turned, and snickered privately at his funny bow ties and squeaky voice. They would have considered his funeral an occasion for a holiday, and the favorite game around the office when he was out of town was writing his obituary, with a prize for the most hilarious one.

The Scorpio employee never joined the game. He was always too busy with his programming. One day, a secretary asked him why he never contributed to the office hobby. He gave her one of those hypnotic Scorpio stares and said, simply, "He pays my salary. I work for him."

"What's that got to do with it?" she wanted to know. "He yells at you in front of the staff every morning and he hasn't given you a vacation for two years. He never pays you a compliment. Don't you have any pride?"

The Scorpio never changed his expression. "I can't deposit compliments at the bank," he said quietly. "I prefer cash."

"But why do you take the way he treats you?" she persisted.

His answer was brief. "When I take a man's money, I take his orders. When I decide to stop taking his orders, I stop taking his money and leave. Do you have the program schedule for next week? I need to check it before I time the commercials."

The secretary silently handed him the schedule, he took out his stop watch and went to work. A few days later, she asked him to bring her a coffee when he returned from lunch. Somehow, he forgot to bring it. He also forgot to send her an invitation to his wedding the following spring. He remembered her insinuation that he had no pride. Scorpions have long memories. That's an excellent illustration of how and when the typical Pluto employee chooses to seek revenge—against whom and why. It also indicates his personal code of loyalty to the man who employs him.

These workers are intense and tenacious. They're quite serious about their careers, and they never lose sight of the goal. Scorpios can be stubborn, rebellious, passionate and overbearing. But you won't often find them wasting office time by writing humorous obituaries. Death is a serious subject to them. So are you. You're the bridge to power. Consequently, you're respected, until the Scorpio has safely passed across the stream to the other side. Smart strategists don't destroy bridges, and Scorpios are smart. Some of them are brilliant. All of them are shrewd and logical. You'll often find Scorpio men and women gravitating to work that involves solving mysteries and penetrating the puzzles of life, machines, facts or human beings. Lots of them are detectives, psychiatrists, scientists, surgeons, policemen, researchers, reporters and even undertakers. They must increase their knowledge each day they live, at the same rate they increase talents, abilities and incomes.

Never pry into Scorpio's private affairs. He will not tolerate that. If he likes you and his job, he'll be generous and fair. He'll give you eight hours work for eight hours pay, and he won't watch the clock if the project holds his interest. But remember that he will always be firmly committed to his own code and ideas. He will be true to them above all other loyalties, including love and ambition. No one but himself can force him to alter his views and opinions. It has to be done through Pluto power, from inside his own nature. If his decision is negative, no one on the face of this earth can slam the door more suddenly or more permanently than a Scorpio, even a door bearing the title Vice-President in gold-leaf letters. He'll take just so much, pay just so high a price. When he thinks the cost is too much, he leaves. That's the way he plays the game. His *real* loyalty, when all is said and done, is to himself. That's not always as selfish as it sounds. When he was very young, his favorite verse began: "This above all: to thine own self be true." He's always figured—if he does that— he can't be false to anyone.

*"You may charge me with murder—
or want of sense
(We are all of us weak at times):
But the slightest approach to a false pretence
was never among my crimes!"*

SAGITTARIUS
the Archer
November 23rd through December 21st

How to Recognize SAGITTARIUS

"I should see the garden far better . . .
If I could get to the top of that hill:
and here's at path that leads straight to it—
at least; no, it doesn't do that . . .
But I suppose it will at last.
But how curiously it twists! . . .
Well then, I'll try the other way."

I would say that finding an example of this Sun sign is as easy as rolling off a log, except that it isn't true. It's much easier than rolling off a log. Pick any party and look at the center of the liveliest group. See that fellow sitting there happily with his rather large foot stuck in his mouth? He's a Sagittarian who has just gone out on a verbal limb, but he doesn't know it yet. When he does, he'll look slightly bewildered—and the group around him will be looking daggers.

The archer will walk up to you, give you a hearty slap on the back and a wide, friendly grin. Then he'll greet you with a remark like, "How the heck do you manage to look so young when you're as old as you are?" Or "Say, that turtleneck sweater sure is flattering. You should wear them all the time. Hides your double chin." After one of these cheery openers, he'll still be wearing his bright grin, but your own smile may start to droop a little. It will take him a while to figure out just what he said that set you back on your heels, and even longer to understand why. Then he'll try to explain. Keep your cool. It gets worse.

Golly, didn't you understand what he meant? He thinks it's fabulous to look only twenty-five years old when you're really thirty-eight (which is six years older than you actually are). As for the double chin, lots of people your age have a little flab in the neck region. The only time you can see it is from the side. You know, when you turn your head. Just don't have any pictures taken in profile.

After he's carefully explained his verbal goofs and got

you feeling all better again, he'll go on his merry way, whistling a tune from the latest Broadway show. When you cut him dead the next time you meet, he'll be heartbroken —and puzzled. There's no use getting angry or embarrassed. Sagittarius is completely free of malice. He blurts out his shockingly direct speech in total innocence. The fact that he usually adds insult to injury when he tries to fix it also escapes him. Don't judge him too harshly. He means well. Not that he needs your sympathy—or mine. Under his tactless manner is an extremely clever mind and high standards. His unique combination of wit, intelligence and fiery drive usually brings the archer straight to the winner's circle. What really gets you is that both male and female Sagittarians are oblivious to their own blunt speech. They are truly convinced that they are the most diplomatic souls in the world. They're always saying, "Why, I wouldn't hurt anyone's feelings for anything. I'm very careful about that." And they honestly believe it. In fact, everything they do is done honestly. Pretense and deception in any form appalls them.

Their physical characteristics aren't hard to learn. Look for a fairly large, well-shaped skull and a high, broad forehead. The features will be open and cheerful, inviting friendship and the exchange of ideas, and the movements will normally be rapid (though you'll find a few who move slowly and deliberately). They will often make wide, sweeping gestures, which may be dramatic and vigorous, but possibly not very graceful. Sagittarius can wave his arms to make a point, and upset the ketchup. He'll stride purposefully forward, head high, and trip over the curbstone. His brief case may snap open at the same time, scattering his papers all over the street.

Jupiter eyes are as bright and alert as a sparrow's, and they sparkle and twinkle with refreshing humor. The archers are either very tall and athletic looking or shorter than average, with strong, sturdy bodies. The tall ones will remind you of thoroughbred horses or spirited colts. In youth especially, many of them have a stray lock of hair which keeps falling over the forehead, like a horse's mane. They'll flip it back with a toss of the head or a quick, unconscious movement of the hand—a habit that may last long after a new hairstyle has been adopted in maturity or after baldness has set in.

Sagittarians are normally restless. They hate to sit or

stand still. The archer is physically conspicuous, if only through his obvious confidence and his disregard for conventional behavior. He walks as if he's really going somewhere. There's no halting or hesitating. (But remember that a conflicting ascendant can slow down the gait.)

When you first meet him, Sagittarius could be perched on a horse or walking his dog. He loves animals passionately. Sagittarian Frank Sinatra once ordered his driver to stop his car when he saw an injured dog lying in the street. He was on his way to a television rehearsal, but musicians, director and camera crew had to wait until the singer had tenderly carried the dog to a vet, was assured he would be fine in a few days, and had found the dog's owner.

Sagittarians with natal afflictions to the birth planets can have, instead, a morbid fear of animals, but it doesn't happen often. Ordinarily, people born under Jupiter's influence fear nothing. The typical Sagittarian is attracted to danger—in sports and in his job or his hobby. An element of risk excites and challenges the archers. They love speed. Fast cars, planes—even roller coasters draw them magnetically. Daredevil test pilots are often Sagittarians. The average Jupiter person enjoys nothing more than a hairbreadth escape of some kind—either physical or emotional. It exhilarates them. They'll take a chance on literally anything (unless a meeker sign on the ascendant dilutes Jupiter's daring).

There's a difference between the legendary bluntness of the archer and the brutal speech of the Scorpio. Scorpio tells the truth, completely conscious of its effect, but still refusing to compromise. Sagittarius is totally unaware of the effect when his direct honesty compels him to speak. Scorpio feels little compunction about the wounds his statements cause. To him, the truth is the truth, and if you can't bear to hear it, don't ask. The Jupiter person, on the other hand, is crushed and dismayed at his own lack of discretion when he discovers he's really cut you. It would be touching if it weren't so infuriating.

What is on the archer's mind and heart is almost instantly on his lips. He's as frank and earnest as a six-year-old. You can take that old advice, "If you want the truth, go to a child," and switch it to "If you want the truth, go to a Sagittarian."

There's a woman in the publishing business in New York

about whom the same thing is said. "If you want the truth, go to Kay—if you can stand it." Kay is not only an authentic archer, she also has additional Sagittarius influences in her natal chart. A Jupiter girl plus, you might say. She's warm and generous, typical of the sign, and she has lots of loyal friends who love her, also typical of the sign. They would have to be loyal, and they would have to love her to survive incidents like the time three years ago when she opened up her big heart and decided to completely outfit her secretary for the winter. The young girl was flat broke, since she had just been through a drizzly financial disaster, and she was touched to tears. Others had sympathized, but until Kay, no one had offered a concrete helping hand. Leave it to Sagittarius. (You can read that several ways.)

One fine fall day, the two of them set forth for Saks Fifth Avenue in a fever of excited female anticipation. The poor secretary was delirious with happiness—until they entered the elevator. Suddenly, the Sagittarian gave her a long, appraising look, and said quite firmly and quite loudly, "We'd better try the Fat Girl's Department first."

Blind ecstasy was instantly replaced by numb shock. The secretary's fiancé had always told her she was "pleasingly plump." Now, in one flashing painful moment of Sagittarian honesty, she had become a baby blimp. To this very day, the young girl remembers how everyone in the car turned to stare at her curiously, as she wondered if her fiancé secretly thought she was grotesque. But good old Kay fixed it. Noticing the girl's discomfiture, she hastily made a joke to jolly her up. "And if we can't find anything to fit you there, we can always try the tents in the camping department." The Sagittarian howled at her own hilarity. So did the people in the elevator.

Just after Kay's warm, generous excursion with her secretary, she cheered up her boss, the publisher, who had been on doctor's orders not to drink for a year. One solid year. He had had infectious hepatitis. No liquor. Not one drop. After going for twelve long months without even wetting his lips, he was justifiably proud of his will power. Kay, just freshly back from Europe, paid him a typical Sagittarian compliment. "About your drinking," she began, and he smiled, waiting. "I hear you've been trying to stay on the wagon." *Trying?* After twelve months without a single drop? *Trying?* As he recovered his composure, she went on. "Say, you know there's a party tomorrow night for

Joe's book? I thought I ought to warn you, but I never get to see you alone." Warn him? Warn him about what? The publisher forgot his chagrin under this new threat. She continued: "We were all hoping that, well, this is embarrassing—but we were all hoping that you wouldn't spoil the party." By now, the publisher was speechless. Not Sagittarius.

"What I mean is, we hope you don't mess up the evening by being a wet blanket about not drinking—and all that. Joe likes his martinis, and after all, his book is a Literary Guild selection. If you slink around like some fugitive from prohibition and make everybody miserable, just because you have this terrible disease, it will throw a damper on the whole thing. Say, can people catch it from being in the same room with you?"

The publisher somehow managed to stammer that she was safe, then gathered his injured dignity together long enough to remind her that he had hosted parties himself for authors like Edna Ferber and Ernest Hemingway without mishap. "I have always been told," he said evenly, between clenched teeth, "that my manners are impeccable." The Sagittarian, blind to her boss's near apoplexy, heartily agreed with him. "That's for sure. You're a fabulous host. No one in the publishing business can figure it out." The publisher had just barely enough breath left to ask, Figure what out? The archer's answer zinged home. "How is it that you can be such a great host and such a perfectly lousy guest? Your own parties are marvelous, but you always pull such big boo-boos every time you go to somebody else's whing-ding. It's really weird."

Then she noticed something else weird. Her boss's face. It was turning purple. Suddenly contrite, the friendly Sagittarian immediately apologized. "Gee, I hope I didn't say the wrong thing. It won't matter how you behave anyway. Joe thinks you're really swell. He was just telling us all today that he's glad he decided to come to us even though his old agent had been against it. He can't understand why he's heard such awful things about you. I told him people were just jealous. Say, you don't look so hot. Are you sure your doctor knows what he's doing?" (There are rumors that Kay's boss went off the wagon that night, permanently.) The Sagittarian? Oh, she's happily helping new authors get over their nervousness at the same publishing company. Fired? He wouldn't dare fire her. As I said in the beginning, everybody loves her.

Few people can resent the archer for very long, because he's so transparently free of harmful intent. You'll see this lovable, likable, intelligent idealist almost anywhere or any time. You may catch him shooting out his careless arrows from your television screen some Sunday night, leaving his guest stars numb and speechless with astonishment at his frankness. He may be your cab driver some Monday morning, the one who cheerfully explains to you why he hates stingy tippers—or you could find him serving you in a restaurant some Friday evening, earnestly advising you not to order the oysters because they're a little on the tired side.

Most archers sincerely try to cheer you up. At least, that's what they start out to do, but sometimes it falls a little short of the good intention. I once had a Sagittarius manager who tried to boost my morale by telling me how much better my hair looked than it usually did when I hadn't washed it or rolled it up for more than a week. But he's still a good friend, so you can see it's useless to get exasperated. Besides, now and then Sagittarians can come up with a dilly of a statement that sends your spirits really soaring, and makes up for all the rest. They can offer profoundly wise counsel, when you've had time to analyze their viewpoints. This is a fire sign, so most archers are extroverts, talkative and forward. There are a few who are painfully shy and timid, but even these are full of original ideas—and they're just as blunt. In fact, the quiet, fey Sagittarians with the reclusive, meek ways can dream the biggest dreams and aim for the highest goals. Introvert or extrovert, the archer is a promoter at heart. The rare one who doesn't say much could be planning something really spectacular to spring on an unsuspecting world. His mind is busy even when his tongue is still, so you have to remember his Sun sign is always there at the bottom of his nature, lest he lull you into not being prepared for his next startling move.

Most of the time the typical Sagittarian is happy and gregarious, but his temper can flare like a sky rocket if he's pushed around by people who abuse his natural friendliness or who get too familiar. Rebellion against authority and stuffy society is also common. Sagittarius will never run away from a fight or call for help. The women can lose their normally pleasant dispositions and let go with a barrage of unexpected plain talk that puts troublemakers right where they belong. The men will use their fists and scorn weapons. A rude, insulting person who has challenged Jupiter's good nature often find himself sprawled on the sidewalk wondering where that truck came from.

High-spirited Jupiter people can't stand to be accused of dishonesty. An unjust accusation or a slur against their integrity will make righteous indignation flame high, but after an especially fiery display of temper, the typical Sagittarian will feel remorse and try to make amends. He'll black your eye and put you in the hospital, but he'll probably shower you with flowers and sympathy the next day. The archer usually speaks and acts first, and considers the consequences later.

Many Sagittarians seek the stage, and no one is happier giving encore after encore for an excited audience. He'll sing himself hoarse or dance his shoes off for the sheer exhilaration of performing. Show business is full of archers.

There's a strong religious streak in Jupiter men and women, especially in their youth. They're intensely interested in church affairs, but as they grow older they can become skeptical of dogma, inclined to question former faiths and search for a perfection of values. It's a rare Sagittarian who doesn't have a matched set of luggage. They love to travel, and there's usually at least one suitcase, well worn from hundreds of trips, that's kept packed and ready for instant use.

You'll always notice something child-like about the typical naive, brave, optimistic Sagittarian. He refuses to accept the seriousness of life, though some of them manage responsibility with admirable conscientiousness in later years. Still, they're never truly happy when they're burdened by it. Jupiter natures rebel against confinement, and too much of it can bring on serious illness. If the Sagittarian can survive that, and the wear and tear of scattering his energies, he'll live to be as old as Methuselah. Most archers retain their faculties, razor sharp and refined by age, to the end. Senility is almost never a problem.

His sensitive areas are the hips, lungs, liver, arms, hands, shoulders, intestines and feet. The Sagittarian love of sports and the outdoors may bring accidents through reckless over-activity. Hospitals can rarely keep him bedded down more than a few days. He gives in to sickness reluctantly, and usually recuperates with amazing swiftness. Life seldom defeats these people permanently. They believe that tomorrow will surely be better than yesterday, and today is pretty interesting. Moody spells are gone almost before the clouds have a chance to obscure the sunshine.

Every Sagittarian is something of a gambler, unless there's a cautious, conservative influence in the natal chart. Very few of them can resist throwing a couple of bills on the green felt. The sound of dice rattling in the dealer's hand attracts some Jupiter men and women like the siren song of Circe. With adverse aspects between the planets at birth, an archer can gamble away a fortune, or throw the rent money on the nose of a favorite horse. Las Vegas attracts Sagittarians like sugar attracts flies. So do the more staid gambles of the stock market and real estate. Fortunately, the majority of them keep the urge to speculate under control, but even these will risk a few dollars now and then on a fast poker game or a lottery ticket.

Both the timid and the forceful ones will take a chance on love anytime. Sagittarians plunge into romance with reckless abandon, but they often stop short suddenly when marriage is mentioned. They think it over, then go ahead and make a mistake after careful consideration. Although the archer is warm and wonderful in love relationships, he's a little tricky to catch. Symbolically he's half horse-half man, which obviously gives him a head start in any game of chase, if he doesn't stumble over his own feet.

Among the most unpleasant traits of some Sagittarians are a tendency to violent temper, a love of too much food and drink, which can lead to obesity or alcoholism, mental brilliance stained by burning sarcasm, or extreme eccentricity and the inability to keep a secret. But none of these need be permanent flaws. They can be easily rooted out with Sagittarian determination. The average Jupiter man will loan you money without ever making you ashamed to ask or even obligated to repay it (barring a stingy Moon sign). The Jupiter housewife will adopt the homeless orphan or the lost animal, and always make room for one more at her table.

Sagittarians have a tendency to go off on tangents. The archer will take on a great cause with blind devotion and believe that the possibilities outweigh the shortcomings, an attitude that results from his brilliant imagination and progressive thinking. He never fails to present his case with cool, reasonable arguments, sometimes cutting the opposition to ribbons with sharp satire, and yet remaining aloof from the fray, somehow. The fire is always ready to leap forth, however, when anyone unfairly attacks his miracle or his cause of the moment. He's a formidable foe, because he aims straight when he takes the time to focus on the victim. His arrows then rarely miss their mark. They're dipped in clever wit and sharp enough to pierce the strongest armor.

Although a few December people are genuinely funny, it's a curious fact that when most of them tell a joke, the timing is slightly off and they fluff the punch line. The audience—at home or in the theater—will roar at the obvious awkwardness, and the jovial Jupiter soul will think everyone is laughing at his great sense of comedy timing. It can be hilarious.

Male or female, the archer can either behave in such a slap-dash fashion, or pretend to have such unassuming manners when he chooses, that you may get the impression his mind isn't too sharp or that he's timid. True, there are a few December-born people who occasionally exhibit eccentric reclusive habits, but that just gives them more opportunity to sharpen their intelligence into genius.

Although Sagittarians have fantastic memories that tell them exactly what they said and where they were on April 14, 1939, and they remember every detail of books and movies, they can forget where they left their coats. Most of them are constantly losing gloves, car keys, wallets—and some people are unkind enough to say they would lose their heads if they weren't fastened on their necks.

A Sagittarian can never successfully tell a lie. No one believes him for a minute. Deceit is unnatural to the archer, and when he tries to dabble in it, the exposure is usually swift and sure. He's always better off to stick to the truth and let the chips fall where they may. Even his observant, highly aware mind won't rescue him from the results of an excursion into deception, unless he has Scorpio rising. I know a secretive archer who has such a Pluto ascendant, and therefore manages very well to play a good chess game. This kind of a Jupiter person is an exception, but be prepared to meet a few.

To the Sagittarian, life is secretly a circus, and he's the clown, rolling and tumbling through purple hoops in a sky-blue suit, His face is smeared with the bright, gay

colors of greasepaint, and his eyes glitter with curiosity
and fun. As the music of the calliope gets louder, he
stumbles and falls, then executes a perfect somersault on
the back of a prancing pony. On his fingers he wears three
turquoise rings; on his toes are bells that ring like the
chimes in a distant church spire that disappears into the
clouds. The archer happily blows a lustrous tin horn, made
of the soft, malleable metal that's barely affected by
moisture. Whether he's bold or backward, the true nature
of this generous idealist is as merry as the Christmas holly
berry. Bravely, he pins a large carnation over his big heart,
and curves his bow toward the sky. When he aims straight,
he shoots higher than man can see—past the stars—to the
place where all dreams are really born.

Famous Sagittarius Personalities

Beethoven	Julie Harris
Arthur Brisbane	Pope John XXIII
William Buckley, Jr.	John Lindsay
Maria Callas	Mary Martin
Andrew Carnegie	David Merrick
Edith Cavell	John Milton
Winston Churchill	Robert Moses
Noel Coward	John Osborne
Sammy Davis	Lee Remick
Joe DiMaggio	Lillian Russell
Walt Disney	Frank Sinatra
Betty Grable	David Susskind
Grimaldi	James Thurber

Mark Twain

The SAGITTARIUS Man

"I hope no bones are broken?"
"None to speak of," the Knight said,
as if he didn't mind breaking two or three of them.
"The great art of riding, as I was saying,
is—to keep your balance properly. Like this, you know—"
He let go the bridle, and stretched out both his arms
to show Alice what he
meant, and this time he fell flat on his back,
right under the horse's feet.

I don't want to discourage you, but Sagittarius men have this odd habit. They leap on a big, white horse and go charging through the streets, waving a sword and defending causes. Then they have another idiosyncrasy. They tumble around like clowns in a circus, indiscriminately mixing with the elephants and the bearded lady, gaily scooping up cotton candy.

He can be captured with certain maneuvers. But first you've got to get him down off that white horse, away from those elephants, and of course the bearded lady has to go. Causes and circuses don't leave much time for family life, let alone sentimental hand-holding.

You have one thing going for you right away. So many Sagittarians charge around and tumble through life that you'll have plenty to choose from. Remember the Victor Herbert refrain: "Give me some men who are stout-hearted men, who will fight for the right they adore; Start me with ten, who are stout-hearted men, and I'll soon give you ten thousand more!"? It happens like that. The idealistic enthusiasm and curiosity of a Sagittarian man is contagious. Of course, sometimes his innocent exuberance can get a little out of hand. Like he'll throw you up in the air in a moment of mad, impetuous exhilaration—and forget to catch you.

There's almost always a crowd around him. That's another obstacle. You'll have to push your way through all

those people to get near him. But don't get pessimistic—
because this man is an optimist supreme. He's so optimistic,
if his enemies mailed him a huge carton of manure, he
wouldn't be offended. He'd just figure they forgot to
include the horse. That kind of optimism can be dangerous.
It's really just another term for blind faith. The Sagittarian
man has stacks of it. Now, blind faith is fine. I'm all for it,
being a fire sign myself. But it can lead to trusting with
such naive belief that he frequently falls into puddles. It's
easy to fall into puddles when you're running with a bow
and arrow, always looking up in the sky for some high goal
no one else has ever had the courage to aim for—or no one
else ever had the lack of common sense to try to reach.

Trusting is great, but trusting the wrong people can slow
down even a race horse. In the strict sense of the word,
he's not a misty dreamer. His dreams are always scrutinized
by Jupiter's intelligent logic and compelling curiosity. If
they stand up under the frank investigation of a Sagittarian, they're probably as practical as they are wild, even
if the world isn't quite ready for them. Once he's established
that there's some hope of fulfillment, he lugs out his paint
pots and colors his practical dreams with the most vivid
and courageous imagination this side of the designers of
the Edsel. But the fuddy duddies are always waiting to
stomp on progressive ideas and strangle them before they've
had the chance to prove themselves, and you know how
many fuddy duddies there are around.

His soaring imagination can cause him to fall down or
go busted. But wonderfully, Lady Luck has a way of
rescuing him just in time. This man is usually so lucky
it's disgusting and illegal. He could go prospecting in the
hills, bring back a bag of rocks, find out they're not gold,
cry awhile, then discover they're uranium. If you pick up
that shiny object at your feet near the subway grating, it
will be a piece of tinfoil from an old chewing gum wrapper. If he picks it up, it will be a chip from the Hope
Diamond Harry Winston dropped when he was hailing a
cab.

Naturally, with that kind of luck, he's optimistic. There's
always that day when a rock is a rock and tinfoil is tinfoil, but the typical Sagittarian recovers quickly from such
crushing blows. Your Jupiter man is very much that way
about love. He's lucky. When he isn't, he recovers quickly.
He discriminates against dishonesty, but that's about all,

which is why he has so many friends and well-wishers. He looks beyond the external appearance of people for a truer, more intrinsic value. Not that he doesn't have enemies. There are a few, but far less than the number accumulated by other Sun signs. People who have been stung by his frank remarks may glare at him and feel like strangling him, but they usually come around to realizing his harmless intent. The sin of the Sagittarian male is tactlessness and thoughtlessness, never deliberate cruelty.

You may have discovered by now that his speech is as direct as his symbolic arrow. He can say outrageous things, and if you're in love with him, he may get away with it. But you'll have every right to take offense when a Sagittarian man who has just met you gazes at you frankly with his bright, alert eyes and remarks that you're just the kind of woman a man would choose for a mistress. Just as you're ready to clobber him, he'll get an innocent, boyish look on his face, and explain with disarming candor that what he really meant was, well, the kings and aristocracy back in the middle ages married for convenience. Their wives, therefore, were often ugly, drab creatures, with good blood lines. But their mistresses were beautiful and brilliant, the kind of girls they would have chosen to fall in love with and marry, if the rules had been different. He's been reading up on it, because he's always been curious about that particular period. You may calm down, and even feel a little smug. You'll also be impressed. How many men spend hours reading history when they don't have to do it? He might even be a genius. Just think, you could be the wife of an intellectual! Wrong. You could be the mistress of an intellectual. By the time he has you ga-ga over his brain, you won't realize that, had your reaction been agreeable to his original proposition—and make no mistake, that's what it was—he would have moved in fast, and you would be a fallen woman.

Of course, not every female would accept such a fumbling explanation of an obvious pass; but it doesn't matter. Even after his victims explode in indignation, they return to be the Sagittarian's close friends again, when their anger cools. That should show you just how much danger you're in with this apparently harmless chap. With that candid, naive grin, he doesn't bear the faintest resemblance to a wolf. He looks more like a Boy Scout troop leader.

But he is not a boy scout in romantic matters. It would pay to keep that in mind when he asks you to go hiking.

The Sagittarius male lives his romantic life on a surface level, but he's honest about it. (After all, if you'll brush those sentimental cobwebs out of your ears, you'll remember he did say mistress. He did not say wife. He is not a king. And these are not medieval times.) Sagittarius seeks casual relationships, and sometimes they can get so casual they're downright promiscuous. Occasionally, the shenanigans of an archer can put a Scorpio to shame, and I promise you it takes a great deal to put a Scorpio to shame.

Let's get back to his honesty. It's a safer subject. If you've learned through bitter experience how fickle other men's vows of eternal devotion can be, you'll welcome his frankness. You won't even flinch when he tells you how many affairs he's had, and what he expects of this one with you, all very clearly and logically. He won't knowingly tie a legal knot with a lie in his heart or on his lips, but somehow, he can get himself involved in a flirtation which tangles itself into a proposal (possibly from the girl, not him), and have to run like sixty to avoid the altar. Since he's a little clumsy, he may trip, and she'll catch him before he gets too far away. In that event, he'll think it over and illogically decide that, since she appealed to him in one way—either physically or mentally, no matter which—she'll eventually appeal to him the other way. He'll give in, get married, and the seeds for another Sagittarian divorce have been planted. His normally dependable reasoning powers seem to desert him when he's romantically trapped.

Women often misinterpret the attitude of a Sagittarian, and think the relationship is more serious than it really is, and this same quality also sometimes makes it appear that he seeks a dark liaison, when he's only after a light, non-physical friendship, or just a girl to pal around with. It seems the archer loses both ways. But he's lucky, and most of his messes turn out straight. He's a flirt, that can't be denied, but he's not looking for sex alone. He likes variety and mental stimulation. If a woman gets sticky when he was only diverting himself, he'll try to pass the whole thing off as a joke. She may definitely miss the punch line. (Remember how unsuccessful the typical Sagittarian is with jokes.) Lots of Sagittarians get accused of making passes at every good-looking receptionist or pretty girl they

see—sometimes even the little old woman who sells newspapers on the corner, or a lady policeman. Now, no man
in his right mind would seriously flirt with a lady policeman—at least, not while she's on duty—so you can see
that unjustified suspicion is annoying to the archer. In all
fairness, most of the time, he was just being breezily
friendly.

If you're a smart girl, who uses her head for something
besides an object to poke under a hair dryer—and you'd
better be, because these men insist on intelligence in a
woman—you'll have caught on by now. Don't be jealous.
Don't be suspicious. Give him lots of rope if you want to
hang him eventually. Don't question him, weep, nag or
threaten to leave him. Smother him with freedom. Imagine
how refreshing that would be to him. If you take life in
the same spirit he does, and take people as you find them,
you have the basic requirements of being his kind of wife-
woman. As long as you're basically honest with each other,
flying kites together can be a ball. Why worry about when
they'll hit the ground? They look so beautiful and free,
soaring up there in the sky. No, you don't have to give
this man everything he wants to get him. Just *be* what he
wants. Be wide-awake—let him direct and dominate your
energies. Love sports. Go camping with him and take your
St. Bernard along for a chaperone. Be generous, affectionate, enthusiastic, and don't try to keep him locked up in
your pantry making fudge every night. Make it clear he
can't keep you all to himself, either. Let him know you're
a free spirit, just as he is. Never throw water on his fiery
ideas, and keep yourself busy with other things while he's
out shooting his arrows at impossible targets. That way,
he'll tell you honestly some lovely night that you are just
about everything he needs in a woman. Once he's gone
that far, then tell him just as frankly that he's okay in
your book, too, but it's time to make a decision. Point out
that you like him so much you'd even consider marrying
him, if he'd promise not to interfere with your freedom.
Otherwise, you really don't have any more time to camp
around with him. It's a shame, you're so compatible, but
you've always been curious what it would be like to have
children. Motherhood is a new kite you'd like to fly. Be
sure to arrange for an old flame to call you on the phone
in the middle of your speech. Accept the date casually,
in front of your archer. When you hang up, smile brightly

and remark that there's no reason why you can't still be good friends. Then invite him to come along on your date, so he won't have to sit around all by himself. That should do it. (You're welcome!)

After you're married, you probably won't have in-law trouble. Many Sagittarians are shockingly disinterested in family ties. They don't accept the theory of loving blood relations unless they deserve loving. Even those who are fond of their parents and brothers or sisters manage to keep a healthy distance. They visit and show warm affection, but they never expect relatives to interfere with their private lives. Better see that your own relatives don't meddle, either.

Keep your suitcase packed. You'll be doing a lot of traveling. You'll still want to take the St. Bernard along on camping trips—not as a chaperone anymore, but because your new husband loves animals. (Tell the dog it's okay now, he doesn't have to stand guard outside the tent flap.) Keep yourself busy and give him as many nights out as he needs. Never question his honesty. When he's in a temper, the archer can break down a door, or punch a hole through a wall. He's just letting off steam, but it does make a lot of work, and how many times can you call the plasterer? It's a lot easier on everyone's nerves not to accuse him of a lack of integrity in the first place. When he does something wrong, he'll almost surely tell you. That will be hard enough to take without worrying about imaginary things. Practice facing his frankness, if that tomorrow ever comes, and be prepared to know he still loves you, instead of chasing after false rumors today. Be as practical as he is about human emotions. You'll be surprised how strong love can grow in such honest soil. Truth has a way of encouraging permanence in a relationship.

You'll have to put in some hours being a Polly-put-the-kettle-on woman. Since he's a sports fan, he'll probably expect you to watch all the big games on TV with him. But he'll also take you along to all his many social activities if you're pretty and fun and you like people. Sagittarians can't stand droopy clinging women who aren't good mixers. He'll be proud of any special talents you have, and do try to have one or two. Read lots of books, and be prepared to defend a few of his causes, especially the lost ones.

He may be a little extravagant, and he'll like an occasional game of chance, but the same impulse will make him pretty generous about your spending money, if he's a typical archer. He probably won't mind if you want to work to buy yourself extras.

Expect a little forthright criticism, often painfully lacking in tact. You should be used to it by now. Let it pass. You'll be busy enough patching up the damage with his friends. You're supposed to understand him, remember? You gave him that, the night you forced the issue.

He'll enjoy the children more when they're older, but babies and toddlers might puzzle him a little. Sagittarius fathers usually love to take the youngsters on outdoor excursions. He may be closer to the boys and share their sports and activities, but he'll be tender with the girls. They'll find him more of a pal than a father image. The older they get, the closer they'll be to him. Now and then, his frankness may disturb them when they need privacy. Children are sensitive about their secrets, and their feelings may suffer from his curious questions and plainspoken observations. Youthful escapades will amuse him rather than anger him, but his very tolerance might keep them in line. He'll probably be strict only if they tell a lie. It will be one of the few occasions they'll feel his displeasure. Don't ignore him for the little ones. When he wants you to fly some kites with him, drop the diaper pins and the talcum, call a sitter (not your mother) and go.

The archer thinks with both his heart and his mind. He won't always be wise. Sometimes he'll be foolishly courageous. He'll stumble and fall, then get up and try again. But you'll forgive him for almost anything, because he'll set your heart free with a very great gift—an honest love.

The SAGITTARIUS Woman

"Then it doesn't matter which way you walk," said the Cat.
"—So long as I get somewhere,"
Alice added as an explanation.
"Oh, you're sure to do that," said the Cat,
"if you only walk long enough."

She's not always going to say the kind of things you want to hear. Most of the time, she'll curl your sideburns with her remarkable, flat statements and her embarrassing questions. But now and then she'll say something so special and splendid it will make you feel like singing.

You may need a sample. Scene: Coffee shop. You've just gotten up the courage to tell her you love her, but before you can say it, she looks at you with wide-open, guileless blue eyes—or forthright, steady brown ones—and asks you curiously, "How do you feel about being so short? Does it make you neurotic or anything?" While you're gulping, trying manfully to recover, she'll add, "You shouldn't care about it. Lots of men were short. Like Napoleon. And Fiorello LaGuardia." That's almost adding insult to injury, but before you get a chance to walk out, thinking no woman ever deserved such ungallant treatment more, she'll muse dreamily, "I hate men who look like bean poles. You're perfect. I noticed when we were walking over here tonight—we measure just right together."

Sit back down. You're staying. For a long time. A friendly, frank Sagittarius girl has just wound herself around your heart with her own, peculiar brand of charm. She'll always be a little outspoken, because she sees the world exactly as it is, even while she's wearing those ridiculous, rose-tinted glasses. That, you must admit, is quite a talent. It's not everyone who can apply clear, reasonable logic to every situation, and retain the happy faculty of believing things will get better or else deciding to accept them for what they are.

Sagittarius females are regular Pollyannas. It will cut when she tells you she wishes you would make more money, but then she'll add, "Of course, too much money can make people selfish. Maybe it's lucky that you're poor." Admittedly, it's sort of a left-handed optimism, but you'll get used to it. This girl will never lie to you. Sometimes, you may wish she would. Show curiosity about how she spends the nights you're not with her, and you'll get a detailed, perfectly honest report of the letters she writes to that handsome intern she met last summer on her vacation and how many dates she turns down on the phone. She may even relate her troubles with insomnia, brought on when she lies awake at night wondering if maybe what she feels for you is friendship instead of love. You'll feel like yelling at her, "For Pete's sake, *lie* a little once in a while, can't you? A man has his pride." Don't yell too loud. You'll offend her, and she's not exactly noncombustible herself. Sagittarius girls have been known to fly into some pretty fiery rages.

She will probably live alone. Sagittarius girls are very independent, and both sexes have a strange aloofness to family ties. Maybe it's because they travel so much, they don't get home often enough to get to know their families well. Even if they only travel to the movies and girl friends' houses, they're restlessly on the go. I don't want to frighten you, but I once knew a Sagittarius woman so unaware of the nuances of family relationships that she invited her rejected beau to come along on her honeymoon with her new husband. The poor thing looked so lonesome. He said he'd pay his own way. Why are you looking at her like that? Did she do something wrong?

There's one thing you'll have to learn right away, or the relationship will never get off the ground. When you want her to do something, ask her. Don't tell her. The cave man technique went out with Tarzan and Jane, as far as she's concerned. She enjoys being protected, but she doesn't want to be ordered around. Not even her mother gets away with that. Who are you, that you should top her mother? She may have an Aries mother, and if a Mars woman can't boss her around, no male on earth is going to do it. However, there's a queer twist to her nature. Although she dislikes being bossed, especially in public, when she's testing you for firmness, be firm. Jupiter women can't stand weak, wishy-washy men. If she gets too high-spirited and her clever tongue gets too sarcastic, or she threatens some action that really incenses you, give her a light touch of the Tarzan treatment. Just enough to keep her in line. Like "You do that and I'll break your neck." She may react with surprising meekness if she thinks you're serious. A Sagittarius female has no intention of giving up her individuality for any male, but she kind of likes to know you think of her as a girl.

She may confuse you, but that's nothing to what she does to herself. Many a Sagittarius girl mistakes friendship for love and love for friendship. If you're one of those old-fashioned men who prefer evasiveness and timidity in your women, you'd better look for another Bingo partner. This young lady has bright, frank ways with men, and she's not going to play any silly games of "Guess how I feel!" or "Guess what I think!" How she feels and what she thinks are identical with how she acts and what she says. Her outspoken bluntness naturally causes misunderstandings, and a good share of fiery battles, let alone hurt feelings, but it doesn't crush her spirit. Jupiter pride comes to the surface and rescues her in a crisis, allowing her to pass off her heartache as the biggest joke of the season. Inside, she may be weeping, but she'll employ such clever wit in answering the questions of friends about the break that they'll decide the whole affair was a harmless flirtation on her part. Little will they guess how she soaks her pillow every night, wondering what she could possibly have said that fractured everything. It might have been when she told him not to stop by her apartment the time he called from the lobby around midnight—because she was "busy talking with a man who had a few problems." Actually, the man was her brother-in-law, but with the peculiar Sagittarius twist of leaving out the core of the story, she neglected to mention that. Why should she have to explain herself? (All Sagittarians show a raging, righteous anger when their integrity is doubted.) Or it could have been when he asked her if she minded him bringing his little sister along to the movies and she blurted out, "Gosh, I hope that doesn't mean she's going to be hanging around all the time when we're married." She may have sincerely liked the young girl, but the natural Sagittarian fear of being suffocated by in-laws brought on her thoughtless and forthright statement. Now she misses his sister as much as the man, but it's too late to explain what she meant. Besides, no one would understand.

Impasses like this are impossible for her to fathom, for all her logical mental processes, and often lead the Jupiter girl into a never-never land of romance, not knowing where the fire might flame up, or why, and afraid of being burned when it does. Then she'll play it too cool and be unable to take anyone seriously, least of all herself. She'll flirt openly, but without any intention of making it a lasting or a forever thing, and gain the reputation of a cold heartless female. A fire sign is never cold or heartless, but then there are a lot of astrologically ignorant men out there who don't know that. If such a state of affairs should happen to lead to spinsterhood, she certainly won't be a dry and bitter old maid. She'll still clown with life and have a barrel of fun. She'll have a dozen interests to replace a man—and enjoy every one of them.

Of course, you're not interested in a Sagittarian spinster. You plan to make one your wife someday. (At least, I hope you have honorable intentions. This poor girl has enough problems without you setting out to seduce her.) Let's stop dwelling on promiscuity, and think about marriage. Like the male Sagittarian, she's a little skittish about wedlock. You'll need to use some bright, colorful pieces of tinsel as bait to get her pinned down (to accepting your proposal, that is). She's breezy and unconventional in her relationships with men. Since she considers herself your equal, she may copy your mannerisms, as well as wear your sweater. If she also likes sports and camping, as lots of Sagittarian females do, you may have trouble distinguishing her from the boys. But she's not the same. For one thing, your sweater looks different on her. Not that Jupiter women are offensively masculine by nature. They can be the softest, most feminine women you ever squeezed. It's just that she pals around with so many men you get used to seeing her in the crowd—everywhere but in the steam room and the gym. Since she's so scrupulously honest and aboveboard, she may be a little careless of her reputation and contemptuous of the hypocrisy demanded by society. If you question her about it, she'll be plain-spoken. She'll probably tell you that waltzing in at midnight doesn't indicate promiscuity any more than coming home at a more conventional hour indicates innocence. She knows her morals are above reproach, and that's all that matters. Naturally she's dead wrong. What other people think matters very much to a female reputation. But try to understand her attitude. Don't think she's fast and loose just because she laughs at a few jokes, usually without the slightest idea of what they're all about (the subtlety of the double-entendre often escapes Sagittarius). So— she stays up to watch the sunrise from the George Washington Bridge (or from the top of a silo, if you live in the country)—that doesn't mean she's the wildest girl in town.

The truth is, she's a trusting child at heart. Her outlook is so naive it makes her vulnerable to wolves, con artists and phonies (though oddly enough, not in other areas, just in romance). Forget about how cleverly she argues and how startlingly logical she can be. All that has nothing to do with her heart. Her mind isn't under discussion. It's bright and intelligent, and well able to take care of itself in any emergency. But her heart is defenseless. It falls down and gets bruised quite often.

That's another thing. She's slightly clumsy. At times when the Sagittarius girl strides down the street like a thoroughbred horse, you'll think she's the most graceful woman you've ever watched—until she stumbles on a crack in the sidewalk, awkwardly grabs the awning over the fruit stand to catch her balance and upsets two crates of oranges. The owner may swear a little, but he'll soon shrug his shoulders, tell her to skip it, and hand her some grapes. The sunny Sagittarian disposition can melt the hardest hearts. Now and then, this girl will remind you of a clumsy puppy dog, wagging its friendly tail, and walking all over your feet. But then friendly puppy dogs do get lots of people to love them and feed them. Of course, dogs are a little cheaper to feed. The typical Jupiter girl has a large appetite. She likes good food and wine, nice clothes, and when she travels, she likes to go first class. Sagittarians are extravagant by nature (unless the Moon is in Capricorn or there's a Virgo ascendant). Money for the sake of money doesn't interest them, and it takes quite a bit of training to teach most of them the meaning of a dollar bill. Check her ascendant carefully before you loan her your credit card.

The Sagittarian girl you're involved with may be in show business, because lots of them are drawn by the lure of the footlights. If so, start out on the right foot by expecting her to put her career first, until she tires of it. The sweet sound of applause and the thrill of the encore will ring in her ears with more conviction than all the romantic phrases you can conjure up. Never force her to choose between pleasing you and the excitement of pleasing whole gobs of people at once with her sunshine personality. After a while she'll grow disgusted with the hypocrisy and artificial glitter she finds all around her in the world of show business, and she'll come running home to try domesticity with someone who is real. You. Someone who believes honesty is beautiful and deception is ugly. You again. Leaving a career won't remove the wings from her heels forever. They were fastened there at birth. The travel bug will always be nearby to give her a case of wandering fever. Vacation with her when you can; otherwise let her go off to ride the carousel herself, and trust her. She loves you, not the clowns and organ grinders she likes to pass the time with.

Because of her casual attitude toward romance and her shyness of marriage, you may think she's lacking in sentiment. You are so mistaken. She'll cry rivers at sad movies and read poetry with wet eyes. She's probably saved every note you ever wrote her, scraps of the flowers you bought her in the rain, and the tickets from the hockey game where she met you.

As for her talent as a homemaker, be brave. And be patient. Sagittarius girls are acutely bored by the confinement of dusting and mopping. No sooner does she make a bed than it gets unmade. Gosh, you'd think the darned thing would stay neat for a few days anyway, it was such a drag tucking in those sheets at the corners. She'll hate it all with a purple passion. When she has a home of her own, however, she'll probably swallow her distaste. She'll prefer that you get her a maid if you can possibly afford one. If not, she'll doggedly keep it shining. Her mother will never believe it. That sloppy child waxing the coffee table? Impossible. Pride and the eternal Sagittarius logic does it. She needs to be surrounded with beauty and cleanliness to be true to herself. The message reaches her that, if she doesn't wipe up the linoleum, no one else will. If she was forced by circumstances to do a lot of chores in childhood, she may rebel at first, but she'll eventually reason it out, and settle down to sweeping the corners with a minimum of resentment.

Her cooking? Well—you can never tell. Maybe you'd just better eat out on weekends. If she manages decent meals through the week, you can't expect her to keep a perfect record on Saturdays and Sundays, too. Most Sagittarian women aren't exactly ecstatic in the kitchen (unless there's a Taurus, Cancer or Capricorn ascendant). But she can whip up a mean, fancy dessert when she's trying to cheer you out of the blues. Her own moods can be terrors, but they're rare, and they last so briefly you'll hardly notice them. When she's really hurt, her tongue can be bitterly sarcastic. But she'll forget what she said almost before she's finished the sentence, and she won't understand why you want to dwell on it. This is not the woman for a brooding, melancholy man. Gloom and pessimism can actually make her physically ill.

Her children will probably adore her. She'll be their buddy, and have a circus playing with them. Once she's over her initial fear of responsibility, she'll cope with diapers and daily baths like a crisp, efficient nurse. Almost everything she does she does well, with grace, when she finally decides to learn it. Just like the big people, the little ones will get a good dose of her cheerful optimism and outspoken remarks. If they survive her blunt truthfulness, they'll grow up thinking she's the greatest big sister a kid ever had. She'll read them funny stories with happy endings, and take them on sudden, impulsive picnics in the woods to look for the three bears. (She half believes they're hiding there herself.) Her youngsters will probably be well-dressed, but not fussily so, and bright-mannered. If they pick up a few unconventional tricks from her, like making footprint curtains by spreading monk's cloth on the floor, stepping barefoot into yellow paint and walking across the material—at least you won't be raising a houseful of conformists. Her honesty will mark their characters. If they don't find those three bears after a careful search under all the fir trees, she'll probably tell them to forget it—it's a phony. But she will have looked first. The child who wrote the editor of the New York *Sun* to ask if there was really a Santa Claus just had to have a Sagittarius Sun sign, Moon or ascendant. She probably raised her own children by the frank, yet idealistic answer of "Yes, Virginia . . ." The Jupiter mother may have to watch a tendency to be lax in discipline, except when she's tired or angry. That's the wrong time for spankings.

You'll have a lovely hostess. No one entertains as graciously as a Sagittarian woman, not even her Leo sisters, who are no slouches themselves in the social department. There's a quality about her sunny, outgoing friendliness that makes people feel deeply welcome, from the garbage man to your boss. A Sagittarian breaks the ice instantly at the stiffest affairs, though she may raise a few eyebrows, too.

As long as you let her call her soul her own, and don't make her feel tied down, your Sagittarius Pollyanna will give you a triple bonus: her loyalty, her trust and her affection. The three are inseparable, because when she gives her love, her friendship trots right along beside it.

The Jupiter woman is an incurable idealist. And here's a secret perhaps she never told you: She fell in love with you many years ago, when she was a little girl and wished on the new Moon for someone to share her honest heart. There were lots of times when she thought she had found you and was disappointed. But when you finally came along, she knew you right away, because you were a gentle clown with a dream or two of your own who took her hand and showed her the way to the stars.

The SAGITTARIUS Child

"There is such a nice little dog near our house. . . .
A little bright-eyed terrier, you know,
with oh! such long curly brown hair!
And it'll fetch things when you throw them,
and it'll sit up and beg for its dinner
and all sorts of things—
I can't remember half of them."

In the building where I live, there's a dark-haired Irish girl who was born in December. She plays a guitar and sometimes writes songs. Once she wrote a line I thought was pretty fabulous, but she was having trouble with the rest of the lyric. She really didn't need to worry, with that opener. It was: "There you were, waving your heart at me. . . ."

Her quaint phrase sums up every Sagittarian from age one week to one hundred years. The calendar doesn't matter. They never grow up, anyway. Take a good look at your little Sagittarius girl. There she is, waving her heart at you, like a friendly sheepdog. Your little Sagittarius son waves his heart just as enthusiastically, needing desperately to be liked for his own honest self. When people don't say "hello" back to them, their tiny hearts droop in disappointment. Sagittarians are happy, playful, miniature clowns, who laugh with tears in their eyes when they're rejected. Even the infants show their sunny natures and desire for comradeship. The Jupiter baby will cry when he's left alone, but wheel his bassinet into the living room where the grownups are laughing and talking, and he'll sleep contentedly, with the warm, reassuring sound of human voices in his tiny ears. His dreams will be all the sweeter for being wrapped in the cozy, familiar atmosphere of loving and happy people. Later, he may grow more removed from family ties, but when he's little, he needs the security of human smells and sights and sounds, exactly as a newborn puppy needs one of your old sweaters in his basket to snuggle up to cozily. If such close, human contact is denied the Jupiter youngster, he'll withdraw and maybe become a little sarcastic. Then he'll adopt a substitute, like the dirty, torn blanket of Linus in *"Peanuts."* It can be a soft pinch pillow or a cuddly teddy bear, with its ears twisted off and its nose missing, but it represents security. He'd much prefer you.

The Sagittarius boy shows his happy-go-lucky nature by wandering into the woods with a makeshift fishing pole and a can of worms, barefoot, cheerfully whistling, talking to everyone he meets, his faithful dog trotting behind him. Sagittarians are informal as youngsters, and they never outgrow it. The little Jupiter girl may go through a tomboy stage, and you'll always be reminding her to "act like a lady" as she grows up. But these girls and boys have their own ideas of what makes "a little lady" and "a little gentleman." It starts out with honesty. Naked, unadorned, brutal honesty. They have it refined to an art and they will expect it from you—or else. Or else what? Or else they will refuse to be docile little slaves, meekly obeying every parental whim.

Your authority is fair game for the Sagittarian child's frank, curious investigation. He'll give in graciously if he's convinced there is logic behind your command. Parental orders must first pass the scrutiny of his inquisitive, reasonable mental processes, and if you don't come out with a good grade in his test, you will get left back. There you'll stand, waving your authority or a switch at him, and there he'll stand, waving his honesty and defiance right back at you. If you're fair and you try to be as honest as he is, the Jupiter youngster will learn to respect your rules. You'll have to be firm when you know you're right and give him a good, solid reason. When you're wrong, you'll have to admit your mistake and come right out with a straightforward confession of stupidity. Let's face it, many times parents insist on obedience to rules they make up for their own convenience, rather than for the well-being of the child. A Sagittarius moppet can smell that kind of dishonesty a mile away as his nostrils quiver like a bird dog's and his muscles quiver with anger, backed by righteous indignation. Better plan to explain all your orders and commands to him calmly, or be prepared to use up a lot of switches before the Jupiter obstinacy in the face of unjustified punishment will show any signs of weakening.

A phrase often used by mothers with December-born children is "curiosity killed the cat." Sagittarian curiosity never ends. The day begins with a question and they fall asleep with a question on their lips. When they're very young, just learning to talk and to explore the huge world, the questions will be, "Why is it naughty to touch the stove?" "Why does candy make my teeth fall out?" "Why do carrots make my hair curly?" "Why does Santa Claus need a letter if he's so magic?" "Why did Daddy wink at you when you were talking about a second honeymoon, and why do you call a Moon honey?" "Why do you talk like there are two Moons when Billy says there's just one?" (Billy is the too-smart-for-his-bluejeans older Aquarian brother, and if you have *that* combination at your house, you're in real hot water!) All through lunch, nap time and supper, the questions drone on. "Why did you and Daddy say Grandpa was henpecked? Is he a chicken?" "Why did my teddy bear tell you I ate the cookies? Why doesn't he ever talk to me like he talks to you?"

You can see that most of the Jupiter youngster's questions are aimed at puncturing adult hypocrisy or grownup smugness and downright deception. It won't do you much good to get all worked up and yell, "Be still! If you say 'why' once more, I'll paddle you. Don't ever say that word again." Then you'll hear the archer's clear little voice giving it to you right between the eyes: "Why not?"

Later, when he or she is older, it will be "Why do I have to come in at a certain time when you say you trust me?" (and you will trust this child, or you should). "Why does it matter what people think? Do you care more about people than you do about me?" That's a tough one. Better practice an answer to it while he's still in diapers. The Sagittarian teenager will never swallow your rules if they're based on social mores rather than on concern for his welfare. There are some good, sound, logical answers to your insistence on his observing certain social customs, of course. They involve a reputation and its precious value, but be sure you have them well-rehearsed and see that they ring true.

The ancient warning, "when children are little, they step on your feet—when they're bigger, they step on your heart," might have been written about a Sagittarian. There's no getting around it. This child is awkward, if not downright clumsy. Keep the medicine chest well stocked with iodine and band aids. Tiny Sagittarians clomp on your feet and get in the way of your dust mop, your vacuum and all your good intentions. You may have a constantly sore toe and a sore ego. But those are nothing compared to the sore heart you may have someday when the Jupiter boy or girl plants a foot on it firmly. His or her strong need for freedom includes freedom from family ties, and these children will strike out on their own extraordinarily early, sometimes neglecting to phone or write for long periods. It can cause some mighty painful stabs in the chest region. The best cure for such parental heartburn is to make sure when your Sagittarian child is little that he's learned to respect you for your sense of honor and tolerance. If you're narrow and prejudiced, you may only see him on holidays, if then. But if you refrain from judging his friends by any yardstick other than their true value—and if you've proved you have faith in his decency and in his dreams, he'll come home to renew his love and trip over your feet to your heart's content. Otherwise, he'll stay out there somewhere with his blanket or pillow or teddy bear in the form of new friends who accept him for what he is and believe in him.

Expect romance to rear its lacy head quite early. The girls will probably not be serious; they're just trying out their femininity, if the right parental attitude precludes using dates as that security blanket. The boys may need a little special tutoring in the subject of birds and bees. An ounce of prevention is worth a pound of cure.

Teach these children economy. They'll spend money like it's made of paper, which they've already discovered it is. They have to learn that when they spend their allowance, it's spent. Don't plug up the holes for them. If they waste their lunch money on comic books or *Mad Magazine*— let them take peanut butter and jelly sandwiches to school for the rest of the week. That may sound a little harsh, but it's necessary. Someday the Diners' Club will thank you.

Both sexes will probably enjoy school. Their multiple-faceted intelligence and great curiosity will make learning a fascinating game, if their bright interest isn't squelched by too much dull, boring routine and too much insistence on strict regulations and rigid study habits. The more progressive education becomes, the better and happier students these children will be. They're restless, and making them sit still constantly or stifling their fanciful imagination will soon kill their incentive, sadly, sometimes permanently. Sagittarian children with severe, intolerant teachers or who are victims of unimaginative teaching methods tend to want to drop out of school and go to work.

The honor system works very well with young archers. A Jupiter child will never cheat in any way, if he's trusted not to do so. Otherwise, he may figure it doesn't matter. If no one believes in him, then why try?

There may be a deep and very serious interest in religion. These are the boys and girls who decide at a tender age to become a priest or a nun, minister, rabbi or missionary in a foreign country. As they grow older, they'll question dogmas, perhaps change faith and church membership, searching eternally for truth. The Peace Corps invariably attracts Jupiter youngsters. They like the idea of seeing the world and the chance to put their idealism to work. A Sagittarian without a cause is like a dog without a bone to chew on. Fighting for causes develops their strength. Without a bone, the puppy may tear the couch or chair to shreds. Without a cause, the Sagittarian youngster may tear into ideas with such fervor and fanaticism that he can shred his future irreparably.

His eyes are fastened trustingly on the stars, and he may take a few spills as he trudges along, not noticing the rocks in his path. He's an independent, honest little archer. Give him lots of room to shoot and to practice drawing his bow. He needs to feel the grass under his bare feet, feel the rain on his face and bake his dreams in the strong, warm sunlight until they're well-done. There he is, waving his happy, optimistic young heart at you. Wave back at him with cheerful faith.

The SAGITTARIUS Boss

"No, no! the adventures first,"
said the Gryphon in an impatient tone:
"Explanations take such a dreadful time."

The first week on the job with a Sagittarius boss may leave you a little confused. You won't know whether to laugh or cry. The gentleman obviously is a dope.

Or is he a genius? No, he's neither—he's clearly just a rude boor. At second glance, he has a touch of Don Quixote. But that couldn't be. Not when he insults you with such relish. Still, he does flatter you with warm sincerity. Look at him—as awkward as a three-legged colt. No, actually he's a graceful as a racehorse. What does he use, trick mirrors?

After the second week, you'll uneasily decide to stay awhile and see what happens next. By now, you're sure his mother spoiled him rotten. (Wrong. She didn't have a chance. Did what he wanted to do.) Well, he's somebody else's problem, not yours. You're leaving soon. She's welcome to the guy—his wife, that is. You've begun to feel sorry for her. (She sheds a few tears of self-pity herself at times, but she leads an exciting life.) You're sure he secretly hates you. (He's crazy about you. Just brutally honest when you make a mistake and painfully frank about your faults.) You think he's going to promote you. (Not yet. He was just a little over-enthusiastic yesterday.) He invited you to lunch this morning. Now you can find out what he's really like. (He cancelled it. He had forgotten he promised to speak at the ASPCA meeting.)

Two months later, both you and your psychiatrist feel it's time to have a serious talk with him. You make up your mind: If he listens to your complaints about his erratic and puzzling actions, and he lets you know where you stand with him and the company, you'll remain on the job. Otherwise you'll quit. You will be firm. (Sorry. He just left for London.) All right, you can wait. So you'll put your cards on the table when he returns, and tell him exactly how you feel. Give him a few days to get back into the swing of things. He looks a little tired. But you're not going to let that impress you. By tomorrow he should be settled down enough to listen to reason. (You'll have to call the airport instead. He's leaving for Tokyo.) *Now wait a minute!* When is he going to light somewhere long enough for you to tell him what's wrong with the way he treats you?

You really want an answer? Never. Your Sagittarius boss greases the ball bearings on his skates each morning and casually glides around town, building one gargantuan promotion after another. He certainly doesn't want to stop long enough to hear you tell him his faults. He thinks he's a pretty good apple. And he is, when you stop to think about it. Often he's shy and helpless, and he needs to be understood.

But he keeps making those outrageous remarks to people. Why should he expect you to make excuses for him? Besides, a person can run out of excuses. (Call his wife. She keeps an alphabetical file of them.)

It's not fair for him to keep smiling so cheerfully while he completely ignores what you're saying and refuses to stick to a schedule. (Call his mother. She'd love to discuss it with you. Been waiting for years to find someone to sympathize with her.) What are you going to do? You simply have to do something.

You might try writing him a letter. Be sure it's logical, with no phony emotion or one-sided arguments which make him the villain and you the righteous one. He's the righteous one. If you make a fair point, he'll consider it, and try to mend his ways, but he doesn't want to spend six hours discussing it. In his opinion, there are more exciting adventures than listening to a recital of why he's wrong. Besides, he's not going to change anyway, so why waste his valuable time? Doesn't he have any virtues at all? Well, yes, he does. Stop right there. Hang on to those, and forget the rest. His mother did. His wife does. Imitate their wisdom.

You could start by checking off a list of his good points. Right away you have to admit he's seldom grumpy. Only once in a while, when somebody tries to dampen the fires of his enthusiasm, or when that stuffy accountant wants him to remember what he meant by those figures in his expense report for last month. Generally your Sagittarius boss is a rather happy-go-lucky, optimistic, cheerful fellow. That's a plus. Now, what else? He's pretty fair about sick leave and vacations. Another good point—he's generous. Lots of bosses wouldn't have understood when you lost all your money at the race track and had to borrow a month's pay in advance. All he said was that you should have asked him which horse was going to win before you picked such obvious losers. But he gave you the advance, and said you could pay it back a few dollars a week later. Another check mark to his credit.

When you impulsively broke off your engagement and then regretted it deeply, he gave you the afternoon off so you could patch it up. Before you left, he happened to remark that he thought you were the most creative employee in the firm, and his obvious sincerity picked up your droopy heart. It gave you the courage to run right straight into someone's arms with confidence, and the broken love affair was mended by nightfall. All right, so he's a pretty great morale booster. Anything more?

You kind of admire him because he's a crusader. He fights hard for what he believes is right, and it gives you a warm feeling to work for a man like that. It's sort of exciting to be around someone who defends lost causes. He's true to himself and his code, whatever it might be. That's refreshing, isn't it? Of course. Add another virtue.

But wait—what about that time you felt like a complete fool when you quoted the wrong figures at a sales meeting, and he led the laughter? Then he tried to fix it up by saying, "That's our boy, Tom, always throwing in a monkey wrench, but we love him anyway." Don't think about those things now. We're dwelling on his good points, remember?

There's no denying a Sagittarius boss can keep you a
little up in the air. It's hard to decide if he's a saint or a
sinner, or a little of each. The latter is probably closer
to the truth. It takes a spell to get used to the Jupiter
executive. He's usualy a hail-fellow-well-met type, but the
Sagittarius honesty and desire to keep everything aboveboard (and I mean everything) can be a shock to more
sensitive natures. This man is so democratic you can't
help liking him. Still, his forthright manner and brutal
frankness are sometimes hard to take. The Sagittarius employer is sincere and friendly, and it's obvious he isn't
the kind of man to hold a grudge or deliberately hurt anyone. He has very few inhibitions, and correcting your mistakes definitely isn't one of them. His criticism is done in
the open, usually with a bare minimum of tact. Even the
gentle archers never think of the wounds they're inflicting
when they cheerfully point out your flaws with deadly
accuracy. True, the compliments and warm appreciation
far outweigh the embarrassments, but those painful moments stand out like sore thumbs. The December-born boss
honestly believes that everyone wants to hear the truth.
So he tells them. When he sees that he has offended, he
can be the soul of contrite regret. Then he apologizes
profusely and explains, frequently making it worse.

You'll seldom know where he is at any given moment.
Sagittarius can be anywhere at a minute's notice. You'll
learn that he's great at spotting phonies, fake salesmen
with false pitches, clients with hidden motives and employees with hidden vices. He's not so clever about his love
life. If he's single, he may keep the office buzzing with
his sentimental journeys and his active romantic adventures.

He probably has a host of friends of all shapes and descriptions. Bank presidents, important politicians, carnival
people, newspaper reporters, ministers, doctors, lawyers,
plumbers, carpenters, radio announcers, society dowagers,
girl weight-lifters, gamblers, chorus girls, architects, bartenders and college professors all trip merrily over his
welcome mat at all hours of the day or night. He sizes up
people with his own ruler. If they measure up to his
standards, he loyally defends them.

He gives orders with a rather regal air, but he's so
jovial about it, and there's normally so much logic in his
methods, it's hard to take offense. Tactless and sometimes
foolish, he nevertheless can call on his powerful intuition

and lucky hunches to pull him out of almost any jam he gets himself into. (The romantic jams may be a little stickier, and harder for him to avoid.) He's a much deeper thinker than his casual nature would lead you to believe. A Sagittarius boss can give any attorney a good argument and normally come out ahead. If he's a typical Jupiter executive, he's probably had an excellent education. Even if he hasn't you'll never guess, what with all the knowledge his inquisitive mind has picked up along the way.

He's basically kind-hearted, but he's also ambitious enough to step on a few toes occasionally. His memory sometimes fails in social situations, but rarely on facts. The archer can roll off the figures of his competitor's gross business and forget the name of his own bookkeeper, who's been with him for several years. Although he walks with a free, active stride, now and then with typical Sagittarian carelessness, he may step into the wastebasket or grind out his cigarette in the paper clips. But though his feet may stumble over the telephone cord, his mind rarely stumbles. His ideas are frequently unpopular, and aimed way over most people's square heads, but nine out of ten of them pay off.

There are some shy Sagittarius bosses, but under the timid surface, Jupiter will control the personality. Even the retiring type of archer shoots his arrows toward the sky, and keeps firm grip on the bow. The extroverted ones love to talk and expound their favorite theories (plus most of their private thoughts). The introverted ones can manage a pretty fair monologue, too, when the mood hits them, and what they have to say is usually interesting or instructive. Your Sagittarius boss loves animals, bright lights, big plans, creative thinkers, good food and drink, travel, loyalty, change and freedom. He's cool to dishonesty, cruelty, selfishness, keeping secrets from him, stinginess, pessimism, possessiveness and hypocrisy. He's usually a lot of fun to work for, and he grows on you. You kind of get the feeling if you ever left him he would somehow lose his way, in spite of his egotism and independence. He won't, but stick with him anyway. Tomorrow may always be a large question mark, but today will never be dull.

The SAGITTARIUS Employee

"It's by far the most confusing thing I ever heard."
"I should like to have it explained," said the Mock Turtle.
"She can't explain it," said the Gryphon hastily.
"Go on with the next verse."

Lots of employees, when you tell them how much money they can make after a year with the firm, plus the financial incentives after five years' service, show a great deal of interest. Your Sagittarius employee will not. He's far more fascinated by what you're going to pay him now—today. Tomorrow is far enough away, but next year is unthinkable and five years is forever. That's play money. He's interested in real cash. What happens later is up to the gods. He'll throw the dice and hope for the best. Usually, the gods will smile on him.

The Sagittarian is a delight to have around the office. He may knock over the filing cabinet or spill coffee on the outgoing mail once in awhile, but what's a little clumsiness when he's so cheerful and willing to help? He's not a whiner or complainer. He's a positive soul, as enthusiastic and optimistic as you were when you first joined the firm, remember? The difference is that he'll stay that way after he's retired. It's part of his nature. Some of it may rub off on you, and who knows, he may shine some light on that dark corner where you lost your illusions, so you can polish them up and try them out again.

Sagittarius never does things halfway. The only thing he's slow to make up his mind about is marriage. In everything else, he's fairly speedy. There are, of course, some archers with Taurus or Capricorn ascendants who move with more caution, but they're not slow pokes in either their emotional or mental attitudes. Normally, the typical Sagittarian is way ahead of you, and he certainly doesn't mind brightly calling your attention to it when he is. Humility is not one of his more noticeable attributes. Some Sagittarians wear a thin veil of modesty over their fiery egos, but if you peek through it, you'll see a self-confident person, who is really quite happy with himself in general. He may be a little unsure of himself in love matters on occasion, but who isn't?

Sagittarius may sometimes seem both casual and careless, but never let that lead you into the grave error of under-estimating the flashing Jupiter intuition and often brilliant mental processes. There will be times when you have no idea where he's going or where he's been either. There will be other occasions when you'll wonder if he's really shy, or just biding his time for that plan he has pressure cooking in his brain. At other times, you won't have any room for doubt. He'll make so bold you'll be aghast at his forthright statements. There will be little that's small about his gestures, ideas or actions. He makes large, grand mistakes and pulls in superduper winnings against enormous odds.

The Sagittarian curiosity may get on your nerves. He'll never be satisfied with simply getting instructions. He'll want to know the why behind your orders, and the reason for your methods. If your logic appeals to him, he'll praise you with his honest approval. If not, you may shrink before his equally frank appraisal of the holes in your procedures. That's before you collect your wits and become angry. Collecting your wits may be a necessary precaution in dealing with a Sagittarian, but getting angry is a shameful waste of adrenalin, because very few people can manage to stay mad at the archer. He's the kind you want to smack and kiss at the same time. Since that's impossible (the first is out if she's your secretary, and the second is out if he's your sales manager), you may as well just give up.

Most Sagittarian employees won't blush when you pay them a compliment. They love applause. You may blush for them, however, when they start to boast about their talents and abilities. One of the minor Jupiter flaws is a happy willingness to promise to deliver anything—the sky is truly the limit—and then not quite following through, because the target was a little further off than he figured. Next time, he'll aim straighter and deliver. The quieter, more discreet archers will, in their own mild way, also tend to bite off a wee bit more than they can chew. Still, both types will come through on top often enough to keep you fascinated.

It's the Jupiter luck that seems to hang over these people. Already fortified at birth by reliable hunches and excellent perceptions which progress toward logical conclusions, they're right more often than they're wrong. Add a little typical Sagittarius luck, and you can see why they're frequently at the head of the parade. A friend of mine recently pointed out what he thought was an exception—a Sagittarius actress who's been trying to get a break for years. Although it now looks as if it's just around the corner, she waited so long and had to work so hard to get recognized he thought Jupiter had deserted her. But her delay in becoming a star had nothing to do with the consistent Jupiter-type good fortune. Everybody's timetable is a little jerky sometimes. Still, she gets the landlord to fix her door knobs while the water is flooding the bedroom in another apartment; she gets to the store just in time to buy the last honeydew melon in the rack; and she finds a new pair of stockings in the refrigerator when she's torn her only pair and doesn't have a dime left until next Tuesday. She got her first really good job because the producer thought she was Sandy Dennis, and then was glad he made the mistake after he saw her act. Those kinds of things are always happening to Sagittarius people. Before the situation gets too black, the sun pops out from some unexpected source and shines on them, as if the sun wanted to reward Jupiter's pure and naive optimism.

Sometimes the Sagittarian luck works in reverse for the archer you employ. He'll fumble the biggest deal your outfit ever had the chance to close, but the day before you fire him, you'll discover that the president of the company he insulted and called a phony was just indicted for selling watered stocks. That crazy Sagittarian's blunder probably saved you from sheer disaster. Your Jupiter secretary who forgot to mail those important letters hardly has time to dry her tears at your cruel abuse before you find out that one of them contained a check made out for more money than your firm could cover at the bank that week.

There are Sagittarians who scoff at their own good fortune and like to give the impression they're real born losers. If you employ one, don't be tricked by his shrewdness. He may be one of those suspicious types with a Scorpio ascendant who thinks that, if he talks about it, his luck will change, but he wins at Bingo as often as the rest of the archers. Last week, he walked into a shoe store to buy the cheapest pair of shoes they had, because he was broke. It turned out that he was the one millionth customer and he won a new pair of shoes every month for five years. He didn't tell you about that, did he? Scorpio ascendant. But Jupiter Sun sign.

Dishonesty is not one of his weaknesses. Neither is tact. You may have to patch up some office squabbles or have to make peace when your brutally frank Sagittarian sympathizes with the bookkeeper about his baldness and suggests a cure—after you've spent years pretending the poor fellow had a full head of hair to keep him happy because he's a Leo. Your gal Friday will never forget the time she was on the telephone with the firm's most important customer, and the Sagittarius member of your staff rushed up to her excitedly and shouted within an inch of the mouthpiece that the pipes were broken and the ladies' room was flooded. It can be disconcerting, but you'll get over these little character deficiencies.

The Sagittarius employee may surprise you with an occasional outburst of temper directed toward anyone from the elevator operator to yourself. (He's not prejudiced.) His fiery, righteous indignation is usually aroused when someone dares to question the honesty of his intentions. He's the soul of integrity, even if he takes some odd, winding back roads to reach the truth. He really is. Doubting him or accusing him of false pretenses can cause him to dip his verbal arrows in flame. They'll pierce your sensitive spots as if he had been trained by Robin Hood himself. In fact, Robin is a very good nickname for him. He probably deeply sympathizes with robbing the rich to help the poor. As for his anger, it never lasts long enough to really burn, and his arrows seldom leave scars. Just little nicks in your ego.

If he can't find an apartment, let your archer move into one of your large, roomy suitcases and pay rent. He'll much prefer living out of a suitcase to living under a roof and between four walls, if they threaten in any way to rob him of his freedom. When he comes in with his brief case covered with travel stickers, he's giving you a subtle message that his toes are getting itchy. Take the hint and send him on a trip. He probably needs it. He'll come back with a full bag of orders and a lighter heart. He's a good salesman, but you may have to train him to curb his hasty enthusiasms. The Sagittarius can dash out after a challenge, and forget to wear his caution. But as impulsive as he is, when his thinking cap is securely fastened on he can beat all the pros with his sound, logical, if a bit startling ideas. Money is important to him, because he has to support himself in the style to which he would like to become accustomed. He's seldom stingy and if you are, he'll move on to more congenial surroundings.

Your Archer can cause you to throw up your hands in despair, but it won't do any good. When he sees you with your arms in the air, he'll just toss you a ball and say, "Catch!" What are you going to do? Catch. The exercise will be good for you.

*"Speak in French when you can't think
of the English for a thing—
Turn out your toes as you walk—and remember
who you are!"*

CAPRICORN
the Goat
December 22nd through January 20th

How to Recognize CAPRICORN

"You are old, Father William," the young man said,
"And your hair has become very white;
And yet you incessantly stand on your head—
Do you think, at your age, it is right?"

It's anything but a breeze to grasp the Capricorn character. You'll learn to recognize this Sun sign, but you'll
need some preliminary practice. Study the quiet spider in
the corner. He hasn't a chance against the fast-flying insects.
But they get caught in his cleverly spun web—and the
spider wins. Remember Aesop's slow tortoise, humorously
crawling in that race. He hasn't a chance against the quick,
bright hare. But the flighty hare goes in all directions, forgetting the goal—the tortoise wins. Observe the goat, as he
scales the mountainside. He hasn't a chance against the
strategy of the smarter humans who pursue him. But the
hunters fall behind as the sturdy goat climbs determinedly
from crag to crag on his uniquely designed hooves—and
the goat wins.

Now study a Capricorn. Where will you find him? Just
about anywhere he can advance or improve himself. Anywhere he can get ahead and further his secret ambitions.
Try a social gathering. The Capricorn is not a carefree
party type, but the goat we're studying is a social climber
as well as a mountain climber. Pick a mixed group, preferably in the upper income level. You can also try the middle
income level, but the lower you go beneath that, the smaller
your chances of finding a Capricorn. He probably won't be
wearing a lamp shade on his head, tap dancing or calling
attention to himself in any way; he'll be the admiring spectator in the background. You may not even notice him
at first as he quietly and calmly watches all the flashy,
pushy, charming, aggressive and brilliant personalities
around him. Everyone in the group will seem to have superior equipment for the race—any race. Lots of them
are bluffing, some of them are afraid, but they're all highly

polished, and the Capricorn doesn't seem to have a chance against them. Yet, he will win.

A couple of years ago, I visited the bookstore of a New York astrologer. As I carelessly scattered my gems of wisdom, gave him unsolicited advice about what books he should stock, and argued astrological theory with him, I learned he was a Capricorn and he learned I was an Aries. Smugly, I guessed his correct ascendant, talked faster, moved faster and seemed to dominate the scene. Before I left, he gave me a charming, gentle smile, and in a fascinating Hungarian accent, he said a funny thing. He said, "Capricorn will always triumph over Aries. The goat will win over the ram." It was spoken lightly, but he was quite serious. Outside the bookstore, I laughed to myself. "Imagine such conceit," I thought. "No one can top a double Aries." Know what? When I can't find certain books I need that have been out of print since Noah built the ark, the Capricorn comes up with them. Gradually, I've been forced to pay respectful tribute to his superiority. Now here I am crediting his Sun sign with qualities I envy, but don't possess. You see? Capricorn won.

Another confession. As an Aries, I hate to take direction. No Aries writer can stand to have anyone edit his work. Recently, it was suggested that a Capricorn woman go over some material I had written. I was infuriated. Outwardly I agreed, but secretly I decided that she wasn't going to change a single word of the product of my genius. I would only pretend to go along. She made her suggestions quietly, almost timidly, and against my will I saw only too clearly how intelligent they were. Why hadn't I thought of cutting that phrase and changing that word myself? After I had grudgingly followed her instructions to the letter, the improvement in the material was painfully obvious. Capricorn won again.

I've finally made up my aggressive Aries mind that it's no use to fight them. You might as well do the same thing. Pity the high pressure salesman who sizes up his Capricorn pigeon and thinks, "This guy is a pushover. I can sell him the Brooklyn Bridge." He has a lot to learn.

Since the goat merges into the group so gently, unconsciously camouflaging himself into the background, it's not always easy to recognize the physical characteristics of this Sun sign. Capricorns can be stocky and muscular, thin and wiry or plump and soft. But no matter how the body is shaped, the goat will give the impression of being rooted to the spot, until he decides to move to another spot. Generally, Saturn people have straight, lank, dark hair, dark, steady eyes, and swarthy olive or tan complexions. You'll see Capricorns with curly blonde hair and blue eyes, but watch them closely. Honestly now, don't they really look as if they should have been born with dark hair, eyes and skin? It's a delicate point, but valid. Take Marlene Dietrich, for example. Dresden china complexion, green eyes and corn silk hair. Look again. Observe her calm, deliberate actions. Listen to her deep, throaty voice. Note her legendary tough business head and her earthy ambition. Aren't these more synonomous with the steady, reliable image of a brunette? Master this subtlety and you'll never be fooled by the appearance of a Capricorn.

There's always a faint aura of melancholy and seriousness surrounding the Saturn personality. None of them completely escape the Saturnine influence of stern discipline and self-denial. Many Capricorns have strong feet and wear sensible shoes. Their hands are capable, their voices usually even and soothing—and you'll probably notice a gentleness that flatters and persuades. Capricorns can look and act as harmless as a feather quilt, but they're as tough as a keg of nails. They hammer away persistently, relentlessly, managing to digest insults, pressures, disappointments and duty as calmly as the goat digests rusty cans, broken glass and cardboard. Like him, they have iron stomachs and dangerous horns. While the gay, laughing extroverts scatter their energies hither and yon, Capricorns never deviate an inch to the left or right. They steadily follow the upward path, with inbred faith in the security of the well-traveled road, and contempt for the enticing short cuts they know are full of pitfalls.

Capricorns have an enormous admiration for those who have preceded them to the top of the mountain, and who have laid down the laws for the journey. They court success; they respect authority and honor tradition. Lots of energetic, impulsive people label them snobbish and stuffy. The goat could conversely label his critics rash and foolish, but usually he's too wise to make unnecessary enemies by indulging in such self-defense. The Saturn-ruled submit. They agree. They adapt. Or do they just appear to do so? Capricorn allows others to walk in front of him, but he often gets there first, against all logic. He's careful to avoid the obstacles, the sharp rocks. No wonder he seldom stumbles. His eyes aren't fastened on the stars. He keeps his gaze fastened ahead, and his feet firmly planted on the ground. Jealousy, passion, impulse, anger, frivolity, waste, laziness, carelessness—are all obstacles. Let others trip and fall over them. Not Capricorn. He may glance briefly behind him with pity for the failures, or in grateful tribute for past advice and help, but he'll soon continue his steady upward climb until his goal is reached.

There are Capricorns who are deliciously romantic—who understand the strange light of the moon and the glorious colors of the butterfly's wing. But they won't let their emotions blind them to the facts. Not if they're typical Saturn people. If Capricorn writes a lovely poem, full of imagination and illusion, the theme will be solid and the punctuation will be correct. It will come to the point, and the sentiment will never be allowed to slosh over the edges. Don't defy the conventions if you want the respect of the goat. Even the more daring ones, and they are the exceptions, will observe at least the outer trappings of social acceptability. Public scenes and raw, naked, uncontrolled passions embarrass them.

An occasional Capricorn will forget to hide his ambition, and refuse to work unless he's at the head of things. Then he becomes a stubborn goat who insists on starting at the top of the ladder, where he feels he belongs. Naturally, such an attitude produces a gloomy, pessimistic, cold and selfish person who's impossible to satisfy. But a couple of hard bumps usually suffice to set him on the right path.

Young Capricorns are typically more contented than older Capricorns, and there's a good reason. In almost Chinese-fashion, the Saturn-ruled youngsters idolize ancestors and elders. Respect for the wisdom of age and experience is ingrained in the Saturnine nature. When they mature and the "honorable ancestors" and the old folks are gone, the wild actions of the modern generation can frighten and bewilder the conservative goats. They go about saying, "Tch, tch!" shaking their heads and murmuring about the good old days. Luckily, however, a fair percentage of them adapt to meet the challenge. It's a warm thing to watch a gray-haired Capricorn cheerfully cavorting with youth, learning for the first time the joys of childhood he missed as a serious youngster. Older Capricorns either behave like frustrated dill pickles, or they happily roll hoops and dance the boogaloo. A few of them, caught in the uncomfortable middle, grin with suppressed excitement as they sit on the sidelines and tap their feet in time to the music, but never quite gather the courage to jump on the carousel.

You'll seldom find the straight, well-shaped Capricorn nose stuck in other people's business or the Saturn tongue wagging in gossip. If the Sun sign is combined with afflicted Gemini or Pisces influences, there may be a little gabbiness, but normally they're content to mind their own affairs. They won't often hand out unsolicited advice, but when you deliberately seek their practical wisdom, they won't hesitate to give it with stern overtones. They'll expect you to accept it, too. The Capricorn has learned to cope with duty and responsibility and to tolerate frustration. If you can't follow his example, he'll waste little time trying to teach you, and allow you only a pinch of sympathy.

You may read that Capricorns marry for money or social position. That's an exaggeration, though I will say that it was doubtless a Capricorn who remarked, "It's just as easy to fall in love with the conductor as it is to have a fling with the second violin." The practical goat rarely leaps into business or marriage unless he's prepared financially for the former and emotionally for the latter. These people will do strange things for security. Old age is constantly on the Saturnine mind. Even the young Capricorns will instinctively enjoy visiting Uncle Jasper or Aunt Minerva. After all, the doting relatives might have a few bonds or some property, besides the fact that they're comfortable and familiar. One certainly wouldn't want to see a fortune willed to a pet canary. You may think such an attitude is cold and calculating, but to the Capricorn, it's sensible. Opportunity never has to knock twice at the goat's door. He'll hear the first knock. In fact, he's been leaning against the door, listening and waiting for it.

In childhood, Capricorns are inclined to be weaker, more sickly than other youngsters, but both strength and resistance to disease increase with age. The sober, temperate nature of the typical goat gives him amazing endurance— and such potential for survival that it's not unusual to find him living past the century mark. Saturn people should be able to avoid doctors and hospitals, but they don't, because fear, uncertainty, worry and gloom are deadlier than germs. No amount of practical diet, conservative habits and stubborn resistance to illness can overcome the dangers of pessimism. Capricorns who want to avoid sickness should have plenty of outdoor exercise, and develop a more positive, outgoing personality. The fresh air of the country and the fresh breezes of tolerance will work magic with Saturnine health. Almost all goats of both sexes have sensitive skin. There may be nervous rashes, allergies, roughness and chapping, some peculiarity of perspiration, enlarged pores or acne. Stomach disorders from incompatible foods and mental distress are common. Broken arms and legs may occur. The knee caps, joints and bones are vulnerable areas, and psychosomatic paralysis, severe headaches and kidney infections are further fruits of Saturnine melancholy.

They will either have beautiful, white, strong teeth—or constant problems with decay and continual visits to the dentist, one or the other. Generally speaking, if they avoid the lingering illnesses caused by lingering depressions, the Capricorn tenacity for life is remarkable. But it's no fun to be the last leaf on the tree if you're suffering from arthritis and rheumatism. The goat must seek the sunlight and laugh at the rain to stay healthy.

He's such a shy, sweet soul, a trifle stubborn perhaps, but gentle about it. He seems so harmless. What a safe person to trust and confide in—how pleasantly he builds your ego. Who could hurt him or suspect him of ambition? All the while, Capricorn is using your own weaknesses, conceits and jealousies to make himself stronger. He's useful and eventually so indispensable that you ask him to take over the reins. Then he'll rule unobtrusively in the corner, modestly pulling the strings of authority. The goat submerges his ego to gain what his ego truly desires—the position of the real leader. With kindly, but stern, cautious wisdom he guards the past from neglect and protects the present from confusion, so you can build tomorrow safely.

He doesn't have to lead the parade with a big brass band. He gives permission for the parade, and plans its route from behind the scenes. All the daring high-wire acts need the Capricorn's strong, safe net when they miscalculate and tumble. The discipline and formality of jet black and navy blue—the solid practicality of brown—the deep, honest dreams of dark green—these are the quiet colors of his enduring rainbow. Walk slowly through his silent forest, carpeted in soft moss and climbing ivy—and seek the eight hidden treasures of Saturn. Rich, red rubies lie buried beneath the Capricorn weeping willow. Stay—and learn the eternal beauty of the pure, smooth onyx. Capricorn lead is solid, and Capricorn coal builds lasting fires.

Famous Capricorn Personalities

Steve Allen	Martin Luther King
Humphrey Bogart	Rudyard Kipling
Pablo Casals	Mao Tse-tung
Nat King Cole	Henry Miller
Benjamin Franklin	Isaac Newton
Ava Gardner	Richard Nixon
Barry Goldwater	Louis Pasteur
Cary Grant	Edgar Allan Poe
Alexander Hamilton	Helena Rubinstein
J. Edgar Hoover	Carl Sandburg
Howard Hughes	Albert Schweitzer
Joan of Arc	Daniel Webster
Johannes Kepler	Woodrow Wilson

Loretta Young

The CAPRICORN Man

"Don't keep him waiting, child! Why,
his time is worth a thousand pounds a minute!
And don't twiddle your fingers all the time . . .
Better say nothing at all.
Language is worth a thousand pounds a word!"

He has a self-made brick wall around him. He's shy, but he's strong and tough. He's pleasant, but he's fiercely ambitious. Like the legendary, silent, earthy cowboy, the Capricorn man seems to prefer to be alone. He doesn't. Not really.

Secretly, Capricorn yearns for adulation. He'd love to

thrill the crowd on a flying trapeze. In his private dreams, the goat is an incurable romantic, but Saturn chains his nature. The stern planet of discipline demands of him calm behavior, practical actions and serious intent. This is his cross, and it's often a heavy one to bear. Sometimes he'll cover his frustration with a brusque manner—and sometimes he'll startle you with unexpected and incongruous humor, although it will always be the ironic tongue-in-cheek variety. But that's often the funniest kind, and Capricorns can be quite a gas when they're wry and dry and juggling the jokes.

Turn a steady, dependable Capricorn male inside out, and you'll find a merry, gentle dreamer who longs for the free wind to blow through his hair and finds the sweet fragrance of compliments intoxicating—who hungers for excitement and thirsts for adventure. Only a chosen few can release this lonely soul from his secret prison.

Sun signs can be wonderfully helpful if you're inclined to judge a book by its jacket. Here you were thinking that Capricorn fellow would make a great school teacher but a miserable lover. You'd just about decided he'd rather be president than be yours. He impressed you as a man who would rather see his name written in the social register than in your diary. Now you discover that he has a heart as warm and friendly as a cozy wood fire on a winter night. I know it's exhilarating, but wait just a moment before you dash off to give him a big bear hug and expect him to fly you to the moon. Those surprises I just described are part of his inner nature. He'll be thrilled and impressed if you guess, but inner nature means just that—*inner* nature. Chances are he'll never let all those gauzy dreams of careless rapture escape and run around loose. Just so you know they're inside him. That's enough. Don't go expecting your Capricorn to dash barefoot through the buttercups. You can't change his basic, Saturnine personality.

What you can do, however, is laugh at his shaggy dog stories until he feels brave enough to tell more sophisticated tales. You can hint that you think there are banked fires beneath his conservative manner until he has the confidence to let a flame or two leap out. You can tell him you find his kind of dreams more colorful, because no dream is as bright as the one that really happens, so he'll be encouraged to weave more of them. Someday, he will reach the top of his special mountain, and you'll be right there beside him, mighty proud of your determined goat—and mighty glad you believed in his practical dreams.

Capricorns pretend they can live without compliments, and the way they behave when they get one is pretty convincing proof. Did you ever say something nice to your Capricorn man and see it fall as flat as the expression on his face? Don't be hasty. Just because the goat is such an expert at fooling himself doesn't mean you have to be fooled, too. Actually, he desperately needs to be told he is good, clever, handsome, desirable and interesting, but since he'll seldom make his need visible, he gets few orchids. Consequently, he may be a little rusty, and won't know quite what to do when someone openly admires him, so he covers his embarrassment by making a wry joke or ignoring it, a reaction which can freeze people into deciding never to risk flattering that poker face again. The impression is created that he hates compliments, so he gets even fewer. It's a vicious circle. Maybe it's your fault more than his. Next time you give your Capricorn a verbal bouquet, look at his ears. See how pink they are? See that faint twinkle in his eye and how his nose twitches ever so slightly? He's as pleased as Sunday punch. Just because he doesn't dance a jig or roll in the grass like Leo, the lion, doesn't mean he hasn't been made deeply happy and ten feet taller. He needs to be seen as the truly great guy he is. Nature and the stars keep him from advertising. You'll have to be his press agent.

This man is what horticulturists would call a late bloomer. He's as serious as an owl in his youth, but he'll relax gradually as he matures, and if he's a typical Capricorn, he may end up as the youngest looking and acting man in the group. Now, that's a point well worth considering. With other men, you have to tolerate flighty foolishness for years and then look forward to a stuffy old age. With a Capricorn, you may have your enthusiasms smothered a bit at first, but just think what you have to look forward to! Your Capricorn lover won't run off to Paris with you in the spring of your romance, but he may take you to see the Taj Mahal by moonlight forty or fifty years later, when other men are complaining of creaking joints. It's not a bad switch. If you're the kind who likes to stuff yourself first with rich appetizers, and then dutifully have your vegetables, he's not for you. A love affair with a Capricorn man, provided it ends in marriage, is like having dessert last, where it belongs.

Naturally, the Capricorn reverse aging process may suggest to you that there's a catch in the faithfulness department. There is. It's true that you'll have few worries about your goat straying when romance is young and dewy. It's also true that he may kick up his heels a little as he grows older. Still, with all that, he's a safer bet for fidelity than most other Sun signs, because the Capricorn man practically burns incense at the family altar. Whatever minor indiscretions he may contemplate when his late blooming begins, they'll never replace the home fires, the children and you. He's almost reverent about family ties. That includes the family he's created with you and his own family, which has been the object of his devotion since childhood.

It wouldn't do to insult his mother or be cool to his brother. Be prepared to love your in-laws, even if they're about as lovable as prickly cactus. Not only will he defend them, but also if you allow disputes to get sticky, the strain of choosing between loyalties to two families can make him morose and gloomy. (If there's anything in this world you don't want to do, it's make a Capricorn morose and gloomy.)

You may bump into a Capricorn who has open contempt for his relatives, or who has bitterly cut family ties and never looked back—but scratch the surface of his independence and you'll find a deep, emotional wound in his past that originally caused such untypical behavior. Many Capricorn men live at home long past the age when their friends are out enjoying the delights of a bachelor pad. They usually fall in love later than most men too—and they seldom marry before they're settled in a career.

With an eye for pedigree and perfection, they'll look around pretty carefully. The goat will pick a girl who will be a good mother. Then she'll have to be a good cook and housekeeper. After that, she'll have to dress well to impress his business associates and friends, and preferably be a cut above them in background, manners, breeding and intelligence. Last of all, he'll make a quick check to see if she's beautiful or if she appeals to his physical senses. You can see right away it's no big deal if your hair is droopy, your perfume bottle is empty or your legs aren't the kind to make the current Miss Universe hate you. Just dig into the trunk for those D.A.R. papers and show him the family

Wedgwood. Take his mother to lunch once a week, and let him see how practical you are with your budget. Invite your four-year-old sister along on your next date. If you're an only child, rent a neighbor's toddler. Wipe her little nose gently and frequently with a proper linen handkerchief, talk about your desire to be on the mayor's committee for civic improvement, walk sedately, drop a few French phrases and gurgle when you see a baby in a buggy. Be sure to respect his father as the wisest gentleman you've ever met, and make casual references to your great uncle, who helped Carnegie build his empire—or your ancestor who fought by George Washington's side in the snows of Valley Forge (it doesn't matter which). If you're pretty, so much the better. But glamor will never replace that afghan you made for his cousin Bessie. I can almost promise that he'll never marry you if you don't pass inspection with his family. There are exceptions, of course, but they're so rare you'd be downright reckless to gamble that your Capricorn man is one of them.

After his family has proposed—or rather after he has proposed—put your foot down. Firmly. Let him know you love his folks dearly, but he's the one whose bed and board you've chosen to share. Otherwise, you'll spend many a Saturday night cooking dinner for his Uncle Charlie or helping his young sister through her painful adolescence.

Since Capricorns are always slightly nervous in the presence of the opposite sex, an occasional one will awkwardly hint at off-color situations, fumble with attempts at innuendo, or appear to be rough, tough and callous. It's just his way of being one of the fellows, a typical method of hiding his embarrassment and curiosity about the purple passions of more aggressive people. Don't ever let it lead you into thinking he wants you to play Bonnie to his Clyde. You are not Mae West or Texas Guinan. You are a lady and don't ever forget it. He may cast a furtive, interested glance at a lady of the evening, but she's definitely not the kind of lady he marries. This may sound like advice from your spinster Aunt Abigail, but if you think it's square, go on and wear your teeny bikini and green mascara—pour on the perfume and kiss him in public. You may eventually walk down the aisle in a white veil, but it won't be beside a Saturn groom.

A nice gift for your Capricorn husband would be a book of poems, the more romantic the better. If you don't train him early in the art of affectionate expression, you may become a well-provided-for wife who's adored and warmly appreciated—with a perfect dear for a husband—but who is also emotionally starved. It won't do any good by that time to complain that he never tells you he loves you. He'll just look at you in injured innocence or grumbling disgust (depending on how strong Saturn was at his birth), and patiently explain that "You're crazy. I distinctly remember telling you I loved you when I gave you your engagement ring and again when little Calvert was born."

He thinks you should know how he feels about you since he supports you, and pays you the tribute of allowing you to bear his children, sweep his floors and polish his trophies. To Capricorn, mushy, verbal declarations are gilding the romantic lily. He may ask, "What do you want, Richard Burton?" That's your cue to say "yes" loudly. It should startle him a little. He won't turn into Richard Burton, but he may be shocked into realizing that a gently murmured "sweetheart" at appropriate times won't harm his masculinity.

As a father, he'll be a Father—the literal personification of the word. He'll always be at the head of the table, and that goes for picnics, too. Even if he's the one sitting on the poison ivy, near the ant hill, around the paper cloth spread under the trees—the spot where the Capricorn daddy sits is the head of the table. He'll demand respect and obedience, and he'll insist on routine and discipline. But he'll repay it with honest devotion, even self sacrifice, probably approve of big, happy birthday parties and a very merry Christmas. Capricorn fathers are highly unlikely to spare the rod and spoil the child. He'll see that they go to the dentist and do their homework, with a few trips to the old woodshed when it's necessary. His own sense of organization and dependability will be emphatically conveyed. It certainly won't hurt the youngsters, though it might take a little starch out of them. Remind him that parenthood can be fun, as well as a serious responsibility. Think of him as a Charles Dickens type papa. Teach the children to give him generous goodnight kisses, and encourage him to take them to the ball game, fishing or swimming. If he's a little strict, remember that they'll profit in the long run, as long as he doesn't overdo it. When the grandchildren bounce on his knee, he'll turn shockingly permissive. Capricorn grandpas make great baby sitters.

I even know one who roller skates around the block with his second generation offspring.

A Capricorn man will seldom marry in haste and repent at leisure. He's more apt to marry at leisure and repent in haste. Most Capricorn marriages are solid, but if the goat makes a mistake, he'll walk out abruptly, and his wife won't get a second chance. Capricorn abhors divorce, so it won't happen often, but when it does, it's final. To be blunt, when he's had it—he has had it.

Your Saturnine husband may regulate love-making to a schedule, along with shopping, correspondence, doing his banking, visiting museums or art galleries and cleaning his gun and trophy collection. It may seem cold and unsentimental, but remember that the practical Capricorn is interested in the physical side of love long after other husbands resort to poetry to express their emotions. Interpreted, that means just what I said back at the beginning. Dessert last. After he's retired, he'll have more time to develop his technique of affection. That's better than insurance. And you'll have that too, with a Capricorn husband—insurance against a rainy day, insurance against loneliness and insurance against the blows of a sordid, ugly world. Any sensible female appreciates the value of Saturn devotion. He won't be a fiery lover who courts you with starry eyes and passionate, flowery speeches. But he'll protect you from all your feminine fears. He's a tough guy with a gentle heart. He'll chop the wood for that cozy fire, then sit with you in front of it and hold your hand tenderly. No matter how many gray hairs, extra pounds or wrinkles you add as the years slip by, to him you'll always look like the girl who made him say "I love you." When you stop to think about it, why should he say it again and again? Once is enough when it lasts that long.

The CAPRICORN Woman

So she got up and walked about—
rather stiffly just at first,
as she was afraid that the crown might come off:
but she comforted herself with the thought
that there was nobody to see her,
"and if I really am a Queen," she said,
as she sat down again,
"I shall be able to manage it quite well in time."

There's no such think as a typical Capricorn female. She can be a museum curator who wears granny glasses for real, or she can be a dancer who wears a glittering G-string for fun. You'll see her crisply running a suburban P.T.A., frying hamburgers in a coffee shop, or organizing the biggest Charity Ball in the city. A Capricorn woman may decorate the society columns, smile demurely behind a political candidate husband or pour mysterious liquids into test tubes. But whatever she's doing and whatever she's wearing, Saturn will rule her actions and her secret aims.

She can be ultra-feminine, flirtatious and charming enough to make a man feel like a giant grizzly bear who can protect her from the cold, cruel world. Or she can be icy, quiet and aloof, sitting securely on her marble pedestal and challenging you to be clever enough to win her superior hand. Whichever personality she projects, underneath her womanly wiles or her practical, sensible manner, she has the same goal—a steely determination to snag the right man, who can become important, make her proud and be a good father to her children.

So many Capricorn women are career girls, you might think love and marriage would always be a second choice. With love, you have a point. With marriage, no. The thing to understand is that the Capricorn goals are security, authority, respect and position. It makes little difference if these needs are supplied in front of a blackboard as a school teacher, behind a desk as an executive, or beside an ambitious husband whose social life and home she can manage with easy grace and careful planning. One way or another, the Capricorn woman will get her recognition. Some of them get it by writing books, lecturing, painting or composing music. It's surprising how many Capricorns of both sexes have unusual artistic talent. Perhaps it stems from an innate sense of balance and harmony, knowing what is pleasing and what is right or correct.

This is a little delicate, but even the Saturn females you find in burlesque theaters or engaging in the world's oldest profession (there will be only a handful) will end up by marrying the top comic or the theater owner in the first instance—or the wealthiest client in the second. The goat must climb. Whether the starting position is high or low, the top of the hill is where she finds the view more satisfying. There's nothing flashy about the Capricorn female. You'll certainly never see her loudly or obviously pushing and shoving for first place; you may even think she's docile enough to contentedly take a back seat to her competition. Wait. See who gets the promotion.

Don't be misled into thinking she'll never sacrifice her career for marriage. Just give this girl half a chance to be a social leader and the mistress of a well-run household, and you'll see how quickly she loses interest in her job (one of the few things she'll do quickly). If you need her to, the Capricorn woman will gladly continue working to help you climb up the mountain of success—she won't be lazy. Otherwise, however, she's happier enjoying her position as your wife, provided the position is a good one, and there's enough financial security.

One of the most typical and delightful things about this woman is her natural breeding and grace of manner. You can meet a Capricorn girl who was raised in a one-room shack across the railroad tracks, or whose father works the swing shift in a coal mine, but unless she decides to reveal her background (which she probably won't), you'll be convinced she comes from an old-line family, and was turned out by one of the best finishing schools. Such is the Capricorn built-in sense of social grace and conservative, conventional appearances.

Any man who's involved in a relationship with the female goat should learn a basic fact about this Sun sign. She seems to be more even-tempered and emotionally steady than she actually is. Her manner may convince you that she's as firm as a rock and nothing can ruffle her calm surface. The truth is that she's subject to many moods. All women are subject to moods, you say, but the Capricorn girl can have some really black and long-lasting ones. If she feels mistreated or unappreciated, she'll brood for days, weeks, even months. She calls it being sensible or practical, but Saturnine gloominess, pessimism and depression are much more deeply rooted than that. They're triggered by fear of the future, worry about the present, shame over the past—or a suspicion that she's being made fun of or is inadequate in some way. These women do not accept teasing lightly. Keep it at a minimum. To be honest, they find it impossible to see the joke when they're the victims. You don't have to bury her in compliments constantly (she'll sense when they're insincere, anyway), but don't kid her about important matters, and praise her often enough to make her realize you know her true value.

It's hard for her to relax in romantic situations. There's plenty of physical desire under the cool Capricorn surface, far more than most people suspect, and it's never satisfied casually. Sitting around and wasting time with breathless hugs and ecstatic kisses while the future is still hanging unsettled is definitely not her favorite hobby—yet once she's decided you're the right man and the finances are secure or your ambition is sufficient, she'll be as warm as a cuddly panda, affectionate, and even passionate. Capricorns don't believe in vague dreams that glide aimlessly through a misty, blue sky. They want to know where the ship of romance is taking them, and that it's sailing on safe waters. Build a firm foundation under your house if you plan to carry a Capricorn girl over the threshold. Make sure there's plenty of insurance and the mortgage is paid off or will be soon.

She'll probably be something of a social butterfly, extremely aware of etiquette, and she'll lean toward quaint customs like engraved napkin rings and needlepoint chairs. Things must be correct and tradition must be observed at all costs. She may have an inconsistent habit of wanting to shop in the most expensive, exclusive stores, yet insisting on a bargain. She doesn't mind buying a dress that's on sale, as long as it bears the right label.

Capricorn women have a fresh beauty of their own. You'll rarely find one who's not unusually attractive. Yet they are timid and unsure about their appearance, and you may find them needing constant reassurance that they're pretty. Although Capricorn females hate dishonesty in all forms, they're not above lying about their ages. They usually get away with it, too, thanks to the odd Saturn aging twist. They look like little old ladies as children, then bloom suddenly into women who look like young girls when they're past the prime of life.

It would be a terrible mistake to snub her family. The man who marries a Capricorn girl marries her relatives. There's no point in thinking that yours is different. She's not. Somewhere along the line, you'll stop laughing at mother-in-law jokes (you may cry instead). Many times, the Saturn female is the sole support of her family, financially or morally or both. She may care for an ill parent with devotion to the point of relinquishing the idea of marriage completely. Often, she'll enjoy the sacrifice because of her honest love for her family, but even if she resents it, her strong sense of responsibility and duty will not permit her to escape.

You might as well resign yourself to flattering your mother-in-law, and hope she's a great gal who's worth it. Don't argue politics with her father, and if you must criticize her brothers and sisters, see that the criticism is constructive, and based on a sincere belief in their potentialities. Frequently, Capricorns find themselves burdened with distressed or invalid relatives, and the typical goats will never let love, however consuming it might be, cause them to neglect such obligations. You'd better start right out by planning to have a guest room or two for visiting relatives. But there's a reverse benefit. You'll have a wife who is kind and considerate toward your own family. The Capricorn girl will understand if you have to allocate a fixed sum to your parents each week, and she'll probably be a companion to your brothers and sisters. She's the kind of girl you take home to meet mother, and mother approves of her immediately. Since men are so contrary, such instant encouragement can cause them to back away. It's always more fun to fight objections for your lady fair. But you'll only be slicing off your nose to spite your heart, because your mother is right. The Capricorn girl, if she's a typical Saturn woman, will make an excellent wife.

The home of a Capricorn woman often looks so effortlessly spotless and smooth-running you'd think there were little fairies and elves hiding in the corners, working away furiously after midnight to shine and polish and cook and clean. Wrong. The very last place you can expect to find such imaginary creatures is around a Capricorn. The Saturn practicality and faith in firm facts ordinarily precludes any sympathy with the unseen. A Capricorn girl wouldn't believe in leprechauns if one sat right on the tip of her nose. In all fairness, however, although she may not be a way-out dreamer or a follower of occult mysteries, once she has the solid facts she's able to see the romance and poetry in the most ordinary situations.

Hers is an earthy kind of beauty that can make even the gross and ugly seem lovely with sheer usefulness. She's not a stranger to the gypsy spell of the north wind, nor is she deaf to the silver song of spring showers and the call of a lonely skylark. Great music stirs her deeply, and she's an enchanted patron of almost any art form. Perhaps she has to see and touch magic to believe in it. A leprechaun would probably get much further with her if he came right out and said where that pot of gold is hidden, instead of hinting about it in fairy tales.

Most Capricorns save their rainbow thinking for history and heroic deeds of the past. Since she worships tradition, and reveres those who have overcome obstacles to gain success, it's easier for her to get sentimental over the Gettysburg address than to get enthusiastic over your latest wild scheme. Actually, she's a true romantic, with greater imagination than the scatterbrains with unreal fantasies. Every January girl has haunting poetry in her soul, but she doesn't have much sympathy for poets who starve in attics. Take care of the food and rent and then pursue the dream, whatever it may be, is the Capricorn motto. Also make sure that the dream is *worth* pursuing. She sees nothing glamorous or magical about failure.

You may have to share your Capricorn wife with causes. She'll be a tireless worker for the poor and the defenseless, but she may prefer to show her charity in group efforts, rather than to individuals. Saturnine sympathies are usually organized, seldom scattered. Female Capricorns are natural leaders of women's clubs.

She'll probably instill both thrift and a respect for quality in the youngsters. She'll teach them to "Eat it up, wear it out, make it do or do without." Still, they'll be served the best cuts of meat, and she'll buy them the finest make of shoes. To her, economy does not have to mean cheap. The children will be expected to be polite to relatives and elders, and they'll probably learn excellent manners. They won't be pampered or allowed to willfully disobey. If you give her a book on child psychology, she may use it to paddle an unruly offspring and get around to reading it later. Sticky kisses may not be welcome, but few mothers are more devoted than the female goat. Her children will get a courteous listening ear. She may be a little strict and unsympathetic to their growing pains, but she'll be a fascinated audience for their achievements. The child who runs home from school and shouts, "Guess what I learned today," won't be ignored by the Capricorn mother, who will never be too busy to give her youngsters her interest and attention. After they become teenagers, there may be a few barriers when the Saturn conservatism clashes with youth's liberalism. At this point, she may need some help in understanding her children's enthusiastic dreams. She may learn the hard way that she can't dictate their friendships and confine them to "acceptable" people. But she's intelligent enough to adjust and pull in her horns if it looks as though she'll lose more than she'll gain.

Since many Capricorn females have sensitive skin, they don't wear much make-up. Lots of them are allergic to it. But nature rewarded them with natural beauty that needs little gilding, and they'll keep it long after the roses have faded from the cheeks of other women. Some of them startle you with lovely complexions, firm features and bright eyes at the age of eighty and older.

Patiently help your Capricorn woman overcome her lack of personal confidence. She's not unimaginative just because she doesn't court delusion. Try on a couple of her practical dreams for size, and you'll find they're surprisingly comfortable. Stubbornness may be one of her vices, but she's not a whiner or a nervous nag. She'll push you toward success, yet be tender and devoted. In spite of her modest, often gentle ways, she'll know just how to twist you around her little finger. There's a deep richness in her love that's more lasting than the brittle, scorching, demanding love of other women. Who says she doesn't believe in fairy tales? Only a wise Capricorn maiden could look deep into the eyes of an awkward frog and see that he's really a prince in disguise. Not only that—if you marry her, you'll never run out of clean socks.

The CAPRICORN Child

"Oh, how I wish I could shut up like a telescope!
I think I could, if I only knew how to begin . . ."

"Pat her on the head,
and see how pleased she'll be! . . .
A little kindness—
and putting her hair in papers—
would do wonders with her—"

If you're one of those people mothers hate, because you think all newborn infants look like little old men and women, save your description for a Capricorn baby, and you won't get so much resistance. Tiny Capricorns do resemble miniature octogenarians. They look old in their youth and young in their old age. That little wrinkled prune of a face in the bassinet will someday be smooth and unlined when other faces are sagging. Maybe it has something to do with being born in January—the old year going out and the New Year coming in. The odd turnabout does match the familiar image of the old man with his care-lined face beside the fresh infant of the New Year with his Ivory soap look.

If you have a Capricorn child, you'll notice the inconsistency soon enough. From the time he's an infant, your self-contained little Cappy will make you feel somewhat uneasy with his strange maturity. You'll say something cheerful to him, like "Does itty bitty Baby Boo want a nicey sugy cake?" and he'll give you a serious, thoughful look, exactly as though he's wondering just how silly you can get. It doesn't take many of those looks to shame the average parent right out of baby talk.

Capricorn youngsters are strong-willed and positive in their tastes, but they don't make a big fuss in expressing them. Your little goat won't throw a temper tantrum or

dramatically pound his fist in the mashed potatoes, but he'll
manage to communicate his negative reactions quite plainly.
A mother may feel vaguely intimidated by a Capricorn
baby, but she can't put her finger on the exact reason.
Somehow he makes her feel—well, he makes her feel foolish and flighty. Let's be very truthful. He makes her feel
like the child, instead of the parent.

This infant isn't the kind to waver or succumb to
wishful thinking. He crawls or waddles deliberately to the
place he wants to reach. You rather get the feeling he
organized it all carefully in his mind while you were
changing his diaper, and now he's going to follow through.
He's nothing if not definite. Capricorns are never coy about
making their wishes known. You get the message clearly.
Then they steadily wait for your answer. Suppose you say
"no." If it isn't anything important, he will probably accept
the disappointment without tearful scenes. If it's something
he's decided he really wants, he'll get it, one way or another. Your "no" will mean little to him. Instead of fighting
it, he'll ignore it and bide his time until he finally wears
you down and you give in.

As he grows older, your Capricorn offspring will begin
to organize his life into a routine. He'll keep his toys in a
certain place, and will be quite put out if you move them or
disturb his system. If he's a typical Saturn child, he'll
usually adapt naturally to mealtime schedules and potty
time, and he'll have less interest in childish tricks or youthful pranks than other youngsters. Even when they're very
small, these boys and girls will show a decided preference
for home life. The little goat would rather go on a picnic
with mother and dad, or sit home and listen to the grownups talk, than run outside with a group of children his own
age. He'll seldom have a gang of friends. There will probably be only a few close companions, or maybe just one
special friend with whom he shares secrets.

School is seldom a struggle for young Capricorn students. Unless he has a conflicting ascendant or the Moon
was in a restless sign at birth, this youngster will be remarkably responsible about homework. He will walk into
the house, hang up his coat, and sit down immediately to
tackle his lessons. If he's a true Capricorn, he can't enjoy
his play until he's first attended to duty.

When he's ready for leisure, the Saturn play often
takes the form of pretending to be an adult. Little Capri-

corn girls love to play dress-up in their mother's clothes. Sometimes they'll suggest, "You be the baby and I'll be the Mommy," which could make you a bit uncomfortable, because the tot will be strangely convincing in the reverse role. You'll feel like a complete fool, standing in the playpen and gurgling while she peers over her big spectacles, wearing your high heels and pearls, and says firmly, "Do be still or you'll go to bed without any supper." You get the impression you'd better stop the play quickly, or she really will put you to bed. Sometimes the Capricorn child will become a "pretend" parent for small pets and be quite serious about the responsibility. Little Capricorn boys like to pretend they're teachers, doctors, executives of big railroads or Daddy. When your little son puts on your husband's topcoat and picks up his pipe, you may get the oddest urge to ask him to drive over to the supermarket and bring home some eggs—until you remember he can't drive anything more complicated than a scooter, and he skins his knees most of the time on that. Capricorn children also like to paint or draw and listen to music, but they won't waste many leisure hours in aimless games. Frequently they'll be absorbed in making something practical. It will have a useful purpose, even if it's a pretty skinny pot holder or a comically wobbly pencil box. They should be encouraged to play outdoors. They won't seek the sunshine and fresh air with much enthusiasm, but it's good for them; it blows those gloomy little Saturn cobwebs out of their young minds.

Teachers usually find the Capricorn child pleasant to instruct, but they may lose patience with his slow, stubborn methods of learning. Still, the teacher will seldom complain of frivolous daydreaming or neglect of studies. These youngsters are normally very good scholars, after they've grasped the fundamentals. They don't learn quickly or project flashy brilliance, but they're thorough and careful. Saturn concentration is nothing to sneeze at. It wins prizes and gets A's.

When your young goat brings home a report card with behavior marks that say he's obedient, studious and reliable, but "he's reluctant to participate in class discussions," "refuses to recite," "is timid, lacks confidence and doesn't mix well with the other students," you'll begin to worry that you've raised an introverted bookworm, a hopelessly anti-social creature. Then one day your little Capricorn will casually mention that he has to be in school early to call the roll. "Why do you have to call the roll?" you'll ask. The answer will be a shock. "Oh, because I'm President of the class." When you exclaim, "Why didn't you tell us?" he'll reply with offhand modesty, "Gee, it isn't that important." But he'll be blushing and pleased. It's the pattern for his adult life. Apparently slower than the others, supposedly a poor mixer and the dark horse, he'll quietly and inevitably end up in some position of leadership, as the extroverts realize he's the one they can trust to be responsible. Capricorn may be left to guard the treasures and keep the records, while the gregarious ones play and dream but he won't feel imposed upon. What he seeks are respect and authority.

An occasional Capricorn youngster will coldly dictate to weaker friends or siblings with a stubborn will, which can amount to childish cruelty, but far more often the Capricorn child will submit to more dominant Sun signs. There may then be a problem of brothers or sisters bossing the little goat, and you'll think he's being pushed around unfairly. Don't worry. He can take care of himself. One little Capricorn girl I know is completely submissive to her older, more aggressive Sagittarian sister. With the patience of the earth signs she takes orders from the more fiery personality. She never talks back or argues. But after an especially severe bossing session, the older sister just happens to find her shoes, her hairbrush or her favorite sweater is "missing." It always turns up eventually, and no one in the family ever has the slightest idea how it got "lost," but for weeks afterwards, the bossy sister is more considerate. Never underestimate the power of Capricorn for self-preservation. Somehow, the odds get evened.

Around members of the opposite sex, little goats will be bashful, but intensely interested. You'll hear remarks like, "Boys are drippy goons," and "Girls are stupid creeps," but they'll get mysteriously excited about Valentine's Day in school, and send a bushel of cards signed "guess who." Romantically, adolescence can be painful. They'll need encouragement and careful handling when dating begins.

It's a blessing to be the parents of a January boy or girl. With very few exceptions, it's like a gift from the gods. Unless he's pushed too far, in which case he can say something bluntly cruel and freezingly painful, the Capricorn child will usually be as sweet as the "sugy cake" he hates.

If you're short on the rent money you can always borrow a few twenties from his fat piggy bank. He'll be polite to his elders, and mind almost without being asked, except for rare stubborn spells. He'll organize his chores, and be serious about his future, though you may have to force him to scrub behind his ears. He'll cling to home and family with honest devotion, and seldom make you wonder where he is. Most of the time, he'll be right there beside you, enjoying every minute. He has his own bright, solid and practical dreams. Don't worry if he snubs *Sleeping Beauty* and *Goldilocks*. When you're old and gray, and feeling lost and forgotten by a thoughtless younger generation, your Capricorn son or daughter will sincerely respect your wisdom. He'll be enthusiastic about inviting you to visit or even to make your home with him. It's for all the world as if the Capricorn youngster is saying—for real this time—"All right, now I'll be the Mommy (or Daddy), and *you* be the baby. You took care of me with love. Now I'll take care of you." There'll be no make-believe about it, but Hans Christian Andersen never wrote a happier ending.

The CAPRICORN Boss

"I told them once, I told them twice:
they would not listen to advice."

"Now I growl when I'm pleased,
and wag my tail when I'm angry.
Therefore I'm mad."

I know a Capricorn boss who's just about as typical of the Sun sign as you can get. He's the major domo of the world of a famous male singer from Hoboken. Few people know it. There are no neon signs spelling his name, and columnists don't print juicy tidbits about his activities. You'll never see his face on the cover of *Time,* but you may have to pass his inspection before you get the chance to try to sell any glamorous ideas to the Idol.

This goat sits firmly behind his desk, efficiently tying up

all the loose ends and dangling strings in the amazingly intricate life of the famous personality. This can range from meeting the singer's relatives at the airport to buying a yacht or renting the floodlights for a premiere. He calmly handles hot potatoes like law suits and tax problems by delegating the right potato into the right accountant's or attorney's oven for baking, making sure it neither stays raw nor gets burned. His phone rings constantly with S.O.S. calls from other members of the widespread entourage; and he knows just who is where and why and when they're coming back. He keeps four million statistics in his head, including top secret information reporters would give an eye tooth to learn, the opening scene of a twenty-year-old movie, the box office figures of a current film, and the fastest source of catered hot spaghetti with Italian cheese sauce.

His day never ends. It starts at dawn, and midnight finds him winding up the schedule of orders he'll see are executed promptly the next morning. Often, he shaves, showers and dresses at the office. Anyone who really knows the score will tell you that certain bedlam would result if he ever disappeared from the frantic scene. He'd look grossly out of place in a discotheque, and he has a vaguely uncomfortable look in nightclubs, where duty demands he show his poker face on occasion.

This particular executive goat has a strange base of operations on an entire floor of a Manhattan building. In addition to the outer rooms and reception hall, there's a huge space for his private den. In one corner is a large circular desk for the mountain of papers that require his daily attention. The rest of his private domain is furnished with two big couches, several over-stuffed chairs, coffee tables, heavy draperies, lamps, book cases and mossy, cushioned carpeting. He even has a dining room, with a table big enough to seat the Mets for lunch, china closets, mirrors, dishes, silver and glasses. The walls are covered with patterned paper, and there are several tanks of expensive tropical fish lining the room. You would think you were in somone's home instead of in the busy office of an important executive.

That's exactly where you are. Since he must spend so many hours away from his home, this Capricorn boss simply brought it with him. Other bosses may enjoy the commercial world, and be glad to get away from home, but not the goat. Home is sacred. At almost any hour, you'll find this particular Capricorn's relatives around. Family life is never neglected for business.

Since he's such a typical Saturn boss his habits tell a lot about all Capricorn executives. He's a kindly father image to those who work for him—stern, but fair. He insists on obedience to duty, and woe betide the employee who forgets to feed his velvet-tailed guppies. He seldom raises his voice to give orders. His tone is gruff, but normally quiet, except on rare occasions when stupidity or careless mistakes cause him to bellow. At these times, he resembles a glaring Monty Woolley. Visitors are sometimes intimidated by his serious, formal manner, but the staff has discovered his soft heart, and they'll brook no criticism of him from outsiders—though they may swear a little under their breath, among themselves, when he cracks the whip. He burns their ears off when they goof, but he comes up with an extra fifty when it's needed, and he'll send his secretary's mother flowers in the hospital. He seldom goes in for compliments or flattery. A mumbled "Yeah, that's good," is about as close as he comes to extravagant praise. But he's a sympathetic listener to his employees' personal troubles, and he makes sure they eat right and wear their boots when it's raining. The staff is like a family, with the Capricorn boss unquestionably the head of the house.

He doesn't hand out Christmas bonuses like Santa Claus, but he's not stingy when an employee gets stuck in Las Vegas on a vacation without the plane fare home, or when the guy Friday he keeps hopping like a jack rabbit has a doctor's bill that can't be paid on his salary. (In the Vegas instance, he'll wire the return trip ticket, rather than the cash, and it will be tourist class. Wastefulness is not one of his hobbies.)

Although he's gruff, he can also be gentle and timid. A compliment will turn his ears pink, though he'll seldom acknowledge that he even heard it. Charity solicitors can always get a check from him, and if the charity is connected with children or the old folks, he'll add an extra zero. He has to be reminded to rest and eat his lunch, since responsibility causes him to neglect his personal needs. Now and then he goes into a black, melancholy mood of Saturnine depression, closes his door, stares out the window on Central Park, and no one dares disturb his privacy. Phone calls are held and office problems kept on ice until the depression lifts. He dresses in conservative, dark colors and subdued styles, and he has a sort of grandfatherly-looking pocket watch he frequently consults. He really looks more as though he's connected with a staid bank than with the leading swinger of these swingin' times. Most of the bric-a-brac around his desk are antiques, and there's a generous sprinkling of faded photos of his wife, children and various, assorted relatives.

That's a simon pure picture of a Capricorn boss. If you keep the image in your mind, you'll have a pretty good idea what to expect from any Saturn executive including your own. If he has any spare time, he won't waste it. He'll expect you to imitate him. Is the switchboard quiet? Good. You'll have time to file those letters. Is the schedule light today? Fine. You can move those cartons in the stock room. Don't spend office time polishing your nails, if you're his secretary—and don't hang on the phone in the back office, talking with your girl, if you're a male employee. Your Saturn boss will materialize out of thin air, like a frowning, avengeful genie. It wouldn't be wise to have your beatnik brother with the beard and guitar visit you at the office. Even the goat's religious devotion to family ties—his own and yours—won't keep him from raising a conservative eyebrow of disapproval. Female employees who reek of perfume and male employees who practice putting in the conference room won't find the office of a Capricorn executive a happy home. As far as he's concerned, the place for heavy perfume is in the bottle, and the place for putting is on the golf course (preferably at the best country club).

He's always impressed with the status of those who have inched a few toeholds above him on the mountain of success, so you'll make a hit if you're familiar with the social register. If you didn't graduate from Vassar or Harvard, then for goodness sakes at least have an aunt or uncle who did.

Make sure he knows you take your mother to lunch every Wednesday, or that you pay your younger brother's tuition at prep school, and you're sure to get promoted. Clean fingernails, courteous manners and perfect grammar are necessities, and efficient work without whining or complaints will be a requirement. Never call him by his first name in front of strangers, and never breathe a word of criticism about his family in front of anybody. For

Christmas, give him a chipped and faded oil painting of Thomas Jefferson you picked up in an antique shop, or a rock you snitched last summer from the back door of Nancy Hanks' birthplace. Capricorns revere history and the past. Just don't tell him you snitched the rock. They also revere scrupulous honesty. Polishing apples won't get you ten cents extra in your pay envelope. But understanding his lonely heart will gain you his confidence. Others may see him as a firm, tough disciplinarian with a heart of stone. Let him know you see him for what he really is: a shy and sensitive soul, who secretly longs to be free and casual, but knows he's chained by Saturn's demands of obedience to order, system and authority. He'll treat you like a son or daughter. You'll get spanked when you're bad and rewarded when you're good. But he won't let you down when you're in trouble or lock the door when you need help. Just don't forget to feed those velvet-tailed guppies.

The CAPRICORN Employee

"If everyone minded their own business,"
said the Duchess, in a hoarse growl,
"The world would go round
a deal faster than it does."

Look around the office and see if you can spot him. No fair sneaking a look at the birthdays in your personnel records. You can forget about that original, creative fellow with the bushy sideburns and the antler tooth necklace. You can also cross off the sport who brags about his pub cruising capers and his candlelight conquests. They're not Saturn types.

Jolly George, who keeps the staff in a state of perpetual panic with his not-quite-practical jokes, definitely isn't a Capricorn. Neither is light-hearted Louie, with the glib tongue and the bouncing baby brainstorms—nor the new promotion manager with the orange silk ascot, who keeps humming *"My Father Was the Keeper of the Eddystone Light"* in sales meetings.

How about that busy worker with the reserved manner who wears suspenders and parts his hair in the middle? The one with the quiet socks and a picture of his family in an ostrich leather frame on his desk. He usually comes in a few minutes early and leaves a few minutes late. His head is fastened firmly to his shoulders, and his pencil points are always sharp. The staff calls him "Sir," salesmen call him "Mister," and you call him when there's trouble. Of course he's a Capricorn.

Who else could you load up with a pile of work that would stagger a horse—but not a goat? He's your dependable safety valve when things get snarled and disorganized, and he comes through for you without making a big fuss about it. I doubt if he ever dashes into your office. He walks in, and he probably checks first to see if you're busy. His clothes and manner are both conservative, and he's the only one in the bunch who never gets caught without his umbrella when it rains. He won't lose his brief case in the subway, or forget where he left his lunch. His lunch? Naturally. What else do you think he carries in that brown paper bag? Restaurants are expensive. Besides, he hates to tip and fight the crowds.

The last time you saw him flash a bright, toothpaste grin was when your secretary mentioned she didn't know how the office could run without him. He's not the grinning type. Or the foolish, frivolous type. He may tell quite a few jokes in his wry and dry way, or take a discreet peek at a pretty girl, but Saturn will never permit him to pull out all the stops. Most of the time, he minds his own business. The Capricorn is more inclined to frown sternly on the casual jollities of the gay extroverts than to join them, although his own brand of cynical humor can be hilarious. When he's in form, it's hard to top him.

You have to admit he has unique and valuable assets. Your Capricorn employee is the one you sic on the tough, suspicious Internal Revenue man. When the goat gets through with him, he's not as suspicious and far less tough. He may even be courteous and respectful. It's not everyone who can successfully intimidate a tax man. Remember that high pressure character who wanted to sell you several hundred dollars worth of perfumed typewriter ribbons in rhinestone studded boxes to pep up your secretaries' morale? After two minutes with your Capricorn man, the poor soul was pressing the down button on the elevator, looking like a fallen souffle.

Somehow, you get the impression your Capricorn employee is going to advance much higher in life, but it's hard to figure how he conveys it. There's nothing aggressive or openly ambitious about him. He's not a flashy, ruthless climber. Let's try that again. He's not a flashy climber. In his own mild, inconspicuous way, the goat is coldly determined to get where he's going. Those who prevent his steady progress or impose on him will soon find he's no Casper Milquetoast. He'll accept his responsibilities without complaint or resentment, but he won't be pushed too far. Capricorns with severe planetary afflictions in their natal birth charts can be astonishingly cruel and ruthless. But the average goat simply gives people a grumpy growl and a black look when they tweak his horns.

Just in case you have one of the exceptions to the rule in your office, I'd better tell you about a Capricorn I knew who worked in a donut shop. He probably had a Leo ascendant or the Moon was in Gemini or Aries when he was born. This goat wore expensive, Italian shoes and big cuff links. He made more romantic conquests in a week than other men do in a lifetime—or said he did. He enjoyed telling off-color stories, and when he wasn't flirting with the women customers or impressing everyone with his toughness, he tossed off some pretty big bubble schemes and way-out promotions. Most people would never peg him as a Capricorn, but they should look a little closer and listen more carefully.

For all his outrageous flirting, when he called his fiancée on the phone his tone was tender and protective. A man who dared to swear in her presence would never have tried it twice. He made it clear that she was a lady. In front of his parents, he was subdued and respectful. Anyone past fifty he treated with a courtesy bordering on reverence. With children, he was as gentle as Whistler's mother. Powerful, famous people with status turned him into a humble, worshiping admirer. He was constantly telling friends and strangers that he once sat next to a glamorous movie actress on a plane or about the time he was invited to a reception at the Governor's mansion. Everything he bought was wholesale, including those Italian shoes. He had the undisputed first prize as the tightest tipper in town. A dollar would never be spent where a dime could be saved. In other words, underneath that false bravado was a typical Saturn nature. This apparently aggressive, extroverted goat turned pink at a compliment and painfully shy in the presence of anyone he thought was upper register. If you need any more proof that he was a Capricorn, he eventually bought the chain of donut shops. And by the way, he didn't risk his own cash on those wild promotions. It was always somebody else's.

The typical Capricorn employee is conscientious almost to a fault. If he makes a mistake or commits an error of judgment, he's miserable. Falling down on his job depresses him. He'll come back to the office and work overtime if you need him, but he won't like it if you make him miss dinner at home with his family too many nights. The goat prefers to tend to his domestic responsibilities first, and return later to the grindstone, if necessary. You won't find him changing jobs often. The Capricorn decides early what the goal will be, and pursues it with unswerving persistence. He is not flighty or undecided about his future. The top of the mountain is never allowed to be obscured by the mist of fanciful dreams and sentimental wishing. Titles usually don't move him. He's not seeking glory. He's after the real position of power: he wants to be the one who guards the fort while the individualists and great idealists are out chasing butterflies. He doesn't need his name in gold letters on the door to feel important. But don't fail to increase his area of responsibility at decent intervals, and make sure you pay him enough money so he can keep up with the Joneses. He has to live in the right neighborhood, send his children to the right schools, and his wife has to dress with more taste than her friends. That takes substantial lettuce. The goat will gladly chew on tough leather, pieces of steel and old light bulbs to earn his dessert of green paper lettuce, sprinkled with the caviar of social distinction. His banker may be his closest friend, next to the members of his immediate family.

Your female Capricorn employee follows the same path as the male up that mountain. Nothing sways her from her determination to seek a position of authority in the firm or marry the boss. It doesn't matter a lot which it is. As long as she comes out ahead. This woman won't wear two sets of false eyelashes or jangling bracelets to work and you'll never catch her spinning daydreams at her desk.

The lady goat is a Lady. She'll rarely raise her voice or indulge in girlish gossip. There are more important things on her mind than who is having an affair with whom and what Emily said about Marilyn getting back late from lunch. After office hours, she may show a little more curiosity. The Saturn woman sometimes lives vicariously on the details of other people's romances, but she usually won't indulge herself in discussing them on the boss's time. That's logical enough. The boss may someday be her husband. In all fairness, there's another reason. All goats have a serious sense of duty, a respect for their superiors, and an inner discipline which makes them abstain from office monkeyshines.

Your Capricorn employees of either sex will be business-like. They disapprove of people who are late to work, and who waste time in idle chitchat. They have no patience with methods that aren't sound or procedures that lack common sense, and they'll rearrange office systems to make sure the organization runs with sensible efficiency. Not all Capricorns are bankers, teachers and bookkeepers. They also make excellent researchers, extremely capable dentists, brilliant engineers and architects, and they're clever at merchandising, manufacturing and politics. Many goats are jewelers, ministers, hotel managers, funeral directors, art dealers or anthropologists, but whatever the occupation, they'll be serious about it.

Don't forget that there's a creative side to Saturn people. Your Capricorn employee may have a hobby that could surprise you. He could be a Sunday artist, and a very good one, too. He could be a weekend musician, dabble in sculpture, sell real estate, apply his green thumb to a garden, sing in a choir or belong to a drama class. Culture is close to his heart. So is Mother Earth. His real loves are his family, his home, his work, money, prestige, books, art and music in just about that order. Get an Aries, Leo, Gemini or Sagittarius employee to travel for your firm. Most Capricorns break out in a nervous rash at the sight of a suitcase. Even if it's not quite that bad, they'll be happier catching a commuter train than catching a jet. Anyway, who would keep things nailed down while he's away? Remember what happened when he took his vacation last summer. Someone in the office went ahead and ordered four dozen of those perfumed typewriter ribbons in the rhinestone studded boxes.

> *'Twas brillig, and the slithy toves*
> *Did gyre and gimble in the wabe:*
> *All mimsy were the borogoves,*
> *And the mome raths outgrabe.*

AQUARIUS
the Water Bearer
January 21st through February 19th

How to Recognize AQUARIUS

"In spring, when woods are getting green,
I'll try and tell you what I mean:
In summer, when the days are long,
Perhaps you'll understand the song."

"For this must ever be
A secret
Kept from all the rest
Between yourself and me."

Lots of people like rainbows. Children make wishes on them, artists paint them, dreamers chase them, but the Aquarian is ahead of everybody. He lives on one. What's more, he's taken it apart and examined it, piece by piece, color by color, and he still believes in it. It isn't easy to believe in something after you know what it's really like, but the Aquarian is essentially a realist, even though his address is tomorrow, with a wild-blue-yonder zip code.

Like the bewildered Alice, taken through the maze of Wonderland by Aquarian Lewis Carroll, you'll have to be constantly prepared for the unexpected with Uranians. Generally kindly and tranquil by nature, Aquarians nevertheless enjoy defying public opinion, and they secretly delight in shocking more conventional people with occasional erratic conduct. These normally soft-spoken and courteous souls can suddenly short circuit you with the most amazing statements and actions at the most unpredictable times. The typical Uranian is half Albert Schweitzer and half Mickey Mouse. His feet can be wearing sandals, boots, oxfords, or hush puppies, and he'll seldom bother to check whether they're appropriate for the occasion. He'll show up barefoot if he feels like it, and laugh at you for laughing at him. Aquarians often deliberately adopt weird attire to show their refusal to conform.

You can often recognize people born under this fixed, air sign by their frequent use of the word friend. Aquarian

Franklin Roosevelt's fireside chats invariably began with, "My friends . . ." and the typical Uranus question after a broken romance is, "Can't we still be friends?" Aquarius is neither jaded nor naive, neither enthusiastic nor blasé. Continuous experimentation simply leaves him curious to penetrate the next mystery, and the next mystery could be you. That person who seems to be either a million miles away mentally, or else dissecting you under an invisible microscope, is probably an Aquarian. It can be disconcerting to discover, after all his intense, flattering curiosity, that he's just as deeply interested in the personal lives of the corner policeman, the bartender, the bellboy, the night club singer or the inmates of the funny house as he is in yours. Politics fascinate him, sports absorb him and children intrigue him. But then so do horses, automobiles, elderly people, medical discoveries, authors, astronauts, alcoholics, pianos, pinwheels and prayers—not to mention baseball and Louis Armstrong. Join the crowd and toss your ego in the wastebasket, or his coolly impersonal approach will be sure to bruise it.

Look for a strange, faraway look in the eyes, as if they contained some kind of magic, mysterious knowledge you can't penetrate. Aquarius eyes are typically vague, with a dreamy, wandering expression, and often (but not always) blue, green or gray. The hair is frequently straight and silky, likely to be blonde, sandy or light brown; the complexion is pale and the height is usually taller than average (though the ascendant can modify the appearance of any Sun sign). You'll notice a marked nobility of profile. Uranus features are finely chiseled, suggestive of Roman emperors cut on old gold coins. True Aquarians will often adopt the pose of the drooping head when they're thinking about a problem, or just after they've asked a question. The head drops abruptly forward, or cocks to one side, waiting for your reaction. Curiously, thanks to the dual sexuality of Uranus, there are often feminine characteristics in the male bodies, such as broad hips, for example—and masculine characteristics in the female body, such as broad shoulders.

Freedom-loving Uranians can be acutely funny, perverse, original, conceited and independent, but they can also be diplomatic, gentle, sympathetic and timid. The Aquarian will almost desperately seek the security of crowds and saturate himself with friendship. Then he'll fall into a gloomy, morose spell of loneliness, and want to be strictly left alone. But whether he's mingling or singling, he'll retain his sharp perception, which is at once both deeper and quicker than others. Uranus makes him a natural rebel who instinctively feels that all old customs are wrong, and that drastic alteration and revolutionary change is what the world and people need (although if he's in politics, he's clever enough not to broadcast his views prematurely and spoil his strategy).

To this end, Aquarians are always analyzing situations, friends and strangers. It can be disturbing when they start asking pointblank questions, with a bare minimum of tact, as they probe into the heart of your private feelings. When they discover the puzzle wasn't so complex after all, they become bored, sometimes even upset. Nothing is more insulting than to have an Aquarian tire of his game of microscopic examination and turn to the next interesting person, just when he's convinced you he thinks you are the most important human being on earth. It stings.

Despite their fixation on friendship, Aquarians don't have many intimates. They seek quantity rather than quality in their associations, and they seldom settle down to a steady relationship for more than a limited period. There's too much to discover around the next corner to remain tied to one or two friendships exclusively. It does little good to make an emotional appeal to such an impersonal nature, but if you touch the heart of an Aquarian (which is not the same thing as mere emotion), he'll usually get off his bicycle and come back to see what he might have missed.

A peculiar sort of isolation hangs over the Uranian, and he's often misunderstood by mankind. That's because mankind hasn't yet caught up with the Aquarian Utopia. Since the water bearer lives in the future, coming back only briefly to the present, he can seem just plain pixilated to more mundane souls. He senses this, and it deepens his sense of isolation. But just because others can't keep up with him is no reason in his opinion to go backwards. So he wanders among his lonely clouds, while we mere mortals wonder what he's doing way out there. Astrology teaches us that "As the Aquarian thinks, so will the world think in fifty years." That may be true, but it certainly doesn't narrow the gap between the Uranus-ruled and the rest of us today. This Sun sign is known as the sign of genius, and so it is, since over seventy percent of the people in the Hall of Fame are either Sun Aquarians or have Aquarian ascendants. On the other hand, a substantially high percentage of those confined in mental institutions, or who drop in for regular couch sessions with an analyst, are also Aquarians. There's a fine line, they say, between genius and insanity, and your Uranian friends can sometimes make you wonder which side of the line they're on. A great deal of the confusion is due to man's tendency to belittle his prophets. The familiar quotes that "they laughed at Fulton and his steamboat," "they thought Edison was mentally retarded," and "they wanted to lock up Louis Pasteur," are examples of the attitude of the materialistic world toward those whose senses are tuned to higher spheres of thought.

Uranians are a curious mixture of cold, practicality and eccentric instability, and they seem to have an instinctive empathy with the mentally disturbed. It's a curious fact that almost any Aquarian can substantially reduce the anxiety of the insane simply by talking to them quietly. He has a marvelous knack for calming hysterical people and soothing frightened children. Is it because of his own thinly-covered, highly acute nervous system that he has such deep understanding?

The Aquarian outlook is so broad that you'll seldom find one who is prejudiced, unless there are severe planetary influences in the natal chart. Even then, he'll be deeply shocked when his prejudice is pointed out. The brotherhood instinct is so strong in him that when a rare Aquarian is guilty of being intolerant, he's not only unaware of it, he hates the label. Ordinarily, everyone is his brother or sister. He'll wander through affluent society and the slums alike with his symbolic jar, gathering the waters of knowledge and pouring them out again, except for those occasional lapses into hibernation. But his hiding out periods seldom last long, and before you get a chance to miss him the Uranian is back gregariously making the rounds again. Don't try to interrupt his solitude. When he wants to be alone, he wants to be alone, but he hasn't retired from the mainstream permanently, even if he does take a sudden Uranus notion to get an unlisted phone number. His address hasn't changed, and neither has he. He can never renounce people for long. Ignore him and he'll soon be walking around town on those home-made stilts, as alert and inquisitive as ever.

Ordinarily, it's difficult to get an Aquarian to make a precise appointment. He'd rather keep it loose, because he doesn't like to be pinned down to specific duties or obligations at specific times. He prefers a casual "I'll see you around—maybe sometime Tuesday" to a definite hour for a meeting. (And he sometimes means the second Tuesday of next week.) However, I will say that once you've succeeded in nailing him and he gives you his word he'll meet you at a particular hour he will be there on the dot. You can count on it, even set your watch by his punctuality, and you'd better not be late yourself. He'll show up dependably, unless he's been kidnapped on the way (which, being an Aquarian, he could be. Anything can happen to these people at any time. I mean but anything).

You can expect him to give his opinion frankly, but he won't try to dictate how you should think or how you should live your life. Conversely, he doesn't intend to let you tell him how he should think or live his. Unlike Aries and Leo or Gemini, he has no desire to hard sell his ideas to others. The Aquarian philosophy is that everyone has his thing, his special yearning. Each person dances to his own fiddle music, and individuality should be respected. It's interesting to see that, as the world moves into the Aquarian Age, the heralds of the new era are the flower people and the Gurus. In exaggerated fashion, they are simply reflecting the Aquarian ideals: equality—brotherhood—love for all—live and let live—seek the truth—experiment—and retire to meditate.

You'll rarely find the Aquarian fighting fiercely for a cause. They live their code, and feel that's enough. Let Aries, Scorpio, Leo and Sagittarius grab the sword and battle gloriously to free the downtrodden. The Uranus-ruled souls are too busy figuring out the reason for the revolution, listening to people's troubles and sharing sympathetic understanding. Aquarius believes in violent change, but he leaves the violence to others. He's not a moral or a physical coward. He just isn't geared for battle. When a fight catches him unaware, he may strike out blindly in confusion, or he may simply agree, to end the argument. His reaction is unpredictable, but one thing is certain. The next day his opinion will be as fixed as it was before. Anyone skilled in debate can usually get the best of him, since his attention can so easily wander to the abstract in a battle of wits. The Aquarian fights best with his hat. He puts it on and leaves. His truth-respecting mind, however, won't budge an inch when he has a firm conviction, despite his distaste for unpleasant confrontations. All the shouting and emotional pressure in the world won't keep him from determinedly going his own way with his independent ideas, while the fireworks explode all around him. Our two Aquarian Presidents, Abraham Lincoln and Franklin Roosevelt, demonstrate this principle perfectly. The concepts were equally original and strikingly unpopular in both cases. There was no aggressive insistence on personal theories, yet the sweeping reforms were made, regardless of lack of cooperation and bitter opposition.

Another reason why Uranians often meet with hostile criticism is that they're so full of surprises. They can lead you west, then suddenly turn and march east, without warning. Aquarius has an obstinate way of not letting you know what he's up to. For weeks, the February-born father of a friend of mine ignored his wife's complaints about a stove that didn't work. He buried himself in his newspaper, oblivious to her desperate hints. Suddenly one day a truck pulled up, two men unloaded a brand new stove and connected it in the kitchen under the surprised eyes of his wife, who should have learned to expect such behavior.

Trusting people doesn't come naturally to the Aquarian until after he's scrutinized your motives, even your soul, if possible. It's easy to grow restive under his intent analysis of your every word and gesture. You get the feeling it's all being filed away in that penetrating mind for future reference, and it is. He may seem to be in a dreamy fog now and then, but don't you believe it. He can probably tell you how many eyelashes you have. Never expect the Uranian to take you at face value. His innate courtesy will never keep him from shining the Uranus spotlight on you from head to toe. He wants to know what's behind that face, and he'll ask some mighty embarrassing questions to find out. But it's comforting to know that once you're accepted he'll be loyal and his friendship will be unshaken by malicious gossip. If you're his real friend, he won't believe the nasty whispers of your enemies, although he'll undoubtedly listen to them out of sheer curiosity. Rest assured, however, that he'll make up his own mind in the final analysis.

Uranus illnesses are usually connected with the circulatory system. Aquarians shiver and shake in the winter, and suffer with the humidity in the summer. They're susceptible to varicose veins and hardening of the arteries in old age, if their emotions are directed into negative channels, and they tend to have accidents to the legs, especially the shin and ankles. The ankle bones are often weak, and there may be pains in the legs, due to poor circulation; frequent sort throats; and sometimes heart palpitation, usually not serious unless there are severe afflictions in the natal chart. Uranians need lots of fresh air, sleep and exercise, but they seldom take advantage of these remedies. They don't get much fresh air because they close their windows, pile on the blankets and still complain that they're freezing. The high frequency nervous tension that accompanies Uranus mental activity keeps them from getting enough sleep, and often the rest they do get is troubled by strange dreams. As for exercise, unless the Aquarian developed an early love of sports by playing stickball in his neighborhood, it's difficult to prod him into moving fast, let alone running around the track. His mind gets a continual workout, but the body needs a strong push. Aquarian health is usually excellent in childhood, barring weird, Uranian complaints—impossible to diagnose. The real troubles don't begin until maturity increases stubbornness. These people are extremely susceptible to hypnosis. Intuitively, lots of them sense this and won't expose themselves to it for love nor money, but this is a mistake, because hypnotic suggestion from a good medical hypnotist could successfully remove their myriad phobias. They're acutely responsive to electrical treatment, too, which can be just as beneficial.

Aquarians don't have the best memories in the world, but then they really don't need to memorize much, since they seem to pick up knowledge out of thin air, with some kind of invisible antennae. Why should they clutter their minds with information they may never need, when they can reach out by osmosis and grasp just about anything they want? They're likely to come home from the store without the most important item on the grocery list, because they can't be bothered with remembering what is, to them, non-essential. The typical Aquarian is the embodiment of the legendary absent-minded professor. I know one who planned to meet his wife in front of the City

Squire Motel at noon. But he arrived early and ran into an old friend. (Aquarians are always running into old friends. In Africa or the Aleutian Islands they will be sure to find somebody they know.) The Uranian was engrossed in conversation with his pal when his wife approached, all smiles. As she came closer he stared at her blankly, gallantly tipped his hat, then turned, took his friend's arm and walked down the street, deep in conversation, leaving the furious, frustrated woman standing on the corner, alone and forgotten.

The Uranus power of concentration can be awesome. Yet, they're also able to pick up things going on around and behind them when they choose, like a radar screen. They can carry on a complicated discussion and still not miss an inflection of what's happening in the other part of the room, if they decide to tune in. Sometimes you could swear the Aquarian paid no attention to anything you said, but the next day he'll repeat it back to you like a tape recorder. Never underestimate the Uranian process of soaking up knowledge while they seem to be oblivious, even though now and then they get lost in concentration, like my friend who left his wife standing on the street, in a mood to kill.

What the Aquarius man or woman thinks is always a clue to tomorrow. The uncanny Uranus ability to plunge into the unknown and absorb mystical secrets without half trying leads to a peculiar sort of intuition which gives them a high degree of psychic precognition. I know one who literally answers the phone before it rings, and what's more, he knows who's on the other end before a word is spoken. Abraham Lincoln had several premonitions of his own death in startling detail. Almost every Aquarian has a unique kind of sensitivity that lets him know your inner desires. Without talk, he understands a need buried so deep that you're almost unaware of it yourself. Using that magical osmosis, the Aquarian can transmit his own thoughts with an unseen charge of electrical current. Even when his back is turned, he can project strong feelings by this strange process. During a long silence on the telephone, he may be sending and receiving vibrations when you think he's fallen asleep. Some Uranians don't need Western Union to send a telegram.

Yet, there's nothing superstitious about their thinking. A true scientist even if he's a mechanic or a musician, the

Uranian won't jump to a conclusion until it's passed the test of his keen mind. However, once he forms an opinon, it remains firmly fixed in his brain, and I do mean firmly. As strongly as he loves change in society and government, he won't change his own idea one iota for anybody. He's completely open-minded about world progress, but his mind clamps shut when it involves his personal behavior, which can be unexpectedly conservative. You can see that his liberalism has its boundaries.

Aquarians despise lying and cheating, and they avoid borrowing and lending. They'll give you money as a gift, but don't ask them for a loan. Did you ever try to touch Aquarian Jack Benny for a fast fifty? Jack may surprise you by saying yes, but be sure you pay him back promptly. A broken promise or bad debt can put a wide crack in your friendship. Aquarians keep their word and pay their bills, and they expect others to do the same. Charge accounts don't normally excite them and credit cards can frighten them. All this love of honesty, however, can sometimes be distorted into questionable behavior. As much as he hates hypocrisy and double-dealing, the Aquarian can somehow answer questions so cleverly that he gives a false impression. Yet he'll be outspokenly indignant if he catches anyone else guilty of such a delicate nuance of deception. He'll seldom tell an outright lie, but he can fool you in very subtle ways, which is hardly the essence of the honesty he so constantly preaches. His un-relenting search for truth and the desire to hide his own motives are incompatible traits, and the Aquarian must eventually face this inconsistency if he's going to learn the real truth about himself.

Aquarians get credit for being idealists, perhaps too much credit, for true idealism consists of blind faith and optimism, and the Uranian is too shrewd to fool himself with lost causes for long. He knows that most dreams are illusions, like the rainbow he has examined so closely and still loves. Tradition and authority leave him unimpressed. He'll politely respect them, but they won't stop his com-pulsive drive to uncover fallacies, distortions and illogical assumptions.

His mind and body must both be as free as the wind. To try to pin down the Aquarian is to try to stabilize the butterfly, to stuff a spring breeze into a closet or confine a winter gale in a bottle. It can't be done, and besides, who in the world would want to try? Though he's so far ahead of his time that you have trouble catching his viewpoint immediately, it's still worthwhile to make the attempt. You'll always come away a little wiser, if a little bewildered. His astrological flower is the daffodil—and now you know the derivation of the word "daffy."

The soul of the water bearer is constantly torn asunder by Uranus, the unpredictable and violent planet of change which lets him see ahead with electric blue clarity to the future. Aquarius belongs to mankind. He represents its truest hopes and its deepest ideals. Even his metal, uranium, is not really a metal, but a radioactive, metallic chemical, found only in combinations. It's important in atomic research, and it can undergo continuous fission. The magnetic majesty of eight bolts of brilliant lightning reflected in the Aquarian sapphire can split open his secrets for those who seek to know him—but only for an instant can you see into his lonely heart, long ago infused with Saturn's ancient wisdom—unless you too live in tomorrow.

Famous Aquarius Personalities

Francis Bacon
Tallulah Bankhead
John Barrymore
Jack Benny
Shelley Berman
George Burns
Lewis Carroll
Katharine Cornell
Charles Darwin
Jimmy Dean
Charles Dickens
Jimmy Durante
Thomas Edison
Mia Farrow
Clark Gable
Galileo

Langston Hughes
Jack Lemmon
Abraham Lincoln
Charles Lindbergh
Somerset Maugham
Jeanne Moreau
Paul Newman
Louis Nizer
Kim Novak
S. J. Perelman
Leontyne Price
Ronald Reagan
Vanessa Redgrave
Norman Rockwell
Franklin Roosevelt
Ann Sothern

Adlai Stevenson

The AQUARIUS Man

All this time the Guard was looking at her,
first through a telescope,
then through a microscope,
and then through an opera-glass.
At last he said, "You're traveling the wrong way,"
and shut up the window . . .

To wade bravely smack dab into the center of the problem, don't expect an Aquarian male to behave the way people in love are supposed to behave. If you do, you're in for quite a jolt, maybe even a series of jolts. When it comes to friendship, he's all you could ask for in a pal or a confidant. Love? Well, as an Aquarian I once knew said, "Anybody can have a girl. But love is something else again." That was an astute observation. It's "something else," all right, with Aquarians.

It's when he acts as though he doesn't like you that he's close to being hooked, and the reason is elementary—simple logic. The Aquarian water bearer likes everybody. Everyone is his friend. He'll even refer to his worst enemy as "my friend." So it means something when he says he doesn't like someone. Just what it means may take some study. The various nuances can be complicated.

An Aquarian man doesn't want to reveal his true feelings, in spite of his favorite pastime of penetrating the feelings of others. His own reactions and motives are complex, and he intends to keep them that way for the pure pleasure of fooling you. Many strange experiences will come to this man, through both love and friendship, and he'll scrutinize each one avidly. Until you get him to the altar, you're just another experience, another experiment, hard as that may be to take. Don't sniffle. He can be tricked, for all his caution. But before you start tricking him, you'd better try to understand how to cope with his unique outlook about people.

He's a group man, and teamwork comes naturally to

him. Aquarius understands the fair play rules of sports as if he had invented them, and he carries these rules into his personal relationships. His interests are scattered all over the place. That's because his love of people is so impersonal; he gives a certain value to everyone he meets, while the rest of us save such efforts for only the very special people in our lives. To an Aquarian, everyone is special. And I mean everyone. Even those he hasn't met yet. Few Uranus men are either selfish or petty. When he does show those qualities, a gentle reminder that he's being narrow-minded will bring him around. Aquarians just can't stand to be called narrow-minded.

He responds to unusually high ideals, thanks to his rigid moral code (though you'd better understand that it's his own code, which may not necessarily reflect or correspond to the one accepted by society in general). He'll almost surely lead a life of change, controversy and unexpected events. Yet there will often be moments of perfect tranquility with him, impossible to find with any other Sun sign. Once he's over the shock that he's allowed himself to become interested in one woman above all of mankind, he can be an extremely considerate lover. The danger area is before he's over the shock. Since he's so accustomed to neglecting his own problems in the interest of the majority, hopefully some of this attitude will rub off on his love life. Don't count on it, though. The chances are just as good that he'll suddenly realize he's devoting his complete loyalty to you when there are all those other nameless faces out there who need him. Then he may lean over backwards to prove to himself that he hasn't lost his love for his friends and the rest of humanity by being attached to just one person.

Forever analyzing, the Aquarian man will frequently ask himself, "I wonder what she meant by that?" He won't rest until he finds it out either. A puzzle drives him simply wild and don't be fooled by his nonchalance. When he senses something is hidden, he just won't sleep at night until he's unraveled the mystery and penetrated the veil. There's always the possibility that he might be disappointed in what he finds, so make sure it's worth discovering. If it isn't, he'll have no qualms about making it painfully evident—and off he'll go to unravel a new veil.

The girl who wants to land him eventually has first to intrigue him. An open book will never pique his curiosity.

He's attracted to closed pages, the more tightly closed, the better to arouse his detective instinct. When a female either ignores him or keeps her own counsel, in the beginning at least, his eyes will open a little wider and he'll get an alert expression, amazingly like that of a bloodhound on the scent of something missing. Why is she so emotional? (You can be emotional, you see, as long as you don't explain why.) Is she really so changeable or is it an act? Why does she wear all that perfume and make-up and such low-cut dresses, and then get insulted when those Leos and Sagittarians and Scorpios whistle at her in front of the drugstore? Does she want male advances or doesn't she? Is she a puritan or promiscuous? What makes her tick? As he probes and questions and examines, the girl is at first flattered, naturally—but when she sees he's just as intently curious about the waitress who just served them (not to mention the bus boy), she begins to cool somewhat. Feeling like an insect trapped under a scientist's cold eye isn't exactly calculated to cause the heart to flutter in any feminine bosom. So she finally drifts (or runs) away to a more fiery or earthy male, and the Aquarian sadly sighs for an instant or two before he begins his next romantic investigation. (If some new invention or unique idea hasn't aroused his interest first. In which case the next female research project must wait.)

Aquarian men can be touchingly gentle and docile, but you'd better tie a bright blue electric string around your finger to remind you that his surface calmness is a mirage. So is his apparent pliability. He won't tolerate an ounce of opportunism from a female. If he thinks he's being exploited, that unpredictable Uranian charm can vanish so quickly you'll think Cary Grant has turned into James Cagney, poised to throw a grapefruit-half in your face. The frightening thing is that an extremely upset Aquarian is perfectly capable of such shocking action. What's even more frightening is that you may forgive him. Don't. At least, not more than once. He admires a woman who holds her ground, if she's not too masculine about it, and if she lets him fly hither and yon, unencumbered by mushy promises and tearful accusations. As for that grapefruit, it's only fair to point out that Aquarians are usually most gallant with the fair sex. But sometimes they can forget to distinguish between the sexes in the throes of excitement.

Couple that with the Uranus unpredictability, and it does add up to a possible squirt of grapefruit juice in the eye.

There's always an excellent possibility that an Aquarian will achieve some sort of prestige during his lifetime. If it's only a trophy for stickball or a brass plaque for being the tallest man in Succatosh County he's sure to be honored with some kind of recognition. It could be something as splendid as winning the Nobel Prize. Lots of Aquarians achieve such distinctions. (On the other hand, a large percentage of disturbed Aquarians are weekly visitors to a head shrinker. It may be kind of tricky to tell the difference.)

Some Uranus-ruled men have a fetish for cleanliness. You may bump into one who shrieks if anyone uses his towel or breathes on his oatmeal. Back of this is an almost neurotic fear of germs and illness. The Aquarian isn't above letting his phobias trail over into his romantic life, when they can serve a purpose, though he may do so unconsciously. Don't be surprised if he complains that he's allergic to your eye shadow and it makes him sneeze. Uranians have a way of developing allergies to things they'd rather avoid, and they can even fool the doctors, let alone innocent, unsuspecting girls.

He's not the type to woo you with extravagant gestures. He's as likely to pull up a dandelion and toss it at you as bring you an orchid. To be honest, more likely. He won't present you with mink coats and diamonds. But life with him can still be glamorous, even without the mink. There's the well-known story about Helen Hayes and her husband, Charles MacArthur. When they first met, he handed her a bowl of peanuts and said, "I wish they were emeralds." Many years and many dollars later, he gave her a cluster of glittering emeralds with the remark, "I wish they were peanuts." I don't know if MacArthur was an Aquarian, but Uranus was certainly prominent in his natal chart. That's exactly the kind of unexpected glory you'll know with an Aquarian lover. Who needs mink?

Now let's face the worst fact courageously. No flinching or wishful thinking. Here it is. Unlike Cancer, Capricorn, Leo and Libra, Aquarians don't take to marriage like a baby takes to candy. To be truthful, most of them avoid it as long as it's humanly possible. A rare Aquarian male will be enticed into a shower of shoes and rice at an early age, but it doesn't happen often enough for the statistics to be encouraging. The way the impasse usually starts is that the Aquarian makes beautiful, wonderful, glorious friendship the basis of the love. (Easier to slide away from later, my dear.) They choose a girl who's also a chum, and who can keep up with the Aquarian interests, including Mickey Mantle's batting average, crossword puzzles, Arabian horses, fireflies on the Mississippi and the Dead Sea Scrolls. Why? That's easy. With so much to talk about, there's less time for lovemaking, which can get him seriously involved and committed. His ideal is the female who is his friend, and who doesn't make heavy emotional demands on him. Where do we go from here? Nowhere, usually.

Aquarian men find it difficult to relax in physical expressions of love. That first goodnight kiss may be a long time materializing. Admittedly, it's often well worth waiting for, and the suspense makes it even more special. But he'll cling to the illusion that he's involved in a nice, safe platonic friendship long after such a palsy-walsy relationship has become impossible for you.

Even after he's mustered the courage to say "I love you," he'll avoid the issue of marriage with every excuse in the book. When those run out, he can think up some pretty imaginative new ones. He'll patiently explain that he can't support you in the manner you deserve, his parents need him at home, or he's not good enough for you. If that doesn't work, he'll claim that the future is too uncertain, what with the threats of nuclear destruction and all. What if his boss sends him to Alaska next year? You might die of pneumonia up there, and he would be grief-stricken the rest of his life. You think he can't top that? One Aquarian man I know was engaged for twelve years to a girl he wouldn't marry because "she would have to sacrifice a great career on Broadway." The fact that the girl had never set foot on a stage in her life was beside the point. *He* thought she had talent. Someday, a producer might just discover her. Then how would she feel if he had held her back by marrying her? Worse yet, how would he feel? Guilty. Just plain selfish and guilty. It's not surprising that this poor female finally escaped to a more positive rival.

But all is not lost. Though it's true that most Aquarians wed late, they do eventually wed—usually. It normally happens after the last bachelor friend has sailed away to a Bermuda honeymoon, and the Aquarian wakes up to realize that here is a mystery other people have solved that he hasn't even investigated. Naturally, he can't stand that, so pop goes the proposal! Suddenly, of course. Uranus, you know.

In the early stages, you may think he needs a lesson and decide to let him think he's lost you to a more aggressive suitor. Let me warn you that you're likely to stay lost. Your broken-hearted Uranian is not nearly as apt to come charging after you with the fire of possession in his eye as he is to shed a couple of quiet tears and say, "Well, I guess the best man won." He'll resign himself to a life without you with insulting ease. He's even liable to ask the unbearable question, "Can't we still be friends?" If you say no emphatically, he'll probably just shrug dejectedly and slowly walk away. If you say yes—well, you're right back where you started—friends.

Jealousy isn't his cup of eggnog. He'll trust you until you show him you can't be trusted. Not because he's trusting by nature, but because his analytical dissection has already satisfied him about your character. Unless there are marked afflictions in his natal chart, he's not capable of unfounded suspicion and possessiveness. If he does have a rare stab of jealousy, you'll never know it if he can help it. He will rarely, if ever, be physically unfaithful himself, mostly because the whole subject of sex, though it's interesting, doesn't consume him. An occasional Aquarian may spend a great deal of time intensely pondering sex, but if you know one of these, you can safely assume there's a heavy Scorpio influence in his natal chart. (And chances are even this type won't pursue it actively and openly.)

Once an Aquarian has chosen a mate, he figures he can concentrate on more important things. He can relax and investigate the boy-girl or man-woman relationship at his own leisure in his own private laboratory (which isn't a bad possibility for its eventual chance of success when you stop to think about it).

Uranian sex is part of a larger image or ideal. Should a temptation to engage in illicit romance arise (illicit in his eyes, that is), he'll usually end the affair abruptly, though it may hurt him deeply, rather than continue what he considers to be a dishonest relationship. The situation that made him feel guilty could be almost anything, from the disapproval of your parents or conflicting religions to an old boy friend not completely discarded, a promise he

made to himself at the age of eight, or something he once
read in a book. But whatever it is, it will somehow have to
be adjusted and resolved before he'll ever renew the
closeness, even if the love is as fated as that of Victoria
and Albert. The Aquarian will always let his heart break
silently, lest his friends hear and ask questions.

He's capable of waiting until he's ninety to claim you,
even if you feel that's a bit long to wait for consummation.
The worst of it is that he'll never give a reason for the
break. That's for him to know and you to find out. He'll
perversely let you think it was just a fantasy from the
beginning, and hold back the real truth that it was genuine
for some hazy future day of forgiveness and reconciliation.
It can be pretty cruel, but that's the way he plays the game.

Your only comfort is the knowledge that he's suffering in
his own way, too. How will you know that? Read "How
to Recognize Aquarius" again. He has his subtle ways of
telegraphing his feelings, and they can be enormously
frustrating—especially when his unique, private communication signals a green go light while he publicly keeps holding out a red stop light until he's ready to switch. It can
make for some nasty romantic traffic snarls. It's hard on
the pedestrian, but he's in the driver's seat, so there's not a
lot you can do—except perhaps think up another mystery
to tempt him with, or maybe shake him a little with some
smashing success to make him curious to talk with you
again—like being the first woman to orbit Venus.

Not that such a feat will change his feelings. If he really
loves you, he'll love you even if you don't orbit any farther
than to the corner delicatessen, but it might interfere with
his fixed strategy. You may gather from all this that a
Uranus man can be pretty stubborn when it comes to love.
You would be so right. His fixity in affectionate matters
can drive you straight into the booby hatch or drive you
to someone else in desperation. That's a big fat waste of
time. He's not jealous, remember? Or he won't show it
if he is. Besides, with his darned Uranian intuition, he'll
know it's all an act. Because he knows what makes you
tick. Don't forget, he studied you for a long time. About the
only thing you can do is hope you'll still be attractive at
ninety or else start practicing those Venus orbits.

Putting the shoe on the other foot, an Aquarian can
arouse a heap of possessiveness in you when the tables are
turned. Don't let it throw you off balance. Thanks to the

everlasting Uranus proclivity for friendship, whenever and wherever he finds it, there may be times when you won't know where he is, even after you're married and you should. Just tell yourself that, no matter how late he sits up with a friend, it's only his normal curiosity at work, his never-ending interest in people. If the friend is a woman, pretend you didn't notice. In all honesty, he most likely didn't. You can expect the truth when you ask him a direct question. But if you doubt him and ask again, he'll figure you don't want the truth. To punish you, he'll make up the wildest story he can dream up (and he can dream up some pretty wild ones). You may regret your suspicions when you spend a few hours in abject misery wondering if he really did tell that redhead she was gorgeous. (That's after he told you he didn't even remember talking to her and you said, "Ha! I just bet you don't remember.") He honestly didn't, but you asked for details, so he gladly obliged with some purely imaginary ones to teach you a lesson. You'll learn fast.

Don't be hurt when he's in one of his solitary moods and prefers to be alone with his silent dreams. He'll return to share them with you, all the more warm and tender for his spiritual retreat and anything that warms him up should definitely be encouraged.

He may not be the best breadwinner around, but he's capable of inventing something beneficial to the world or being the first man to land on Mars. He'll feel right at home there, too. There's always a surprise just around the corner with an Aquarian husband, even when the budget is shaky. Naturally, there are a few Uranian men who are wealthy, even millionaires, but a high income bracket is seldom a burning ambition. All the rich Aquarians you see probably stumbled on it. It's certain they didn't greedily grasp for it. If he has a fat bank book, the chances are it gained weight while he was attempting to improve some product or idea for the good of humanity in general—or he's saved it to support his eccentric old age. Who knows? He might want to take a trip in a time machine someday, and he wants to be sure to have the fare. Most of the time he'll be reasonable about money, but save when you can, and don't run up charge accounts. He'll never recover from sheer extravagance on your part. Sometimes he can surprise you with a burst of generosity, but he won't go overboard, unless he has an Aries, Leo, Sagittarius or Pisces ascendant. Even then, he won't be a big butter and egg man.

The children will find him the greatest listener on the block. He'll be fascinated at the perfect breath control of the wolf when he blew down the three little pigs' pad— and curious about how the old witch pickled the poisoned apple that put the whammy on Snow White. A small boy's trouble learning how to strike a home run and a little girl's tears over a broken doll are simply the problems of a couple of pals in trouble to an Aquarian father. He's a whiz at complicated arithmetic questions, too.

Don't let your career make you neglect to feed him or sew on his buttons. Don't encourage your girl friends to camp on his couch or tie up the telephone for hours, and don't get engrossed in TV or a novel when he wants you to find his old soft ball in the attic or pull a splinter out of his finger. He married you for several reasons. Though romance may play its part, the most important reason was to have you around—so he would always have someone to mash his baked potato, cross-stitch his buttonholes, find his lost articles and operate on an occasional splinter. He won't cotton to your letting television, reading or female chums interfere with those duties. His idea of a good wife and mother is quite simple: a woman who keeps at it almost constantly. Even the more liberal Aquarian husbands will frown on a glamorous gadabout. But you won't mind it too much. He's so full of interesting surprises himself you won't need soap operas, women's magazines and tête-à-têtes with girl friends to keep your mind and emotions challenged. (He may be about all the challenge you can take.) You can always catch up on the female gossip and such when he's engrossed in some new project and gets a little absent-minded about what you're doing. But just be sure to be there when he has a sore finger, because he can be a real sorehead when he's neglected.

Strangely, since he's so realistic about most things, the Aquarian will never forget his first love. (Not the first date, but the first girl who ever gave him a rainbow. There's a difference.) Uranians frequently marry childhood sweethearts years later, or cling to a faded illusion. An Aquarian can usually describe his first love in detail, which can be annoying to a wife. The solution is to be that first love. You may have to wait a long time to wear orange blossoms, but at least you won't be replaced by a ghost. Who else could turn peanuts into emeralds or vice versa, never mind a little grapefruit juice in the eye? Despite his general romantic clumsiness, he can come up with sudden phrases which could only have been invented by the angels. He can forget your wedding anniversary, but he'll bring you violets in January. Christmas? Who says it has to be on December 25th? It can be any time you want it to be. He may go for days or weeks or months without a single word of romance or affection. Then some morning while you're slicing his blueberry pie, he'll look deep into your eyes and ask gently, "Do you know how beautiful you are?" There will be something about the way he says it that will make your knees weak.

Jingle bells on the seashore, birthdays at dawn, Valentine's Day on Halloween, rainbows at midnight. Pin a red heart on an orange pumpkin, roll Easter eggs in the snow, light the candles on the cake on top of a ferris wheel— you're in love with an Aquarian, didn't you know? I wish you a Frank Merriwell ending. But be careful. You can get lost out there in Wonderland.

The AQUARIUS Woman

But Alice had got so much into the way
of expecting nothing but out-of-the-way things to happen
that it seemed quite dull and stupid
for life to go on in the common way . . .

Put cats in the coffee, and mice in the tea—
And welcome Queen Alice with thirty times three!

The safest way to enter into romance with an Aquarian female is to remember she's as paradoxical in love as she is in everything else. That way, you won't be expecting Priscilla Alden and get Pocahontas.

This girl has all the faithfulness of the fixed signs when she's in love, but she also has the detachment and lack of emotion of the air element. It's possible to have a happy relationship with the Uranus woman if you leave her free to pursue her myriad interests and circulate among her friends. Never try to tie her to the stove or the bedpost. Ask the man who's tried. She can suddenly decide to study ballet, meditate in the mountains or join the Peace Corps. Remember the story of the princess with the long, golden hair who lived high in a tower? That's the Aquarius female. Cutting off her flowing tresses won't change her any more than it did in the fairy tale. She dreams different dreams than you or I. She hears a distant drummer—and follows a star most of us have never seen.

She belongs to everyone, and yet to no one. Her love can be tender and inspired, but there will always be a vaguely elusive quality about it, like a half-remembered song. You can hum the melody, but the lyrics keep slipping away. The Aquarian girl's demand for freedom is insistent, but her allegiance to anyone who can accept romance within such limits is boundless. Here's something you'll like: She won't be terribly interested in your bank book (unless Cancer or Capricorn or Taurus is on her ascendant). Money is never the prime consideration of the typical Aquarian woman. She won't care if you're not the richest man in town, but she'll expect you to be respected in some way for your intellectual achievements. Dr. Christian Barnard and his heart transplants or Wernher von Braun and his rockets interest her far more than J. Paul Getty and his billions.

When you set out to catch this butterfly in your net, remember that she'll never spend her unpredictable life with a man who isn't true to himself. Her own code of ethics may be as weird as anything you've ever come across, and quite different from the accepted codes of society, but she lives up to it totally. She'll understand that your rules may also be highly individual. That's fine with her, but don't compromise those rules. If you're looking for a passion flower, you've picked the wrong daisy. Passion is not her forte if she's a typical Aquarian. She'll think physical love is pleasant enough, if it's not overemphasized. In other words, she can take it or leave it alone. Uranus females can respond to lovemaking with a haunting, deep intensity, but if you prefer to keep it platonic for long periods of time, that's all right, too. Like all Aquarians, she may have an unconscious fear that desire for one person will imprison the spirit in some way, and keep her from being true to her one great love—freedom. Freedom to experiment and investigate and freedom to give time to humanity. Also freedom to pursue her rather kicky, off-beat fancies.

She's an ideal girl if you're planning a political, scientific or educational career. You couldn't do better, unless you happen to run across an Aquarian girl with adverse planetary positions in her natal chart who enjoys shocking people by walking barefoot down Main Street or smoking big black cigars on buses. There are some pretty wild, way-out Uranian females here and there. But the average girl born under the sign of the water bearer is a social delight. She's graceful, witty, bright as a penny, and extremely adaptable to all forms of society, high and low and in the middle.

Her lack of suspicion under normal circumstances is a special bonus. A traveling salesman should find his dream girl in the typical Aquarian female. If she actually catches you being unfaithful, it will cause a deep wound to her sensitive nature. You'll know it the minute you look into those strange, dreamy eyes. But she won't suspect you without cause, and she'll rarely doubt your word. The typical Uranus woman will never check up on you after you leave, phone you at the office, inspect your handkerchiefs for lipstick stains or look for blonde hairs caught in your cuff link. Deception will have to be brought forcibly to her attention; she won't go out looking for it. Before you give her too much credit, consider that her lack of passionate jealousy is due to something more than strength of character. First of all, she probably dissected your psyche under a microscope before she gave you a second glance. Besides, she has so many outside interests and so many people who turn her on to talk with, there's not much time for her to worry about what you're doing when you're out of sight. Out of sight can often mean out of mind for Aquarians of both sexes. Absence seldom makes the Uranus heart grow fonder. Occasionally, an Aquarian woman will suffer a promiscuous or flirtatious mate, because there's something she needs which she can find only with him, so she looks the other way. On the other hand, if she doesn't really need you, that moral strength will work in reverse at the first actual proof of infidelity. She'll simply walk away. Don't try to kindle the embers, they're stone cold dead. Of course, you can still be friends. Why not?

She's willing. It never embarrasses an Aquarian girl to be chummy with ex-lovers or husbands. She's forgotten the past and wiped the slate clean of memories.

There is one peculiar and notable exception to the rule. Like the Uranus man, the Uranian female will remember the first true and honest love for a lifetime. Only the first, however. Are you wondering whether that Aquarius girl you once knew still remembers you? The answer lies in her definition of love. It could have something to do with the first boy who gave her a bunch of sweet peas when she was nine—the boy who walked her through the park in the rain—or the one with the funny ears who knew the clown at the circus, and used to feed her peanuts.

Uranus women involved in extra-marital affairs are rare. They can be tempted in exceptional situations, but a dishonest relationship goes against their chemistry. It won't be long until an undercover romance is broken off for good. Yet, there are many Aquarian divorcees. There's a reason. If a situation becomes intolerable, the Uranian nature turns cold suddenly. They can disappear overnight, and never look back. They don't seek or enjoy divorce, but it isn't the shock to them it is to their more sentimental sisters. Uranus rules change, you know. Since she's such an individualist, with a list of friends several miles long, the Aquarian female never hesitates to make her way alone if the need arises.

Expect her to probe into your heart until you haven't a secret left, or a dream that hasn't been analyzed. But don't try to dissect her private thoughts. That's not the way the game is played with Aquarians. She'll keep her motives hidden, and sometimes take a perverse pleasure in deliberately confusing you. She'll usually be truthful to a fault, but remember, with an Aquarian, telling a lie is one thing. Refraining from telling the whole story is another.

It's comforting to know that an Aquarian girl is pretty cagey with a buck. That is, it's comforting to know unless you're planning to hit her for a loan. She might say yes a time or two, but if you let your credit rating slip, she can be colder than the guy at the bank when you skip your car payment. On the rare occasions when she accepts a small loan herself, you'll get back every penny with no stalling, excuses or feminine wiles, if she's a typical Uranus female. As for every man's nightmare of charge accounts, you'll have little worry on that score. Aquarian women are uncomfortable about owing money. Bad debts don't fit in with the Uranus code.

Her appearance is puzzling. Most Aquarian women are lovely, with a haunting, wistful beauty. But they're changeable. They can give an impression of smooth whipped cream, then suddenly switch to salty pizza as quickly as a bright, blue, zig-zag bolt of Uranian electricity. Next to Librans, Aquarian females are often the most beautiful women in the zodiac. At the very least, they're interesting-looking. The Aquarian manner of dressing can stop you dead in your tracks. There are a few of them who could grace the cover of a fashion magazine, but the average Aquarian girl is anything but conventional about her costumes. She can wear some outfits a gypsy would envy, and her naked individuality can produce some mighty unique combinations. She'll usually be the first to wear a new fad, no matter how zany it is, yet she can also stick to Grandma's styles—even great-grandma's styles. With typical Aquarian indifference, she'll mix yesterday's lace snood with today's metallic jump suit, and the effect can be a little startling. She'll wear her lace nightgown to a formal banquet, ostrich feathers to the supermarket, bell bottom slacks to the opera, sneakers to the theater, diamonds when she visits the zoo—and top it all off with a faded Mother Hubbard she picked up in a thrift shop.

Your Aquarian girl will probably have an unusual way of wearing her hair. Her tresses are as unpredictable as her personality. They can be worn braided, pig-tailed, pinned in a bun, flowing down like a waterfall, short as a marine's, in Mary Pickford curls or as straight as a poker. One thing you can depend on. Her hair won't look like the hair of any other female on this planet.

A conversation with her can be remarkable, to say the least. She has charming manners, and usually behaves in a timid, almost reserved way. Then comes one of those sudden Uranus urges, and out will pop a remark with absolutely no relation to what anyone is saying. You'll be talking about the fluctuations of the stock market, and she'll interrupt out of nowhere with: "Did you know that Woodrow Wilson, Jack Kennedy, Herbert Hoover, Harry Truman, Calvin Coolidge, Benjamin Harrison, Franklin and Theodore Roosevelt and William McKinley all have double letters in their names?" There's only one way to answer a question like that. Tell her she missed Millard

Fillmore, Ulysses Grant and Thomas Jefferson. Then gently, but firmly, lead the discussion back to the stock market. Other minds may progress in fairly logical steps, but hers zigs into tomorrow, then zags back into today with no more sense of direction than a flash of lightning. Now and then she'll toss off an unexpectedly poignant phrase. You'll ask her what she thinks of space travel and she'll answer, "When I was a little girl, I thought the stars were holes in the floor of heaven where the light shone through." If she's in a different mood, you'll say that melted snowmen make you sad, and she'll counter with: "A melted snowman is just a pile of slush, Charlie." First misty—then practical. First timid—then rowdy. Aquarian women will rudely ridicule flying saucers, then tell you a story about a polka-dotted elf on a windowsill. Never talk down to an Aquarian female. She'll resent not being considered your equal, and an unsympathetic attitude will cause her to retreat and become unapproachable.

Since Uranus rules the future, you might imagine that these girls would be natural mothers. Children do, after all, belong to the future. But the average Aquarian woman may be bewildered by motherhood in the beginning. She has to adjust to devoting all her attention and energy exclusively to one human being for a period of time, when she's used to spreading herself far and wide, and this can take some practice. Her natural aloofness may make it difficult for her to demonstrate warm affection outwardly. The typical Aquarian mother is devoted to her offspring, but also somewhat detached toward them. But she'll probably be the most willing PTA worker in the neighborhood. She'll talk happily for hours with their small friends on their own level without patronizing them, and she'll give up her afternoons to work for a school project. The children will learn the lessons of brotherhood and humanity from her by observation. Aquarian mothers are never fiercely protective of their children. They take a tolerant view of the most startling confession. A Uranus woman will seldom punish a child for telling the truth, no matter what he's done. With her unprejudiced viewpoint, she'll gain the complete confidence of her little ones. She's great at reassuring young minds about everything from monsters hiding under the bed to the pain of being ignored in the playground. She can turn their tears to laughter in minutes. Your children will find her jolly fun, a little helter-skelter, relaxed about housework, helpful with homework and gentle when they're ill. She won't smother them with affection, and she'll seldom nag. Maybe Tommy didn't wash his hands the third time he was told, but she's more interested in what he learned in science class.

We may be a little ahead of ourselves. Even though Uranus likes to reverse the existing orders of things, before your Aquarian girl becomes a mother she has to become a wife. And before she becomes your wife, you'll have to convince her that marriage isn't synonymous with Alcatraz. She won't exactly rush into matrimony. She's in no hurry to take your name until she's weighed you, sorted you, tested you, and found out what makes you tick. The opinions of her friends and family will mean nothing, though she may ask them what they think out of curiosity. She has her own yardstick for measuring you. Assuming you pass her test, marriage to an Aquarian girl can be confusing. She'll listen pleasantly when you give her advice, but there's something in the Uranian make-up that prevents her from following directions explicitly. She can't stick to the recipe when she bakes one of her angel food cakes anymore than she can park the car exactly where you told her to. There's some kind of a snag in her thinking that causes her to believe just a little twist will improve anything. But she'll smile agreeably as she goes on her own sweet way. There's a constant urge to experiment with a different way to make the coffee, fill her pen, fasten her ice skates or cross the street. She'll wear a sweater backwards, mix her brandy with milk, arrange flowers in a fish bowl, rinse her hair in shaving lotion or make a rock garden on your desk. But don't ask her why. She doesn't know herself. The unique and unusual is her wave-length, that's all.

Because her nature is so impersonal, expressions of deep feeling won't come easily. Except for those sudden remarks that sound likes a combination of Robert Frost and Yogi Berra, she has few words with which to express her love, and her pattern of physical passion is woven closely with threads connected to the mind and soul. Although the unique Uranus outlook leads some Aquarian girls into peculiar attachments, once they find the right mate their marriages are usually models of happiness.

Your Aquarian woman can float through her days and nights with all the grace of a proud swan, but she may behave like a clumsy bear in romantic situations. The line between friendship and love is often all but invisible to Aquarius. Love songs about people who only have eyes for each other strike her as silly. There are so many miracles in the world for eyes to behold, it seems to her a terrible waste for two pairs of them to do nothing but gaze into each other's depths. She'll be glad to let you take her hand and walk beside her as she looks with happy delight on the sunrise, an antique car, the milkman's horse, a yellow garbage pail, a stuffed owl or a red balloon caught in a church steeple. But don't distract her with too much togetherness. Let her wander through her wonderland alone when she chooses, and she'll never question your pinochle games with the boys.

The quickest ways to lose her are to show jealousy, possessiveness or prejudice; to be critical, stuffy or ultra-conservative. You'll also have to like her friends, who will come in odd, assorted sizes and shapes.

She's susceptible to sudden flashes of inspiration, and her intuition is remarkable. Her judgment may not seem sound or practical at first, because she sees months and years ahead. The Aquarian girl lives in tomorrow, and you can only visit there through her. What she says will come true, perhaps after many delays and troubles, but it will come true. I suppose, after all, that's the most special thing about your February woman. She's a little bit magic.

The AQUARIUS Child

The dream-child moving through a land
Of wonders wild and new,
In friendly chat with bird or beast—
And half believe it true.

According to Mother Goose, if your offspring is dressed in blue, he's made of snips and snails and puppy-dog tails. It baby is wearing pink, she's made of sugar and spice, and everything nice. But if he or she was born in February, dress him in an aquamarine cap and electric blue booties and forget that old rhyme. This infant is made of the raw material of Uranus, and he's going to make you chase him into tomorrow.

He's a quivering, sensitive, stubborn, independent mass of invention and electrical impulses. Even if he has a slow and careful Taurus ascendant, his mental processes will be as fast as Uranian lightning. His thoughts will vibrate like high frequency radio beams, and as he grows up, you may feel like sending out an S.O.S. yourself.

Every mother and father think their child is special—different and unique, compared to other youngsters. But this one is just ridiculous. Lots of parents of a young Aquarian puzzle whether to send him out on the farm, where he won't frighten neighbors, or let the word casually get around that he may win the Pulitzer prize someday. Which route should you take? You have a problem. Yes, you do. The Pulitzer is possible, but my advice would be to try the farm for a few summers and watch. Observe. Wait. He's liable to invent a new plow, or just eat them out of house and home. It depends. There's never a cut and dried rule with Aquarians.

I know one New York mother who just called her Uranian son "the Bronx Wonder" and let it go at that. At least her relatives and neighbors were as mystified as she was. Nobody knew if the nickname meant he had three heads or he was headed for the Hall of Fame. As it turned out, he was a pretty good basketball player, and most folks thought that's why he had the tag. But they shouldn't have been so hasty. The story's not over yet. He's presently rotating between composing the score for a musical which may go on Broadway or in the wastebasket, playing bit parts in detective films, and making himself available for TV commercials. (The kind that need men from Mars types for flying saucer approaches on soft-sell automobile spots.) He's also working on an invention in his bedroom (between watching the Mets play and eating pickle sandwiches), but since he won't tell anyone what it is, I can't give you any clues. He has a kind of thing about clocks and watches, so it may have something to do with a time machine (a common Aquarian obsession). Well, we'll see. There's no rush. Lots of Aquarians don't break loose and shower electric sparks of genius on a waiting world until they're a young fifty. It makes it all a little nervewracking, waiting around like that. Of course, there are quite a few

Aquarian child prodigies, but we're tangled up enough trying to figure out your average Aquarian youngster (and I use the term average loosely).

He may end up working for the FBI or a private eye outfit (he loves to figure out mysteries), and become an ordinary, sensible, conservative citizen. (Don't hold your breath, but it's a possibility.) We'd better concentrate on his tender years. That way, you'll have a fighting chance to guide this Uranus rocket in some kind of direction.

Until maturity has mellowed Uranian influences, and society has molded more conventional attitudes, an Aquarian youngster can be strongly negative. The immediate reaction to a command (or even a pleasant suggestion) is often an emphatic no. But let him think about it, mull it over, and it's surprising how many times his final reaction will be sensible—the answer he found by himself correct and acceptable.

These boys and girls can be calm and sweetly docile on the surface, but the north wind can turn them suddenly topsy turvy. (Except that, with an Aquarian, it could be turvy topsy. You can expect anything.) Unpredictable in their behavior, but lovable and often amusing, the February child can be quite a spinning propeller to contend with. I used that analogy because Aquarians and Uranus rule air flight, planes and Charles Lindbergh and things like that. Yet, these youngsters are so full of contradictions, instead of taking to flight naturally, many of them have a strange, unreasonable fear of planes and elevators—even electricity (also ruled by Uranus). It isn't easy to direct them or channel them. They have no idea where they're going, but they have definite ideas about how to get there.

Raising and teaching these "wonders" can be a big responsibility. Their minds combine fixed practicality with uncanny perception and sharp, probing logic. Mix it all up and it can be acutely embarrassing, like when your little Aquarian asks your best friend why she got her face lifted (she did)—or asks your Uncle Elmer why he cheated on his income tax in front of the Internal Revenue man (he did).

They love to do favors for friends. Buy your little Aquarian boy a brand new pair of boots and he's likely to wear them out the first day—smoothing down the snow to make it slick so the neighborhood kids can use their sleds.

Expect your February child to have a dream and hold it fast—until he gets another one. With a girl, it's likely to be a projection of herself as a prima ballerina, with a pure dedication to her art that would put Pavlova to shame, a thirst to be the first woman president or a hunger to follow in the footsteps of Madame Curie. With the boys, it could be an oceanographer, ichthyologist, archaeologist, anthropologist, an exterminator or a tree surgeon. Normal career choices like nurses, secretaries, clerks, salesmen, teachers, bankers and brokers are too mundane for the average Aquarian child's fantasies. He may have to settle for one eventually, but the original dream will be tucked under his left ear and not forgotten. It's eerie, but Aquarians can sometimes cause a thing to happen by simply concentrating on it and waiting.

You'll never know quite what to expect from day to day. This is a child who may not want to stay indoors when it rains. He'll be out with your best sterling silver tablespoon, digging a drain so the hill in back of the house won't wash away.

Remember the old verse you heard as a child that went, "The bear went over the mountain—the bear went over the mountain—the bear went over the mountain—to see what he could see. The other side of the mountain—the other side of the mountain—the other side of the mountain—was all that he could see." Your Aquarius youngster will have better luck. He'll find something there. Maybe it will be a pot of gold or just a new species of woodpecker, but none of his exploratory journeys will ever result in a dead end or a total loss.

I skipped over the infant stage because these children are never infants. They are born middle-aged. However, many of them do go through the toddler stage, and during that precarious period you might be wise to consider buying a seeing-eye dog. Keep the dog until your little Uranian is at least ten. He may have trouble navigating the block without an incident. Off on his own private cloud, he'll lope down the street in a fog, and ram right into a telephone pole or a mailbox. Aquarian absent-mindedness brings on twisted ankles, broken bones and the wrath of teachers. You may be torn between pride, when the school reports he or she is a budding genius—and shame, when you receive a note saying, "Oliver simply won't pay attention in class. He stares out the window all day and plays with

his two-way wrist watch." Or ".Gertrude refuses to concentrate. Instead of studying, she just sits there and flexes
her arches in those silly ballet slippers." A lecture to Oliver
and Gertrude will result in a shrug of bored impatience.
What's all the fuss about? He was trying to figure the
effect of the summer solstice on Greenwich Mean Time,
and she was wondering what makes a caterpillar turn into
a butterfly. To their minds, that's perfectly logical. Chee!
What a square school. Granted, they are on the right track.
But this may not be the century to prove it.

Teachers often complain that the Aquarian child refuses
to explain, step by step, how he arrived at his remarkable
answer to a complicated math problem before she finished
writing it on the blackboard. There's a good, sensible
reason. His Uranian intuition, that works by some kind
of unseen radio waves, forced his mind through those
steps so quickly he just can't remember. Almost all
Aquarian children were behind the delivery-room door
when memory was passed out. Forgetting their address is
frequent, forgetting their last name is uncomfortably possible, and forgetting what time to come home is par-for-the-
course. Your brilliant—and he most likely is—Uranus
youngster must be taught that his aim should encompass
more than being a human computer. He needs to learn the
importance of organizing his thoughts in logical order.
Otherwise, a potential genius, philosopher, engineer, scientist, doctor, lawyer—gardener or cab driver (the last two
if you're lucky) can turn into an eccentric adult, headed in
several directions at once, and end up going around in
interesting, but not very profitable, circles.

Encourage him to participate in physical activity or a
harmful inertia can take over and he'll daydream the hours
away. It often takes an emergency to spur Aquarian children to physical action, though they can have a great love
for sports. Mentally, they're speed demons. But the body
may be a bit slower, at least around the house. They may
have an empathy for birds, trees, nature and the seashore.
They'll always prefer their own independent discovery to
organized activity. You'll have to watch for a tendency to
say "I can't" to rationalize the urge to avoid responsibility.
The Aquarian child may take the path of least resistance
if you let him. Teach him that he's only fooling himself.
Let him make his own decisions, but encourage him to act
on them.

Unspoken tension can deeply disturb him. These young-sters can almost see into the souls of others, and hear thoughts which haven't even been audibly expressed, which can disturb them and leave lasting feelings of unhappiness. Better encourage tranquility and harmony, concentration and memory, if you don't want an eccentric, nervous, absent-minded bachelor or spinster with unfulfilled dreams on your hands in thirty years or so.

Be careful what you say and how you say it with Aquarian youngsters. Suggestions planted in these fertile, remarkably acute Uranian minds in childhood can take firm root and form fixed adult opinions. Undue emphasis on clean hands, repeated warnings, "Don't drink out of my glass, it's dirty," can cause the Aquarian youngster to grow up with exaggerated fears and carry his own goblet in his pocket when he goes visiting. Being so accident prone, you can imagine what will happen if he sits down suddenly with that goblet there. And he does do almost everything sud-denly.

Aquarian boys and girls have multitudes of friends. They make at least ten new ones per day, from the street cleaner to the truant officer and the ex-parachutist who runs the candy store. He might even bring home a little friend named Rockefeller for lunch someday, too, but don't let it shake you. You're not raising a social snob. He won't know him from the dog catcher. He's just an-other "pal."

Adolescent problems of romance may never bother you. In fact, the Aquarian child may have to be reminded which sex is which. Few of these youngsters are boy crazy or girl crazy. Just plain crazy is more of a possibility, especial-ly when they start wearing those weird clothes and parting their hair in such an odd way. This may be about the time his hidden love of poetry emerges, which should be encouraged. Your little Uranian has frogs in his pockets and stars in his eyes, but he's very special. He's a hu-manitarian. He loves people. Do you know how rare that is? As society moves into the Aquarian age, his un-prejudiced wisdom is leading us. Aquarian boys and girls have been chosen by destiny to fulfill the promise of to-morrow—frogs and stars, pickle sandwiches and all. Just nickname him the "Twentieth Century Wonder," and let the neighbors guess why.

The AQUARIUS Boss

"What sort of things do you remember best?"
Alice ventured to ask.
"Oh, things that happened
the week after next."

First of all, check again. Are you sure his birthday is late January or early February? Are you absolutely positive your boss is an Aquarian? Uranus-ruled executives are as rare as albino pandas. If you have one for a boss, you can't very well sell him to a zoo, but consider him a collector's item, anyway. Someday, he may be extremely valuable.

Seriously, the typical Aquarian would just about prefer starvation to the usual nine-to-five office routine. Most Aquarians dislike making decisions, they are uncomfortable giving orders, they have no particular desire to direct others and they're totally incompatible with stuffy board meetings, let alone stuffy vice presidents. This doesn't mean Aquarians are not competent bosses. Uranus is full of surprises, and the totally unqualified Aquarian boss who turns out to be absolutely indispensable is one of them.

When an occasional Aquarian wanders into an executive position, burdened by all the above negative qualifications, he simply pulls a couple of new tricks out of his bag. He may be absent-minded and forgetful, eccentric and unpredictable, by turns shy and then bold, but he also has a mind like a bear trap hidden behind those strange, vague eyes and that detached, distant attitude. Add to that a highly tuned, perceptive intuitiveness which makes you think he has a crystal ball tucked in a pocket. Throw in his uncanny ability to analyze, dissect and weigh the facts with insight as keen as a razor blade—and for good measure—his sure instinct in making a warm friend of everyone from the office boy to the firm's biggest customer. Back it up with the broad, liberal Uranus philosophy which sees miles into tomorrow, and catches the big picture in all its scope while others are floundering over details—and you see what I mean by surprises. Unfitted as the average Aquarian is for an executive role, he tosses off the job as casually as if he had been born to it, which he definitely was not.

There's the other side of the coin, too. He may possibly refer to you as "My secretary, Miss . . . ah . . . ah . . . Miss . . . uh . . . what was your name again?" He can be maddening when he plans complicated programs behind your back and springs them on you at the last minute. And I'm sure you've chafed under his frustrating habit of giving you a completely new and unexpected job to do, blithely neglecting to explain the reason behind the change. But confess now, under it all he really is rather a lovable old dear, isn't he? Most Aquarians are, once you get used to their peculiar ways, sudden changes and unexpected surprises. Also, I might add, their fixed opinions when they've made up their mind.

If I were you, I wouldn't try to borrow money from an Aquarian boss. If he's a typical Aquarian, he doesn't approve of people living beyond their income. Some Aquarians, of course, live in comfortable luxurious surroundings —but most of them are quite capable of living in one shabby room while they spend twenty hours a day promoting better housing for the poor. He won't be impulsive about giving raises, but then, he won't be stingy either. You'll get just about what you deserve with your Aquarian boss. No more and no less. He can be most generous when he thinks someone has done a top job beyond the call of duty. Make no mistake. He'll expect your best—your very best. Anything less brings the danger of being politely and kindly, but firmly dropped. Kerplunk—like that. An Aquarian has no use for people who goof off or give half a day's work for a full day's pay. To him, that's a form of dishonesty, and he hates dishonesty in approximately the same degree that a cat hates the water.

When it comes to your personal life, the Aquarian boss hasn't the slightest desire either to judge you or advise you. He does have a desire to know about it, however, and you may find it hard to escape that probing Uranus curiosity when it comes to your private affairs. But you can tell him anything at all without worrying that he'll be shocked. Nothing shocks him. He's the best student of human nature in the zodiac, and he'll never look down on you (anymore than he'll look up to you). Both your vices and your

virtues blend into an interesting and colorful pattern, as
far as he's concerned. He takes it all in stride, and it
doesn't make a ripple in his opinion of you. The town
drunk and the silly, giggling teenager are as much his
friends and as close to him as the president of the local
university and the state senator. You'll find literally no
prejudice or discrimination if he's a true Aquarian. In
other words, you're in danger of being fired if he catches
you stealing stamps or hiding an unfinished report in your
desk—but if he discovers you're a bigamist, that your
father served two terms in prison, your son smokes pot
or your wife practices yoga on the back porch in her birthday suit, he'll just shrug, figure it's your life and probably
defend you to your critics. The Aquarian boss won't be
bothered one whit if you're a conservative politically and
you paste a picture of Calvin Coolidge next to his painting
of Franklin Roosevelt. He won't bat an eye at the news
that you had to be poured into a taxi after the last office
party. Just don't cheat him, lie to him or—heaven forbid
—break your word to him. Promises and ethics and such
are where he falls into the narrow-minded category.

Unlike the Aries or Leo boss, he won't exert energy
trying to convince you that you're making a mistake in
voting for that man, dating that girl or wearing that color
tie. And, unlike the Cancer, Capricorn or Libra boss, he
won't hint and use persuasive strategy to change your
viewpoint. Live your life the way you choose and more
power to you for being an individualist is his creed. On
the other hand, don't ever attempt to dictate his personal
code to him, either. He won't show any anger, or probably even feel any. He may even smile and nod thought-
fully, with that faraway look in his eyes, but you might as
well talk to the wall. He'll listen to almost anybody. Listen.
That's all.

Although he forms his own code of ethics and keeps his
own counsel in relation to his personal and private life,
business decisions are another matter. He's very likely,
if he's like the average Uranian man, to request everyone's
opinion on projected procedures—and sometimes even ask
a subordinate to make the final decision. There's a method
to this madness, and it's not the same as with the indecisive Libran. Aquarius isn't passing the buck. He enjoys
sitting back with an I-told-you-so look when the decision
you made (against his acutely accurate intuition) falls as

flat as a pancake—to teach you a lesson. You do have to watch that. Aquarian bosses are usually willing to give you all the rope you need to hang yourself with and another several yards besides, if you ask for it. You're lucky if he explains even once just exactly why he thinks you're on the wrong track. When he's done that—which is unusual enough—he won't explain a second time. You take it from there. Catch it clearly the first time or you'll get some confusing double-talk to remind you to pay attention to what he says.

He expects you to be able to wiggle your antennae and pick up anything you've missed out of the atmosphere. He doesn't realize that other people don't have his Uranian gift for absorbing information from three people talking all at once while he peels an orange, dials a phone number and shuffles through a stack of inter-office memos.

Don't get too set in your ways around an Aquarian executive. You're liable to walk in some morning and find your office has been moved to another floor and he forgot to tell you. There's always change in the air around this man. You may have the unsettling experience of having him sweep down unexpectedly one day with a big, warm, friendly grin and throw your entire system out the window —the system the office has been using since the Civil War. In its place he'll substitute a new method, faster and less cluttered with detail. You say you can't adjust that quickly? You need at least six months to make the change and the new system is Greek to you at this point? He can't understand that. It's perfectly clear to him. Don't worry, you'll catch on. He'll wait. He's patient.

And that he is. The normal Uranus-ruled mind may be full of nervous curiosity just beneath the surface, but generally the Aquarian takes it fairly easy, and projects an image of calm and thoughtful deliberation. You'll notice I said generally. Of course, there was the time he actually ran out of the office to catch those six fire trucks, the turtle race he staged on his carpet with real turtles, and the day he had those miniature TV sets delivered to each desk during the World Series. And of course there was that morning he took over the switchboard, just to see what it was like, mixed up all the calls, disconnected everyone, accidentally got a big TV network veep on a crossed wire and sold him a half a million dollar deal—then forgot the man's name when he came in to sign the contract. But normally he's placid and controlled. So he's a little eccentric now and then: he has the water cooler moved once a month so you can't find it, and he likes to change your day off with no notice. What are a few minor annoyances like that when you work for a boss who's sincerely fascinated by that book you're writing on Kansas City jazz? And how can you stay mad at a boss who doesn't mind if the bookkeeper grows a beard, his secretary wears white fur boots with rhinestone heels to work or the new filing clerk parks his bicycle in the reception room?

He may spend one day talking your ear off, and the next week secluded inside his office, ignoring staff, customers and suppliers, deep in lonely thought. He's resting his soul, and those periods of retreat are necessary. Regardless of how recently you joined the firm, he'll consider you his friend. He's even good friends with the competition. No matter what it says on your company letterhead, the real business of your Aquarian boss is friendship. Somebody discussing today's corporate conformity recently said, "Give me back the good old-time individualist executive with the gravy spots on his tie, who got things done without calling a committee meeting for every little snag." The poor man was undoubtedly undergoing a rush of nostalgia for an Aquarian boss he had years ago.

Those of you who work for a Uranian probably don't have the common problem of the boss's wife dropping in unexpectedly while things are a mess and the painters are tearing the reception room apart. She's lucky if she knows where he works, let alone has permission to drop in on him. Aquarians don't confide every little activity to their wives. I used to live next door to the February-born executive of a research firm who once didn't get around to telling his wife he had to fly to Europe on business until he arrived there and noticed he didn't have any clean shirts. (He was quite put out about it, and he told her so when he phoned her from London. Somehow, it was all her fault. She should have anticipated he might make a trip.)

Funny how you kept remembering all the idiosyncrasies of your own Aquarian executive last week while you watched him get the *Man of the Year* award from the mayor at that big formal banquet. You had just decided that, regardless of his unpredictable ways and his dippy habits, he was actually one of the most distinguished bosses

a person could have. Then you happened to look down
under the table—and there were his feet tapping the rug
impatiently, clad in neat black dress shoes, wearing one
blue sock and one yellow sock.

The AQUARIUS Employee

Twinkle, twinkle, little bat!
How I wonder what you're at!
Up above the world you fly,
Like a tea-tray in the sky.

You shouldn't have any trouble spotting your Aquarian employee. He's the one with all the friends. You know, the
one who forgot his brief case this morning—the same man
who casually dropped in your office last month to borrow
your fountain pen and left behind a production idea which
has saved your company $30,000 in overtime so far, ac-
cording to the latest check by the auditor.

It should also be a snap to remember the day you hired
him. He's that fellow you thought came in to sell you a box
at Yankee Stadium—then you decided he was soliciting
funds for Shakespeare-in-the-Park, finally figured he was
taking one of those political polls—and didn't realize until
after he left that he had actually stopped by to apply for a
job. If you don't remember him, it's five-to-one your
secretary does. Aquarius men seem to make an instant
and lasting impression on women, even those who look
like neglected, underfed puppy dogs with figures loosely
resembling Ichabod Crane's. Some people might jump to
the hasty conclusion this is the mother-instinct, but they
would be wrong. The real Uranus attraction for females
is the Aquarian's absolute indifference to their existence.
It drives them to distraction. He's a challenge they can't
resist—so they either retaliate by trying to vamp him
or by snubbing him back, neither of which makes the
slightest impression on your Aquarian employee. He can be
totally blind to a female co-worker for weeks, literally not
seeing her, then one fine spring morning suddenly startle

her with the information that her eyes are the exact shade of a robin's egg he once found in a tree, and she's gone. I mean, completely lost. She may not type a word the rest of the day.

Life with an Aquarian employee can be exhilarating and leave you a little breathless. It's not that they're extroverts or flamboyant or practical jokers. Quite the reverse. Many Aquarians are sober, cool, aloof and removed from the mad world around them. The only trouble is that they've removed themselves fifty years ahead, and when they rocket back to the present every few days or so, they've bagged some unusual ideas from the stratosphere. If you're a smart boss, you'll invite the Uranus man to your office for a chat once a week. It could be profitable. Who knows what you might pick up? When he tells you in the proper technical language exactly what's wrong with that loose screw under the fourth bolt in the new machine that keeps breaking down, you may start to wonder if he *has* been to Mars and back since you saw him on the elevator yesterday. Especially after you check personnel records and see that he didn't take a course in science or mechanics at college. Still, the informal conference with him may not always turn out so profitably. He may leave after that little confidential talk with your check for a few thousand dollars for the preservation of Basketball on Indian Reservations—or the Research Society for Investigating Psychic Phenomena in Smyrna. The Aquarian interests are worldwide.

Chances are this seemingly quiet, brilliant and friendly young man won't stay around long enough for you to remember his face. The Aquarian male will either begin at the top, work his way up there in a few weeks, decide to go it alone as a composer, photographer, ornithologist, dancer, singer, clown, writer, juggler, athlete, geologist, radio or TV announcer, etc.—or leave you to drift from job to job "looking for himself." Someday he'll find himself, too. When he does, he usually stays in one place for a lifetime. Until that moment of truth, however, our Uranus-ruled friends spend a period of time just roaming around, experimenting, learning, looking, investigating, and picking up new friends.

He's not sentimental by nature. He has a scientific attitude, but there's also a strong interest in people, what makes them laugh and what makes them cry. An Aquarian does not lean toward emotionalism (except rarely when he's in the clutch of an eccentric rush of behavior, perhaps a reaction to some very disturbing personal experience). Unfortunately, his ideas and opinions are often considered irrational and impractical, but that's just because his critics aren't tuned to his frequency—half a century ahead. Imagine how your grandmother felt when some Aquarian back in the nineties tried to describe color television and astronauts landing on the moon. That gives you a fair idea of the reception Uranus-ruled people get today when they start in on their theory of a time machine, and how it could be designed with safety valves so a defective switch won't get you lost somewhere in 1770.

You may notice the Aquarian employee with a different friend each week or so. It's difficult for him to be satisfied with any one individual at a time, since his sympathies run into so many channels. It's common for him, therefore, to give more friendship than he receives.

The first thing you may have to do is decide which kind of Aquarian you have employed. There's only one basic Uranus type—but there are two ways in which the Aquarian nature can manifest itself. The first kind is the suave, pipe-smoking professor type, with a relaxed manner and not a few eccentric habits, who lives in an elegant but curious apartment full of Egyptian mummies, a tree from India planted in the center of the room, bells from Sumatra, 16th Century tables and early American rockets, plus a mod painting or two and maybe an old airplane propeller hanging over the fireplace. He dines on gourmet foods like roasted grasshoppers and steak tartar with ants' eggs sprinkled on top. He's usually brilliant.

The other kind lives in a tiny room over the subway, eats mustard sandwiches and watches his favorite TV show on the first set ever manufactured. He scatters his inventions all over the corner table, picks out tunes on a dusty piano, and washes the dishes once a week. He is also brilliant. The trouble is, when you get them both out in normal society, it's hard to tell the difference.

Both are conscientious workers. Both have a high degree of intelligence, as well as uncanny perception and a fine sensitivity to everyone around them. They each soak up knowledge while appearing to be engrossed in some abstract theory. Their memories are weak but their intuitive powers more than make up for it. They're extremely odd in their habits, kind and sympathetic, usually very courteous, and they wear unusual combinations of clothing. They're each loyal, honest and have a strict code which is never violated. Both are bachelors, and they number about five thousand good friends each, ranging from Leonard Bernstein and Joe Namath to Scarface Al and Minnie, the apple lady who takes numbers. So you see? An Aquarian is an Aquarian. A pipe, a mustard sandwich or a couple of Egyptian mummies between a couple of lotus trees have nothing at all to do with it.

You can be safe in assuming your Aquarian worker is giving you a full day's work for his pay. Although he's probably the real cause of your secretary's severe skin rash her doctor can't diagnose or cure, he may end up on the front page of *The New York Times* someday, being presented with a plaque or something and you can say "I knew him when." He can also contribute some pretty sane, concrete thinking to your firm which will possibly even result in bringing it up to the Twentieth Century. He's utterly trustworthy with company secrets, and probably the best customer's man you can find, because he'll make friends with your coldest client and wonder why everyone thought he was so tough to deal with. To the Aquarian, he's just another human with some intriguing aspect to his personality to be uncovered with a few polite, direct questions and a little observation.

This employee isn't likely to nudge you constantly for a raise, because money is usually down there on the bottom of his list, along with women. But he's shrewd enough to know his worth, and it wouldn't be wise to take advantage of him. He may cause some raised eyebrows, but he'll seldom cause any scandal or petty office gossip. You won't find him filled with much intense, driving ambition, yet he has one of the finest minds in the zodiac. If you should decide he knows enough to make him your partner, he'll never steal the business from you—and he can be a most decided asset, possibly even bring worldwide prestige to the firm someday.

When he does eventually decide to get married, you may lose a good secretary (he won't want his wife to work), but you want the poor girl's skin rash to clear up, don't you?

Child of the pure, unclouded brow
And dreaming eyes of wonder!
Though time be fleet, and I and thou
Are half a Life asunder,
Thy loving smile will surely hail
The love-gift of a fairy-tale.

PISCES the Fish

February 20th through March 20th

How to Recognize PISCES

Hush-a-by lady, in Alice's lap!
Till the feast's ready, we've time for a nap:
When the feast's over, we'll go to the ball—
Red Queen, and White Queen, and Alice, and all!

Then fill up the glasses with treacle and ink,
Or anything else that is pleasant to drink.

If you should happen to see a Pisces behind a teller's cage, or sitting at a bank president's desk, you'll be viewing a rare kind of fish. Very few of these people can stand being confined for long in one place. You'll have better luck if you wander into a spiritual seance, visit an art gallery, walk through a convent or a monastery, attend a concert or catch a floor show in a nightclub. You might check an Authors League meeting, drop backstage after a play, or try some sunbathing on a yacht.

The chances are you'll come up with a pretty good catch in any of those streams of life. The more creative and artistic, the more leisurely and esoteric the surroundings, the more fish you'll find. The net will be full of colorful, shimmering types, if you spread it out at cocktail parties or gala balls. You might even hook a couple of mollies, or an exotic species, like Princess Lee Radziwill.

There's little worldly ambition in Neptune people. Most of them wouldn't give a minnow for rank, power or leadership, and wealth holds little attraction. Few Pisces people accumulate money by the bushel, unless they marry it or inherit it. Mind you, they have nothing against cash. They'll gladly accept any old coins you can't use. But they're more aware than most of us of its temporal qualities.

Whoever said, "I don't want to be a millionaire—I just want to live like one," was truly reflecting the Piscean philosophy. The typical Neptune heart is free of greed. There's a lack of intensity, almost a carelessness about tomorrow. There's also an intuitive knowledge of yesterday and a gentle tolerance of today. It's never easy for either real or human fish to struggle and fight their way upstream. It's more common, and it takes less effort, to go with the current wherever it takes them. But to swim upstream is the challenge of Pisces—and the only way he ever finds true peace and happiness. Taking the easy way is a trap for those born under this Sun sign, a glittering bait that entices them, while it hides the dangerous hook —a wasted life.

You'll be impressed with the Piscean charm of manner and lazy good nature. He's indifferent to most limiting restrictions, if they don't rob him of his freedom to dream and feel his way through life. He's even more indifferent to insults, recriminations and other people's bristling opinions. Tell a Piscean that society is decadent, the government is cracking, air pollution will put us all in our graves and the world is coming to a dead stop, and he'll yawn, or smile enchantingly, or look vaguely sympathetic. Very little will excite him to violent action or reaction. Of course, the fish is not completely bland. He does have a temper. When he's finally aroused, he can be bitingly sarcastic, with a clever, caustic tongue. Neptunians can lash their tails angrily and spill forth a torrent of nervous irritability, but the typical Pisces will normally take the path of least resistance, and the cool waters of Neptune continually wash away his anger. To arouse the fish to a display of temper is rather like tossing a pebble into a clear, mirror-smooth lake, You'll create some ripples, but the surface will soon be calm again.

When you meet Pisces people, look first at their feet. They'll be quite noticeably small and dainty (including the men's), or else they'll be huge and spread out like a tired washerwoman's. The Pisces hands will also be tiny, fragile, and exquisitely formed—or else big ham bones that look as though they belong behind a plow. The skin is silky soft; the hair is fine, often wavy, and usually light (though you'll find a goodly number of brunette fish). Pisces eyes are liquid, heavy-lidded, and full of strange lights. Frequently, but not always, they're slightly protruding, bulbous and extremely compelling. Some Piscean eyes are simply beautiful. There's no other word to describe them. The features are elastic and mobile, and you'll usually find more dimples than wrinkles. Few Pisceans are tall; Neptune bodies are sometimes awkwardly built, but with their extraordinary grace, it's seldom discernible. They seem to sort of flow along, instead of walking—as if they were swimming across the room or down the street. Sometimes they really are. Where's the liquid? It may be nearby, and the fish is attracted to it.

It can be a love of ice water, the habit of a dozen cups of tea or coffee a day, a hankering for soda pop—or a yen for something stronger. Like Scorpios and Cancerians, Pisces people are wise to stay miles away from alcohol. Very few Neptunians can have a social cocktail, then leave it alone. There are some, naturally. But too many Pisceans find enticing relief from trouble in liquor. It lulls them pleasantly with a false sense of security and it's a dangerous lullaby. Of course, every Pisces who drinks a pousse-café doesn't become an alcoholic, but the percentage is higher than it ought to be.

The fish was born with the desire to see the world through rose-colored spectacles. He knows well enough about the seamy side of humanity, but he prefers to live in his own watery, gentle world, where everyone is beautiful and all actions are lovely. If reality becomes too terrible to face, he often escapes into rosy daydreams with powder puff foundations and not a prayer of coming true. When life dumps him with a splash—a real belly-smacker—into a stagnant river of dismal failure and hopeless conditions, instead of leaping out of the murky danger, he's more inclined to hide behind his pale green illusions which keep him from making practical decisions. The rejected Pisces is too inclined to face the ugliness of failure by deepening his false hopes, when a determined switch of course or some new, forceful action might shower him with real, instead of imaginary, success.

Not every March-born person falls into such a typical Neptune trap, but enough of them do to make it a necessary warning. The Pisces writer may be tempted to lounge for years in bars, telling himself he's gathering material, when he's really just gathering moss and unpaid bills. The Pisces artist who can't get the patronage he seeks may stroll through the park, day after day, mumbling into his beard that he's studying nature as a background for his great masterpiece, while his paint brushes gather dust. Where is the angel who will support him while he splashes canvases with glory? The Piscean woman, left alone, with just enough fixed income to keep a roof over her head and a little seaweed in the cupboard, will tend to dream away the hours, tenderly remembering yesterday, hazily hoping for tomorrow, and wasting the bright sunlight of today. The actor, composer, musician—you fill in the stories.

You may have read that the Pisces symbol of two fish, swimming in opposite directions, indicates that the Neptunian is torn by dual desires. It's not so. Dual desires belong to Gemini. The two fish in reversed directions symbolize the choice given Pisces: to swim to the top—or to swim to the bottom and never quite reach his goals. Pisces must learn that he is to serve mankind in some way, and eschew worldly possessions. Piscean Einstein, who swam upstream, formulated a whole new world of relative time. Pisceans who swim downstream serve by washing dishes or shoveling snow. The choice is always there, because there's never a lack of unusual talent, but the fish, with eyes that see clearly on both sides, sometimes has difficulty seeing straight ahead. Pisces often retreats—either to the sublime heights of a dedicated professional life, or to stimulants, artificial emotions and false excitement.

Although Pisceans shrink from competition, the strong pull of Neptune sends many of them, even the shy ones, toward the bright footlights, where they can use their fabulous powers of interpretation to project myriad emotions. In spite of their natural timidity, they often become some of the finest performers in the theater. But only if they fight their distaste for the hard work of grueling rehearsals, and the dullness of the dreary, but necessary years of experience. Sometimes the sharp wounds of the critics leave such a scar on sensitive Pisces souls that a potential Barrymore or Bernhardt retires when fame was just ahead. Memorization is seldom a problem. The Pisces memory is legendary, although with an afflicted Moon or Mercury they can forget their own telephone numbers.

To every Pisces, from the fisherman on the wharf to the nurse in the children's hospital, life itself is a huge stage. In the reflective eye of the fish, the entire scene is elusive and fleeting. Knowing this, Neptunians accept most storms with tranquil equilibrium. Despondency, however, is always threatening to swoop down and bring peculiar dreams or weird nightmares which are often precognitive. When Pisces has a feeling something will happen, it usually does.

If he tells you not to get on that plane or in that car, you'd better plan to swim or walk.

Astrologers who speak of an old soul refer to a soul which has gone through many lives, retaining the wisdom of each. Often they refer to Pisces, because a life as the fish is either the most difficult obligation a soul can choose —or a chance to reach perfect fulfillment. While Aries represents birth in the zodiac, Pisces represents death and eternity. The fish is the twelfth sign, a composite of all that's gone before, and his nature is a blend of all the other signs, which is quite a lot to cope with. His surprising ability to organize and concentrate on detail which pops up now and then, as well as his gentleness, reflects his inner knowledge of the lessons of Virgo. His judgment is as fair and detached as that of Libra, and his love of pleasure is also purely Libran. Pisces people have the crazy sense of fun of Cancer, as well as both the Cancerian sympathy and crabbiness. They're sometimes full of the Sagittarian outspoken frankness and generosity, as fun-loving and outgoing as Leo, yet as devoted to duty as Capricorn, and often just as envious of social distinction. There may also be a smattering of the Saturnine melancholy. Perhaps more than just a smattering. The fish can be as moody as a Moon child and as happy as a lion. He likes to tease and analyze in Aquarian fashion. He's often overflowing with Aries idealism and enthusiasm, but usually without the Mars drive. A Pisces person can zip around with Gemini quickness, talk just as fast and think just as cleverly. He can also be as lazy and peaceful as Taurus. He has the clever wit of Mercury and the soft grace of Venus, and he combines it with the mystic penetration of Scorpio, without the Scorpio's ruthlessness.

Pisces holds within himself the fondness of debate of all the air signs, the love for nature of all the earth signs and the flaming aspirations of all the fire signs. But he is neither fixed nor cardinal. The fish is mutable always; in this respect he is undiluted. The one and only quality which originates with his own sign is his strange power to stand outside himself and see yesterday, today and tomorrow as one. The Piscean love of music and art, and his highly developed senses and versatility he owes to other signs, but his deep wisdom and compassion belong only to him, culled from the combined knowledge of every human experience. Now that you understand all that, is it any wonder that your Pisces friends are a bit of a puzzle at times, not to mention being outright kooky odd balls on occasion?

Pisceans tend to think they can live forever, and they often act as though they believed it fervently. The fish typically doesn't take very good care of himself. Chances are he spends most of his excess energy (and he doesn't have too much to spare) helping relatives in trouble or taking on the burdens of friends. Their troubles can be emotional or financial, but either can be a serious drain on Piscean health, which is rarely robust to begin with. The fish must conserve his energy and refrain from succumbing to stimulants or sedatives, fatigue and other people's emergencies. Weakest as infants, seldom sturdy as children (unless there's a strong Mars influence in the natal chart), Pisces people seem to have slow metabolisms, which is why they often wake up sleepy-eyed and listless. Poor eating habits can bring troubles with liver and intestinal functions and digestive troubles. Accidents to, or some abnormalities of the feet, hands or hips are common, also colds, flu and pneumonia. The lungs are not strong, and weak toes and ankles may result from March births. The fish seem to have fallen arches and metatarsal injuries or superbly strong and supple feet. There's no inbetween. They have a hidden inner resistance, however, and one of the challenges of Neptune is to discover this latent strength and call on it. Pisceans can literally hypnotize themselves into or out of anything they choose—including fear of cats, mice, heights, subways, elevators and people.

Humor is one of their secret weapons. Pisceans grin to cover unshed tears. They're masters of satire, and you may cringe from a bright remark thrown at you so casually that you're unable to pin down the exact meaning or the intent. Yet, you'll have a decidedly uncomfortable feeling. The fish can scatter caustic observations around like flashing lights which wink on and off so fast you can't keep up with them. He's an excellent practical joker, great at pulling hilarious lines while he keeps his own elastic face mournful and straight. He can move gracefully from slapstick to brittle, sophisticated jokes. Sometimes the fun is warm and harmless, sometimes it's cold and merciless; but it's always a cover for another emotion the fish wants to hide, seldom spontaneous of itself. Pisces wears his laughs as a mask, and they disguise him well.

There's a great feeling of pity and a desire to help the sick and weak. Pisces may share compassion for the ill with Virgo, but he takes the extra step to try to understand the hearts of the burdened and the friendless, the failures and the misfits, no matter how weird or how rejected by society. The fish will gently comfort those whom Virgo feels are weak by choice, and therefore undeserving. If you need a dime or a dollar, a large loan, or just a small encouragement that no one else would give, go to Pisces. You'll get no lectures and no glances of superiority. He judges no man—thief, murderer, addict, pervert, sinner, saint, hypocrite or liar. Greed, lust, sloth and envy will bring no critical wrath, if he's a typical Neptunian. His understanding overflows, along with whatever practical help he's able to offer. He senses every vice and virtue, and he knows each pitfall. Many fish, for this reason, don the robes of the priest or monk, and spend their lives in prayer or contemplation.

To help is his first instinct. There are Pisces people who are crusty and brusque, but it's only a fragile shell, worn for protection. The fish soon learns how vulnerable he is. The world is not yet tuned to the sensitive Piscean wavelength, so to avoid ridicule (as well as to avoid being taken for every last dime he owns), he sometimes feigns indifference. The impositions of those who would trample him force the fish to hide his true spirit. Since the depth of Neptune's waters causes him to absorb every pain and joy as if they were his own, it's little wonder many Pisceans pretend disinterest in hearing sad stories. But remember that they are pretending. If you've been rebuffed once, try twice, and the real fish will surface.

The glorious Piscean imagination, their marvelous elfin humor and the Neptunian sense of beauty can create the most delicate, yet eternally lasting prose and poetry. Indeed, the world couldn't do without their artistic efforts and their gentle compassion for a moment. It would stop spinning. You'll frequently find fish who have buried their personal dreams to brighten odd corners of the lives of relatives and friends, or to bring the gift of tears and laughter to the public through the stage, at the cost of the privacy Pisces seeks and needs. Yet Neptune is a deceptive planet, capable of giving birth to natures that twist and turn in two directions at once, distorting the truth, an influence which often causes Pisces to hide his real emotions.

This thespian quality is obvious if you've ever tried to pin down the elusive, flashing fish. He hates to answer a direct question with a yes or a no. It's always maybe. A simple curiosity about what play he just saw or what book he just read can bring an evasive answer for no reason in particular. He can turn on tears, then turn on sunshine by pressing another invisible switch. Neither is truly real. All is illusion with Pisces, and they find it hard to tell the difference themselves. Their internal nature is as unfathomable as Neptune's great oceans. The altruistic fish is filled with an inexhaustible, tender love for every living creature which is truly saint-like, when it's not turned inward in self-pity and self-love. Typically Piscean are the gregarious housewives with hearts big enough for the troubles of all the neighbors, and the patient bartenders who listen sympathetically to hundreds of tales of woe each week.

Hanging somewhere between the silent waters of the sea below and the vast, star-studded mist above, only barely touching the earth from necessity, Pisces lives his life in lonely understanding of truth too deep to express in words. Those who want him for a friend, those who love him, must use their imagination to grasp the strange planes of his mind and emotions. The other two water signs—Scorpio and Cancer—are symbolized by half land–half water creatures, amphibious and flexible—but the fish can't breathe air. He must live in cool green water, sometimes muddy, always moving.

Pisces is represented, not by iron or mercury or gold or lead, but by the vibrations of the indefinable, artificial metals—again, an echo of the unreal and the illusionary. He sees his reflection in three dimensions in the violet amethyst and the clear emerald; and his natal flowers are the water lily and the lotus. Their blossoms are pink and white and delicate, but their stems and leaves are made of strong fibers, tough and indestructible, unless they're torn up by the roots. Few can follow Pisces and probe his aquamarine nature, whether he swims downstream to oblivion, just another lashing speck in the large, moving school of fish—or fights his way upstream to conquer the swift current and find serenity in pure waters. He is stronger than he thinks and wiser than he knows, but Neptune guards this secret until he discovers it for himself.

Famous Pisces Personalities

Edward Albee	James Madison
Harry Belafonte	Michelangelo
Elizabeth Browning	Zero Mostel
Luther Burbank	Vaslav Nijinsky
Enrico Caruso	Rudolf Nureyev
Frederic Chopin	Auguste Renoir
Grover Cleveland	Rimsky-Korsakov
Albert Einstein	David Sarnoff
Jackie Gleason	Dinah Shore
Handel	Earl of Snowden
Rex Harrison	Svetlana Stalin
Ben Hecht	John Steinbeck
Victor Hugo	Elizabeth Taylor
Ted Kennedy	Earl Warren
Gordon MacRae	George Washington

The PISCES Man

We are but older children, dear,
Who fret to find our bedtime near.

William Shakespeare was a Taurus, but he left this message for anyone who is considering becoming involved with a Pisces man:

There is a tide in the affairs of men,

Which, taken at the flood, leads on to fortune;

Omitted, all the voyage of their life

Is bound in shallows and in miseries.

If you're about to fall over the dam for a Neptunian, you should paste those lines on your compact mirror, where you can see them every time you powder your nose. They may possibly make or break your future, not to mention your heart.

Try to untangle your probably rosy state of mind and make sure that Pisces fellow you're about to join in a moonlight swim knows when the tide is coming in. If he

takes it at the flood, you're as lucky as any girl can be.
On to fame and fortune! But if, perchance, your Pisces lad
can't see the tide for the stardust in his eyes, and he misses
that big flood—well, let me warn you that those Neptunian
shallows can result in some of the most dismal miseries
you'll ever know.

A Pisces man can be everything you want him to be—
or everything you don't want him to be. A tide in his
affairs is synonymous with opportunity. It requires a firm
decision, determined action, and the ability to drown any
old, soggy dreams that prevent success. The trouble is
that some Pisces men never recognize that tide at its flood,
even when it sloshes over their feet.

The Pisces man isn't weak. It's just that he may linger
too long on a fading, silver star, and miss the bright sunlight of success. Not all Pisceans are gentle dreamers. But
more of them than you can scatter with a pebble are.
However, there is hope. There's always hope, where there's
life. Although the world needs his lovely imagination only
too desperately, there comes a time when the Pisces male
has to go about the business of earning his potatoes. When
he does that, he has a snap of it, because the Neptune
intuition coupled with his clever mind can turn him toward
sensible goals which could bring him fame and recognition—even wealth and immortality. If not all that (you
can't hit the jackpot every time), then at least respectability
and comfortable security. Let's hope that's the kind of
Pisces male you're sailing with. Practically no other Sun
sign can stop his potential under those circumstances.

However, if, say by the age of twenty-five or so, he
hasn't recognized that tide in his affairs, frankly, his future
isn't too hopeful. You think that's unfair? All right, make
it by the age of thirty-five, but you're gambling. When I
said his future isn't too hopeful, I meant with you. As a
wife—with the family routine. His personal future can be
more or less satisfactory. Lots of Pisces men who can't
bury stale dreams and dig up fresh ideas for success live
fairly contented lives. That's because all they need is that
dream, rusty as it is around the edges. Add a jug of wine,
a loaf of good rye bread, and he's as happy as most of us
other misfits. Ah! You noticed I stopped short of one item.
It's a loaf of bread, a jug of wine and Thou—right? I'm
glad you're up on the Rubaiyat. But you see, I left "Thou"
out on purpose. The dreamy, sensitive, artistic fish can

exist nicely on bread and wine—even thrive on it. But such
a diet won't feed a wife, one to five little bundles of joy,
and who knows, maybe even some goldfish and guppies
(considering his Sun sign). You need things like stockings
and cosmetics and shoes and spinach and rent money and
celery and milk and light bulbs and, well, you know what
I mean.

There's only one way out with this kind of fish: Be an
heiress. No, there is another way out: Get two jobs—one
for you and one for him, and work at both of them yourself like the very dickens.

Now, I didn't say you wouldn't be happy in the romantic
hours. That's one thing no kind of Pisces ever born will
ever be short of—romance. They fairly breathe it. It's just
that it's no substitute for spinach and baby shoes, or your
sanity. The planets, in their wisdom, take care of such com-
plications of life by giving oodles of chances for this
dreamy, unworldly type of Piscean male to become a
protégé. If he finds a patron or patroness (much more
likelihood of the latter, but it can be either), he can turn
into a great painter, a great writer, a great composer, a
great musician—or at least just a great guy. But how is he
going to find a patron, let alone a patroness, if he has you
and those bundles of joy and the goldfish and the guppies
and all cluttering up the artistic simplicity of his existence?

You have to admit it just won't work. Better say farewell
to him right now. You'll cry a little, and it may hurt—even
deeply. But not as much as being married to a walking,
talking dream, and having to face the landlord with nothing
but empty wishes in your pocketbook. That really hurts.

Now that we've been brave and practical about the
bread and wine type, we can talk about the other kind of
Pisces, the one who grabbed the tide at its flood. Obviously,
he's a real catch for any girl. There's always the chance he
could turn out to be an Einstein or a George Washington,
which would be simply wonderful. You couldn't ask for
much more, though I suppose Einstein might have been a
little engrossed in his equations on weekends and George
may have brought a few problems home from the office
at night. But you don't have to seek perfection. Even
a super practical Capricorn or an aggressive, driving Aries
man can have little flaws. The point is that a Piscean who
fights his way upstream will have plenty of chances to lay

the twin gifts of fame and fortune at your feet. And he's quite a guy in other ways, too.

A Pisces man has no prejudices. He'll never judge an Indian until he's walked a few miles in his moccasins, or a nudist until he's tried going barefoot. Even then he'll understand and not pass critical judgment. He's very short on cold accusations and very long on warm tolerance. He'll even make a stab at trying to understand his mother-in-law, and how many men do that? The Neptune male possesses a rare sympathy of spirit. His friends confide in him and never worry that he'll be shocked. It takes a real blockbuster to shock the fish. If you and I and your Piscean were all three sitting in a room, and a man walked in and told us he was a little worried because he was a bigamist, with four different wives in four different states—you might glare at him and think he deserved to go to jail; I might sneer at him and call him a skunk; but your Pisces man would probably ask, "What four states? Were you in love with any of them?" The fish is curious, but totally shockproof. As far as he's concerned, the fellow needs heaps of sympathy and a darned good lawyer.

He might tell a secret or two accidentally, never on purpose. Pisces sometimes speaks before he realizes the possible damage. It's a little tough for him to comprehend that what he says could perhaps be interpreted in the wrong light by more severe souls with less relenting attitudes. (It would take some thought, for example, for him to grasp that people like his sister or your mother wouldn't understand the domestic difficulties of that poor bigamist.) However, once the fish has been specifically requested to keep it under his fin, he'll be close-mouthed and reliable, and you can trust him with your darkest secrets.

An occasional Pisces who's the victim of an afflicted Mercury talks very fast, fluently and frequently. But the typical Neptunian speaks slowly, thinks gently, and tries to mind his own business, even though he's continually subjected to the problems of friends, relatives and neighbors. They flock to him because Neptune listens so beautifully. You'll find yourself tempted to confide your own little worries with the broken hair dryer, your father's sinus trouble and your overdrawn bank balance, but try to go easy. If there's anything a Pisces husband or boy friend doesn't need, it's more tribulations dropped in his lap. Others have been dropping them all day. Bundles of them. He needs some relief when he's with you. People don't mean to impose on Pisces. They seldom realize that the Neptune nature is so receptive it just soaks up all the vibrations around, good or bad, joyful or fearful, dark or light. The life of an absorbent, spiritual sponge can be kind of wearing on the psyche, as any mystic can tell you. (Many of them are Piscean.) The very fact that he's sensitive means that he vividly feels the emotions of those who seek his ear and get his heart. Pisces people often have to rest for long periods. The Neptune soul must be alone at times so fresh breezes can blow through to heal the wounds of all those vicarious troubles and bring back calm, undefiled individuality. So never begrudge your Pisces man his moments of silence. He sorely needs them. If he feels like being alone or taking a walk by himself, let him go. Too much togetherness can spoil the beauty of Pisces love. It needs space to grow untangled.

Remember that the fish is sensitive and can be easily hurt. His shyness is due to a painful consciousness of his own limitations, whatever they may be, and he feels them keenly. He needs to know that his virtues are counted by someone he admires. You. Never hold back encouragement from him.

He may try Yoga and Zen, or experiment with occult beliefs, and he'll probably be interested in astrology and numerology, even reincarnation. Like the Scorpio, he was born with an understanding of esoteric principles, and these things are usually good for him. They help keep his emotions stable, and they provide an anchor for his vivid imagination. Pisces men get upset now and then, but their anger is seldom violent or long lasting. When it's over, the waters grow placid again, and life is just as peaceful as before. Some Neptune males do a little yelling around the house, but it's harmless. It's almost impossible for the fish to really bellow, like Taurus the bull, for example. See how lucky you are?

Although he's difficult to fathom himself, Pisces has no problem in seeing all the subtleties of others clearly. It's difficult to fool him; he'll look right through to the other side. Yet, he can fool you when he takes a notion to do so, through some quirk he has which makes him want to keep his personal affairs safely hidden from close scrutiny.

One Piscean I know carries this trait so far he has actually been able to fool the government, and that's no easy trick. All his life he has managed to avoid the census taker. The Internal Revenue knows less about him than they know about a native in Pago Pago. He gets away with it because he's a writer. His phone is listed under a fictitious name, and he's never applied for a social security card or a driver's license. He has a horror of some imaginary Big Brother turning him into a number and knowing all his private secrets.

Your fish may not be quite so neurotic about it, but there will probably be times when he'll tell you he was at the cleaner's when he was really buying a cigar. Why? I really don't know. Nor does he. It's a sort of mild deception the Piscean (also the Geminian) seems to enjoy. As long as he's wearing green suspenders and people think he's wearing orange suspenders—or no suspenders—he feels secure, somehow. Since it makes him happy, let him have his little mysteries. Why make a big deal of it? Even if you know he wasn't at the cleaner because you saw him in the cigar store yourself, ask him if his slacks were ready. When he tells you the man said they won't be ready until Monday, remark that the cleaner is as slow as molasses and let it go at that. He could have far worse habits than practicing a little harmless make-believe just to keep his vivid imagination oiled up and in top working condition.

There won't be many tremendous surges of jealousy. Or if there are, he's such an excellent natural actor (if you let him practice) that he'll probably pretend them away. But he's a man, for all his poetic, tender nature, so he'll expect your technical loyalty when everything is said and done. You may have to control your own jealousy, however, because he'll have warm friends of both sexes, and he'll be sympathetic to them, sometimes at odd hours. It's his nature to be gregarious. He can't help it. There's danger here if you're the violently possessive type. An Aries or Leo girl had better chase another moonbeam. He does admire beauty, and he may stare at pretty legs from time to time. But you can keep that in bounds and innocent with a little extra effort, and your reward will be a gentle husband who's both a romantic lover and a companion who can talk about everything under the sun.

When those spells of loneliness and depression cause the gloom to gather, toss your apron in the corner behind the aquarium, throw on a yellow dress and a golden smile, buy some green tickets to a happy show, and trick him right out of it. Pisceans are particularly vulnerable to suggestion. You may hit a few snags trying to get him to be economical and cautious about money. Neptune people, frankly, aren't noted for their triple A credit ratings (unless he has a Capricorn ascendant or strong planets in Taurus, Aquarius or Cancer, for example). He'll learn, but don't compound the situation by being extravagant yourself, if you can help it. One loose spender per family goes a long way—toward the poor house. He needs a good example. It's surprising how that works with the Pisces character in a sort of follow-the-leader manner. That is, if the leader is close to him and someone he respects. The Piscean nature is vividly receptive to the vibrations around him, especially if they're intensified by emotion.

The children will find him one whale of a lot of fun. Chances are he'll take them boating and swimming and snorkel diving. He'll play the part of the Wicked Crocodile and Little Boy Blue until they think they've found a human nursery rhyme, in living color. He may sprinkle them with a little way-out philosophy, sing them some mildly salty ballads, or teach them to stand on their heads, yoga style. They'll probably adore him, and they just may turn out to be well-balanced, well-adjusted adults, thanks to his rare ability to hold a tiny bird in his hand without crushing it or frightening it. You do the spanking and he'll do the listening to their young problems—you keep their noses and their clothes clean and he'll keep their minds active. It should work out fine.

Never tread on this man's dreams—he won't forgive that, or forget it. Give him a chance to turn them into realities by helping him find a good, firm star to hitch his wagon to —one that will sparkle instead of fizzing out in an eclipse of common sense. In love, Pisces is a leaner emotionally, which means he needs boundless reassurance and faith, but it also means you musn't lean on him with imaginary complaints. His enthusiastic hopes need to be watered with understanding affection, and make sure you supply the rich soil of a happy home life. Keep the deadly insects of nagging and criticism away from the roots, and someday those wild and crazy hopes of his will change from useless weeds into tall money trees in the backyard, high enough to reach a few of your own private dreams. Hope springs eternal in the Piscean heart. Don't knock it. It may shower

you with some gigantic and surprising luck if you nurture
it tenderly.

You may have heard or read that Pisces is the sign of
"self-undoing," and that could make you all nervous and
negative, but don't let it frighten you. True, there's always
a bit of self-undoing in all Neptune men, but just "do him
back up again," like you would a package that comes un-
tied. If you make the knots tight enough, it won't happen
often. Serve him a dream for breakfast, a clever joke for
lunch, and Chopin for dinner, with Browning for a chaser.
After that, you're on your own. Don't be afraid to jump
in. The water's fine.

The PISCES Woman

*"Well, what are you?" said the Pigeon. "I can see you're
trying to invent something!"*
"I—I'm a little girl," said Alice, rather doubtfully.

*She found herself at last in a beautiful garden,
among the bright flower-beds and the cool fountains.*

The line forms to the right. And please don't crowd. There
may not be enough Pisces women for every man, but that's
no reason to be unruly. You'll have to take your turn, and
hope for the best.

Even without astrology, rumors have spread about the
charms of a Pisces female. She has her negative points, to
be sure, but at first glance she's every man's grade school
valentine, with maybe just a touch of a Playboy bunny to
add some pepper. We might as well admit that the modern,
emancipated woman, with her cast-iron image, has made
the Pisces girl's value shoot even higher. With all that freedom from the feminine mystique clouding the air over
lover's lane, the demure, pretty, helpless Neptune creature
has to beat off the men with big sticks.

It's hardly surprising that she's at a premium. The
Neptune female seldom tries to overshadow her man, married or single. She hasn't the slightest hidden, neurotic de-

sire to dominate him in any way. He can pull out her chair, put on her coat, whistle for the taxi, light her cigarette and talk about how wonderful he is to his heart's content. All she wants is that he should protect her and care for her. She's happily content to lean on his big broad shoulder and let him know, with wide-eyed wonder, how strong he is, and how much she needs him in this scary world. Just think of all those wolves out there, waiting to devour Red Riding Hoods. It's enough to make a girl get out her smelling salts. Even if she isn't quite as Victorian as all that (though plenty of girl fish are), she'll be a charming listener to all his troubles, and what is referred to as a good egg through every crisis.

A Pisces woman thinks her mate, lover, boy friend, brother, father—in fact, any man—can lick the whole world with one hand tied behind his back, and it takes a surprisingly small amount of her touching faith to convince them of the same thing, men being the way they are. And you wonder why she's so popular? The Pisces girl is a cozy, calm haven of tranquility for her proud male, far from the noise of the traffic and the ticker tape machines. The lights in her fish pond are soft and dim. They soothe tired eyes which have been blasted by neon and all those silly little figures at the stock market she couldn't understand to save her life. (Though if it would really save her life, she would sharpen her pencil.)

In the winter she wears fluffy angora mittens. In the spring she wears dainty, full skirts. Summers will find her in a brief bikini. In the fall she'll look adorable sitting beside you at football games, with her hands in your pockets to keep them warm, and asking you the score. She is eternally feminine in all seasons. At the risk of making an understatement, men are drawn to her like bumblebees to a honey pot.

A short conversation with her, and a man instantly relaxes. He pictures a glowing, crackling fire on a chilly night, or he sees himself in a hammock on a balmy spring day, with no one to nag him. She makes it clear that she'll never blame him for any problems in his career or any accidental mistakes. It's always someone else's fault. Not her man's. She'll never press him to get ahead faster. His own pace is perfect with her. Need I explain why the female fish makes the most dangerous other woman of all the Sun signs? *Flash!* Maritime warning: After marriage she may nudge a little. To be truthful, she may nudge a lot. In a way, it serves you right for letting yourself be so blinded by her charms. Lots of times she'll even be bitterly sarcastic, but every woman has to have some flaws, and the Pisces girl will be gentle far more often than she's quarrelsome. She has to be goaded by extreme cruelty or laziness in a mate to be a shrew—and who's to say a cruel or lazy husband doesn't deserve it? Not me. I'm with her.

Besides, her delectable femininity covers any minor deficiencies, and most of the time the typical Neptune girl is soft, dreamy and womanly. Since the fish swims in both directions at once, she adapts beautifully and quietly to conflicting situations that would turn other women into nervous Nellies. Of course, now and then, some cranky words and irritable chatter may bubble up from her normally placid stream of thought. Occasionally a sensitive Neptune female who has suffered harsh treatment at an early age will allow bitterness to break the two symbolic fish of her sign apart—and this can be very sad. She becomes a lonely, miserable Piscean, always swimming furiously, and meeting herself everywhere she dives down to escape—never realizing that the turning inward of her endless love and sympathy toward herself is the real poison. Drugs and drink and false illusions hide the truth from her and blind her to the rocks in the river that might destroy her. But the average Neptune girl keeps both symbolic fish joined firmly together in smooth action, gliding softly first back, then a little forward, so you're never quite sure exactly which way she's headed. Pisces is said to be a deep, mysterious sea, into which all rivers flow. You'll have a better chance of catching her if you know some of her elusive secrets. What makes her swim?

First of all, she's subtle. Ask Nicky Hilton, Michael Wilding, Eddie Fisher and Richard Burton—each of whom married a Pisces. As a matter of fact, the same Pisces. She is not only subtle, she's sometimes a bit deceptive when she practices her art of wrapping you around her emerald earrings.

Now, you may know a Neptune lady who wears a gingham apron and a shy smile, and who is the epitome of the devoted wife, homemaker and tender mother. You're thinking that she's neither subtle nor deceptive. Forgive my directness, but you are wrong. As for that Pisces lady you think is different, I know her, too, or one just like her.

She's a widow who lives in the Bronx, and her name is Pauline. She also wears a gingham apron and a shy smile —the whole setup. How can such a Fannie Farmer image be subtle or deceptive? I'll tell you. First of all, she wraps everyone around her apron strings. (She doesn't have any emerald earrings. Next year, maybe.) She's a short woman who has managed to stand up to the loss of a dear child, heartbreak, boredom, tragedy, fear, poverty, and even the confusion of sudden, very brief riches. She's coped with little boys' bruised knees, braces, lost galoshes; a husband's sloppy Sunday cook-ins in her neat kitchen—and the biggest mixture of in-laws—all speaking eight languages at once—you ever saw outside the United Nations. She has faced all this mishmash of fate like Rocky Graziano. That's gentle? That's delicate? To this very moment, her two sons think of her as a charming, girlish, helpless, fluttery and soft little creature, who needs to be protected, and who can't quite understand how the lock works on the front door.

She's delightfully vague and dreamy. She doesn't know a thing about economics, but she manages to dress as though she was turned out by Sophie of Saks, cook frequent seven-course dinners for assorted grandchildren, pay the rent on time, and send exquisite gifts on holidays and birthdays— all on a monthly income about the size of one of Jack Benny's tips. She has the open love and affection of two daughters-in-law, and an incongruous group made up of the librarian, the super, the owner of the corner delly, the fruit man, half a dozen stray cats and children, the butcher, the newsboy, and would you believe it, even the landlord. She may have one enemy. The man she turned down before she married her husband. He probably joined the Foreign Legion in disappointment, and now I doubt if she even remembers his name. Heartless females, these Pisces women. Subtle and deceptive. (But don't try to tell their neighbors that.)

Like the March winds, your Pisces girl will have many a mood. She's terribly sentimental, and when her feelings are wounded she can cry buckets. She'll look at you so reproachfully you'll feel as if you'd just shot a small rabbit. Pisces females sometimes get the idea they're hopelessly unequipped for the fierce battles and driving ambition required to survive. Then deep depression sets in. At these times you'll have to tell her she's admired for her deep, mysterious wisdom and her blessed understanding by every single human she has ever graced with her friendship. It's usually the gospel truth. The hardest lesson she has to learn is to overcome her timidity and her doubts. If the fears go deep, she'll shut herself off from others, then wonder why she's lonely. She's often afraid of imposing, pushing too hard, taking advantage, when such thoughts are in no one's head but hers.

Now and then a Pisces girl will cover her shyness and vulnerability with wisecracks, a sophisticated veneer and a frigid independent personality, but it's merely a cloak of protection, worn to hide her uncertainty from the prying eyes of rough people who would bruise her gentle heart if she exposed it. I know one who pours out her real soul by writing lovely song lyrics with a secret message woven in the shades of her soft, very private dreams. When she's not writing, she's the picture of the brittle, callous, career woman she wants people to see. Yet, even this type of Pisces is unable to fight her Sun sign. With all her make-believe independence she waits on the curb and lets the man whistle for the cab. There are some things one just doesn't do, as far as Neptune women are concerned; not acting like a lady in public is one of them. She fools a lot of men who could quiet her inner fears and make her take back her frequent claim of, "Who needs a husband? They only mess up your life." Imagine a statement like that from a Piscean, who needs to belong to someone more than she needs to sleep, eat or breathe.

A Pisces girl will give all of her heart to her children, except for the large chunk she saves for you. She'll love them all, but the ones who are uglier, weaker, smaller or sicker may have a slight edge with her. Only a Pisces movie star would pass up the little dimpled darlings and adopt a tiny, crippled tot with frightened eyes. Female fish are the greatest women in the world for understanding the shyness of small boys and the growing pains of awkward adolescent girls. A Piscean mother spins a thousand wispy, cobweb dreams over each bassinet. She'll sacrifice anything so her children can have what she was denied as a child. She may be too permissive. Administering discipline is difficult for her, and she must realize that a lack of firmness is often as bad as severe neglect. In a way, it is neglect, of building the small characters in her care, who need firm guidance to learn to swim alone. If she's guilty of too much softness, explain it to her kindly. She'll comprehend without bitterness, and begin to give the hairbrush a workout. Still many Neptune mothers manage a happy medium between discipline and kindness, and their offspring do them credit.

A Pisces woman will gladly let you earn the bacon and eggplant. She'll probably prefer not to enter the brutal competition of the commercial world, unless you desperately need her to. She had enough of that (if she's a typical Neptune girl) when she worked for that big, confusing company while she was waiting for you to rescue her. Some, not all, but some Pisces women are a wee little bit extravagant. She may need some help figuring out why the bank's balance doesn't reconcile with her stubs, written in Sanskrit. Still, when an emergency forces her to adapt her champagne taste to a skim milk pocketbook, she'll manage.

She listens to the ocean, and it tells her things. In the midst of the city, she still hears the waves of Neptune whispering to her Pisces heart more, perhaps, than she wants to know. Don't forget her birthday or your anniversary or the day you proposed. She won't. I'll always remember the Pisces friend I went to school with in West Virginia. She was tiny, with long, dark hair and those strange Neptune lights in her greenish brown eyes. She married (among several other men) a big football star; it was a totally unexpected elopement. I remember when she asked him why he proposed. She was curious. "Well," he told her, "it was the funniest thing, Shorty. I didn't have the slightest idea of proposing that day. We were in the park, near the pool. The chicks who were lying around getting a tan had wet, stringy hair from swimming, and they looked all hot and sweaty on the benches. You were sitting there under that tree in a white lace dress, and you looked so cool and different from the others. You looked like—well, I guess you sorta looked like a girl." That's the subtle secret of the Pisces woman. Whether she follows Neptune's call as a dedicated nun in a convent or as a sultry songstress in a noisy nightclub—she's a girl. All girl. One hundred percent.

The PISCES Child

Eager eye and willing ear,
Lovingly shall nestle near.
In a Wonderland they lie,
Dreaming as the days go by,
Dreaming as the summers die:

Ever drifting down the stream
Lingering in the golden gleam—
Life, what is it but a dream?

Most babies, as everyone knows, were found under a cabbage leaf. A few are carried in that long diaper, hanging from the stork's bill or were brought to the hospital in the doctor's black bag. Not your little Pisces bundle. He came straight from fairyland, clutching a moonbeam. If you look closely, you'll still see the reflection of elves and magic wishing trees in his dreamy little eyes, maybe even a trace of stardust smudged behind his left ear. His wings may have disappeared by the time he gets to the delivery room, but there's probably a small bump where they were once fastened.

You've seen those congratulation cards for new mothers, with pictures of dimpled, pink and white painted babies, fragile and gauzy, flying around over the verse. The artist used your Pisces babe as a model. This could make you think you can lead your Neptune child by the toe, or that after you've scrubbed that shiny stardust out of his ears you can mold him into any shape you like. Why not, when he's such a gentle, delicate little lump of clay? Think again. He'll get his own way just as surely as the yelling red-faced Aries baby, the demanding, regal Leo baby or the stubborn, tough little Taurus baby. The only difference is that he'll get it by charming you to death, and drowning you in oceans of sweet smiles and winning ways.

As soon as the ink is dry on the birth certificate, turn in the name of your little Pisces boy for the lead in the first

future production of *Peter Pan* or the girl for *Alice i.
Wonderland*. Peter Pan and Alice will be the Neptun
children's favorite roles, and they won't need a stage t
act the parts superbly. They'll still be starring in then
when they're eighty. Parents who breathe the age-ol
prayer, "I wish baby never had to grow up," will get thei
wish if baby was born under the sign of the fish. Th
years won't leave any lasting impression: there will alway
be a childish, dreamy, magical quality of make-believ
hanging like a mist over the Pisces. It will drench him i
mystery and unreality forever-and-three-days.

By the time he's old enough to crawl into the jam pot an
hide, this strange child of yours will show a preference fo
living in a world of fancy. He'll enjoy diversions that ar
far removed from everyday patterns and routines. Wher
he's in the high chair, he'll eat like an angel, if you pretend
you're a queen or a clown while you're feeding him. Wea
a lampshade, dripping with all your old, sparkling necklaces, or a mop for a wig; smear lipstick and chalk on
your face. His imagination will supply the rest. When he's
a little older, he'll play happily on the front porch while
you do the washing if you hang up a few balloons, put
some music on the record player, toss around his stuffed
animals, give him some popcorn and tell him he's at the
circus.

When he's old enough to start to school and begin to
have those peculiar dreams at night, you'll be tying his
shoes one ordinary spring morning and get a shock. "Guess
who I saw last night?" he'll remark confidentially. You'll
mumble a polite rejoiner—now where on earth is his green
sweater? Oh, there it is—on the teddy bear he dressed up
yesterday, when he was pretending it was his best friend.

"Who did you see?"

He'll answer casually, "Grandma Stratton. We talked
for a long time, then she had to go. She said to tell you to
be sure to water her geraniums and send Uncle Clarence
the money."

Since Grandmother Stratton died before he was born,
this could unnerve you a little, on an empty stomach, before coffee. But it's nothing to the prickly sensation you'll
get after breakfast, when he's in school and the mailman
delivers a letter from your Uncle Clarence from whom
you haven't heard in five years, asking for a loan to start
a new business.

The wisest parents have difficulty arranging a schedule that will stick with a Pisces offspring. Schedules and routines are his natural enemies, and he'll do everything in is fertile imagination to avoid them. Babies who live upside down—sleep all day and stay awake all night—are often Neptune infants. He wants to eat when he's hungry, sleep when he's tired and play when something attracts his fancy, whenever that might be. Trying to get him to eat, sleep or play at any other time is quite a task. Actually, it's rather a sensible attitude, but the times he gets hungry, tired or playful may vary considerably from day to day and night to night. You might as well adjust your schedule to his. He'll seldom throw tantrums, scream or balk to get you to come around to his way, but he'll gradually win you over by evasive, elusive tactics, and confuse you into capitulation. You may even get charmed yourself by the sheer freedom of it. Not feeling guilty when you chat with neighbors over coffee during the feeding hour, playing a fascinating game of "Princess and Frog" in the still magic hours of dawn—or sharing a bowl of vegetable soup and a cup of hot chocolate with him in the middle of a dreary, gray winter afternoon can become strangely attractive. He might even teach you there's no reason to let that silly clock be a cruel, infallible dictator over your life. It's only a ticking hunk of metal.

The Pisces child will require a healthy amount of attention and appreciation. He'll have to be noticed and encouraged, because he's uncertain about his abilities. Give him as many bushels of it as he needs. He'll also require his moments of privacy. When he goes into one of his mysterious moods of withdrawal, let him be. His mind is a million light years away, and you can't follow. He'll return in plenty of time for his vegetable soup and hot chocolate. Only by now, he'll have changed his lunch hour to mid-evening. If he tells you he was out flying on a saucer with a man from Mars, believe him. It just might be so.

Teachers are always confused when they try to put this odd-shaped peg into a round or square educational hole. He may not fit into either. You'll probably have heaps of struggles between his unique methods of learning and the school's stale routines. He'll simply refuse to conform to a pattern not his own. Don't blame him too much. The educational system has yet to catch up with Neptune's wisdom. Many Pisces boys and girls are artistic, and most of them love music and dancing. Typical Neptunian youngsters are light on their feet, regardless of their weight. The little girl often longs to be a ballerina; the little boy usually chooses heroes like Beethoven, Michelangelo, the astronauts or Saint Anthony over scientists, presidents and generals. They love all kinds of books and English may be a favorite subject, since Pisces is a good story-teller. They love words, and poetry often enchants them. Neptunian may find math hard to understand at first, but they'll have an uncanny grasp of the abstract theories behind algebra and geometry later on.

There may be a lack of responsibility, which can be frustrating. Pisces children follow their own rules. They're sensitive and easily stabbed to the quick by harshness. Tears may be frequent. These youngsters ordinarily prefer the company of adults to playing with other children. Even at a tender age, they have a deep wisdom and sympathetic understanding of situations over their heads. A child of Neptune is often accused of lying, yet they aren't lies to him. There's no malicious or cowardly intent. His young mind swims in fluid imagination which whispers a thousand secrets, so utterly delightful and filled with such sheer beauty he can't help trying to make them live in the cold real world. The fact that these lovely dreams soon die in the sterile, arid soil of a materialistic society is heartbreaking. He needs your deepest pity, or he'll retreat into silent, moody despair.

The Piscean child hears songs of the sea he can never describe. The cold, ugly, naked truth is too brutal for him to bear. He must dress it up occasionally or try to warm it and color it with Neptune shades of romance. It's not fair to call it lying. Instead, encourage him to gather all his clouds and moonbeams and weave them into poems, plays or paintings. Soon enough, he'll learn to adapt to the normal world of brutality, selfishness, cruelty and greed. Why thrust him into it rudely? He may have trouble learning to conform to social and scholastic demands that stifle his individuality. But his parents and teachers can learn from him the value of compassion, understanding, beauty, tolerance, imagination and gentleness. It all depends on the kind of diploma you want from life.

Someday, either the Piscean philosophy of freedom of

expression or the conformist concept will win. My money is on Pisces. Of course, your friendly, warm-hearted little Neptunian must be taught that people expect him to adjust eventually to their crazy-quilt, upside-down concepts in order to survive. But if he's shoved too hard by stern, negative adults, he'll lose his way back to the other side of the looking-glass. Don't steal his key. He needs to slip over there now and then, to refresh himself with the true wisdom of the Red Queen and the White Knight. Then he can better cope with the real world of war, poverty, disease, hypocritical ethics and ingratitude. Your little fish needs a cloak of protection against the cold winds to come. Knit it yourself with bright, gay sturdy yarn. Try to understand his Neptune ways. Guide him tenderly, wisely, and when he's tall enough, he may someday suddenly reach out and catch one of his silver stars to bring home to you. Then you'll be glad you didn't laugh at his dreams. Better clear off a spot on the mantle right now.

The PISCES Boss

"You are old," said the youth; "one would hardly suppose
That your eye was as steady as ever;
Yet you balance an eel on the end of your nose—
What made you so awfully clever?"

Sample conversation in an office about a typical Pisces executive:

"What's the name of that new boss the firm hired last week?"

"You mean the one who took his coffee break with us yesterday?"

"No. The one who left this morning."

With only slight exaggeration, that's about the normal length of time the average Piscean will remain in an executive position. There are a limited number of streams for Pisces bosses, and we'll concentrate on those. In most corporate and industrial areas, the Neptunian chief is as rare as a bathing suit at the North Pole. The great majority of Neptune's children prefer to swim alone—unconfined—as writers, salesmen, creative artists, actors, wandering minstrels or soldiers-of-fortune.

However, there are a few areas where he can apply his talents and make himself an indispensable boss. He has top qualifications for radio stations, TV networks, advertising and public relations outfits. Running any of these operations, he'll go around happily dispensing creative ideas from his superabundant fountain of imagination. Pisces sees no reason to blurt out the plain and often brutal truth, as certain other Sun signs do. Unlike Gemini, Sagittarius and Scorpio, the fish prefers not to tell it like it is. He would rather tell people what he thinks will have the best effect on them in the long run, or what they want to hear. It's not because he's dishonest. He's learned through bitter experience that society does not want to hear the cold and naked truth. Besides, he feels the soul requires the added dressing of ritual and beauty painted over sound facts. Madison Avenue loves him.

He's a superlative director of stage and screen, also a capable producer (if he has a good company manager). He can run a dance studio like a dream. As the head of a detective or research bureau, his uncanny psychic ability to penetrate mystery leads him straight to the top of the heap. Lots of travel agencies have Pisces executives, and they're usually tremendously successful. He's often found as the head of a charitable organization. Many fish happily lead orchestras or bands, and keep rehearsals running smoothly, not to mention producing great music. They're unexcelled as executive managers of country clubs or hotels (if there's a good bookkeeper around). They can run a progressive publishing company, magazine or newspaper competently, even brilliantly. You'll often find the fish heading up a service business of some kind, and he's certainly in home waters as the director of a camp, or in an official capacity in a church or synagogue. But that's just about it, except for teachers and professors and a few administrators in medical or law schools. Pisceans aren't cut out to be bosses, in the strict sense of the word.

With his sensitive nature, Pisces was born to serve mankind, not to accumulate power or build huge empires. He can be a capable and competent stockbroker and a shrewd trader, but he'll almost never take over as the head of a brokerage or bond house. Too much responsibility. However, thanks to his quick, clever mind and his sometimes uncanny grasp of figures, the fish can have a lot of fun juggling the points of fluctuating shares, though it will be more like a game to him than actual work.

If your boss was born in March, he may be the type to behave like a crosspatch when he's irritated by something. He has a gift of words, and when he's being brusque, it's a caustic brusqueness that can scald a little, but he'll seldom be aggressively domineering or truly mean and petty. One minute he may shock you with his unconventional ideas, then he'll do a rather slippery turnabout and appear to be a conformist. You'll eventually catch on that he's neither a great liberal nor a cautious conservative. On different occasions, he takes either view, to find out what your ideas are. He can be, in other words, a mite tricky. When he finds your ideas and your conversation interesting, your Pisces boss will listen with flattering concentration, silently and sincerely, maybe even offer you a glass of sherry to create a relaxed atmosphere. If he finds what you say boring, his mind will wander. He'll probably daydream about far-off people and places while you're talking, carefully keeping a fixed smile on his face. Since every one of them is a born actor, you'll think he's being attentive, but after a certain period, he'll get tired of his mental wanderings, notice that you're babbling away, and suddenly interrupt. Then he'll do the talking and you'll do the listening, sometimes for hours—and hours—and hours.

He may be well-traveled, and if he isn't, he'll soon make up for lost time. Like the Sagittarian and Geminian boss, the Pisces executive will keep a packed suitcase behind the couch in his office. If not, he should. Why don't you suggest it to him? He'll probably think it's a splendid idea. Besides, the knowledge that the bag is zipped and ready to take off can give him strange comfort on dreary rainy days, or in the dead of a slushy, bitter winter when he feels like jumping off the penthouse roof with boredom. He'll have his depressed moods and they will be real humdingers. Better stay away from him at those times, hum cheerful melodies while you're working, and make sure he has his hot toddy, laced with the best bourbon.

Be nice to his wives—I mean his wife. (It's a natural mistake. Along with your Gemini and Sagittarius boss, the Pisces boss is more apt to undergo multiple double-ring ceremonies than other bosses.) His wife is probably a nice, sensible, practical girl. If she were as imaginative and original as her husband, they'd likely both drown together in an ocean of misty dreams and fancies.

The Piscean executive is somewhat partial to the creative thinkers in his firm. If you tend more toward caution than imaginative strategy, you may not get as many glasses of sherry or as many comradely smiles, but you probably won't get fired. He may enjoy the others more, but he needs you. He leans on your practical approach and your organizational ability. The favored, highly inventive employee of a Pisces boss is often shocked right out of his sparkling ideas when the firm has an economy drive and the fish gently lets the ax fall on him, and keeps the steady, reliable, rather stodgy worker on the payroll. The Pisces will wave farewell sadly, but he is a shrewd judge of human nature, including his own. Although he enjoys the company and the progressive contributions of the imaginative employees, his own brand of creativity works more smoothly when it's backed up by the careful planning and office discipline of the old gray heads of wisdom, even if they're young, blonde or brunette heads. Discretion and conservatism aren't his greatest assets, and he's clearly aware of his deficiencies. He can always find another daring, enthusiastic dreamer when business picks up, but when the profits dip a little, he can't afford to be without the workers whose noses are worn down by the grindstone. Meanwhile, he figures he'll take care of the daring, enthusiastic dreams department himself until things get better and he can put some more compatible blue-sky people on the payroll. Of course, there are always exceptions to any rule, but it won't hurt to let your Pisces boss know that you can be serious and sensational at the same time.

You've probably already learned that he's installed a Capricorn or Taurus as a middleman to deal with employees who seek raises. He knows better than to let you appeal to him personally. The Neptune nature is so constituted that he finds it almost impossible to say no to a fellow human being who has a sincere need, or even just a sincere desire. He learns early to insulate himself as best he can.

Remember, he lives in two different worlds. Such a division of nature can cause a confused personality, but it can just as easily cause brilliance. His thoughts may be as abstract and deep as Piscean Einstein's, who once

said, "God doesn't throw dice." Einstein meant that the
law of mathematical probability isn't necessarily sacrosanct.
Your Neptune boss feels the same way about accepted
business procedures, and time usually proves his first
instincts are right, no matter how visionary they may sound
when he expresses them. He's a mystic at heart, a secret
believer in the unseen and the supernatural, though he
may be a little bashful about it. He won't practice Voodoo
at his desk or meditate in the lotus position at the water
cooler, because he fears ridicule if people discover the
undercurrent of his psychic vibrations. But they find out
anyway, for all his clever playing of the role of tough
realist.

Remember that time your heart was broken by a boy
friend who flew the coop and took your engagement ring
and all your dreams with him? Your Pisces boss casually
invited you to dinner, filled your sad head with the nicest
compliments, then hurried you to the theater. Afterwards,
he took you backstage, introduced you to the leading
players, and then treated everyone to a late supper. With
all that food and wine and glittering conversation, he took
your mind right off your fickle fiancé. Though sometimes
he was gruff deliberately, so it wouldn't look obvious, for
weeks afterwards, he found little ways to cheer you up
until the ache stopped aching. You hadn't told a soul in
the office about the breakup. Now, how did he know you
needed help over that black period? The gypsy who read
his fortune one day by the lines in his hand could have
told you. She noticed right away that he has a rare mark on
his palm—which means he's a compassionate genius.
There aren't very many of them around. That's why he's
a rare fish.

The PISCES Employee

"It was much pleasanter at home," thought poor Alice,
"when one wasn't always growing larger and smaller,
and being ordered about by mice and rabbits.
I almost wish I hadn't gone down that rabbit-hole—
and yet—and yet—it's rather curious, you know,
this sort of life!"

The abilities of the Piscean employee depend entirely on which pond he swims in. He can be such a miserable misfit in an incompatible occupation or career that he drifts from one place to another, until he eventually realizes that he's better off going it alone with his own dreams for company.

To work successfully with other people or be part of a team, the fish must be doing something that doesn't offend his sensitivity. It has to be a position that gives him the opportunity to utilize his unsurpassed understanding of human suffering, or that allows him to channel his unique imagination toward a progressive path. A job that fails to supply one or both of these deep-seated Neptune needs will create a lazy, disinterested, not to mention disheartened employee. When his needs are satisfied, however, he can be a gem of a worker, often one-of-a-kind in his field—difficult, if not impossible, to replace. There's a side to the fish that allows him to surprise you with his painstaking attention to detail, when he's in the mood. It seems to be totally inconsistent with his obvious mystical bent, but these people were born under the Sun sign that encompasses the qualities of all other signs. It can be the "dust bin of the zodiac," as it's often called in astrology, or the turning path to shining glory. The glory needn't be achieved hanging from a star. It can be realized in a quiet way, right in your office, if the fish is happy and content with what he's doing.

The most common remark heard around an office where there's a Pisces employee is, "I can't understand him.

What's he up to?" They may never know. The Piscean man or woman is compelled, possibly by inner doubt and confusion, to disguise motives and keep his true aims hidden. If the fish revealed his entire nature it would startle or shock most people, so he keeps his counsel. All the chattering of the occasional talkative Pisces is deceptive. It still won't reveal what he really thinks, even if he talks all night, as some of them do. The quiet ones can also drive you wild by keeping their most interesting thoughts and ideas a secret. You never know what's going on inside those dreamy Neptune heads.

He'll work with a terrific sense of duty if he's happy with his job. When he's not happy, he withdraws. Only his body is there. Eventually it will also disappear, leaving only the memory of his grin and his wise eyes. It's not easy to keep this slippery employee peaceful. When the water gets stagnant, he swims away before you have a chance to filter the pool, and that can be frustrating. If he would be more open about his true desires, compromise might be reached, but too often the fish chooses abrupt change to long, honest discussion that might turn things rightside up again.

There's no doubt that the Pisces man or woman is more often found in the world of the arts, but the term can cover more than you might suppose. Pisces is happy adjusting the lights in a theater, hanging canvases in museums, stitching the lace on doll dresses, polishing the brass of musical instruments or designing the cover of a book. He or she can spend hours blissfully teaching tots to dance, blowing up balloons for a party, arranging flowers, planning a poster advertising campaign, engrossed in creative writing, or experimenting with unusual hair styles. Now and then you'll find a Piscean engaged in a mechanical occupation relating to mathematics, engineering or computing, but he will always attack such subjects from the abstract point of view.

Pisces people make excellent teachers, with uncanny insight into the natures of their students and a deep grasp of the subject they teach. They seem to have a special knack for both preparing and merchandising food and drink, either serving it in posh restaurants or supervising the operation with social grace.

If your business concerns medicine, hospitals or pharmaceuticals, the Pisces employee is probably your right arm. No one makes a finer nurse or servant to the sick. They're right at home with drugs and medicines, too. Unfortunately, however, the Piscean receptivity can cause them to saturate themselves in their surroundings, with occasional adverse effects on their own mental, emotional and physical health. If Pisces controls his instinct for instant empathy, he can be a shining light in the field of health. Needless to say, social work is also a Pisces occupation, and you'll find lots of Neptunes efficiently dispensing welfare to unfortunate humanity.

The fish takes on the color of his surroundings. If you shut your Pisces employee in a small cubicle with drab furnishings, bare floors and drapeless windows, he'll begin to look like the office itself. You'll look up one day and there he'll be—an exact imitation of his immediate working world. His conversation will be drab, his ideas bare and dull. As you stare at this listless, plain, cold and colorless creature with nondescript clothing and a mousy personality, you'll wonder what happened to that person you hired who was bright, sunny and full of fresh imagination, whose conversation was rich and sparkling and who wore vivid, cheerful clothes. Believe me, such a Neptunian transformation is easier to remedy than other personnel problems. Just hang some gay green drapes in his office, cover the floor with soft emerald carpeting, and plunk a vase of happy daisies on his desk. Pipe in some soft, low music, smile at him once an hour on the hour, and the fish you hired will reappear in his true colors. The Piscean personality is elusive, but it's amazingly easy to reel it in when you use the right bait.

Your Pisces secretary may be a little sloppy at home, but she'll probably be neat at the office. She'll daydream on her own time and try to be methodical during working hours. Of course, there are exceptions, when her mind can wander in odd directions. There's a Pisces girl I used to work with in a radio station who had the most peculiar filing system. I don't think it was permanent. It may have had something to do with the fact that her mind was on a novel she was writing on weekends. One day the boss asked her why the drawer in the filing cabinet marked "L" was so full it was always popping open and cracking him on the shin. Her answer was unexpected, to say the least. "Because of all those letters," she informed him efficiently. In all fairness to Pisces, however, she did have a

Sagittarius ascendant and an Aquarius Moon, which can make for a little loopiness when they're mixed up like that.

After she left to peddle her novel in New York, the filing problems became really tangled for a spell. The first week she was gone, one of the announcers needed a music theme for a Notre Dame football game. Rushing over to the record file, he hurriedly checked under N for Notre Dame. (He was looking for the song that goes, "Cheer, cheer, for old Notre Dame" . . .) Not finding it under N, he checked the letter C, thinking perhaps she had filed it under the lyric. It wasn't there, either. Perspiring nervously, for it was now one minute to game time, he realized she might have tucked it away under the title, "Victory March." He flipped open the file. No such luck. The game went on the air sans music that day. Weeks later, the record turned up. The Pisces had filed it under F. Why? You can't guess? For "Fighting Irish," of course. It was perfectly logical to her. That's how everybody referred to the team in the office pool. Well, it does make some sense.

The average female fish will be a little more conventional. She'll be gentle and considerate, and get along beautifully with the other members of your staff. She may even be a sort of den mother, if you can call the office a den. The other employees will go to her with all their troubles, minor and major. You may cry on her shoulder yourself on occasion, she's such a sympathetic listener. This girl may read the cards for fun (though she'll secretly take it seriously), and it's a cinch she'll be able to read your mind—so be careful what you're thinking when she passes your desk.

An occasional Pisces employee can be fussy or critical, but they usually won't be energetic enough about it to be really annoying. These people need nearly as many compliments as Aries and Leo to feel secure, but be sure you're sincere, because they'll sense it quickly if you're not. If you have reason to scold a Pisces, you may wonder where the fish went for a day or so. He didn't leave. Not yet. There he is, hiding behind the outgoing mail basket on his desk, trying to pretend he's invisible by not speaking, barely moving and hardly breathing. He has been hurt, and you'll have to do something very sweet and lovely to make him brighten. The fish is ultra sensitive, remember. When your mood changes, so will his. Pisces has a way of cutting

himself off from others when situations become painful
He seeks the sunlight and rosy, beautiful emotions. When
gray or black appears, he dives down deep to escape. A
thoughtless word can make him weep inside, although he'll
probably tell a joke to disguise it. Pisces has a way with
a clever line, and his humor, though it's not ever obvious,
is seldom faraway.

Money won't mean a lot to your Pisces employee. He'll
talk a good salary and bonus, but he'll hardly notice if
he has to take a temporary cut in pay when business is
slow (unless he has a large family to feed). Actually,
many Pisces men and women are happy with a reasonable
wage, as long as you're open-minded about loans. The fish
will often approach you with empty pockets and a big
smile a day or so before payday, and charmingly ask for
a light touch to see him through. He may forget to pay it
back unless you remind him. His intentions are honest,
but there's always something extra he needs. The chances
are just as good he gave it to someone else. Money
ordinarily passes through Pisces like water through a
sieve. He's sort of a middle man for cash. He'll borrow a
hundred from you, then turn around and hand it to a man
whose wife needs an operation. As neglectful as Pisces may
be to repay your loan to him, he'll happily give you his
last dime if you're temporarily short, and he probably
won't be in any more of a hurry to get it back than he
was to return the hundred he got from you earlier. In fact,
it sometimes gets so confusing you may forget who owes
what to whom. That's the way the typical Pisces sees the
whole monetary setup anyway. In a hazy way, he feels
money was created to spread around. When a person needs
it, the cash should be there. When you don't need it, you
pass it on. It's a kind of bread-cast-on the-waters theory.
It works surprisingly often for the fish, but such Neptune
philosophy can bewilder other Sun signs. (Of course, a
Virgo, Cancer or Capricorn ascendant, or perhaps an
Aquarius or Taurus Moon can spoil all the fun.)

More Pisces employees quit than are fired. They're too
elusive and too shrewd about human nature to wait for
the painful hook. Sensing your displeasure in advance, the
fish will wriggle away before you get a chance to embarrass
him. You'll find the single Piscean man less apt to leave
a job lightly than the married one, whose wife probably
works. In fact, her willingness to work if necessary may

have been one of her main attractions, though romantic love was probably equally important. The girl fish may only be marking time until some man comes along to rescue her from repulsive competition, unless she's involved in a creative endeavor she thinks of as a career.

There's little danger the Pisces employee is after your job. He probably secretly pities you for the responsibilities you carry. After all, it's tough to move around with burdens on your back, and Pisces seeks a changing scene. The length of time he brightens your office will depend on the variety of changes it offers his wandering nature. When the snails begin to bore him, or when the whales and sharks threaten to devour him, he'll glide away. The Neptune employee will never get stuck in a bunch of seaweed.

Afterword

Shake her snow-white feathers, tune in to her nonsensical
wave-length, and old Mother Goose may show us a secret
message. There may be a pearl of wisdom hidden in the
apparently childish prattle of her nursery rhyme.

How many miles to Babylon? It seems to be quite a
leap from the sandal-clad people of Chaldea and the
jeweled, perfumed Pharaohs of Egypt to the space age—
from the lost continent of Atlantis to the jet-propelled
Twentieth Century. But how far is it, really? Perhaps only
a dream or two.

Alone among the sciences, astrology has spanned the
centuries and made the journey intact. We shouldn't be
surprised that it remains with us, unchanged by time—
because astrology is truth—and truth is eternal. Echoing
the men and women of the earliest known civilizations,
today's moderns repeat identical phrases: "Is Venus your
ruling planet?" "I was born when the Sun was in Taurus."
"Is your Mercury in Gemini too?" "Wouldn't you just
know he's an Aquarian?"

Astrological language is a golden cord that binds us to
a dim past while it prepares us for an exciting future of
planetary explorations. Breath-taking Buck Rogers advances in all fields of science are reminding us that "there

are more things in heaven and earth, Horatio, than are dreamt of in your philosophy" (even if your name is Sam or Fanny instead of Horatio). Dick Tracy's two-way wrist radio is no longer a fantastic dream—it's a reality— and Moon Maid's powerful weapon has been matched by the miracle of the laser beam, the highly concentrated light that makes lead run like water and penetrates the hardest substances known to man. Jules Verne and Flash Gordon are now considered pretty groovy prophets, so there were obviously important secrets buried in those way out adventures twenty thousand leagues under the sea and many trillions of leagues above the earth.

Could it be that the science fiction writers and cartoonists have a better idea of the true distance between yesterday, today and tomorrow than the white-coated men in their sterile, chrome laboratories? Einstein knew that time was only relative. The poets have always been aware—and the wise men, down through the ages. The message is not new. Long before today's overwhelming interest in astrology, daring men of vision like Plato, Ptolemy, Hippocrates and Columbus respected its wisdom; and they've been kept good company by the likes of Galileo, Ben Franklin, Thomas Jefferson, Sir Isaac Newton and Dr. Carl Jung. You can add President John Quincy Adams to the list; also great astronomers like Tycho Brahe, Johannes Kepler and Dr. Gustave Stromberg. And don't forget R.C.A.'s brilliant research scientist John Nelson, famed mathematician Dr. Kuno Foelsch and Pulitzer prize winner John O'Neill. None of these men were high school drop-outs.

In 1953, Dr. Frank A. Brown, Jr. of Northwestern University made a startling discovery while he was experimenting with some oysters. Science has always assumed that oysters open and close with the cycle of the tides of their birthplace. But when Dr. Brown's oysters were taken from the waters of Long Island Sound and placed in a tank of water in his Evanston, Illinois laboratory, a strange pattern emerged.

Their new home was kept at an even temperature, and the room was illuminated with a steady, dim light. For two weeks, the displaced oysters opened and closed their shells with the same rhythm as the tides of Long Island Sound—one thousand miles away. Then they suddenly snapped shut, and remained that way for several hours.

Just as Dr. Brown and his research team were about to consider the case of the homesick oysters closed, an odd thing happened. The shells opened wide once again. Exactly four hours after the high tide at Long Island Sound—at the precise moment when there would have been a high tide at Evanston, Illinois, if it were on the sea coast—a new cycle began. They were adapting their rhythm to the new geographical latitude and longitude. By what force? By the Moon, of course. Dr. Brown had to conclude that the oysters' energy cycles are ruled by the mysterious lunar signal that controls the tides.

Human energy and emotional cycles are governed by the same kind of planetary forces, in a much more complicated network of magnetic impulses from all the planets. Science recognizes the Moon's power to move great bodies of water. Since man himself consists of seventy percent water, why should be be immune to such forceful planetary pulls? The tremendous effects of magnetic gravity on orbiting astronauts as they get closer to the planets is well-known. What about the proven correlation between lunar motion and women's cycles, including childbirth—and the repeated testimony of doctors and nurses in the wards of mental hospitals, who are only too familiar with the influence of the Moon's changes on their patients? Did you ever talk to a policeman who had to work a rough beat on the night of the full Moon? Try to find a farmer who will sink a fence rail, slaughter a pig or plant crops without astrological advice from his trusted *Farmer's Almanac*. The movements of the Moon and the planets are as important to him as the latest farm bill controversy in Congress.

Of all the heavenly bodies, the Moon's power is more visible and dramatic, simply because it's the closest body to the earth. But the Sun, Venus, Mars, Mercury, Jupiter, Saturn, Uranus, Neptune and Pluto exercise their influences just as surely, even though from further away. Scientists are aware that plants and animals are influenced by cycles at regular intervals, and that the cycles are governed through forces such as electricity in the air, fluctuations in barometric pressure and the gravitational field. These earthly forces are originally triggered by magnetic vibrations from outer space, where the planets live, and from where they send forth their unseen waves. Phases of the Moon, showers of gamma rays, cosmic rays, X-rays, undulations of the pear-shaped electro-magnetic field and other influences from extraterrestrial sources are constantly penetrating and bombarding the atmosphere around us. No living organism escapes it, nor do the minerals. Nor do we.

Dr. Harold S. Burr, emeritus Professor of Anatomy at Yale's Medical School, states that a complex magnetic field not only establishes the pattern of the human brain at birth, but continues to regulate and control it through life. He further states that the human central nervous system is a superb receptor of electro-magnetic energies, the finest in nature. (We may walk with a fancier step, but we hear the same drummer as the oysters.) The ten million cells in our brains form a myriad of possible circuits through which electricity can channel.

Therefore, the mineral and chemical content and the electrical cells of our bodies and brains respond to the magnetic influence of every sunspot, eclipse and planetary movement. We are synchronized, like all other living organisms, metals and minerals, to the ceaseless ebb and flow of the universe; but we need not be imprisoned by it, because of our own free will. The soul, in other words, is superior to the power of the planets. Yet unfortunately, most of us fail to use our free will (i.e., the power of the soul), and are just about as helpless to control our destinies as Lake Michigan or an ear of corn. The purpose of the astrologer is to help us gain the knowledge of how to avoid drifting downstream—how to fight the current.

Astrology is an art as well as a science. Though lots of people would like to ignore that basic fact, it can't be overlooked. There are astrologers who tremble with anger at the mere mention of intuition in relation to astrology. They send out fiery blasts against any hint of such a correlation, and frantically insist that "Astrology is an exact science, based on mathematics. It should never be mentioned in the same breath with intuitive powers." I regard their opinions as sincere, but logic forces me to ask why these must be so totally separate. Should they be? Even the layman today is attempting, through books, games and parlor or laboratory testing, to determine his or her ESP potential. Why not astrologers? Are they supposed to bury their heads in the sand like ostriches concerning the development of a sixth sense, or the existence of it in some individuals?

Granted, the calculation of an astrological chart, based

on mathematical data and astronomical facts, is an exact science. But medicine is also a science, based on fact and research. Yet, all good doctors admit that medicine is an art as well. The intuitive diagnostician is recognized by his colleagues. Physicians will tell you that they each have, in varying degrees, a certain sensitivity, which is an invaluable aid in interpreting the provable facts of medicine. To synthesize medical theories, to interpret the results of laboratory tests in relation to the patient's individual history, is never cut and dried. It simply couldn't be done without intuitive perception on the part of the doctor. Otherwise, medicine could simply be computerized.

Music is also scientifically based—on the inflexible law of mathematics—as everyone who has ever studied chord progressions knows. Musical interludes are governed by ratios of whole numbers—a science, indisputably. Yet it's also an art. Anyone can be taught to play *Clair de lune* or *The Warsaw Concerto* correctly, but it's the sensitivity or intuitive perception of a Van Cliburn that separates him from the rest of us. The notes and chords are always the same, mathematically exact. The interpretation, however, is different—an obvious reality which has nothing to do with the present definition of the word science.

Many intelligent people can study or teach astrology successfully, even brilliantly, but few are able to add the dimension of sensitive interpretation or intuitive perception that makes the science of astrology ultimately satisfying as an art. Of course, one doesn't have to be a psychic or a medium to give an accurate and helpful astrological analysis, yet any intuition on the part of the astrologer is clearly an asset to his synthesis of the natal chart. Naturally, the intuitive astrologer must also be well versed in mathematical calculation and must strictly observe the scientific fundamentals of his art. Assuming he is and does, he's using a powerful combination of both conscious and subconscious abilities, so you needn't be frightened into avoiding competent professionals who are able to make both an art and a science of their work. If anything, you'll be lucky to find one. Sensitive perception is rare in any field.

The popularity of astrology today is bringing all the quacks out of the woodwork, and there aren't as many qualified astrologers and teachers as there should be. Possibly within the next decade, astrologers will be recognized professionals who have graduated from an "astral science" course in a leading college. The important study of the influence of the planets on human behavior will be then taught in the modern halls of ivy, as it was once taught in the great universities of Europe. Students will be accepted only if their natal charts reveal an ability to teach or research in astrology or to give a personal analysis; and the courses will be as tough as those in any law or medical school. The subjects of magnetic weather conditions, biology, chemistry, geology, astronomy, higher mathematics, sociology, comparative religions, philosophy and psychology will be required—as well as instruction in calculating an astrological chart and interpreting it—and graduates will proudly set up a shingle reading: "John Smith—Astrologer, D.A.S." (Doctor of Astral Science).

At the present stage of research and acceptance, the safest and sanest approach to astrology by the layman is to become thoroughly acquainted with the twelve signs, which is on a par with becoming acquainted with the theories of medicine by studying first aid or sensible health rules.

Mankind will someday discover that astrology, medicine, religion, astronomy and psychiatry are all one. When they are blended, each will be whole. Until then, each will be slightly defective.

There is an area of confusion in astrology about which opinions clash. Reincarnation. There's not a person today who doesn't have either a positive or negative approach to the law of karma. You can't avoid hearing and reading about it any more than you can avoid exposure to the ouija board or Jeanne Dixon, under the Uranus influence of this Twentieth Century movement into the Aquarian age.

Esoteric astrologers believe, as I do, that astrology is incomplete unless properly interpreted with the law of karma as its foundation. There are others who emphatically deny this, especially in the western world, to which astrology is comparatively new. You needn't accept reincarnation to derive benefit from astrology; and the proof of the soul's existence in previous lives, however logical, has never been scientifically established (though some mighty convincing circumstantial evidence is available, including documented cases and the Bible itself). Because of its very nature, reincarnation may forever elude absolute, tangible proof. The ancients taught that the evolved soul must reach the point of seeking the truth of karma, in order to end the cycle of re-birth. Therefore, faith in reincarnation is a gift—a reward for the soul advanced enough to search for the meaning of its existence in the universe and its karmic obligations in the present life. Proof of this deep mystery would remove the individual free will of discovery, so perhaps man must always look for the answers to reincarnation in his own heart. But he should do so only after intelligent study of what other minds have found to be both false and true. Books written about the amazing prophet Edgar Cayce will give the curious layman a better understanding of what it's all about, and there are many other excellent works on the market concerning reincarnation, which will help you establish for yourself whether the subject is worthy of your consideration or just so much black magic. That's the only way to approach such a personal matter as life and death—by yourself—after a thorough examination of the pros and cons.

We are heading in the direction of new respect for unseen influences, and the current interest in mental telepathy is a good example. Huge sums of money have been and are being spent by NASA in ESP tests with selected astronauts to determine the possibility of transferring mental messages through sense perception, as an emergency measure against a breakdown of present communications between earth and astronaut. Russia is rumored to be far ahead of us in this area of research, another reason why dogmatic, materialistic thinking must go.

The excitment of distinguished scientists about experiments with these invisible wave-lengths between human minds has gained attention of the medical doctors. Medicine has long admitted that such ailments as ulcers and strep throat are brought on by mental strain or emotional tension, and now physicians are advancing serious theories that there is a definite relationship between the personality of the patient and the growth and development of cancer. Recent articles by well-known doctors have urged the cooperation of psychiatrists in determining in advance which patient may be susceptible, so the disease can be treated early or even prevented. Yet astrology has always known that disease is triggered by the mind and emotions, and can be controlled or eliminated the same way; also that people born under certain planetary influences are either susceptible or immune to particular diseases and accidents. The knowledge medicine seeks is in the patient's carefully calculated, detailed natal chart, clearly shown by his planetary positions and aspects at birth.

The astrologer-physicians in ancient Egypt practiced brain surgery with refined techniques, a fact recently proven by archaeological and anthropological discoveries. Today's progressive doctors are quietly checking the astrological sign the moon is transiting before surgery, imitating the Greek physicians of centuries ago, who followed Hippocrates' precept of: "Touch not with metal that part of the anatomy ruled by the sign the Moon is transiting, or to which the transiting Moon is in square or opposition by aspect." There's much that's compelling and important to say about medical astrology and its value to the physician in the cause and prevention of illness, but it's such a huge subject, it must wait for another volume.

Moving from medicine to travel, several insurance companies and airlines are secretly investigating the possible relationship between fatal plane crashes and the natal charts of the passengers and crew. So time marches on— from ancient knowledge of planetary influences—retrograding back to materialistic thinking—and forward again to truth. Down through the centuries the planets remain unchanged in their grandeur and their orbs. The stars which shone over Babylon and the stable in Bethlehem still shine as brightly over the Empire State Building and your front yard today. They perform their cycles with the same mathematical precision, and they will continue to affect each thing on earth, including man, as long as the earth exists.

Always remember that astrology is not fatalistic. The stars incline, they do not compel. Most of us are carried along in blind obedience to the influence of the planets and our electromagnetic birth patterns, as well as to our environment, our heredity and the wills of those stronger than us. We show no perception, therefore no resistance; and our horoscopes fit us like a fingerprint. We're moved like pawns on a chess board in the game of life, even while some of us scoff at or ignore the very powers which are moving us. But anyone can rise above the afflictions of his nativity. By using free will, or the power of the soul, anyone can dominate his moods, change his character, control his environment and the attitudes of those close to him. When we do this, we become movers in the chess game, instead of the pawns.

Do you refrain from following your star by saying, "I just wasn't born with the strength or the ability?" You were born with more of each than Helen Keller, who called on the deep, inner power of her will to overcome being blind, deaf and dumb. She replaced these natal afflictions with fame, wealth, respect and the love of thousands, and she conquered her planetary influences.

Do constant fears keep you from seeing tomorrow? Do melancholy and pessimism color your rainbows gray before you even reach out to touch them? Actress Patricia Neal substituted iron nerve for gloomy apprehension. She smiled at tragedy, and her grin gave her enough emotional energy to astound her doctors by literally forcing the paralysis of a near fatal stroke to vaporize.

Do newspaper headlines have you convinced America is doomed to oblivion in the near future through the stalemate of hot and cold wars, lack of national and international understanding, rising crime rates, injustice, prejudice, moral decadence, loss of ethics and the possibility of nuclear destruction? Winston Churchill once faced certain defeat for himself personally—and for his country. But he put a twinkle in his eyes, a piece of steel in his spine and a prayer in his heart. That triple combination wrought a miracle, as the courage of one man aroused thousands to blind optimism and stubborn strength. The resulting magnetic vibrations melted the lead of fear, inspired the world and made victory the prize. He refused to be a pawn of the planets or to let his country be the pawn of their influence.

You say such people are special? But these could be your miracles. All of them. There's enough magnetic power in you to make you immune to the strongest planetary pulls, now or in the future. What a pity to submit so easily and let your potential remain unrealized.

When hate and fear are both conquered, the will is then free and capable of immense power. This is the message of your own nativity, hidden in the silent stars. Listen to it.

An ancient legend tells of a man who went to a wise mystic to ask for the key to power and occult secrets. He was taken to the edge of a clear lake, and told to kneel down. Then the wise one disappeared, and the man was left alone, staring down at his own reflected image in the water.

"What I do, you can do also." "Ask, and you shall receive." "Knock, and it shall be opened unto you." "Seek the truth and the truth shall set you free."

"How many miles to Babylon? Three-score-miles-and-ten. Can I get there by candlelight? Yes—and back again!" Is it a poem, or is it a riddle? Each thing in the universe is part of the universal law, and astrology is the basis of that law. Out of astrology grew religion, medicine and astronomy, not the other way around.

There's a sculptured zodiac in the temple of Thebes, so old that its origin has never been determined. Atlantis? Perhaps. But wherever it's from and whoever carved its symbols, its message is eternal: You are endless galaxies —and you have seen but one star.

ABOUT THE AUTHOR

LINDA GOODMAN was born and brought up in Parkersburg, West Virginia. She worked first as a columnist and feature writer for the PARKERSBURG NEWS-SENTINEL and the CLARKSVILLE (TENNESSEE) COURIER. Since then she has been a staff writer for several radio and television stations, including three years at NBC writing "Monitor" and "Emphasis."

At present she is completing the book and lyrics for a Broadway musical—in the time she can spare from preparing astrological charts and conferring with a sizable clientele.

She lives in New York with her husband and four children.

YOUR GUIDES TO THE STARS

Bantam has a wide range of books on Astrology from which to choose. Check to see which titles are missing from your bookshelf.

DON'T MISS
THESE CURRENT
Bantam Bestsellers

] 26807	**THE BEET QUEEN** Louise Edrich	$4.50
] 26808	**LOVE MEDICINE** Louise Edrich	$4.50
] 25800	**THE CIDER HOUSE RULES** John Irving	$4.95
] 26554	**HOLD THE DREAM**	$4.95
	Barbara Taylor Bradford	
] 26253	**VOICE OF THE HEART**	$4.95
	Barbara Taylor Bradford	
] 23667	**NURSE'S STORY** Carol Gino	$3.95
] 26322	**THE BOURNE SUPREMACY**	$4.95
	Robert Ludlum	
] 26056	**THE CLEANUP**	$3.95
	John SKipp & Craig Spector	
] 26134	**THE EMBASSY HOUSE** Nicholas Proffit	$4.50
] 25625	**A CROWD OF LOVERS** Laddie Marshak	$3.95
] 26659	**DREAMS & SHADOWS**	$4.50
	Rosemary Simpson	
] ‘6850	**GOLDEN FIRE** Jonathan Fast	$4.50
] ‘6888	**THE PRINCE OF TIDES** Pat Conroy	$4.95
] ‘6892	**THE GREAT SANTINI** Pat Conroy	$4.95
] 26574	**SACRED SINS** Nora Roberts	$3.95
] 26798	**THE SCREAM**	$3.95
	Jonathan Skipp & Craig Spector	

Prices and availability subject to change without notice.

Buy them at your local bookstore or use this page to order.

- -

Bantam Books, Dept. FB, 414 East Golf Road, Des Plaines, IL 60016

Please send me the books I have checked above. I am enclosing $_____ (please add $2.00 to cover postage and handling). Send check or money order —no cash or C.O.D.s please.

Mr/Ms _____

Address _____

City/State _____ Zip _____

FB—6/88

Please allow four to six weeks for delivery. This offer expires 12/88.

Special Offer
Buy a Bantam Book
for only 50¢.

Now you can have Bantam's catalog filled with hundred
of titles plus take advantage of our unique and excitin
bonus book offer. A special offer which gives you th
opportunity to purchase a Bantam book for only 50
Here's how!

By ordering any five books at the regular price pe
order, you can also choose any other single boo
listed (up to a $5.95 value) for just 50¢. Som
restrictions do apply, but for further details why n
send for Bantam's catalog of titles today!

Just send us your name and address and we will ser
you a catalog!

BANTAM BOOKS, INC.
P.O. Box 1006, South Holland, Ill. 60473

Mr./Mrs./Ms. _____
(please print)

Address _____

City _____ State _____ Zip _____
FC(A)—10/87
Please allow four to six weeks for delivery.